Lecture Notes in Computer Science 13162

More information about this subseries at https://link.springer.com/bookseries/7410

Lejla Batina · Stjepan Picek ·
Mainack Mondal (Eds.)

Security, Privacy, and Applied Cryptography Engineering

11th International Conference, SPACE 2021
Kolkata, India, December 10–13, 2021
Proceedings

Editors
Lejla Batina
Radboud University
Nijmegen, The Netherlands

Mainack Mondal
Indian Institute of Technology Kharagpur
Kharagpur, India

Stjepan Picek
Radboud University
Nijmegen, The Netherlands

TU Delft
Delft, The Netherlands

ISSN 0302-9743 ISSN 1611-3349 (electronic)
Lecture Notes in Computer Science
ISBN 978-3-030-95084-2 ISBN 978-3-030-95085-9 (eBook)
https://doi.org/10.1007/978-3-030-95085-9

LNCS Sublibrary: SL4 – Security and Cryptology

This Springer imprint is published by the registered company Springer Nature Switzerland AG
The registered company address is: Gewerbestrasse 11, 6330 Cham, Switzerland

Preface

The 11th International Conference on Security, Privacy, and Applied Cryptography Engineering 2021 (SPACE 2021) was held during December 10–13, 2021. This annual event is devoted to various aspects of security, privacy, applied cryptography, and cryptographic engineering. This is a challenging field, requiring expertise from diverse domains ranging from mathematics and computer science to circuit design. It was first planned to host SPACE 2021 at IIT Kharagpur, India, but it took place online due to the worldwide COVID-19 crisis.

This year we received 42 submissions from authors in many different countries, mainly from Asia and Europe. The submissions were evaluated based on their significance, novelty, technical quality, and relevance to the SPACE conference. The submissions were reviewed in a double-blind mode by at least three members of the Program Committee, which consisted of 51 members from all over the world. After an extensive review process, 13 papers were accepted for presentation at the conference, leading to an acceptance rate of 30.95%.

The program also included two invited talks and three tutorials on various aspects of applied cryptology, security, and privacy, delivered by world-renowned researchers: Christof Paar, Ahmad-Reza Sadeghi, Nele Mentens, Peter Schwabe, and Blase Ur. We sincerely thank the invited speakers for accepting our invitations in spite of their busy schedules. As in previous editions, SPACE 2021 was organized in cooperation with the International Association for Cryptologic Research (IACR). We are grateful to the general chair, Debdeep Mukhopadhyay, for his willingness to host it physically at IIT Kharagpur and his assistance with turning it into an online event.

There is a long list of volunteers who invested their time and energy to put together the conference. We are grateful to all the members of the Program Committee and their sub-reviewers for all their hard work in the evaluation of the submitted papers. We thank our publisher, Springer, for agreeing to continue to publish the SPACE proceedings as a volume in the Lecture Notes in Computer Science (LNCS) series. We are grateful to the local Organizing Committee, especially to the general chair, Debdeep Mukhopadhyay, who invested a lot of time and effort in order for the conference to run smoothly.

Last but not least, our sincere thanks go to all the authors who submitted papers to SPACE 2021, and to all of you who attended it virtually. At least due to the COVID-19 crisis we were able to have so many of you attending the conference online and registering for free. We sincerely hope to meet some of you in person next year.

December 2021

Lejla Batina
Stjepan Picek
Mainack Mondal

Organization

General Chair

Debdeep Mukhopadhyay	Indian Institute of Technology, Kharagpur, India

Program Committee Chairs

Lejla Batina	Radboud University, The Netherlands
Stjepan Picek	Radboud University and TU Delft, The Netherlands
Mainack Mondal	Indian Institute of Technology, Kharagpur, India

Program Committee

Amr Youssef	Concordia University, Canada
Aniket Kate	Purdue University, USA
Anupam Chattopadhyay	Nanyang Technological University, Singapore
Bodhisatwa Mazumdar	Indian Institute of Technology, Indore, India
Bohan Yang	Tsinghua University, China
Chester Rebeiro	Indian Institute of Technology, Madras, India
Chitchanok Chuengsatiansup	University of Adelaide, Australia
Claude Carlet	University of Bergen, Norway, and University of Paris 8, France
Daniel Moghimi	University of California, San Diego, USA
Diego Aranha	Aarhus University, Denmark
Dirmanto Jap	Nanyang Technological University, Singapore
Domenic Forte	University of Florida, USA
Eran Toch	Tel Aviv University, Israel
Fan Zhang	Zhejiang University, China
Fatemeh Ganji	Worcester Polytechnic Institute, USA
Guilherme Perin	TU Delft, The Netherlands
Ilia Polian	Stuttgart University, Germany
Ileana Buhan	Radboud University, The Netherlands
Jakub Breier	Silicon Austria Labs, Austria
Jean-Luc Danger	Télécom Paris, France
Johanna Sepulveda	Airbus, Germany
Kazuo Sakiyama	University of Electro-Communications, Japan
Kerstin Lemke-Rust	Bonn-Rhein-Sieg University of Applied Sciences, Germany
Kostas Papagiannopoulos	University of Amsterdam, The Netherlands
Luca Mariot	TU Delft, The Netherlands
Lukasz Chmielewski	Radboud University, The Netherlands

Marc Stoettinger	Hessen3C, Germany
Marc Manzano	Sandbox@Alphabet, Spain
Martin Henze	Fraunhofer FKIE, Germany
Md Masoom Rabbani	KU Leuven, Belgium
Naofumi Homma	Tohoku University, Japan
Oğuzhan Ersoy	TU Delft, The Netherlands
Olga Gadyatskaya	Leiden University, The Netherlands
Pedro Maat C. Massolino	PQShield, Oxford, UK
Peter Schwabe	MPI-SP, Germany, and Radboud University, The Netherlands
Rajat Subhra Chakraborty	Indian Institute of Technology, Kharagpur, India
Ruben Niederhagen	University of Southern Denmark, Denmark
Sandeep Shukla	Indian Institute of Technology, Kanpur, India
Sandip Chakraborty	Indian Institute of Technology, Kharagpur, India
Shahram Rasoolzadeh	Radboud University, The Netherlands
Shivam Bhasin	Nanyang Technological University, Singapore
Sikhar Patranabis	Visa Research, USA
Silvia Mella	STMicroelectronics, Italy
Somitra Sanadhya	Indian Institute of Technology, Jodhpur, India
Soumyajit Dey	Indian Institute of Technology, Kharagpur, India
Sk Subidh Ali	Indian Institute of Technology, Bhilai, India
Vishal Saraswat	Bosch Engineering and Business Solutions, Bengaluru, India

Additional Reviewers

Anirban Chakraborty
Soumyadyuti Ghosh
Arnab Bag
Ipsita Koley
Arpan Jati
Manaar Alam
Nikhilesh Kumar Singh
Sayandeep Saha
Vikas Maurya
Reetwik Das
Aneet Kumar Dutta

Contents

Symmetric Cryptography

Computing the Distribution of Differentials over the Non-linear Mapping χ

Joan Daemen[1], Alireza Mehrdad[1], and Silvia Mella[1,2](✉)

[1] Radboud University, Nijmegen, The Netherlands
silvia.mella@ru.nl

[2] STMicroelectronics, Agrate Brianza, Italy

Abstract. When choosing the non-linear layer in a symmetric design, the number of differentials with given differential probability (DP) gives information about how such non-linear layer may perform in the wide trail strategy. Namely, less differentials with high DP means less opportunity to form trails with high DP over multiple rounds. Multiple cryptographic primitives use the χ mapping as basis of their non-linear layer. Among them, KECCAK-f, ASCON, XOODOO, and Subterranean. In the first three, the χ mapping operates on groups of few bits (5 in KECCAK-f and ASCON, and 3 in XOODOO), while in Subterranean it operates on the full state, that is on 257 bits. In the former case, determining the number of differentials with given differential probability is an easy task, while the latter case is more involved. In this paper, we present a method to determine the number of differentials with given DP over χ operating on any number of bits.

Keywords: Differentials · Differential probability · χ mapping

1 Introduction

Many block ciphers and cryptographic permutations are iterative: they consist of the repeated application of a round function alternated by the application of round keys or constants. An important class of round functions for block ciphers and permutations is the one indicated with the term *Substitition-Permutation network (SPN)*. A round in an SPN treats the bits of the intermediate result (often called state) in a uniform way and consists of a non-linear layer and a linear layer. The non-linear layer typically splits the state in a sequence of 4-bit or 8-bit chunks and applies a non-linear permutation to each of these chunks. This non-linear permutation is called an S-box. The S-boxes are the source of non-linearity in the round function, often denoted by the term *confusion* and the linear layer takes care of the mixing of different parts of the state, often denoted by the term *diffusion*.

Modern linear layers often consist of two steps: a mixing step that makes output bits dependent on multiple neighbouring input bits and a shuffle step

L. Batina et al. (Eds.): SPACE 2021, LNCS 13162, pp. 3–21, 2022.
https://doi.org/10.1007/978-3-030-95085-9_1

that moves neighbouring bits to remote positions and vice versa. In many cases the mixing step and the shuffle is specified in terms of nibbles or bytes rather than bits and we speak of an *aligned* round function.

The best known example of a primitive with an aligned round function is the AES [DR02]. AES is specified fully on bytes: the S-boxes operate on individual bytes, the mixing layer operates on column vectors containing 4 statebytes by the multiplication with a so-called maximum-distance separable (MDS) matrix and the shuffle moves bytes in a column to 4 different columns.

There exist also unaligned round functions, where the systematic grouping of bits in bytes or nibbles is avoided. The grouping is still present in each step, but these groupings are different. The best known example of a primitive with an unaligned round function is the KECCAK-f permutation [BDPA11] used in SHA-3 [NIS15]. It has a 3-dimensional state with horizontal 5-bit rows, vertical 5-bit columns and, orthogonal to these two, 64-bit lanes. The non-linear layer groups the bits in rows and applies a 5-bit S-box to them. The mixing layer does not split the state at all but tends to follow the column partition and the shuffle operates at lane-level.

The design of both AES and KECCAK-f is motivated by the *wide trail strategy*, that underlies the design of round functions to have good resistance against differential and linear cryptanalysis. In a nutshell, it aims at the absence of high-probability differential propagation patterns, called *differential trails*, and high-correlation propagation patterns, called *linear trails*, by having relatively lightweight S-boxes but a strong diffusion.

When reasoning about and identifying differential trails, the differential propagation properties of the S-boxes play an important role. In particular, one needs the probabilities of the propagation of a difference b at the input of the S-box to a difference a at its output. An ordered pair of an input difference b and an output difference a is called a differential and denoted as (b, a). The probability that b propagates to a is called its differential probability and denoted as $\mathrm{DP}(b, a)$. An n-bit S-box has 2^{2n} differentials (b, a). The DP values of all differentials are usually arranged in a 2^n by 2^n array, called the difference distribution table (DDT). For usual dimensions of S-boxes the DDT has manageable size: $n = 4$ gives a DDT of $2^8 = 256$ entries and $n = 8$ a DDT of $2^{16} = 65536$ entries.

However, not all round functions have a non-linear layer consisting of small S-boxes. A predecessor of KECCAK-f, RadioGatún [BDPA06], makes use of an *S-box* that operates on 19 bits. The corresponding DDT has 2^{38} entries, something that is non-trivial to manage. This S-box is an instance of so-called χ mapping, that is defined by a local map and can operate on a number of bits *arranged in a circle* of any circumference (length). If the length is odd, the mapping is invertible. The χ mapping lies as the basis of the non-linear layer of multiple cryptographic primitives including KECCAK-f [BDPA13], XOODOO [DHAK18], and ASCON [DEMS21]. In these three, the length of the circles is either 5 or 3 and the DDT approach works fine. However, in the cryptographic primitives Subterranean [Dae95] and Cellhash [Dae95] that were proposed in the 90's of the previous century, the length of the circle is 257 and the DDT approach completely breaks down. These primitives are still relevant as Subterranean was slightly adapted to Subterranean 2.0 [DMMR20] and turned out to be the candidate in the NIST lightweight cryptography competition with the lowest energy consumption per processed bit in dedicated hardware implementation.

The difference propagation properties of χ lend themselves to an analytical approach. Given a differential (b, a), it is easy to determine whether $\text{DP}(b, a) > 0$, in other words, whether they are *compatible* through χ. And given a differential (b, a) with b and a compatible, it is straightforward to determine $\text{DP}(b, a)$. Additionally, it is easy to describe the space of possible output differences a that an input difference can propagate to as they form an affine space [Dae95]. Given an output difference a, it is feasible to determine its compatible input differences b at the cost of some more effort. So analysis of differential trails is manageable in round functions that for their non-linear layer make use of χ with large circles.

However, there is one aspect that is easy to compute for S-box layers and that is not solved yet for big-circle χ. This is determining the number of differentials with given DP. The number of differentials with given DP gives information about how a non-linear layer may perform in the wide trail strategy: less differentials with high DP means less opportunity to form trails with high DP over multiple rounds. This is especially relevant in non-aligned round functions where the absence of high DP trails cannot be systematically avoided but one relies on the absence of *accidents*. Namely, high-DP round differentials that happen to be chainable to high-DP differential trails. The more high-DP differentials there are over the non-linear layer, the higher the probability of such accidents. Therefore, when making a choice of a non-linear layer in a non-aligned design, it is useful to have the histograms with the number of high-DP differentials for the alternatives. In this paper, we provide a method for the computation of such histograms for big-circle χ.

Organization of the Paper. In Sect. 2, we recall concepts related to differential cryptanalysis and the χ function. In Sect. 3 we introduce a method to compute the number of differentials with given weight for χ operating on circles of any length. Finally, in Sect. 4 we present histograms for some well-known ciphers and compare the case of parallel instances of χ on small circles with the case of a single instance of χ on a big circle.

2 Preliminary

In this section, we start by defining circular strings and presenting our notations. Then we recall differential probability and the concept of restriction weight. Finally, we specify the χ transformation and recall the formula to compute restriction weight over χ as introduced in [Dae95, Sect. 6.9.1].

2.1 Circular Strings

We denote binary strings by lowercase letters s and the i-th bit of s as s_i, where we start indexing from 0. We denote the length of a string by $|s|$. Hence we have $s = s_0 s_1 s_2 \ldots s_{|s|-1}$.

We allow indexing of bits in a string outside the range $[0, |s| - 1]$ by reducing the index modulo $|s|$. Hence the strings we consider are *circular*: the first bit s_0 and last bit $s_{|s|-1}$ are neighbors.

We say s' is a sub-string of s if $|s'| \leq |s|$ and there exists an offset i such that $s'_j = s_{j+i}$ for all $j \in [0, |s'| - 1]$. As an example, we say $s' = 11000$ is a sub-string of $s = 00110011100$ since $s'_j = s_{j+7}$.

We write $s \| s'$ for the concatenation of two strings s and s'. Given a string s, we denote by $(s)^m$ the string $s\|s\|\ldots\|s$. We use the notation 1^ℓ for an all-one string of length ℓ. We call such string a *1-run*.

2.2 Differential Probability and Restriction Weight

Let $B, B^* \in \mathbb{F}_2^n$ be two inputs of a function α over $\mathbb{F}_2^n$, and $A, A^* \in \mathbb{F}_2^n$ be their corresponding outputs, respectively. We call $b = B - B^*$ an input difference to α and $a = A - A^*$ an output difference. A *differential* over α consists of a couple (b, a).

We now introduce some terminology used in the rest of the paper.

Definition 1 (Active/Passive bit). *Let $s_i \in \mathbb{F}_2$ be a bit of difference s, then we say s_i is an* active *bit if $s_i = 1$ and is a* passive *bit otherwise.*

Definition 2 (Hamming weight). *The* Hamming weight *of a difference $s \in \mathbb{F}_2^n$ denoted by $H_w(s)$ is the number of active bits in s.*

Definition 3 (Differential Probability (DP)). *The differential probability of a differential (b, a) for a function α over $\mathbb{F}_2^n$, denoted as* $\mathrm{DP}(b, a)$, *is defined as*

$$\mathrm{DP}(b, a) = 2^{-n} \cdot |\{B \in \mathbb{F}_2^n \mid \alpha(B - b) - \alpha(B) = a\}|.$$

Definition 4 (Restriction weight). *The restriction weight of a differential (b, a) for a function α over $\mathbb{F}_2^n$, denoted as $\mathrm{w_r}(b, a)$ is defined as*

$$\mathrm{w_r}(b, a) = -\log_2 \mathrm{DP}(b, a).$$

2.3 χ Mappings

We use the symbol χ to denote non-linear layers that can be seen as the application of parallel instances of the mapping χ_ℓ to a n-bit state partitioned in $\frac{n}{\ell}$ circles of length ℓ. We refer to such non-linear mapping as a *composite* χ mapping. We speak of a *single-circle* χ mapping if the size of the state that χ_ℓ operates on is n. Namely, if $\ell = n$.

Definition 5 (χ_ℓ). *The map χ_ℓ is a transformation of $\mathbb{F}_2^\ell$ with local map*

$$A_i = B_i + (B_{i+1} + 1) \cdot B_{i+2}, \tag{1}$$

where B denotes the input of χ_ℓ, $A = \chi_\ell(B)$ its output and all indices are taken modulo ℓ.

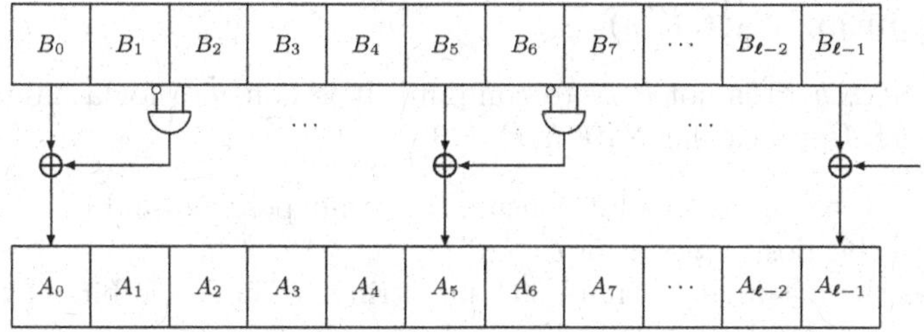

Fig. 1. χ_ℓ transformation.

An illustration of χ_ℓ is given in Fig. 1.

As shown in [Dae95, Sect. 6.9], since the algebraic degree of χ_ℓ is two, the restriction weight of any differential (b, a) over χ_ℓ is fully determined by b, and it can be computed using Proposition 1 and 2.

Proposition 1. *The restriction weight of a non-fully active input difference* $b \in \mathbb{F}_2^\ell \backslash \{1^\ell\}$ *equals the Hamming weight of b plus the number of sub-strings* 001 *in it, denoted by* $\#_{001}(b)$*:*

$$\mathrm{w_r}(b) = H_w(b) + \#_{001}(b). \tag{2}$$

If b is known from the context, we simply write H_w and $\#_{001}$ instead of $H_w(b)$ and $\#_{001}(b)$, respectively.

Proposition 2. *For a fully active input difference* $b = 1^\ell$ *the restriction weight is* $\ell - 1$.

3 Number of Differentials in χ_ℓ with Given Weight

In this section, we provide a method to compute the number of ℓ-bit differences with given restriction weight w. Our analysis is simplified by the fact that χ_ℓ has algebraic degree two and that we can apply Proposition 1.

We denote the number of ℓ-bit differences with weight w by $\mathrm{N}(\ell, w)$. The number of differentials with restriction weight w is then simply $2^w \mathrm{N}(\ell, w)$.

We denote the number of strings of length ℓ with Hamming weight h and containing r 001 sub-strings by $\mathrm{N}_3(\ell, h, r)$.

Due to Proposition 1, the number of ℓ-bit strings with weight w for $w < \ell - 1$ can be written as

$$\mathrm{N}(\ell, w) = \sum_{r=0}^{\lfloor w/2 \rfloor} \mathrm{N}_3(\ell, w - r, r). \tag{3}$$

For $w = \ell - 1$ we have

$$\mathrm{N}(\ell, w) = 2\ell + 1.$$

These are the all-1 string, the ℓ strings with a single zero and the ℓ strings with two zeroes, that are consecutive.

3.1 Computing $\mathrm{N}_3(\ell, h, r)$

In general $\mathrm{N}_3(\ell, h, r)$ is not easy to compute. It is non-zero for a limited range of parameters. In particular $\mathrm{N}_3(\ell, h, r) = 0$ if

- $h + 2r > \ell$: as any active bit consumes one bit position and every 001 consumes two bit positions out of ℓ.
- $r > h$: as there cannot be more 001 sub-strings than active bits. This is also why r is bounded by $\lfloor w/2 \rfloor$ in Eq. 3.
- $r = 0$ and $2h < \ell$: as it is not possible to position less than $\ell/2$ active bits without leaving a gap of two zeroes.

For the other cases, we can compute $\mathrm{N}_3(\ell, h, r)$ by partitioning the set into subsets characterized by two more properties:

- If a string exhibits a sub-string 101, shortening it by removing the zero in the middle leaves the weight intact as it leaves the Hamming weight and $\#_{001}$ invariant. We call the zero in 101 a *hole* and we denote the number of holes by $\#_{101}$.
- If a string exhibits a sub-string 000, shortening it by removing the leading zero leaves the weight intact as it leaves the Hamming weight and $\#_{001}$ invariant. We call the leading zero in 000 a *pause* and denote the number of pauses by $\#_{000}$.

Definition 6 (minimal string). *A string without pauses and holes is called a* minimal string, *i.e., it satisfies* $\#_{101} = 0$ *and* $\#_{000} = 0$.

A minimal string can be written as a sequence of 1-runs interleaved with sub-strings 00.

Any string s is associated to a unique minimal string, that we call its *parent* minimal string. The parent string of a string s can be obtained by removing holes and pauses from s.

We specify an algorithm to find the parent minimal string of a string in Algorithm 1. First, s is transformed by removing holes with the recursive procedure REMOVEHOLES. This procedure scans s and removes the middle 0 from the first 101 sub-string that is encountered. This procedure stops when the string does not contain any more 101 sub-string. Then, s is transformed by removing pauses by applying the recursive procedure REMOVEPAUSES. This procedure scans s and removes the leading 0 from the first sub-string 000 it encounters. This procedure stops when the string does not contain any 000 sub-string.

Example 1. Let $s = 010010101000001000$. First, holes are removed.
Since $s_4 s_5 s_6 = 101$, then s_5 is removed obtaining $s = 01001101000001000$. Similarly, since $s_5 s_6 s_7 = 101$, then s_6 is removed obtaining $s = 0100111000001000$.
Since no more 101 sub-strings are contained in s, pauses are removed from s.
Since $s_7 s_8 s_9 = 000$, then s_7 is removed obtaining $s = 010011100001000$.
Since $s_7 s_8 s_9 = 000$ again, then s_7 is removed obtaining $s = 01001110001000$.
Since $s_7 s_8 s_9 = 000$ again, then s_7 is removed obtaining $s = 0100111001000$.

Algorithm 1. Computing the parent minimal string of a string s

```
procedure REMOVEHOLES(s)
    ℓ ← |s|
    for i ← 0 to ℓ − 1 do
        if s_{i−1} s_i s_{i+1} = 101 then
            s ← s_0 ... s_{i−1} || s_{i+1} ... s_{ℓ−1}        ▷ remove hole in position i
            return REMOVEHOLES(s)
    return
end procedure

procedure REMOVEPAUSES(s)
    ℓ ← |s|
    for i ← 0 to ℓ − 1 do
        if s_i s_{i+1} s_{i+2} = 000 then
            s ← s_0 ... s_{i−1} || s_{i+1} ... s_{ℓ−1}        ▷ remove pause in position i
            return REMOVEPAUSES(s)
    return
end procedure
```

Then, since $s_{10}s_{11}s_{12} = 000$, then s_{10} is removed obtaining $s = 010011100100$. Finally, since $s_{10}s_{11}s_0 = 000$ again, then s_{10} is removed obtaining $s = 01001110010$. Since s does not contain any 000 sub-string, s is a minimal string.

Lemma 1. *For a string of length ℓ, Hamming weight h, number of* 001 *sub-strings r, number of holes $\#_{101}$ and number of pauses $\#_{000}$ we have:*

$$\ell = h + \#_{000} + \#_{101} + 2r.$$

Proof. The length of a string ℓ is the sum of the number of active bits and the number of passive bits. The former is simply the Hamming weight h of the string. The latter is the number of passive bits in each 001 sub-string (i.e. 2) plus the number of passive bits that are removed from the string when reducing it to its parent minimal string. Namely, the middle bit of each 101 sub-string and the leading bit of each 000 sub-string. This gives $\ell = h + \#_{000} + \#_{101} + 2r$.

Example 2. Let $s = 010010101000001000$ with $\ell = 18$ as in Example 1. The Hamming weight of s is $h = 5$ and the number of passive bits is 13. The number of 101 sub-strings is 2 and thus the number of holes is 2. The number of 001 sub-strings is 3 and thus the number of passive bits in 001 sub-strings is 6. Finally, the number of 000 sub-strings is 5 and thus the number of pauses is 5. The sum of such bits gives 13.

We denote the number of strings of length ℓ with Hamming weight h and containing r 001 strings, y pauses and x holes by $\mathrm{N}_5(\ell, h, r, y, x)$. Lemma 1 implies that

$$\mathrm{N}_3(\ell, h, r) = \sum_{x=0}^{\ell-h-2r} \mathrm{N}_5(\ell, h, r, \ell - (h + x + 2r), x). \tag{4}$$

3.2 Computing $\mathrm{N}_5(\ell, h, r, y, x)$

Since each string can be associated to a unique minimal string, it follows that the set of strings can be partitioned in classes, where strings in the same class have the same associated minimal strings. Strings in the same class can be built by adding holes and pauses to the corresponding minimal string in all possible ways.

Specifically, the set of strings of length ℓ, Hamming weight h and number r of 001 sub-strings with y pauses and x holes can be built by first generating the strings of length $\ell - x - y$, Hamming weight h and number of 001 sub-strings r with $x = y = 0$ and then adding for each state x holes and y pauses in all possible ways.

The number of ways to add x holes and y pauses to a minimal string depends on its Hamming weight and its number of 001 sub-strings, but also on the value of its leading and trailing bits. Namely, it depends on whether the minimal string has a 11 sub-string or a 001 sub-string that spans the boundaries.

Example 3. Let $s = 1100111001$ be a minimal string of length $\ell = 10$ and $x = 1$. The hole can be place between any pair of adjacent active bits. But if we consider the pair at indexes $(\ell - 1, 0)$, then the hole can be placed either at the end of the string or at its beginning. In the former case we obtain the string 11001110010 and in the latter case the string 01100111001.

Example 4. Let $s = 011100110$ be a minimal string of length $\ell = 9$ and $y = 1$. The unique pause can be place before any 001 sub-string. If we consider the 001 sub-string at indexes $(\ell - 1, 0, 1)$, then the pause can be placed only between positions $\ell - 2$ and $\ell - 1$ giving the string 0111001100.

Similarly, let $s = 111001100$ be a minimal string of length $\ell = 9$ and $y = 1$. If we consider the 001 sub-string at indexes $(\ell - 2, \ell - 1, 0)$, then the pause can be placed only between positions $\ell - 3$ and $\ell - 2$ giving the string 1110011000.

Example 5. Now, let $s = 0011111$ be a minimal string of length $\ell = 7$ and $y = 1$. If we consider the 001 sub-string at indexes $(0, 1, 2)$, then the pause can be placed between positions $\ell - 1$ and 0 in two different ways, giving the strings 00011111 and 00111110. Similarly, for the same string if $y = 2$, we can build the strings 000011111, 000111110, 001111100.

We denote the pair $(s_0, s_{\ell-1})$ formed by the leading bit and the trailing bit of a minimal string s by S. Of course, S is in $\{(0,0), (0,1), (1,0), (1,1)\}$.

Since s is minimal, $S = (0,0)$ and $S = (1,0)$ imply that there is a 001 sub-string that crosses the boundaries as in Example 4, while $S = (0,1)$ implies that the string starts with a 001 sub-string as in Example 5. Finally, $S = (1,1)$ implies that there is a 11 sub-string that crosses the boundary as in Example 3.

We denote the number of minimal strings with Hamming weight h, r 001 sub-strings and given S by $\mathrm{N}_{min}(h, r, S)$.

It holds that:

$$\mathrm{N}_5(\ell, h, r, y, x) = \sum_S \alpha(h, r, x, S) \times \beta(h, r, y, S) \times \mathrm{N}_{min}(h, r, S)\,, \tag{5}$$

Table 1. Combinatorial expressions to compute the number of minimal states of length ℓ, Hamming weight h and leading and trailing bits specified by S, and the number of ways to add x holes and y pauses to them.

S	$\mathrm{N}_{min}(h, r, S)$	$\alpha(h, r, x, S)$	$\beta(h, r, y, S)$
$(0, 1)$	$\binom{h-1}{r-1}$	$\binom{h-r}{x}$	$\binom{y+r}{y}$
$(0, 0), (1, 0)$	$\binom{h-1}{r-1}$	$\binom{h-r}{x}$	$\binom{y+r-1}{y}$
$(1, 1)$	$\binom{h-1}{r}$	$\binom{h-r-1}{x} + 2 \cdot \binom{h-r-1}{x-1}$	$\binom{y+r-1}{y}$

where $\alpha(h, r, x, S)$ denotes the number of ways to add x holes and $\beta(h, r, y, S)$ the number of ways to add y pauses to a minimal state of length ℓ, Hamming weight h and leading and trailing bits specified by S.

The factors in the right hand side of (5) are summarized in Table 1 and we show how we derived them in the remaining part of this section.

Case: $S = (0, 1)$.

- $\mathrm{N}_{min}(h, r, S) = \binom{h-1}{r-1}$, that is the number of ways of putting $r - 1$ pairs of passive bits between the $h - 1$ pairs of active bits. The position of one 001 sub-string is in fact specified by S.
- $\alpha(h, r, x, S) = \binom{h-r}{x}$, which is the number of ways to distribute x holes over $h - r$ positions, where each position can have at most one hole.
- $\beta(h, r, y, S)$ is the number of ways to distribute y pauses over r positions, where there are no restrictions on the number of pauses per position. Since $S = (0, 1)$ implies that the minimal string starts with a 001 sub-string, then the pauses that are put before it can be placed either at the beginning of the string or at its end, as shown in Example 5. It means that there are actually $r + 1$ positions to place the y pauses. It follows that $\beta(h, r, y, S) = \binom{y+r}{y}$.

Case: $S \in \{(0, 0), (1, 0)\}$.

- $\mathrm{N}_{min}(h, r, S) = \binom{h-1}{r-1}$ as in the previous case.
- $\alpha(h, r, x, S) = \binom{h-r}{x}$, as in the previous case.
- $\beta(h, r, y, S) = \binom{y+r-1}{y}$, which is the number of ways to distribute y pauses over r positions, where there are no restrictions on the number of pauses per position.

Case: $S = (1, 1)$.

- $\mathrm{N}_{min}(h, r, S) = \binom{h-1}{r}$, that is the number of way of putting r pairs of passive bits between the $h - 1$ pairs of active bits remaining after excluding the pair at the boundaries.
- $\alpha(h, r, x, S)$ is the number of ways to distribute x holes over $h - r$ positions, where each position can have at most one hole. Since the minimal state starts with a 1 and ends with a 1 then the hole that is placed between these two

ones can be placed either at the beginning of the state or at its end, as shown in Example 3. For any other pair of active bits, there is a unique way to put the hole. The total count is thus

$$\alpha(h, r, x, S) = \binom{h-r-1}{x} + 2 \cdot \binom{h-r-1}{x-1}$$

where $\binom{h-r-1}{x-K}$ for $K \in \{0, 1\}$ is the number of ways to distribute $x - K$ holes between the $h - r - 1$ pairs of ones remaining after excluding the pair across the boundary.

- $\beta(h, r, y, S) = \binom{y+r-1}{y}$, as in the previous case.

4 Experimental Results

We experimentally verified the correctness of our formula for $\ell \in [3, 32]$ by applying two checks.

The first check consists in exhaustively generating all ℓ-bit states, compute their weight and check that the number of states with given weight corresponds to the number obtained by applying our formula.

The second check is based on the following observation. Since χ_ℓ is a translation-invariant transformation, a state that is obtained by rotational shift of another state will have the same weight. It follows that the set of ℓ-bit states can be partitioned in equivalence classes where the states in each class have the same weight and are one the translated-version of another. When ℓ is prime each equivalence class has cardinality ℓ, except for the class that contains only 1^ℓ. It follows that the number of states with a given weight w should be divisible by ℓ for any $0 < w < \ell - 1$.

In the remaining part of this section, we discuss some well-known primitives where χ_ℓ is used.

4.1 257-Bit State as in Subterranean

We applied the method introduced in this paper to compute the number of differentials with given weight for Subterranean, where χ_ℓ operates on the full state of 257 bits. In Fig. 2a we report the obtained histogram, while in Fig. 2b we report the number of differentials with weight up to a given target.

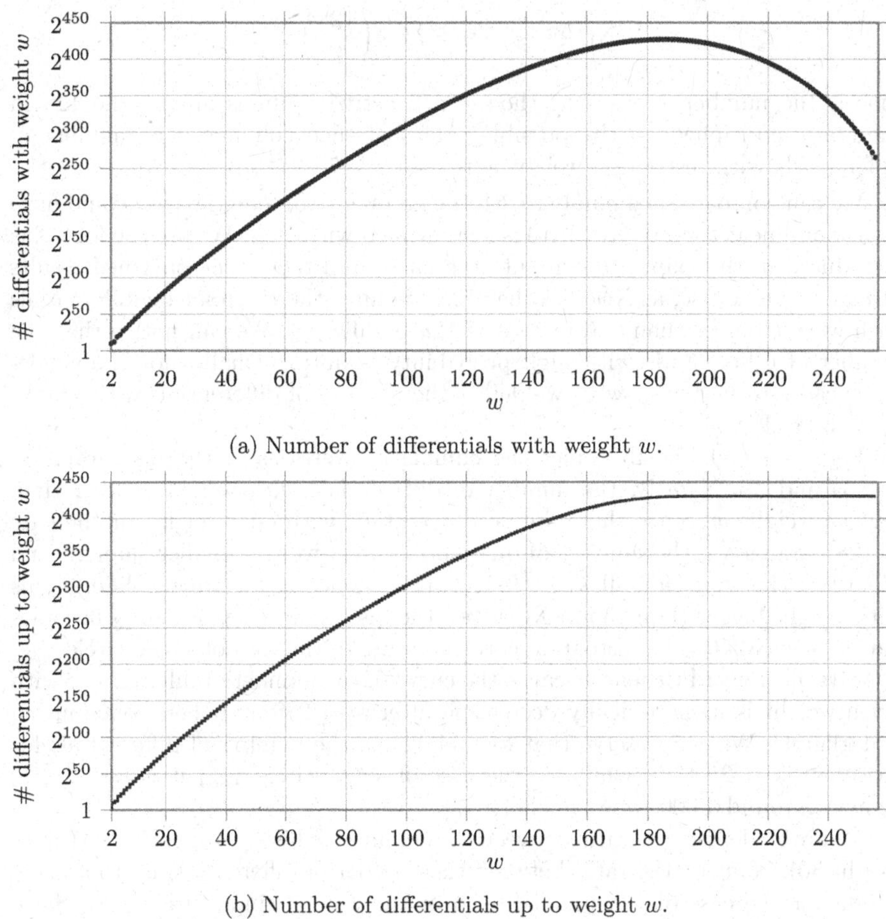

(a) Number of differentials with weight w.

(b) Number of differentials up to weight w.

Fig. 2. Number of differentials for single-circle χ_{257} (as in Subterranean).

4.2 384-Bit State as in Xoodoo

In the permutation XOODOO, the state is composed by 384 bits arranged in an array of shape $4 \times 3 \times 32$. The non-linear layer is a composite χ mapping of 128 circles of length $\ell = 3$. We denote the number of differences in this non-linear layer with weight w as $\mathrm{N}(128 \times 3, w)$. In general, if we have a composite χ mapping of q circles of length ℓ, we denote the number of input differences with weight w by $\mathrm{N}(q \times \ell, w)$. Clearly if $q = 1$ the mapping is not composite and we have $\mathrm{N}(1 \times \ell, w) = \mathrm{N}(\ell, w)$.

In the case of XOODOO, the number of differences in the composite χ mapping with weight w is easy to compute. Since the weight of any 3-bit circle is 2, there are no differences with odd weight. Therefore, $\mathrm{N}(128 \times 3, w) = 0$ for w odd. For w even,

$$\mathrm{N}(128 \times 3, w) = 7^{\frac{w}{2}} \cdot \binom{128}{\frac{w}{2}}$$

that is the number of ways to choose $w/2$ active columns among the 128 in the state, multiplied by the possible values of such columns. The number of differentials with restriction weight w is then $2^w \cdot 7^{\frac{w}{2}} \cdot \binom{128}{\frac{w}{2}}$.

We can compare such number with the number of differentials we would have if the non-linear layer of XOODOO is instantiated with χ_{384}. We use the formulas introduced in this paper to compute the latter and report the obtained results in Fig. 3a. Of course, as XOODOO has 128 columns, there cannot be differentials with weight bigger than 256 in case of 128 parallel χ_3. We can notice that the number of differentials with high probability is always smaller for the single-circle case. To better show it, we depict the number of differentials with weight up to 30 in Fig. 3b.

Figure 4a and Fig. 4b depict the cumulative versions of the histograms in Fig. 3a and 3b. Namely, the number of differentials with weight smaller than a given weight w. Since there are no differentials with odd weight for the case of 128 parallel χ_3, the number of differentials with weight smaller than $2k$ and $2k+1$ is the same for all $k \in \{0, 1, \ldots 127\}$. Since there are no differentials with weight bigger than 256 in XOODOO, the histogram for parallel χ_3 becomes flat after $w = 256$. The histogram corresponding to the case of single-circle χ_{384} appears flat toward the end because the curve of the number of differentials with given weight is monotonically decreasing after $w = 288$ and their contribution is negligible. We can observe that for weight 30, the number of differentials for XOODOO is $\approx 2^{135.636}$, while for the case of single-circle χ_{384} it is $\approx 2^{123.793}$. Namely, around 4,000 times smaller.

Figure 5b depicts the ratio between the cumulative histogram in Fig. 4b (up to weight 30). Namely, the ratio between the number of differentials up to a given weight for the case of 128 parallel χ_3 over the case of single-circle χ_{384}. Since there are no differentials with odd weight for the case of 128 parallel χ_3, and thus for all $k \in \{0, 1, \ldots 127\}$ the number of differentials with weight smaller than $2k$ and $2k+1$ is the same, the curve presents a zigzag trend.

Figure 5a depicts the full ratio between the cumulative histogram in Fig. 4a.

4.3 400-Bit State as in Keccak-*f*[400]

In KECCAK-f[400], the state is organized as an array of $5 \times 5 \times 16$ bits. The non-linear layer is a composite χ mapping of 80 circles of length 5. Therefore, we denote the number of differences in this non-linear layer with weight w as $\mathrm{N}(80 \times 5, w)$.

In general, if we have a composite χ mapping of $q > 1$ circles of length ℓ, we can efficiently compute the number of differences with weight w by q-fold convolution using the following recursion:

$$\mathrm{N}(q \times \ell, w) = \sum_{0 \leq x \leq w} \mathrm{N}((q-1) \times \ell, x)\mathrm{N}(\ell, w - x)\,.$$

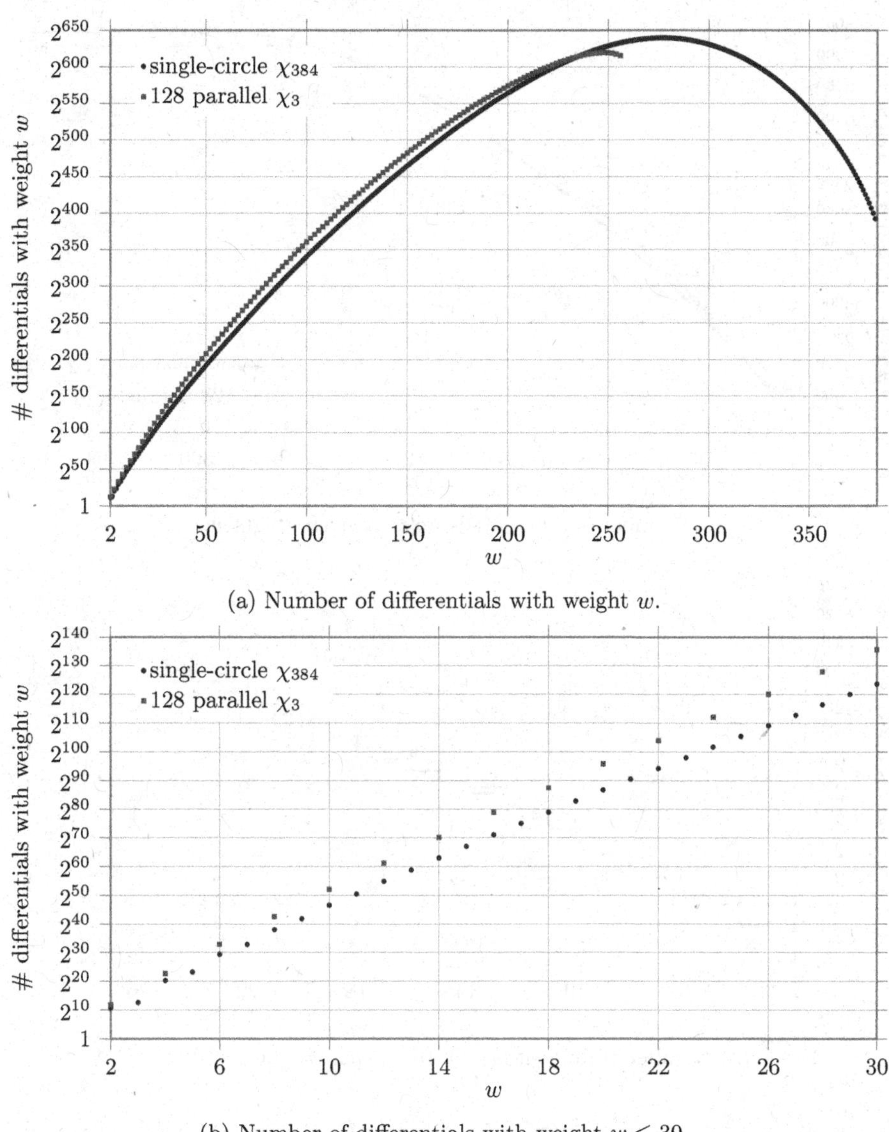

(a) Number of differentials with weight w.

(b) Number of differentials with weight $w \leq 30$.

Fig. 3. Number of differentials with given weight for the case of 128 parallel χ_3 (as in XOODOO) and the case of single-circle χ_{384}.

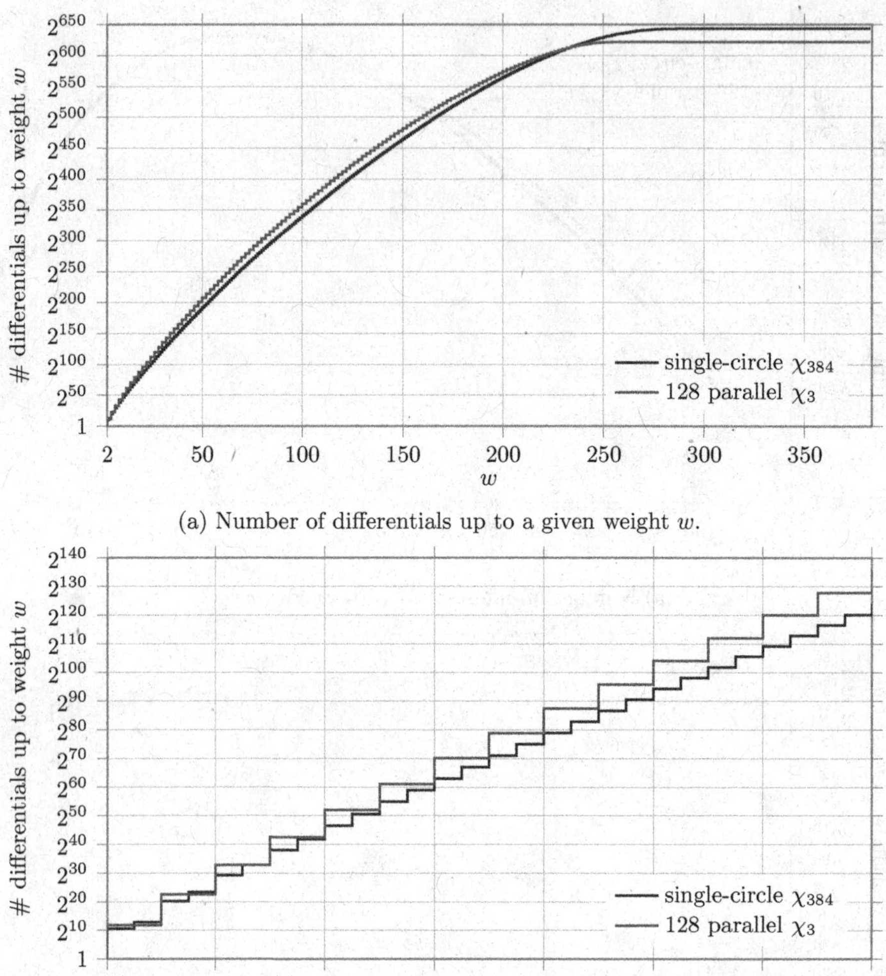

(a) Number of differentials up to a given weight w.

(b) Number of differentials up to a given weight $w \leq 30$.

Fig. 4. Number of differentials up to a given weight for the case of 128 parallel χ_3 (as in XOODOO) and the case of single-circle χ_{384}.

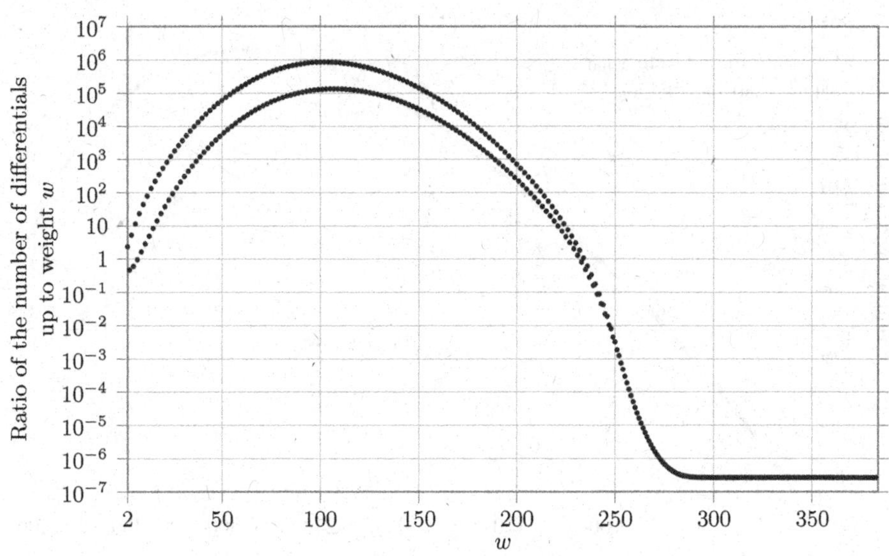

(a) Ratio between the number of differentials up to weight w.

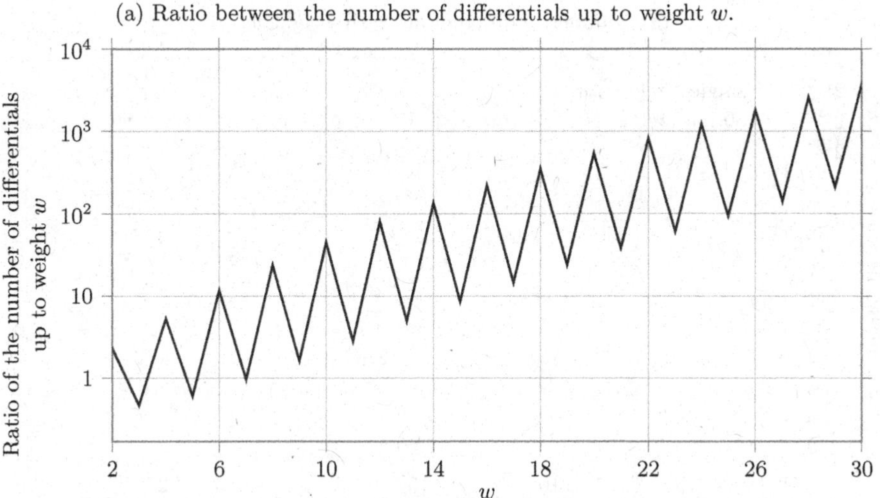

(b) Ratio between the number of differentials up to weight $w \leq 30$.

Fig. 5. Ratio between the number of differentials up to weight w for the case of 128 parallel χ_3 (as in XOODOO) over the case of single-circle χ_{384}.

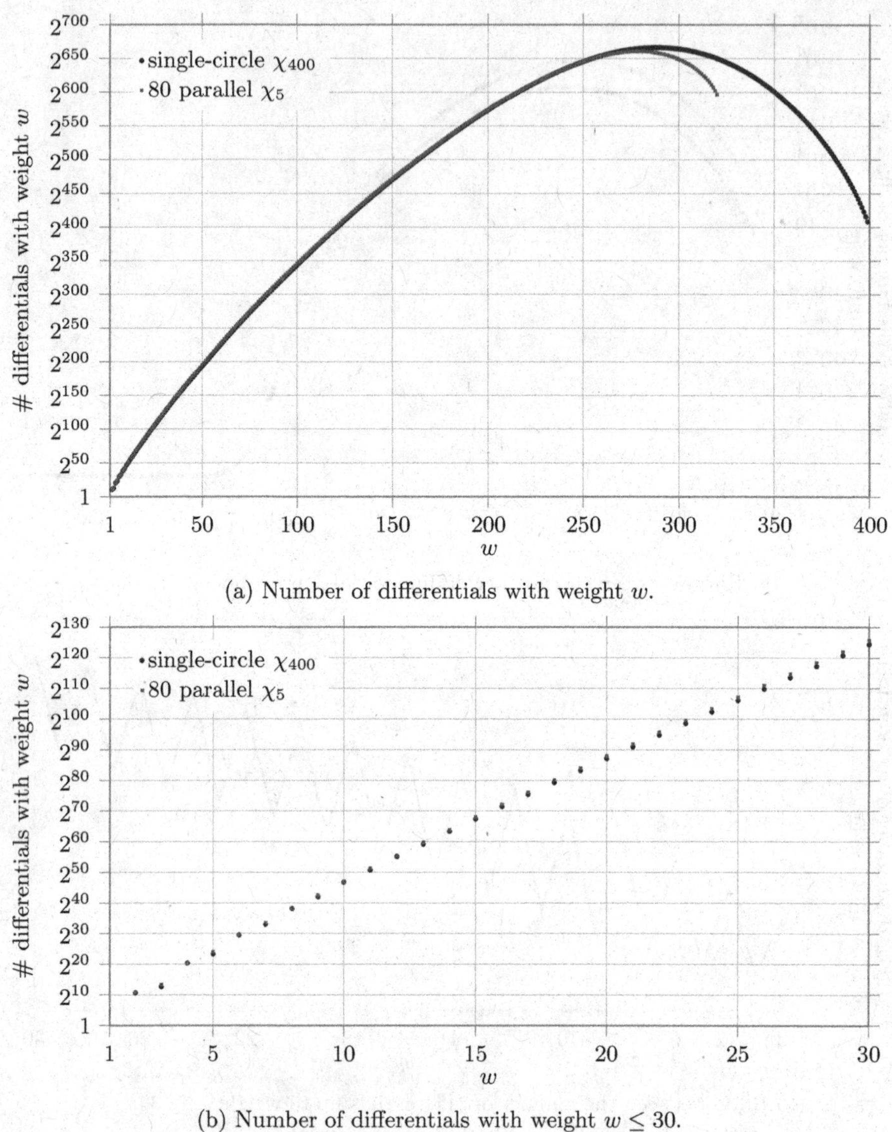

(a) Number of differentials with weight w.

(b) Number of differentials with weight $w \leq 30$.

Fig. 6. Number of differentials with given weight for the case of 80 parallel χ_5 (as in KECCAK-f[400]) and the case of single-circle χ_{400}.

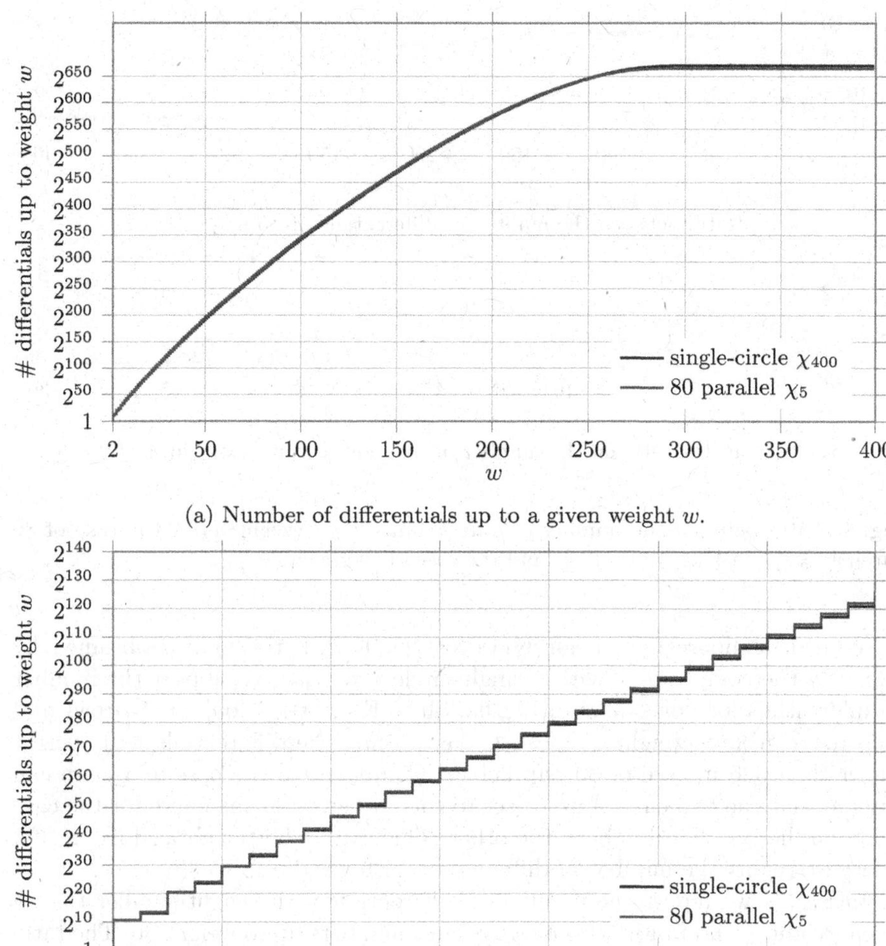

(a) Number of differentials up to a given weight w.

(b) Number of differentials up to a given weight $w \leq 30$.

Fig. 7. Number of differentials up to a given weight for the case of 80 parallel χ_5 (as in KECCAK-$f[400]$) and the case of single-circle χ_{400}.

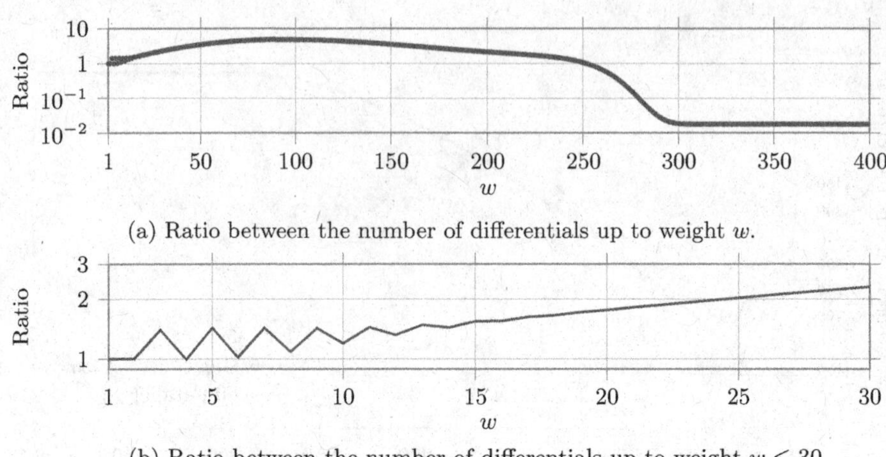

(a) Ratio between the number of differentials up to weight w.

(b) Ratio between the number of differentials up to weight $w \leq 30$.

Fig. 8. Ratio between the number of differentials up to weight w for the case of 80 parallel χ_5 (as in KECCAK-f[400]) and the case of single-circle χ_{400}.

We can compare figures for KECCAK-f[400] with the figures obtained by replacing the composite χ with a single-circle $\chi = \chi_{400}$. We report the number of differentials for both cases in Fig. 6a. Since KECCAK-f[400] has 80 rows and each row can have weight at most 4, there cannot be differentials with weight bigger than 320 in case of 80 parallel χ_5. Compared to the case of χ_3, we can observe that the two curves are closer to each other, with the curve for the case of 80 parallel χ_5 slightly above the other. This can be better noticed in Fig. 6b, where we report the number of differentials with weight up to 30.

In Fig. 7a we report the number of differentials with weight smaller than a given weight w and in Fig. 7b we report such numbers up to weight 30. The ratio between the two cases is depicted in Fig. 8a. We can observe that the number of differentials with weight smaller than 30 for the case of 80 parallel χ_5 is only 2.3 times larger than the case of single-circle χ_{400} (Fig. 8b).

5 Conclusions

We introduced a method to compute the number of differentials with given DP over the non-linear map χ_ℓ for any size of ℓ. This is a useful tool to evaluate and compare the alternatives available to instantiate a non-linear layer based on χ_ℓ. One can for instance choose to use parallel instances of χ_ℓ operating on small circles or to use a single-circle χ_ℓ operating on the whole state.

We used our method to compute the number of differentials with given DP over the non-linear layer of Subterranean, which consists of a single-circle χ_ℓ with $\ell = 257$.

Then we used our method to compare the non-linear layers of XOODOO and KECCAK-f[400], which can be seen as the application of parallel instances of

χ_ℓ on small circles, with non-linear layers instantiated with single-circle χ_ℓ. We observed that in the case of XOODOO, where $\ell = 3$, the use of single-circle χ_ℓ seems more advantageous, as the number of differentials up to a given weight is smaller compared to the parallel χ_ℓ case. Instead, for $\ell = 5$ this difference is significantly reduced and almost disappears.

Acknowledgements. Joan Daemen and Alireza Mehrdad are supported by the European Research Council under the ERC advanced grant agreement under grant ERC-2017-ADG Nr. 788980 ESCADA.

Silvia Mella is supported by the Cryptography Research Center of the Technology Innovation Institute (TII), Abu Dhabi (UAE), under the TII-Radboud project with title *Evaluation and Implementation of Lightweight Cryptographic Primitives and Protocols.*

References

[BDPA06] Bertoni, G., Daemen, J., Peeters, M., Van Assche, G.: RadioGatún, a belt-and-mill hash function. Cryptology ePrint Archive, Report 2006/369 (2006). Presented at the Second Cryptographic Hash Workshop, Santa Barbara, 24–25 August 2006

[BDPA11] Bertoni, G., Daemen, J., Peeters, M., Van Assche, G.: The keccak reference (2011)

[BDPA13] Bertoni, G., Daemen, J., Peeters, M., Van Assche, G.: Keccak. In: Johansson, T., Nguyen, P.Q. (eds.) EUROCRYPT 2013. LNCS, vol. 7881, pp. 313–314. Springer, Heidelberg (2013). https://doi.org/10.1007/978-3-642-38348-9_19

[Dae95] Daemen, J.: Cipher and hash function design, strategies based on linear and differential cryptanalysis. Ph.D. thesis. K.U. Leuven (1995). http://jda.noekeon.org/

[DEMS21] Dobraunig, C., Eichlseder, M., Mendel, F., Schläffer, M.: Ascon v1.2: lightweight authenticated encryption and hashing. J. Cryptol. **34**(3), 33 (2021)

[DHAK18] Daemen, J., Hoffert, S., Van Assche, G., Van Keer, R.: The design of Xoodoo and Xoofff. IACR Trans. Symmetric Cryptol. **2018**(4), 1–38 (2018)

[DMMR20] Daemen, J., Massolino, P.M.C., Mehrdad, A., Rotella, Y.: The subterranean 2.0 cipher suite. IACR Trans. Symmetric Cryptol. **2020**(S1), 262–294 (2020)

[DR02] Daemen, J., Rijmen, V.: The Design of Rijndael: AES - The Advanced Encryption Standard. Information Security and Cryptography, Springer, Heidelberg (2002). https://doi.org/10.1007/978-3-662-04722-4

[NIS15] NIST. SHA-3 Standard: Permutation-Based Hash and Extendable-Output Functions (2015). https://www.nist.gov/publications/sha-3-standard-permutation-based-hash-and-extendable-output-functions

Light-OCB: Parallel Lightweight Authenticated Cipher with Full Security

Avik Chakraborti[1(✉)], Nilanjan Datta[2], Ashwin Jha[3], Cuauhtemoc Mancillas-López[4], and Mridul Nandi[5]

[1] University of Exeter, Exeter, UK
[2] Institute for Advancing Intelligence, TCG CREST, Kolkata, India
nilanjan.datta@tcgcrest.org
[3] CISPA Helmholtz Center for Information Security, Saarbrücken, Germany
ashwin.jha@cispa.de
[4] Computer Science Department, CINVESTAV-IPN, Mexico City, Mexico
cuauhtemoc.mancillas@cinvestav.mx
[5] Indian Statistical Institute, Kolkata, India

Abstract. This paper proposes a lightweight authenticated encryption (AE) scheme, called Light-OCB, which can be viewed as a lighter variant of the CAESAR winner OCB as well as a faster variant of the high profile NIST LWC competition submission LOCUS-AEAD. Light-OCB is structurally similar to LOCUS-AEAD and uses a nonce-based derived key that provides optimal security, and short-tweak tweakable blockcipher (tBC) for efficient domain separation. Light-OCB improves over LOCUS-AEAD by reducing the number of primitive calls, and thereby significantly optimizing the throughput. To establish our claim, we provide FPGA hardware implementation details and benchmark for Light-OCB against LOCUS-AEAD and several other well-known AEs. The implementation results depict that, when instantiated with the tBC TweGIFT64, Light-OCB achieves an extremely low hardware footprint - consuming only around 1128 LUTs and 307 slices (significantly lower than that for LOCUS-AEAD) while maintaining a throughput of 880 Mbps, which is almost twice that of LOCUS-AEAD. To the best of our knowledge, this figure is significantly better than all the known implementation results of other lightweight ciphers with parallel structures.

Keywords: Authenticated encryption · Lightweight · tBC · Light-OCB, Parallel

1 Introduction

From the recent past, lightweight cryptography is enjoying high popularity due to an increase in the demands of security for lightweight IoT applications such as healthcare applications, sensor-based applications, banking applications, etc., where resource-constrained devices communicate and need to be implemented with a low resource. Lightweight cryptography involves providing security in these resource-constrained environments. The importance of this research

L. Batina et al. (Eds.): SPACE 2021, LNCS 13162, pp. 22–41, 2022.
https://doi.org/10.1007/978-3-030-95085-9_2

domain has been addressed by the ongoing NIST Lightweight Standardization Competition (LWC) [17] followed by the CAESAR [8]. Hence, in recent years, the cryptographic research community has seen a surge in new lightweight authenticated encryption proposals.

One popular design approach for lightweight AE schemes is to use a blockcipher based parallel structure as it can be efficient for both lightweight and faster implementations. Blockcipher (BC) based parallel AE schemes popularly use XEX structure. It processes all the inputs in parallel and finally integrates them. Thus, blockcipher-based parallel AE schemes can be well described by the underlying blockcipher, and the final integration function. Consequently, the efficiency and the hardware footprint of the AE scheme also largely depend on these two components. In the following part, we assume that the underlying blockcipher is ultra-lightweight and efficient to instantiate the AE scheme. The efficiency of a construction is primarily dependent upon the *rate*, the number of data blocks processed per primitive call where the upper bound on the rate value is one. Here, we only concentrate on rate-1 authenticated encryptions with a small hardware footprint such that we can achieve a lightweight construction as well as a high throughput construction.

1.1 Parallel Authenticated Encryption

Parallel AE modes, such as OCB [21], OTR [15], COPA [1], ELmD [7] have mainly been designed to exploit the advantage of parallel computations needed for several high performance computing environments. These constructions mainly concentrate on efficiency in software as well as on faster implementations in hardware. Among them, OCB and OTR are efficient, achieve rate one, and COPA and ELmD achieve rate half. One of the disadvantages of such schemes are large state size. For example, OCB has $3n + k$ and OTR, COPA and ELmD require $4n + k$-bit state size where n and k are the block size and the key size respectively. Furthermore, both of them are only birthday bound secure in the block size n. This means they need at least an 128-bit block cipher to satisfy the NIST criteria (which says that when the key size is 128 bits, any cryptanalytic attack should need at least 2^{112} computations in a single key setting). This large state size makes these designs inefficient for lightweight applications. One possible way out is to improve the security, and thereby instantiate with 64-bit primitives such as PRESENT [6], SKINNY [4], or GIFT [3] that have ultra lightweight implementation with decent throughputs. In [16], Naito proposed a variant of OCB, called ΘCB+, which offers beyond the birthday bound security but does not meet NIST's security criteria if instantiated with 64-bit primitive. This raises the important question of whether it is possible to design AE schemes using 64-bit primitives that satisfies the NIST criteria.

1.2 LOCUS-AEAD

Chakraborti et al. answers the above question in a positive direction by proposing LOCUS-AEAD [10] that employs OCB style encryption with nonce-based derived key that boosts the design by providing full security, and hence realizable by 64-bit primitives. Additionally, the novel use of short-tweak tweakable block ciphers handles all the domain separation, and makes the design simple and compact. To achieve RUP security, the construction uses two primitives in a sequential manner to process each message block, which degrades the throught, and hence the speed of the cipher, which is the primary focus for parallel constructions. So, we ask the question

"Can we design a rate-1 parallel authenticated cipher with full security?"

1.3 Our Contribution

We answer the above question in an affirmative way by presenting a new *rate one* parallel, nonce based authenticated encryption mode of operation with full security named Light-OCB. As the name suggests, Light-OCB follows the general design paradigms of popular NAEAD modes OCB [12,13]. However, we update Light-OCB introduces several key changes (see Sect. 3.1 for more details) in order to add new features. Some of the important changes include nonce-based rekeying and short-tweak based domain separation similarly as used in [10].

Light-OCB achieves higher NAEAD security bounds with lighter primitives. It allows close to 2^{64} data and 2^{128} time limit when instantiated by a block cipher with 64-bit block and 128-bit key. Light-OCB is a single pass, online, fully parallelizable, rate-1 authenticated encryption mode. This mode is extremely versatile, in the sense that, it is equally suitable for lightweight memory constrained environments, as well as high-performance applications. We provide concrete AE security proof for Light-OCB in the ideal-cipher model.

We instantiate Light-OCB with TweGIFT-64 [9,10], a tweakable variant of the GIFT-64-128 [3] block cipher. TweGIFT-64 is a dedicated design, built upon the original GIFT-64-128 block cipher, for efficient processing of small tweak values of size 4-bit. TweGIFT-64 provides sufficient security while maintaining the lightweight features of GIFT-64-128. We propose Light-OCB [TweGIFT-64], the TweGIFT-64 based instantiation of Light-OCB.

Finally, we also provide our own hardware implementation results for Light-OCB on FPGA. The implementation result depicts Light-OCB is significantly better than LOCUS-AEAD in throughput (twice the value for LOCUS-AEAD). In fact, Light-OCB also improves the hardware area over LOCUS-AEAD.

1.4 Applications and Use Cases

The most important feature of Light-OCB is its scope of applicability. At one end of the spectrum, the parallelizability of Light-OCB make them a perfect candidate for applications in high-performance infrastructures. On the other end, there overall state size is competitively small with respect to many existing lightweight candidates, which makes them suitable for low-area hardware implementations. We would like to emphasize that Light-OCB is inherently parallel and can be implemented in a fully pipelined manner keeping a comparable area-efficient implementation. Hence, it is well-suited for protocols that require both lightweight and high-performance implementations e.g., lightweight clients interacting with high performance servers (e.g., LwM2M protocols [19]). Some real life applications, where our proposed mode would best fit includes vehicular applications and memory encryptions.

1.5 Light-OCB in DSCI Light-Weight Competition

In 2020, National CoE, the joint initiative of the Data security council of India and the Ministry of Electronics and IT (MeitY), announced a lightweight cryptography competition named "Lightweight Cipher Design Challenge 2020" [18]. One of the primary objectives of the challenge is to design new lightweight authenticated ciphers, and the best designs will be considered for developing the prototype for ready industry implementation. The algorithm Light-OCB has been nominated as one of the top three candidates in the challenge and has been selected for the final round. Interestingly, this is the only construction that supports full pipelined implementation alongside a very hardware footprint, making it to be the most versatile design in the competition.

2 Preliminaries

2.1 Notations and Conventions

For $n \in \mathbb{N}$, we write $\{0,1\}^*$ and $\{0,1\}^n$ to denote the set of all binary strings including the empty string λ, and the set of all n-bit binary strings, respectively. For $A \in \{0,1\}^*$, $|A|$ denotes the length (number of the bits) of A, where $|\lambda| = 0$ by convention. For all practical purposes, we use the little-endian format for representing binary strings, i.e., the least significant bit is the rightmost bit. For any non-empty binary string X, $(X_{k-1}, \ldots, X_0) \xleftarrow{n} x$ denotes the n-bit block parsing of X, where $|X_i| = n$ for $0 \leq i \leq k-2$, and $1 \leq |X_{k-1}| \leq n$. For $A, B \in \{0,1\}^*$ and $|A| = |B|$, we write $A \oplus B$ to denote the bitwise XOR of A and B.

We use the notation $\widetilde{\mathsf{E}}$ to denote a tweakable block cipher. For $K \in \{0,1\}^\kappa$, $T \in \{0,1\}^\tau$, and $M \in \{0,1\}^n$, we use $\widetilde{\mathsf{E}}_{K,T}(M) := \widetilde{\mathsf{E}}(K,T,M)$ to denote invocation of the encryption function of $\widetilde{\mathsf{E}}$ on input K, T, and M. The decryption function is analogously defined as $\widetilde{\mathsf{D}}_{K,T}(M)$. We fix positive even integers n, τ, κ, r, and t to denote the *block size*, *tweak size*, *key size*, *nonce size*, and *tag size*, respectively, in bits. Throughout this document, we fix $n = 64$, $\tau = 4$, and $\kappa = 128$, $r = \kappa$, and $t = n$.

We sometimes use the terms (*complete*) *blocks* for n-bit strings, and *partial blocks* for m-bit strings, where $m < n$. Throughout, we use the function ozs, defined by the mapping

$$\forall X \in \bigcup_{m=1}^{n} \{0,1\}^m, \quad X \mapsto \begin{cases} 0^{n-|X|-1}\|1\|X & \text{if } |X| < n, \\ X & \text{otherwise,} \end{cases}$$

as the padding rule to map partial blocks to complete blocks. Note that the mapping is injective over partial blocks. For any $X \in \{0,1\}^+$ and $0 \leq i \leq |X|-1$, x_i denotes the i-th bit of X. The function chop takes a string X and an integer $i \leq |X|$, and returns the least significant i bits of X, i.e., $x_{i-1} \cdots x_0$.

The set $\{0,1\}^\kappa$ can be viewed as the finite field $\mathbb{F}_{2^\kappa}$ consisting of 2^κ elements. Addition in $\mathbb{F}_{2^\kappa}$ is just bitwise XOR of two κ-bit strings, and hence denoted by $\oplus$. $P(x)$ denotes the primitive polynomial used to represent the field $\mathbb{F}_{2^\kappa}$, and α denotes the primitive element in this representation. The multiplication of $A, B \in \mathbb{F}_{2^\kappa}$ is defined as $A \odot B := A(x) \cdot B(x) \pmod{P(x)}$, i.e., polynomial multiplication modulo $P(x)$ in $\mathbb{F}_2$. For $\kappa = 128$, we fix the primitive polynomial

$$P(x) = x^{128} + x^7 + x^2 + x + 1.$$

2.2 (Ideal) Tweakable Blockcipher

The notion of tweakable blockciphers was first formalized by Liskov et al. [14]. Additional to a plaintext X and a key K, it takes a third input - a tweak T, which is generally public. An ideal tweakable blockcipher provides an independent permutation for each new key and tweak pair (K, T). More formally,

$$\widetilde{\mathscr{E}} : \mathcal{K} \times \mathcal{T} \times \{0,1\}^n \to \{0,1\}^n.$$

Here, $\mathcal{K}$ and $\mathcal{T}$ are called the keyspace and the tweak space respectively. To ease the notation, for a fix K and T we denote $\widetilde{\mathscr{E}}(K, T, \cdot)$ by $\widetilde{\mathscr{E}}_K^T(\cdot)$. Hence, according to the definition $\widetilde{\mathscr{E}}_K^T$ is a permutation (for K and T).

2.3 Authenticated Encryption in the Ideal Cipher Model

Authenticated encryption (AE) is a cryptographic scheme that provides both privacy of the message and authenticity of both the message, the nonce, and the associated data. It takes as input, a plaintext $M \in \{0,1\}^*$, a nonce $N \in \{0,1\}^n$ (typically one block data) and an associated data $A \in \{0,1\}^*$, such that the encryption function of AE, $\mathcal{E}_K$, outputs a ciphertext-tag pair (C, T) such that $|C| = |M|$ and $|T| = t$ (t is called the tag length). Throughout the paper, we assume that t is fixed and $n = t$. There is a corresponding decryption function, $\mathcal{D}_K$, that takes (N, A, C, T) as the inputs and outputs the corresponding ciphertext M if (N, A, C, T) is successfully verified, otherwise $\mathcal{D}_K$ rejects the (N, A, C, T) tuple denoted by the symbol $\perp$.

Privacy in the Ideal Cipher Model. Given an adversary $\mathcal{A}$, we define the *privacy-advantage* of $\mathcal{A}$ against $\mathcal{AE}$ in the ideal cipher model as

$$\mathbf{Adv}^{\mathsf{priv}}_{\mathcal{AE}[\widetilde{\mathscr{E}}]}(\mathcal{A}) = |\Pr[\mathcal{A}^{\mathcal{AE}_K, \widetilde{\mathscr{E}}^{\pm}} = 1] - \Pr[\mathcal{A}^{\$, \widetilde{\mathscr{E}}^{\pm}} = 1]|,$$

where \$ returns a random string of the same length as the output length of $\mathcal{AE}_K$. Where the maximum is taken over all adversaries running in time t and making q_e many queries to the encryption oracle with an aggregate of σ_e blocks and q_p many the primitive queries.

INT-CTXT Security in the Ideal Cipher Model. We say that an adversary $\mathcal{A}$ *forges* an AE scheme $(\mathcal{AE}, \mathcal{AD})$ in the INT-CTXT security settings in the ideal cipher model if $\mathcal{A}$ is able to compute a tuple (N, A, C, T) satisfying $\mathcal{AD}_K(N, A, C, T) \neq \perp$, without querying (N, A, M) for some M to $\mathcal{AE}_K$ and receiving (C, T), i.e., (N, A, C, T) is a non-trivial forgery. The *forging advantage* for an adversary $\mathcal{A}$ is written as

$$\mathbf{Adv}^{\mathsf{int\text{-}ctxt}}_{\mathcal{AE}}(\mathcal{A}) = \Pr[\mathcal{A}^{\mathcal{AE}_K, \mathcal{AD}_K, \widetilde{\mathscr{E}}^{\pm}} \text{ forges}],$$

and the maximum forging advantage for all adversaries running in time t, making q_e encryption queries with an aggregate of σ_e blocks, q_p ideal cipher oracle queries and q_v forgery attempts with an aggregate of σ_v blocks is denoted by

$$\mathbf{Adv}^{\mathsf{int\text{-}ctxt}}_{\mathcal{AE}}((q_e, q_v, q_p), (\sigma_e, \sigma_v), t) = \max_{\mathcal{A}} \mathbf{Adv}^{\mathsf{int\text{-}ctxt}}_{\mathcal{AE}}(\mathcal{A}).$$

2.4 Coefficients-H Technique

We briefly describe the Coefficients-H technique proposed by Patarin [20]. This technique is used to find the upper bound of the statistical distance between the outputs of two interactive systems. This is traditionally used to prove the information theoretic pseudo randomness of constructions. Here, we assume a computationally unbounded adversary (hence deterministic) $\mathcal{A}$ that interacts with either the real oracle, i.e., the construction of our interest, or the ideal oracle which is usually considered to be a uniform random function or permutation. The tple of all the interactive queries and responses that $\mathcal{A}$ made and received to and from the oracle, is called a *transcript* of $\mathcal{A}$, which is typically denoted by ω. We often let the oracle release additional information $\mathcal{A}$ only if $\mathcal{A}$ is done with all its queries and replies but before it outputs its decision bit.

Let Λ_1 and Λ_0 denote the probability distributions of the transcript ω induced by the real oracle and the ideal oracle respectively. The probability of realizing a transcript ω in the ideal oracle (i.e., $\Pr[\Lambda_0 = \omega]$) is called the *ideal interpolation probability*. Similarly, one can define the *real interpolation probability*. A transcript ω is said to be *attainable* with respect to $\mathcal{A}$ if the ideal interpolation probability is non-zero (i.e., $\Pr[\Lambda_1 = \omega] > 0$). We denote the set of all attainable transcripts by Ω. Following these notations, we state the main lemma of H-Coefficient Technique as follows:

Lemma 1. *Suppose we have a set of transcripts, $\Omega_{\mathsf{bad}} \subseteq \Omega$, which we call* bad *transcripts, and the following conditions hold:*

1. *The probability of getting a transcript in Ω_{bad} the ideal oracle $\mathcal{O}_0$ is at most ϵ_1,*
2. *For any transcript $\omega \in \Omega \backslash \Omega_{\mathsf{bad}}$, we have $\Pr[\Lambda_1 = \omega)] \geq (1 - \epsilon_2) \cdot \Pr[\Lambda_0 = \omega]$.*

Then, we have

$$|\Pr[\mathcal{A}^{\mathcal{O}_0} = 1] - \Pr[\mathcal{A}^{\mathcal{O}_1} = 1]| \leq \epsilon_1 + \epsilon_2. \tag{1}$$

Proof of this lemma can be found in [22].

3 Specification

We propose a short-tweak tweakable block cipher based authenticated encryption algorithm Light-OCB instantiated with the underlying tweakable block cipher TweGIFT-64. The instantiation is denoted by Light-OCB [TweGIFT-64].

3.1 Light-OCB Mode

During the encryption phase, Light-OCB mode receives an encryption key $K \in \{0,1\}^\kappa$, an associated data $A \in \{0,1\}^*$, a nonce $N \in \{0,1\}^\kappa$, and a message $M \in \{0,1\}^*$ as inputs and generates a ciphertext $C \in \{0,1\}^{|M|}$, and a tag $T \in \{0,1\}^n$ pair. The corresponding decryption function receives a key $K \in \{0,1\}^\kappa$, an associated data $A \in \{0,1\}^*$, a nonce $N \in \{0,1\}^\kappa$, a ciphertext $C \in \{0,1\}^*$, and a tag $T \in \{0,1\}^n$ pair as inputs, and returns the corresponding plaintext $M \in \{0,1\}^{|C|}$, if T is matched. Light-OCB is tweakable block cipher based with an underlying primitive $\widetilde{\mathsf{E}}$. The tweaks are very short with 4-bit length, and are mainly used for domain separation. The 4-bit tweaks vary from 0 to 13. Light-OCB can process data with a maximum $2^{64} - 1$ block message and a maximum $2^{64} - 1$ block AD.

Initialization. In the initialization phase, a κ-bit nonce N is added to the κ-bit master secret key K to output a κ-bit nonce-based encryption key denoted by K_N. Next, Δ_N, a nonce dependent masking key is generated by double encrypting a constant 0^n with K and K_N successively with $\widetilde{\mathsf{E}}$.

Associated Data Processing. In this phase, we divide the data into n-bit blocks and the blocks are processed following the hash layer of PMAC [5]. For each of the associated data blocks, we first update the current key value by field multiplying it by 2. Next, we add this block with Δ_N and encrypt it with $\widetilde{\mathsf{E}}$ under the fixed tweak 0010 (also denoted by 2 in integer representation) and K_N. The encrypted output is finally accumulated by adding it to the previous checksum value. For domain separation, if the final block is partial the tweak 0011 is used (also denoted by 3) to process it. Output of this associated data processing phase is denoted as AD checksum. This phase is described in Fig. 1 and Algorithm 1.

Plaintext Processing. In this phase, we divide the message into n-bit blocks and the blocks are processed following OCB's [21] message processing. Each message block is first masked and then encrypted with the tBC. Next, it is again masked to compute the ciphertext block. The Δ_N masking along a query is done following OCB and plaintext checksum is computed by adding all the message blocks. For the last plaintext block, we first apply XEX on the block length (instead of applying it on the last plaintext block) and add the output with the last plaintext block. This ensures a similar process technique of the complete or incomplete last blocks. Note the, we also update the key by multiplying it by 2 before each block processing. It is described in Fig. 2.

Tag Generation. In this phase, tweak 0100 and 0101 (4 and 5 respectively) are used for non final and final blocks respectively. Here, XEX transformation is applied on the sum of the plaintext checksum and AD checksum. Algorithm 1 describes this phase in detail.

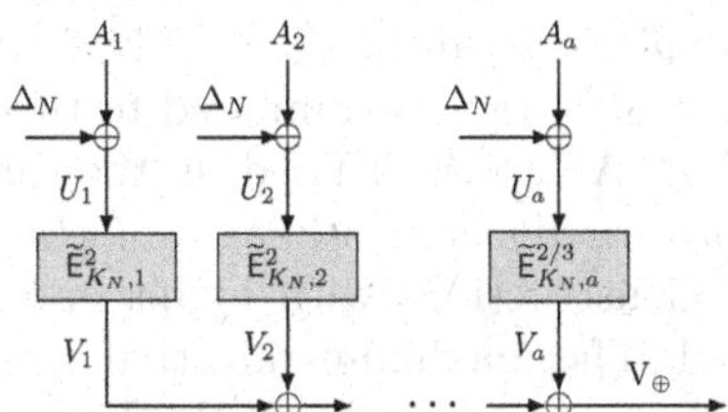

Fig. 1. Associated data processing for Light-OCB. Here $\widetilde{\mathsf{E}}^t_{K_N,i}$ denotes invocation of $\widetilde{\mathsf{E}}$ with key $2^{i+1} \odot K_N$ and tweak i. For the final associated data block, the use of $\widetilde{\mathsf{E}}^{2/3}_{K_N,a}$ indicates invocation of $\widetilde{\mathsf{E}}$ with key $2^a \odot K_N$ and tweak 2 or 3 depending on whether the final block is full or partial.

3.2 Features

Here we discuss the salient features of our proposal and possible applications:

1. **High Security:** Light-OCB provides beyond the birthday bound security as it uses nonce-based encryption key and masking key. Actually, Light-OCB provides the optimal security with the level $DT = O(2^{n+\kappa})$, such that D and T are the data and time complexity, respectively. We assume, $D < 2^n$, and $T < 2^\kappa$.
2. **Lightweight:** Light-OCB satisfies all the lightweight requirements of the NIST lightweight standardization process. In fact, Light-OCB uses a 64-bit block cipher and optimizes the state size. TweGIFT-64 can perfectly fit with Light-OCB.
3. **Parallel:** Light-OCB has a parallel structure and hence the implementation of Light-OCB can be fully pipelined. This can help to achieve high throughput.

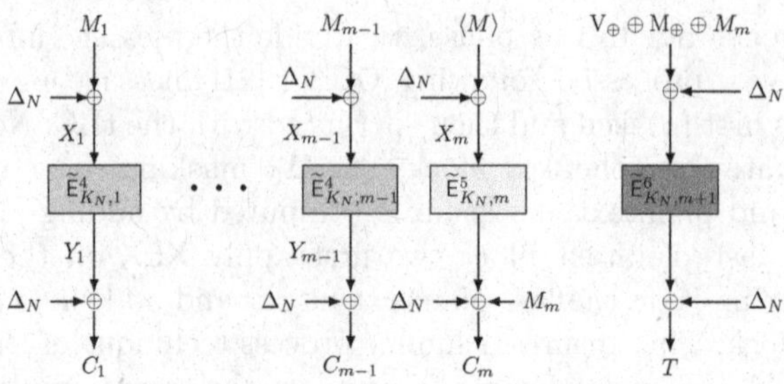

Fig. 2. Processing of an m block message M and tag generation for Light-OCB. $\langle \text{len} \rangle_n$ denotes the n bit representation of the size of the final block in bits. $M_\oplus$ denotes the plaintext checksum value and $V_\oplus$ denotes the AD checksum value. $\widetilde{E}^t_{K_N,i}$ is defined in a similar manner as in Fig. 1.

4. **Single Pass:** Light-OCB makes only one pass through the data while maintaining both confidentiality and authenticity. This, in turn reduces the computational cost by a factor of two as compared to two-pass schemes.
5. **Rate-1:** The *rate* of an AEAD is defined as the number of blocks of the message (plaintext) processed per non-linear (block-cipher, field multiplication, etc.) operation. Constructions with higher rates have shorter latency and achieve high speed. The maximum rate that a secure AEAD construction can achieve is 1, and our mode Light-OCB achieves the rate. This signifies extremely high speed and low latency which is ideal for high-speed applications.
6. **Optimal:** An authenticated encryption scheme is called *optimal* if the number of non-linear operations it uses is the minimum possible. For nonce based AEAD, the minimum number of non-linear operations required to process a data with a block associated data and m block plaintext is $(a + m + 1)$ [11]. Light-OCB is an optimal construction, and hence it performs excellent especially for short messages.
7. **Versatility:** As mentioned already, the parallelizability and small state size together makes the design extremely versatile.

3.3 Recommended Instantiation

We instantiate Light-OCB with the short-tweak tweakable block cipher TweGIFT-64. Here, the key size is 128 bits, nonce size is 128 bits, and tag size is 64 bits. Here we briefly describe the tBC TweGIFT-64 or more formally TweGIFT-64/4/128 [9]. It is a 64-bit tweakable block cipher with 4-bit tweak and 128-bit key. As the name suggests, it is a tweakable variant of GIFT-64-128 [3] block cipher. TweGIFT-64 is composed of 28 rounds and each round consists following operations:

SubCells: TweGIFT-64 uses a 4-bit S-box as GIFT-64-128 and parallelly applies it to each nibble of the cipher state. Table 1 below defines the S-box.

```
function Light-OCB_Ẽ.Enc(K, N, A, M)
    C ← ⊥, M_⊕ ← 0, V_⊕ ← 0
    (K_N, Δ_N) ← init(K, N)
    if |A| ≠ 0 then
        (K_N, V_⊕) ← proc_ad(K_N, Δ_N, A)
    if |M| ≠ 0 then
        (K_N, M_⊕, C) ← proc_pt(K_N, Δ_N, M)
    T ← proc_tg(K_N, Δ_N, V_⊕, M_⊕)
    return (C, T)

function init(K, N)
    Y ← Ẽ^0_K(0^n)
    K_N ← K ⊕ N
    Δ_N ← Ẽ^1_{K_N}(Y)
    return (K_N, Δ_N)

function proc_ad(K_N, Δ_N, A)
    L ← K_N
    (A_{a-1}, ..., A_0) ←^n A
    for i = 0 to a − 2 do
        U ← A_i ⊕ Δ_N
        L ← L ⊙ 2
        V ← Ẽ^2_L(U)
        V_⊕ ← V_⊕ ⊕ V
    U ← ozs(A_{a-1}) ⊕ Δ_N
    L ← L ⊙ 2
    V ← (|A_{a-1}| = n)? Ẽ^2_L(U) : Ẽ^3_L(U)
    V_⊕ ← V_⊕ ⊕ V
    return (L, V_⊕)

function proc_pt(K_N, Δ_N, M)
    L ← K_N
    (M_{m-1}, ..., M_0) ←^n M
    for j = 0 to m − 2 do
        M_⊕ ← M_⊕ ⊕ M_j
        X ← M_j ⊕ Δ_N
        L ← L ⊙ 2
        Y ← Ẽ^4_L(X)
        C_j ← W ⊕ Δ_N
    L ← L ⊙ 2
    X ← ⟨|M_{m-1}|⟩_n ⊕ Δ_N
    Y ← Ẽ^5_L(X)
    C_{m-1} ← chop(Y ⊕ Δ_N, |M_{m-1}|) ⊕ M_{m-1}
    M_⊕ ← M_⊕ ⊕ M_{m-1}
    C ← (C_{m-1}, ..., C_0)
    return (L, M_⊕, C)
```

```
function Light-OCB_Ẽ.Dec(K, N, A, C, T)
    M ← ⊥, M_⊕ ← 0, V_⊕ ← 0
    (K_N, Δ_N) ← init(K, N)
    if |A| ≠ 0 then
        (K_N, V_⊕) ← proc_ad(K_N, Δ_N, A)
    if |C| ≠ 0 then
        (K_N, M_⊕, M) ← proc_ct(K_N, Δ_N, C)
    T' ← proc_tg(K_N, Δ_N, V_⊕, M_⊕)
    if T' = T then
        return M
    else
        return ⊥

function proc_ct(K_N, Δ_N, A, C, T)
    L ← K_N
    (C_{m-1}, ..., C_0) ←^n C
    for j = 0 to m − 2 do
        Y ← C_j ⊕ Δ_N
        L ← L ⊙ 2
        X ← D̃^4_L(Y)
        M_j ← X ⊕ Δ_N
        M_⊕ ← M_⊕ ⊕ M_j
    L ← L ⊙ 2
    X ← ⟨|C_{m-1}|⟩_n ⊕ Δ_N
    Y ← Ẽ^5_L(W)
    M_{m-1} ← chop(Y ⊕ Δ_N, |C_{m-1}|) ⊕ C_{m-1}
    M_⊕ ← M_⊕ ⊕ M_{m-1}
    M ← (M_{m-1}, ..., M_0)
    return (L, M_⊕, M)

function proc_tg(K_N, Δ_N, V_⊕, M_⊕)
    L ← K_N ⊙ 2
    T ← Ẽ^6_L(V_⊕ ⊕ M_⊕ ⊕ Δ_N) ⊕ Δ_N
    return T
```

Fig. 3. The encryption and verification-decryption algorithms of Light-OCB.

Table 1. The GIFT S-Box GS. Each value is a hexadecimal number.

x	0	1	2	3	4	5	6	7	8	9	A	B	C	D	E	F
$GS(x)$	1	A	4	C	6	F	3	9	2	D	B	7	5	0	8	E

PermBits: PermBits also uses the same permutation as used in GIFT-64-128. It maps the ith of the cipher state to the $GP(i)^{th}$ bit, where

$$GP(i) = 4\lfloor i/16 \rfloor + 16\Big((3\lfloor (i \bmod 16)/4 \rfloor + (i \bmod 4)) \bmod 4 \Big) + (i \bmod 4).$$

AddRoundKey: Here a 32-bit round key is extracted from the master key and added to the cipher state. This also follows the same as used in GIFT.

AddRoundConstant: A single bit "1" and the bits of a 6-bit round constant are added to the cipher state at the 63rd, 23rd, 19th, 15th, 11th, 7th and 3rd-bit respectively. The 6-bit constants are generated using a 6-bit affine LFSR (same as that of SKINNY [4] and GIFT-64-128 [3]).

AddTweak: The 4-bit tweak is first expanded to a 16-bit expanded tweak by the linear code Exp and then XOR this expanded tweak to the state at an interval of 4 rounds (starting from the 4th round) at bit positions $4i + 3$, for $i = 0, ..., 15$. Exp takes as input a 4-bit tweak $t = t_1 \| t_2 \| t_3 \| t_4$ and outputs a 16-bit expanded tweak $t_e = t \| t' \| t \| t'$, such that $t' = s \oplus t_1 \| s \oplus t_2 \| s \oplus t_3 \| s \oplus t_4$ and $s = t_1 \oplus t_2 \oplus t_3 \oplus t_4$.

3.4 Design Rationale

In this section, we briefly describe the various design choices and rationale for our proposals.

Choice of the Mode Light-OCB. We mainly target to design a lightweight AEAD that should be efficient as well as provides high-performance capability. The AEAD can be efficient by incorporating one-pass data process. It can be parallelizable to provide high-performance capability.

We take the approach to start with the well-known mode OCB. OCB is online, one-pass as well as fully parallelizable. OCB also provides birthday bound security, and thus we need 128-bit blocks that satisfy the NIST criteria. This in turn, increases the state size while keeping the main features intact.

The associated data is processed following the hash layer of PMAC, and the computation is fully parallel in order to maximize the performance in parallel computing environments.

Light-OCB mainly updates the use of nonce and position dependent keys. OCB achieves only the birthday bound security level. This is due to the fact that collision probability at any two distinct block cipher calls (as two calls share the same encryption key). Light-OCB overcomes this by changing the key and tweak tuple for each block cipher invocation. Hence, even if there is a collision the security remains intact as the key, tweak tuples are distinct. Actually, Light-OCB achieve full security up to a data complexity 2^n, and time complexity 2^κ, and combined data-time complexity up to $2^{n+\kappa}$ (see the security analysis in Sect. 4). This helps us to design a secure aead using a ultra lightweight block cipher TweGIFT-64.

Choice of Short Tweakable Block Cipher: TweGIFT-64. We choose a tweakable block cipher TweGIFT-64, that can handle short tweaks. This is essential for instantiating our mode Light-OCB. There are several efficient tweakable ciphers like SKINNY [4] but they are designed to handle general purpose tweaks and are optimized for handling short tweaks. On the other hand, TweGIFT-64 is designed over GIFT-64-128 to handle such short tweaks.

Tweak expansion is done using a simple (only 7 XORs are needed) high distance linear code (distance 4) to convert a 4-bit tweak value into a 16-bit codeword. This high distance code ensures strong differential characteristics for TweGIFT-64.

The expanded codeword is XORed to the block cipher state to the third bit of each nibble. The choice of this position has been made due to the fact that the other three positions are already masked by the round key and round constant bits. In addition, tweak addition after 4 rounds ensures low differential probability for TweGIFT-64.

3.5 Light-OCB vs LOCUS-AEAD

In this section, we briefly discuss how Light-OCB differs from LOCUS-AEAD. We first discuss on the difference between the two modes from specification point of view, and then demonstrate the advantages of Light-OCB over LOCUS-AEAD.

Structurally, both the modes are very similar in the sense that they both are parallel authenticated encryption schemes following the XEX paradigm, both use nonce based derived key, and short tweak tweakable block cipher. However, the modes have the following subtle differences:

1. While processing the message, Light-OCB uses one primitive call per message block, while LOCUS-AEAD requires two primitive calls per message block.
2. Light-OCB computes plain text (or message) checksum for generating the tag, while LOCUS-AEAD uses an intermediate checksum to generate the tag.

Due to the above two structural modification, Light-OCB achieves the following advantages over LOCUS-AEAD:

High Throughput: In LOCUS-AEAD, processing each message block requires 2 block-cipher invocations. On the contrary, Light-OCB requires only 1 block-cipher invocation per message. Hence, to process a message block of 64-bits Light-OCB requires only 1 clock-cycle as compared to 2 clock cycles required for LOCUS-AEAD. This gives a double speed-up, and improves the overall throughput by a factor of 2.

Efficient Short-Message Processing: Another notable advantage of Light-OCB as compared to LOCUS-AEAD is efficiency in short message processing. Light-OCB requires only $(a+m+1)$ primitive invocations to process a message of m blocks with a block associated data, and this is the optimal number of non-linear invocations for any nonce based authenticated encryption scheme. The optimality ensures that the construction achieves extremely high throughput even for very short messages.

We would like to point out that these advantages are obtained at the cost of RUP security. However, we emphasize the fact that the RUP security is only required in some unconventional settings, and practical applications where RUP setting is necessary are limited. On the other hand, these modification allows the design to boost the speed and throughput up to a factor of 2, which is critical, specially for high-speed applications such as memory encryption, and vehicular security applications.

4 Security Analysis of Light-OCB

4.1 Privacy Security of Light-OCB

Theorem 1. *Let $\mathcal{A}$ be a non-trivial nonce-respecting adversary against* Light-OCB$[\widetilde{\mathscr{E}}]$ *that makes q_e many encryption queries (with an aggregate of σ_e many blocks) to the construction and q_p many queries to the primitive. The privacy advantage of $\mathcal{A}$ in the ideal cipher model satisfies*

$$\mathbf{Adv}^{\mathsf{priv}}_{\mathsf{Light\text{-}OCB}[\widetilde{\mathscr{E}}]}(\mathcal{A}) \leq \frac{q_p}{2^k} + \frac{4q_pq_e}{2^{n+k}} + \frac{4q_p\sigma_e}{2^{n+k}}.$$

Proof. We employ the coefficient-H technique to prove Theorem 1. In the same spirit, we assume that $\mathcal{A}$ is deterministic. As per convention, $\mathcal{A}$ makes q_e many encryption queries to the construction oracle, with an aggregate of total ν_e many associated data blocks and μ_e many message blocks. We write $\sigma_e = \mu_e + \nu_e$. In addition, $\mathcal{A}$ makes q_f many forward queries and q_b many backward queries to the underlying primitive oracle, i.e. the tweakable ideal cipher $\widetilde{\mathscr{E}}$. We write $q_p = q_f + q_b$ to denote the total number of primitive queries. The proof is given in the rest of this subsection.

Oracle Description. The two oracles at hand are: $\mathcal{O}_1 := (\mathsf{Light\text{-}OCB}[\widetilde{\mathscr{E}}], \widetilde{\mathscr{E}}^{\pm})$, the real oracle, and $\mathcal{O}_0 := (\$, \widetilde{\mathscr{E}}^{\pm})$, the ideal oracle. We consider a stronger version of these oracles, the one in which they release some additional information.

Description of the real oracle, $\mathcal{O}_1$: The real oracle $\mathcal{O}_1$ has access to Light-OCB$[\widetilde{\mathscr{E}}]$ and $\widetilde{\mathscr{E}}^{\pm}$. We denote the transcript random variable generated by $\mathcal{A}$'s interaction with $\mathcal{O}_1$ by the usual notation Λ_1, which is a collection of construction and primitive query-response tuples. For $i \in [q_e]$, initially, the i-th construction query-response tuple is of the form $(\mathsf{N}^i, \mathsf{A}^i, \mathsf{M}^i, \mathsf{C}^i, \mathsf{T}^i)$, where N^i is the i-th nonce, A^i is the i-th associated data consisting of a_i many blocks, M^i is the i-th message consisting of ℓ_i many blocks, C^i is the i-th ciphertext consisting of ℓ_i many blocks and T^i is the i-th tag value. Clearly, $\mathsf{Light\text{-}OCB}[\widetilde{\mathscr{E}}](\mathsf{N}^i, \mathsf{A}^i, \mathsf{M}^i) = (\mathsf{C}^i, \mathsf{T}^i)$ for all $i \in [q_e]$. For $i \in [q_p]$, the i-th primitive query-response tuple is of the form $(\hat{\mathsf{K}}^i, \hat{\mathsf{T}}^i, \hat{\mathsf{X}}^i, \hat{\mathsf{Y}}^i)$, where $\hat{\mathsf{K}}^i$: the i-th key, $\hat{\mathsf{T}}^i$: the i-th tweak, $\hat{\mathsf{X}}^i$: the i-th input of $\widetilde{\mathscr{E}}$ and $\hat{\mathsf{Y}}^i$: the i-th output of $\widetilde{\mathscr{E}}$. Clearly, $\widetilde{\mathscr{E}}(\mathsf{K}^i, \mathsf{T}^i, \mathsf{X}^i) = (\mathsf{Y}^i)$ for all $i \in [q_p]$. Once the query-response phase is over $\mathcal{O}_1$ releases the secret key K, and the internal variables, $(\mathsf{U}^i, \mathsf{V}^i, \mathsf{X}^i, \mathsf{W}^i, \mathsf{Y}^i, \mathsf{V}^i_{\oplus}, \mathsf{W}^i_{\oplus}, \mathsf{K}^i_{\mathsf{N}}, \Delta^i_{\mathsf{N}})_{i \in [q_e]}$, which are defined analogously as in Fig. 3. Additionally it also releases $\Delta_0 = \widetilde{\mathscr{E}}(\mathsf{K}, (0,0), 0)$. Finally, we have

$$\Lambda_1 = \left\{(\mathsf{N}^i, \mathsf{A}^i, \mathsf{M}^i, \mathsf{C}^i, \mathsf{T}^i, \mathsf{U}^i, \mathsf{V}^i, \mathsf{X}^i, \mathsf{Y}^i, \mathsf{V}^i_\oplus, \mathsf{M}^i_\oplus, \mathsf{K}^i_\mathsf{N}, \Delta^i_\mathsf{N}, \Delta_0, \mathsf{K})_{i\in[q_e]}, (\hat{\mathsf{K}}^i, \hat{\mathsf{T}}^i, \hat{\mathsf{X}}^i, \hat{\mathsf{Y}}^i)_{i\in[q_p]}\right\}.$$

Description of the ideal oracle, $\mathcal{O}_0$: The ideal oracle $\mathcal{O}_0$ has access to \$ and $\widetilde{\mathscr{E}}^{\pm}$. The ideal transcript random variable Λ_0, is also a collection of construction and primitive query-response tuples. For $i \in [q_e]$, initially, the i-th construction query-response tuple is of the form $(\mathsf{N}^i, \mathsf{A}^i, \mathsf{M}^i, \mathsf{C}^i, \mathsf{T}^i)$, where N^i is the i-th nonce, A^i is the i-th associated data consisting of a_i many blocks, M^i is the i-th message consisting of ℓ_i many blocks, $\mathsf{C}^i \leftarrow_\$ \{0,1\}^{n\ell_i}$ is the i-th ciphertext consisting of ℓ_i many blocks and $\mathsf{T}^i \leftarrow_\$ \{0,1\}^n$ is the i-th tag value. For $i \in [q_p]$, the i-th primitive query-response tuple is of the form $(\hat{\mathsf{K}}^i, \hat{\mathsf{T}}^i, \hat{\mathsf{X}}^i, \hat{\mathsf{Y}}^i)$, defined analogously as in the real world. Once the query-response phase is over $\mathcal{O}_0$ defines the internal variables in the following order

1. $\mathsf{K} \leftarrow_\$ \{0,1\}^k$ and $\Delta_0 \leftarrow_\$ \{0,1\}^n$.
2. $\mathsf{K}^i_\mathsf{N} = \mathsf{K} \oplus \mathsf{N}^i$.
3. $\Delta^i_\mathsf{N} \leftarrow_\$ \{0,1\}^n$.
4. $\forall i \in [q_e]$, $j \in [a_i]$, $\mathsf{U}^i_j = \mathsf{A}^i_j \oplus \Delta^i_\mathsf{N}$, and $\mathsf{V}^i_j \leftarrow_\$ \{0,1\}^n$.
5. $\forall i \in [q_e]$, $j \in [\ell_i - 1]$, $\mathsf{X}^i_j = \mathsf{M}^i_j \oplus \Delta^i_\mathsf{N}$, $\mathsf{Y}^i_j = \mathsf{C}^i_j \oplus \Delta^i_\mathsf{N}$.
6. $\forall i \in [q_e]$, $\mathsf{X}^i_{\ell_i} = \langle \ell_i \rangle \oplus \Delta^i_\mathsf{N}$, $\mathsf{Y}^i_{\ell_i} = \mathsf{C}^i_j \oplus \Delta^i_\mathsf{N} \oplus \mathsf{M}^i_{\ell_i}$.
7. $\forall i \in [q_e]$, $\mathsf{V}_\oplus = \bigoplus_{j\in[a_i]} \mathsf{V}^i_j$, $\mathsf{M}_\oplus = \bigoplus_{j\in[\ell_i]} \mathsf{M}^i_j$, and $\mathsf{CS}^i = \mathsf{M}^i_\oplus \oplus \mathsf{V}^i_\oplus$.

At this point, we have the complete ideal transcript random variable, i.e.,

$$\Lambda_0 = \left\{(\mathsf{N}^i, \mathsf{A}^i, \mathsf{M}^i, \mathsf{C}^i, \mathsf{T}^i, \mathsf{U}^i, \mathsf{V}^i, \mathsf{X}^i, \mathsf{Y}^i, \mathsf{V}^i_\oplus, \mathsf{M}^i_\oplus, \mathsf{K}^i_\mathsf{N}, \Delta^i_\mathsf{N}, \Delta_0, \mathsf{K})_{i\in[q_e]}, (\hat{\mathsf{K}}^i, \hat{\mathsf{T}}^i, \hat{\mathsf{X}}^i, \hat{\mathsf{Y}}^i)_{i\in[q_p]}\right\}.$$

Note that, for brevity we used identical notations to describe the real and ideal random variables. Since we never consider the joint probability of Θ_1 and Θ_0, this abuse of notation should not cause any confusion.

Bad Transcripts: Definition and Analysis. Let Ω be the set of all attainable transcripts. We say that a transcript

$$\omega = \left\{(N^i, A^i, M^i, C^i, T^i, U^i, V^i, X^i, Y^i, V^i_\oplus, M^i_\oplus, K^i_N, \Delta^i_N, \Delta_0, K)_{i\in[q_e]}, (\hat{K}^i, \hat{T}^i, \hat{X}^i, \hat{Y}^i)_{i\in[q_p]}\right\},$$

is bad, denoted as $\omega \in \Omega_{\mathsf{bad}}$, if one of the following three cases occurs.

Case 1: Key-guessing primitive query: We say that a primitive query-response tuple is key guessing if the following condition is true:

$$\exists\, i \in [q_p], \text{ such that } \hat{K}^i = K.$$

Case 2: Inconsistent primitive-construction queries: We say that the primitive and construction query-response tuple is inconsistent if one of the following conditions is true for some $i \in [q_e]$ and $i' \in [q_p]$:

- P_1 : $\exists\, j \in [a_i]$, such that $(\hat{K}^{i'}, \hat{T}^{i'}, \hat{X}^{i'}) = (K^i_N, (0,j), U^i_j)$.

- $\mathsf{P}_2: \ \exists\, j \in [\ell_i]$, such that $(\hat{K}^{i'}, \hat{T}^{i'}, \hat{X}^{i'}) = (K_N^i, (1,j), X_j^i)$.
- $\mathsf{P}_3: \ (\hat{K}^{i'}, \hat{T}^{i'}, \hat{X}^{i'}) = (K_N^i, (0,0), CS^i)$.
- $\mathsf{P}_4: \ (\hat{K}^{i'}, \hat{T}^{i'}, \hat{Y}^{i'}) = (K_N^i, (1,0), \Delta_0)$.
- $\mathsf{P}_5: \ \exists\, j \in [a_i]$, such that $(\hat{K}^{i'}, \hat{T}^{i'}, \hat{Y}^{i'}) = (K_N^i, (0,j), V_j^i)$.
- $\mathsf{P}_6: \ \exists\, j \in [\ell_i]$, such that $(\hat{K}^{i'}, \hat{T}^{i'}, \hat{Y}^{i'}) = (K_N^i, (1,j), Y_j^i)$.
- $\mathsf{P}_7: \ (\hat{K}^{i'}, \hat{T}^{i'}, \hat{Y}^{i'}) = (K_N^i, (0,0), T^i \oplus \Delta_N^i)$.
- $\mathsf{P}_8: \ (\hat{K}^{i'}, \hat{T}^{i'}, \hat{Y}^{i'}) = (K_N^i, (1,0), \Delta_N^i)$.

Let B_1, and B_2 denote the event that cases 1, and 2, respectively, are satisfied for Λ_0. Therefore, the probability that $\Lambda_0 \in \Omega_{\mathsf{bad}}$, is given by

$$\Pr[\Lambda_0 \in \Omega_{\mathsf{bad}}] = \Pr[\mathsf{B}_1 \vee \mathsf{B}_2] \leq \Pr[\mathsf{B}_1] + \Pr[\mathsf{B}_2] \tag{2}$$

Upper bound on $\Pr[\mathsf{B}_1]$: For a fixed i, $\hat{\mathsf{K}}^i = \mathsf{K}$, happens with at most 2^{-k} probability (K is uniform and independent of $\hat{\mathsf{K}}^i$). There are at most q_p many choices for i. So, we get $\Pr[\mathsf{B}_1] \leq q_p 2^{-k}$.

Upper bound on $\Pr[\mathsf{B}_2]$: By the definition of B_2, we have

$$\Pr[\mathsf{B}_2] \leq \sum_{i=1}^{8} \Pr[\mathsf{P}_i] \leq \frac{4q_p q_e}{2^{n+k}} + \frac{4q_p \sigma_e}{2^{n+k}} \tag{3}$$

The proof of Eq. (3) is given in Appendix A of the full version at eprint.

$$\Pr[\Lambda_0 \in \Omega_{\mathsf{bad}}] \leq \frac{q_p}{2^k} + \frac{4q_p q_e}{2^{n+k}} + \frac{4q_p \sigma_e}{2^{n+k}}. \tag{4}$$

Good Transcript Analysis. Let us fix a transcript $\omega \in \Omega \backslash \Omega_{\mathsf{bad}}$, where ω has the usual form. In Eq. (5), we claim that the ratio of real to ideal world interpolation probabilities is at least 1. The proof of this claim is available in Appendix B of the full version at eprint.

$$\frac{\Pr[\Lambda_1 = \omega]}{\Pr[\Lambda_0 = \omega]} \geq 1. \tag{5}$$

Theorem 1 follows by using Eq. (4) and (5) in Eq. (1) of the coefficient-H technique. □

4.2 INT-CTXT Security of Light-OCB

Theorem 2. *Let $\mathcal{A}$ be a non-trivial nonce-respecting forger against* Light-OCB $[\widetilde{\mathscr{E}}]$ *that makes q_e and q_d many encryption and decryption, respectively, queries (with an aggregate of σ_e many encryption query blocks) to the construction and q_p many queries to the primitive. The INT-CTXT advantage of $\mathcal{A}$ in the ideal cipher model satisfies*

$$\mathbf{Adv}^{\mathsf{int\text{-}ctxt}}_{\mathsf{Light\text{-}OCB}[\widetilde{\mathscr{E}}]}(\mathcal{A}) \leq \frac{2}{2^n} + \frac{q_p}{2^k} + \frac{16q_p}{2^{n+k}} + \frac{4q_p q_e}{2^{n+k}} + \frac{4q_p \sigma_e}{2^{n+k}}.$$

Proof. As per convention, $\mathcal{A}$ that makes at most q_e many encryption queries and at most q_d many RUP queries to Light-OCB$[\widetilde{\mathscr{E}}]$. In addition $\mathcal{A}$ also makes q_f many forward queries and q_b many backward queries to $\widetilde{\mathscr{E}}$. We write $q_p = q_f + q_b$ to denote the total number of primitive queries. We will reuse the notations used in Sect. 4.1. In particular, the i-th encryption query-response tuple is denoted by $(\mathsf{N}^i, \mathsf{A}^i, \mathsf{M}^i, \mathsf{C}^i, \mathsf{T}^i)$, and the i-th primitive query-response tuple is denoted by $(\hat{\mathsf{K}}^i, \hat{\mathsf{T}}^i, \hat{\mathsf{X}}^i, \hat{\mathsf{Y}}^i)$. The intermediate variables are also analogously defined. In addition the i-th decryption query-response tuple is denoted by $(\mathsf{N}'^i, \mathsf{A}'^i, \mathsf{M}'^i, \mathsf{C}'^i)$, where A'^i, and M'^i contains a'_i, and ℓ'_i many blocks, respectively. Note that, $(\mathsf{N}^i, A^i, \mathsf{M}^i, \mathsf{C}^i) \neq (\mathsf{N}'^j, \mathsf{A}'^j, \mathsf{M}'^j, \mathsf{C}'^j)$ for all $i \in [q_e]$ and $j \in [q_d]$.

Finally, $\mathcal{A}$ tries to forge with $(\mathsf{N}^\star, \mathsf{A}^\star, \mathsf{C}^\star, \mathsf{T}^\star) \neq (\mathsf{N}^i, \mathsf{A}^i, \mathsf{M}^i, \mathsf{C}^i)$ for $i \in [q_e]$. Let Forge denotes the event that $\mathcal{A}$ submits valid forgery. We define the transcript random variable corresponding to $\mathcal{A}$'s interaction with Light-OCB$[\widetilde{\mathscr{E}}]$ as

$$\Lambda_1 := \left\{(\mathsf{N}^i, \mathsf{A}^i, \mathsf{M}^i, \mathsf{C}^i)_{i \in [q_e]}, (\mathsf{N}'^i, \mathsf{A}'^i, \mathsf{M}'^i, \mathsf{C}'^i)_{i \in [q_d]}, (\hat{\mathsf{K}}^i, \hat{\mathsf{T}}^i, \hat{\mathsf{X}}^i, \hat{\mathsf{Y}}^i)_{i \in [q_p]}, (\mathsf{N}^\star, \mathsf{A}^\star, \mathsf{C}^\star, \mathsf{T}^\star)\right\}.$$

Let multi(x) denote the number of $i \in [q_p]$ such that $\hat{\mathsf{K}}^i = x$. Let Bad denote the event that Λ_1 satisfies one of the following properties:

- $\mathtt{G}_1$: $\exists i \in [q_p]$, such that $\hat{\mathsf{K}}^i = \mathsf{K}$.
- $\mathtt{G}_2$: $\exists i \in [q_p]$, such that $(\hat{\mathsf{K}}^i, \hat{\mathsf{X}}^i) = (\mathsf{K}^\star_\mathsf{N}, \widetilde{\mathscr{E}}_\mathsf{K}(0))$.
- $\mathtt{G}_3$: $\mathsf{multi}(\mathsf{K}^\star_\mathsf{N}) \geq 2^{n-1}$.
- $\mathtt{G}_4$: $\exists i \in [q_p]$, such that $(\hat{\mathsf{K}}^i, \hat{\mathsf{Y}}^i) = (\mathsf{K}^\star_\mathsf{N}, \mathsf{T}^\star \oplus \Delta^\star_\mathsf{N})$.
- $\mathtt{G}_5$: $\exists i \in [q_p]$, such that $(\hat{\mathsf{K}}^i, \hat{\mathsf{X}}^i) = (\mathsf{K}^\star_\mathsf{N}, \mathsf{U}^\star_{a_\star})$.
- $\mathtt{G}_6$: $\exists i \in [q_p]$, such that $(\hat{\mathsf{K}}^i, \hat{\mathsf{Y}}^i) = (\mathsf{K}^\star_\mathsf{N}, \mathsf{Y}^\star_{\ell_\star})$.
- $\mathtt{G}_7$: $\exists i \in [q_e], i' \in [q_p]$, such that $(\hat{\mathsf{K}}^{i'}, \hat{\mathsf{X}}^{i'}) = (\mathsf{K}^i_\mathsf{N}, \widetilde{\mathscr{E}}_\mathsf{K}(0))$.
- $\mathtt{G}_8$: $\exists i \in [q_e]$, such that $\mathsf{multi}(\mathsf{K}^i) \geq 2^{n-1}$.
- $\mathtt{G}_9$: $\exists i \in [q_e], j \in [a_i], i' \in [q_p]$, such that $(\hat{\mathsf{K}}^{i'}, \hat{\mathsf{X}}^{i'}) = (\mathsf{K}^i_\mathsf{N}, \mathsf{U}^i_j)$.
- $\mathtt{G}_{10}$: $\exists i \in [q_e], j \in [\ell_i], i' \in [q_p]$, such that $(\hat{\mathsf{K}}^{i'}, \hat{\mathsf{Y}}^{i'}) = (\mathsf{K}^i_\mathsf{N}, \mathsf{Y}^i_j)$.

Observe that if Bad is satisfied, then $\mathcal{A}$ can forge with very high probability. On the other hand, we will show that given that Bad is not satisfied, $\mathcal{A}$ cannot succeed with significant probability. Formally, we have

$$\Pr[\mathtt{Forge}] \leq \Pr[\mathtt{Bad}] + \Pr[\mathtt{Forge} | \neg \mathtt{Bad}]. \tag{6}$$

We make two claims, given as follows

$$\Pr[\mathtt{Bad}] \leq \frac{q_p}{2^k} + \frac{16 q_p}{2^{n+k}} + \frac{4 q_p q_e}{2^{n+k}} + \frac{4 q_p \sigma_e}{2^{n+k}} \tag{7}$$

$$\Pr[\mathtt{Forge} | \neg \mathtt{Bad}] \leq \frac{2}{2^n}. \tag{8}$$

The proof for claims in Eq. (7) and (8) are is given in Appendix C and D respectively of the full version at eprint. The result follows from Eq. (6), (7), and (8). □

5 Hardware Implementation

In this section, we describe a lightweight implementation of Light-OCB. Light-OCB is structurally simple with tweakable blockcipher and a few XORs. In this section we provide hardware implementation details of Light-OCB instantiated with the TweGIFT64 blockcipher.

5.1 Clock Cycle Analysis

We provide a conventional way for speed estimation, i.e., the number of clock cycles per byte (*cpb*). This is a theoretical way to estimate the speed of the architecture. We consider round-based architecture with 64 bit datapath. To process a data block of $d = a + m$ blocks (a is the number of associated data blocks and m is the number of message blocks), we need $29d$ clock cycles. We use one TweGIFT64 call to process one data block. Our block cipher is optimized to process a bulk data, and the reset is required only to indicate that the stream processing starts. We observe that the *cpb* values for different sized data are constant as there is no initialization overhead and the overhead for the tag generation (constant small number of clock cycles) is negligible for long messages. Our design accept 64-bit or 8-byte data blocks and hence the *cpb* is $29d/8d = 3.625$.

5.2 Hardware Architecture

Light-OCB is based on E-t-M paradigm and the message blocks are processed in parallel to generate the ciphertext blocks and the tag. Here, the blockcipher tweak values for the three types of input data (N, A and M) are required to distinguish. Below, we provide brief hardware architecture details. For simplicity, we omit the control unit from Fig. 4. The main components in the hardware circuit are as follows.

State Registers. The architecture for Light-OCB contains four registers.

- A 64-bit state register to store the encryption state,
- an 128-bit register to store the blockcipher master secret key,
- a 64-bit register to store the checksum and
- the 64-bit Δ register to store Δ_N.

Module TweGIFT. The TweGIFT module computes one round of the underlying tweakable blockcipher. This module internally uses a 64-bit register for the blockcipher internal state and an 128-bit register fr the master key. In addition, TweGIFT also uses internally a control unit. We are omitting this for the sake of simplicity.

Accumulator Module. The accumulator module *ACC* is used to compute the checksum of the ECB layer and the last block for computing the tag.

Remark 1 (Combined Encryption and Decryption). In this implementation, we mainly focus on a combined encryption-decryption circuit. We observe that we can also implement encryption-only circuits even with a small decrease in hardware area and with the same throughput.

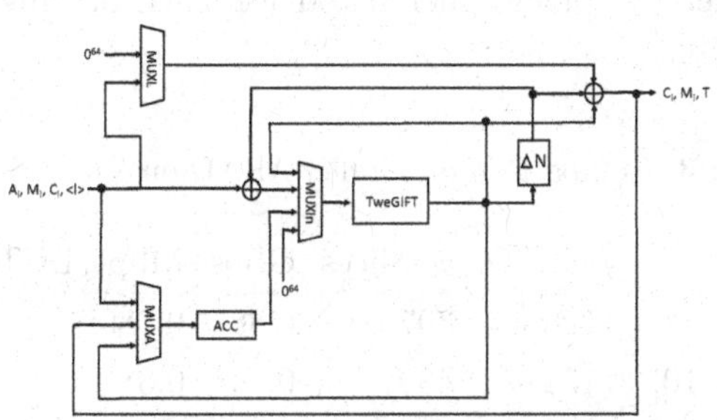

Fig. 4. Hardware architecture diagram

5.3 Implementation Results

We implement Light-OCB on Virtex 7 (xc7v585tffg1761-3), using VHDL and the VIVADO tool. We use exactly the same implementation for TweGIFT64 as used in the implementation of LOCUS-AEAD [10]. The results are presented in Table 2. The implementation follows the RTL approach and a basic iterative type architecture with 64-bit datapath. The areas are reported in the number of flipflops, LUTs and slices. We also report the Frequency (MHz), Throughput (Gbps), and throughput-area efficiencies. The mapped hardware results are reported in Table 2. For the sake of comparison, we also provide the implementation results for LOCUS-AEAD taken from [10].

Table 2. FPGA implementation comparison between Light-OCB and LOCUS-AEAD

Design (platform)	Slice registers	LUTs	Slices	Frequency (MHz)	Throughput (Gbps)	Mbps/LUT	Mbps/Slice
Light-OCB (Virtex 7)	428	1128	307	400	0.88	0.780	2.866
LOCUS-AEAD (Virtex 7)	430	1154	439	392.20	0.44	0.38	1. 002

5.4 Benchmarking

We benchmark our implemented results using the existing FPGA results on Virtex 7. We provide comparisons with the implementation results of the well known designs in Table 3 below. Note that, all the candidates for benchmarking in Table 3 either parallel in structure or can have almost parallel implementation. We did not consider the blockcipher based feedback designs or sponge based feedback designs.

Table 3. Comparison of parallel AEAD on Virtex 7 [2].

Scheme	# LUTs	# Slices	Gbps	Mbps/LUT	Mbps/Slice
LIGHT-OCB	1128	307	0.88	0.780	2.866
LOCUS-AEAD [10]	1154	439	0.44	0.38	1.00
LOTUS-AEAD [10]	865	317	0.48	0.55	1.50
CLOC-TWINE [2]	1552	439	0.432	0.278	0.984
SILC-AES [2]	3040	910	4.365	1.436	4.796
SILC-LED [2]	1682	524	0.267	0.159	0.510
SILC-PRESENT [2]	1514	484	0.479	0.316	0.990
JAMBU-SIMON [2]	1200	419	0.368	0.307	0.878
AES-OTR [2]	4263	1204	3.187	0.748	2.647
OCB [2]	4269	1228	3.608	0.845	2.889
AES-COPA [2]	7795	2221	2.770	0.355	1.247
AES-GCM [2]	3478	949	3.837	1.103	4.043
CLOC-AES [2]	3552	1087	3.252	0.478	1.561
ELmD [2]	4490	1306	4.025	0.896	3.082

References

1. Andreeva, E., Bogdanov, A., Luykx, A., Mennink, B., Tischhauser, E., Yasuda, K.: Parallelizable and authenticated online ciphers. In: Sako, K., Sarkar, P. (eds.) ASIACRYPT 2013. LNCS, vol. 8269, pp. 424–443. Springer, Heidelberg (2013). https://doi.org/10.1007/978-3-642-42033-7_22
2. Authenticated Encryption FPGA Ranking. https://cryptography.gmu.edu/athenadb/fpga_auth_cipher/rankings_view
3. Banik, S., Pandey, S.K., Peyrin, T., Sasaki, Yu., Sim, S.M., Todo, Y.: GIFT: a small present - towards reaching the limit of lightweight encryption. In: Fischer, W., Homma, N. (eds.) CHES 2017. LNCS, vol. 10529, pp. 321–345. Springer, Cham (2017). https://doi.org/10.1007/978-3-319-66787-4_16

4. Beierle, C., et al.: The SKINNY family of block ciphers and its low-latency variant MANTIS. In: Robshaw, M., Katz, J. (eds.) CRYPTO 2016, Part II. LNCS, vol. 9815, pp. 123–153. Springer, Heidelberg (2016). https://doi.org/10.1007/978-3-662-53008-5_5
5. Black, J., Rogaway, P.: A block-cipher mode of operation for parallelizable message authentication. In: Knudsen, L.R. (ed.) EUROCRYPT 2002. LNCS, vol. 2332, pp. 384–397. Springer, Heidelberg (2002). https://doi.org/10.1007/3-540-46035-7_25
6. Bogdanov, A., et al.: PRESENT: an ultra-lightweight block cipher. In: Paillier, P., Verbauwhede, I. (eds.) CHES 2007. LNCS, vol. 4727, pp. 450–466. Springer, Heidelberg (2007). https://doi.org/10.1007/978-3-540-74735-2_31
7. Bossuet, L., Datta, N., Mancillas-López, C., Nandi, M.: ELmD: a pipelineable authenticated encryption and its hardware implementation. IEEE Trans. Comput. **65**(11), 3318–3331 (2016)
8. CAESAR: Competition for Authenticated Encryption: Security, Applicability, and Robustness. http://competitions.cr.yp.to/caesar.html
9. Chakraborti, A., Datta, N., Jha, A., Mancillas-López, C., Nandi, M., Yu, S.: Elastic-tweak: a framework for short tweak tweakable block cipher. IACR Cryptology ePrint Archive, 2019:440 (2019)
10. Chakraborti, A., Datta, N., Jha, A., Mancillas-López, C., Nandi, M., Sasaki, Yu.: INT-RUP secure lightweight parallel AE modes. IACR Trans. Symmetric Cryptol. **2019**(4), 81–118 (2019)
11. Chakraborti, A., Datta, N., Nandi, M.: On the optimality of non-linear computations for symmetric key primitives. J. Math. Cryptol. **12**(4), 241–259 (2018)
12. Krovetz, T., Rogaway, P.: The software performance of authenticated-encryption modes. In: Joux, A. (ed.) FSE 2011. LNCS, vol. 6733, pp. 306–327. Springer, Heidelberg (2011). https://doi.org/10.1007/978-3-642-21702-9_18
13. Krovetz, T., Rogaway, P.: OCB(v1.1). Submission to CAESAR (2016). https://competitions.cr.yp.to/round3/ocbv11.pdf
14. Liskov, M., Rivest, R.L., Wagner, D.: Tweakable block ciphers. In: Yung, M. (ed.) CRYPTO 2002. LNCS, vol. 2442, pp. 31–46. Springer, Heidelberg (2002). https://doi.org/10.1007/3-540-45708-9_3
15. Minematsu, K.: AES-OTR v3.1. Submission to CAESAR (2016). https://competitions.cr.yp.to/round3/aesotrv31.pdf
16. Naito, Y.: Tweakable blockciphers for efficient authenticated encryptions with beyond the birthday-bound security. IACR Trans. Symmetric Cryptol. **2017**(2), 1–26 (2017)
17. NIST. Lightweight cryptography. https://csrc.nist.gov/Projects/Lightweight-Cryptography
18. National Centre of Excellence. Light-weight Cipher Design Challenge. https://www.dsci.in/ncoe-light-weight-cipher-design-challenge-2020/
19. OMA-SpecWorks. Lightweight-M2M (2019). https://www.omaspecworks.org/what-is-oma-specworks/iot/lightweight-m2m-lwm2m/
20. Patarin, J.: The "coefficients H" technique. In: Avanzi, R.M., Keliher, L., Sica, F. (eds.) SAC 2008. LNCS, vol. 5381, pp. 328–345. Springer, Heidelberg (2009). https://doi.org/10.1007/978-3-642-04159-4_21
21. Rogaway, P., Bellare, M., Black, J.: OCB: a block-cipher mode of operation for efficient authenticated encryption. ACM Trans. Inf. Syst. Secur. **6**(3), 365–403 (2003)
22. Vaudenay, S.: Decorrelation: a theory for block cipher security. J. Cryptol. **16**(4), 249–286 (2003). https://doi.org/10.1007/s00145-003-0220-6

MILP Based Differential Attack on Round Reduced WARP

Manoj Kumar and Tarun Yadav(✉)

Scientific Analysis Group, DRDO, Metcalfe House Complex, Delhi 110054, India
{manojkumar,tarunyadav}@sag.drdo.in

Abstract. WARP is a 128-bit lightweight block cipher presented by S. Banik et al. at SAC 2020. It is based on 32-nibble type-2 Generalised Feistel Network (GFN) structure and uses a permutation over nibbles to optimize the security and efficiency. The designers provided a lower bound on the number of active S-boxes but they did not provide the differential characteristics against these bounds. In this paper, we model the MILP problem for WARP and present the 18-round and 19-round differential characteristics with the probability of 2^{-122} and 2^{-132} respectively. We also present a key recovery attack on 21 rounds with the data complexity of 2^{113} chosen plaintexts. To the best of our knowledge, this is the first key recovery attack against 21-round WARP using differential cryptanalysis.

Keywords: Block cipher · Differential cryptanalysis · Lightweight cryptography · MILP

1 Introduction

Lightweight cryptography is used for encryption and authentication on small computing devices *e.g.* RFID tags, sensor networks and smart cards [9]. The block cipher PRESENT is the first notable lightweight design which was published in 2007 [4]. There are numerous lightweight block ciphers which were designed in the past two decades. Initially, the 64-bit block with a key size of 80 or 128 bits was used for designing the lightweight version of block ciphers. Nowadays, the block size of 64 or 128 bits with a 128-bit key is preferred to design the lightweight block ciphers. The 128-bit lightweight block ciphers can serve as good candidates to replace the AES [6] in resource constrained scenarios. NIST has started a competition in 2018 to standardise the lightweight cryptographic algorithms due to increased importance of lightweight cryptography [14]. Therefore, security analysis of the new lightweight block ciphers is required to assess their strength against the basic cryptanalytic attacks.

The differential attack is a basic cryptanalytic technique proposed by E. Biham and A. Shamir in 1990 [3]. This exploits the non-uniform relations between the input and output differences. The probability of the best differential characteristic is used to provide a bound on the security of block cipher

L. Batina et al. (Eds.): SPACE 2021, LNCS 13162, pp. 42–59, 2022.
https://doi.org/10.1007/978-3-030-95085-9_3

against the differential attack. High probability differential characteristics are essential for a successful key recovery attack on a block cipher. The automatic techniques based on branch-and-bound [12], MILP [13] and machine learning [7,20] are used to construct these differential characteristics. M. Matsui proposed the branch-and-bound based technique to search the high probability differential characteristics in 1993 [12]. There are limitations in this technique to search differential characteristics for large block sizes. In 2012, N. Mohua et al. proposed a new technique using mixed integer linear programming (MILP) to search differential characteristics for block ciphers [13].

MILP deals with the optimization problems with an objective function subject to the constraints. These constraints are represented as linear equations. There are various commercial linear programming problem (LPP) solvers *e.g.* Gurobi [8] and CPLEX [5]. These solvers provide the solution for an LPP problem very efficiently. Mouha et al. proposed a framework to convert the differential characteristic search problem into an MILP problem and used these MILP solvers to minimize the number of active S-boxes in the differential characteristics. At Asiacrypt 2014, Sun et al. presented the MILP based attack on the bit oriented block ciphers using the H-Representation of convex hull for all differential patterns of the S-box to find the differential characteristics [16,17]. The differential characteristic search problem can be divided into two modules. In first module, a lower bound on the number of differentially active S-boxes is computed. While, the differential characteristics with high probability are constructed in the second module. At CT-RSA 2019, Zhu et al. optimized the probability of differential characteristics for lightweight block cipher GIFT using the MILP model consisting of the probability of each possible propagation [21].

The designers of WARP [2] provided a security bound against the differential attack. They used the MILP-aided search to compute a lower bound for the number of differentially active S-boxes. However, they did not search for the differential characteristics containing these bounds. According to the designers analysis, there are at least 61 active S-boxes in any 18-round differential characteristics of WARP. Similar bound for the 19-round differential characteristic is given as 66 active S-boxes which requires 2^{132} chosen plain text pairs. In this paper, we construct the differential characteristics for the 18-round WARP using the MILP-aided search. Firstly, we compute a lower bound on the number of differentially active S-boxes which is equal to the designers bound. Secondly, we construct the differential characteristics for the 18 and 19 rounds with the probability of 2^{-122} and 2^{-132} respectively. We also present a key recovery attack on 21 rounds which is the best differential attack against WARP till date.

We organise the remaining paper in the following manner. In Sect. 2, we provide a brief introduction to the lightweight block cipher WARP. In Sect. 3, we model the MILP problem for WARP to compute a lower bound on the number of differentially active S-boxes. We also construct the 18-round and 19-round differential characteristics using the MILP-aided search in this section. We present a key recovery attack on the 21-round WARP in Sect. 4. The paper is concluded in Sect. 5.

2 Description of WARP

The base structure of the lightweight block cipher WARP is a type-2 Generalised Feistel Network (GFN) structure. There are many 64-bit block ciphers, with 16 branches, designed using the type-2 GFN structure. The slow diffusion in 64-bit block with 16 branches is a security challenge. The GFN was revisited by S. Banik et al. [2] and 128-bit block size with 32-branches is considered more suitable to design a 128-bit lightweight block cipher.

2.1 Encryption Algorithm

WARP encrypts the 128-bit plaintext block using a 128-bit key and generates a 128-bit ciphertext block. There are total 41 rounds and round function can be explained in various equivalent forms [2]. We discuss the LBlock like equivalent form of WARP to describe its encryption process. The encryption algorithm encrypts 128-bit input X using a 128-bit key K (Algorithm 1). The key expansion algorithm is not required for WARP. The Key K is divided into two 64-bit keys and it is expressed as $K = (K_0, K_1)$. In the odd rounds, the left part K_0 is used and even rounds use the right part K_1. We express the 128-bit input X using 32 nibbles $x^1_{31}, x^1_{30}, \cdots, x^1_0$, where x^1_0 is the least significant nibble and size of each nibble is 4-bit. The initial permutation (IP) is applied on X to get two 64-bit words X^1_0 and X^1_1. In each round ($1 \le r \le 41$), the constants (Table 1) are XORed with the first two nibbles of X^r_1. The S-box layer (Table 2) is applied on each 4-bit nibble in X^r_0 and output of the S-box layer is XORed with the round key and nibble permutation (N_P) (Table 3) is applied thereafter to get a 64-bit output U. The cyclic rotation by 24 bits is applied on X^r_1 to get a 64-bit output V. To get X^{r+1}_0, U and V are XORed while X^r_0 becomes X^{r+1}_1 due to the Feistel structure. This process is applied 40 times iteratively and the last round is performed without the rotation and permutation operations.

Algorithm 1: Encryption Algorithm

Input: $X = (x^1_{31}, x^1_{30}, \cdots, x^1_0)$ and $K = (K_0, K_1)$
Output: $X^{42} = (x^{42}_{31}, x^{42}_{30}, \cdots, x^{42}_0)$
IP: $X^1_0 = (x^1_0, x^1_2, \cdots, x^1_{30})$, $X^1_1 = (x^1_1, x^1_3, \cdots, x^1_{31})$
for *r=1 to 40* **do**
  $x^r_1 = x^r_1 \oplus RC^r_0, x^r_3 = x^r_3 \oplus RC^r_1$
  $Y = S(X^r_0)$
  $U = N_P(Y \oplus K_{(r-1) mod 2})$
  $V = X^r_1 \lll 24$
  $X^{r+1}_0 = U \oplus V$
  $X^{r+1}_1 = X^r_0$
end
$x^{41}_1 = x^{41}_1 \oplus RC^{41}_0, x^{41}_3 = x^{41}_3 \oplus RC^{41}_1$
$X^{42}_0 = X^{41}_0$
$X^{42}_1 = S(X^{41}_0) \oplus K_0 \oplus X^{41}_1$

Round Constant: In each round, the 4-bit constants given in Table 1 are used.

Table 1. Round constants

r	1	2	3	4	5	6	7	8	9	10	11	12	13	14	15	16	17	18	19	20	21
RC_0^r	0	0	1	3	7	f	f	f	e	d	a	5	a	5	b	6	c	9	3	6	d
RC_1^r	4	c	c	c	c	c	8	4	8	4	8	4	c	8	0	4	c	8	4	c	c
r	22	23	24	25	26	27	28	29	30	31	32	33	34	35	36	37	38	39	40	41	
RC_0^r	b	7	e	d	b	6	d	a	4	9	2	4	9	3	7	e	c	8	1	2	
RC_1^r	8	4	c	8	4	8	0	4	8	0	4	c	c	8	0	0	4	8	4	c	

S-box: The 4-bit S-box (Table 2) is applied in the S-box layer of WARP.

Table 2. S-box

x	0	1	2	3	4	5	6	7	8	9	A	B	C	D	E	F
S(x)	c	a	d	3	e	b	f	7	8	9	1	5	0	2	4	6

Nibble Permutation: The output from the S-box layer is divided into 16 nibbles. The nibble permutation (N_P) is applied on these 16 nibbles (Table 3).

Table 3. Permutation

i	0	1	2	3	4	5	6	7	8	9	10	11	12	13	14	15
$N_P(i)$	3	7	6	4	1	0	2	5	11	15	14	12	9	8	10	13

3 Differential Characteristics Search in WARP

3.1 Differential Cryptanalysis

In differential attack, the propagation of input differences is studied to find the highly probable output differences. These non-uniform relations between the input and output differences are used to recover the round subkeys and we need a high probability (p) differential characteristic for the target cipher. The data requirement is inversely proportional to the probability p of the differential characteristic. Therefore, we need p^{-1} chosen plaintext pairs to distinguish the r rounds of an n-bit block cipher. In general, a differential characteristic can be extended to more rounds, till the bound $p^{-1} \gg 2^n$, where n is the block size [10].

To cover more rounds, additional rounds are added on the head and tail of the high probability differential characteristic. For a key recovery attack, plaintext pairs with a chosen input difference are generated and corresponding ciphertext pairs are obtained under a fixed key. The round subkeys involved in these additional rounds are guessed and the counter of each key is incremented after a match with the expected input or output difference. The correct subkey guesses are expected to have higher counter value while wrong key guesses are expected to have lower counter value. The subkey guess with highest counter value is considered as the right subkey used for the encryption.

3.2 MILP Modeling to Search the Differential Characteristics

A high probability differential characteristic is the first and foremost requirement to launch the key recovery attack on a block cipher. There exists several automatic tools to search the optimal differential characteristics for block ciphers. The technique based on MILP converts the differential characteristic search problem into a linear programming problem and solves it using the optimization problem solvers [13]. In MILP model, round function of a block cipher is represented with linear inequalities. The linear components of the round function, viz. nibble permutation and XOR operations, can be easily represented by linear inequalities. The non-linear part of the block cipher, viz. S-box, can not be easily represented by linear inequalities. There are two approaches to build such a system of linear inequalities that represent the solution space of the S-box viz. H-representation of convex hull and logical computation model [19]. In both the approaches, linear inequalities are generated to define the solution space. We use SageMath tool [15] to generate the linear inequalities based on H-representation of convex hull of the S-box.

3.2.1 Difference Distribution Table

The S-box is the only non-linear function used in a block cipher. To generate a system of linear inequalities, we construct the difference distribution table (DDT) of the 4-bit S-box used in WARP (Table 4). The DDT represents the propagation of input and output differences of S-box (Δ_i, Δ_o). Each non-zero entry in the table corresponds to a probable propagation and zero entries (subspace $\mathbb{R}$) provide a list of impossible patterns.

3.2.2 Linear Inequalities for Minimizing the Number of Active S-Boxes

In this module of MILP problem, we minimize the number of differentially active S-boxes. For a given subspace, $\mathbb{R} \subset \mathbb{F}_2^4$, a system of linear inequalities is required so that $\mathbb{F}_2^4 - \mathbb{R}$ covers the solution space. For 4-bit S-boxes, SageMath generates linear inequalities and MILP problem with large set of inequalities can not be solved efficiently. Therefore, it is necessary to minimize the number of linear inequalities to reduce the time complexity of the MILP problem. There are three approaches which can help in the minimization process. In the first approach, the greedy search algorithm [16] is used to minimize the number of linear inequalities obtained from SageMath tool while impossible patterns in the DDT are used to reduce the number of inequalities in the second approach [18,19]. In the

Table 4. DDT of WARP S-box

(Δ_i, Δ_o)	0	1	2	3	4	5	6	7	8	9	a	b	c	d	e	f
0	16	0	0	0	0	0	0	0	0	0	0	0	0	0	0	0
1	0	2	4	0	2	2	2	0	2	0	0	0	0	0	2	0
2	0	4	0	0	4	0	0	0	0	4	0	0	4	0	0	0
3	0	0	0	0	2	0	4	2	2	2	0	0	0	2	0	2
4	0	2	4	2	2	2	0	0	2	0	0	2	0	0	0	0
5	0	2	0	0	2	0	0	4	0	2	4	0	2	0	0	0
6	0	2	0	4	0	0	0	2	2	0	0	0	2	2	0	2
7	0	0	0	2	0	4	2	0	0	0	0	2	0	4	2	0
8	0	2	0	2	2	0	2	0	0	2	0	2	2	0	2	0
9	0	0	4	2	0	2	0	0	2	2	0	2	2	0	0	0
a	0	0	0	0	0	4	0	0	0	0	4	0	0	4	0	4
b	0	0	0	0	2	0	0	2	2	2	0	4	0	2	0	2
c	0	0	4	0	0	2	2	0	2	2	0	0	2	0	2	0
d	0	0	0	2	0	0	2	4	0	0	4	2	0	0	2	0
e	0	2	0	0	0	0	0	2	2	0	0	0	2	2	4	2
f	0	0	0	2	0	0	2	0	0	0	4	2	0	0	2	4

third approach, the Logic Friday tool [11] is used to minimize the number of inequalities which minimizes the product of sum of boolean functions [1]. We follow the second approach to minimize the number of linear inequalities for WARP S-box.

We use SageMath to construct the linear inequalities to represent the DDT of WARP S-box. The DDT of WARP S-box is represented by 239 linear inequalities $z_j (0 \le j \le 238)$. The input and output patterns in the DDT can be represented with 8 variables $(x_0, x_1, x_2, x_3, y_0, y_1, y_2, y_3)$. The total number of such patterns is $2^8 (= 256)$ while the number of possible and impossible patterns are 97 and 159 $(R_0, R_2, \cdots, R_{158})$ respectively. To minimize the number of linear inequalities, we construct a solution space to remove the impossible patterns corresponding to the zero entries in the DDT[1].

The inequalities which exclude the pattern R_i from the solution space are selected and pattern $R_i (0 \le i \le 158)$ is excluded by adding a constraint. Then, the number of inequalities are minimized subject to these constraints. We assign a variable $z_j (0 \le j \le 238)$ corresponding to each inequality obtained from SageMath. We generate a set corresponding to each $R_i (0 \le i \le 158)$ with '0' and '1' entries, where '0' is assigned corresponding to an inequality satisfying the pattern and '1' otherwise (Table 5).

We write a new system of linear inequalities corresponding to each $R_i, (0 \le i \le 158)$. For example, the pattern $R_{158} = (0, 0, 0, 0, 1, 0, 0, 0, 0, 1, \cdots, 0, 0, 0, 0, 0)$

[1] Source code is available at https://github.com/tarunyadav/WARP-MILP.

Table 5. Reduction of inequalities using impossible patterns

Impossible patterns	z_0	z_1	z_2	z_3	z_4	z_5	z_6	z_7	z_8	z_9	$\cdots$	z_{234}	z_{235}	z_{236}	z_{237}	z_{238}
R_0	0	0	0	0	0	0	0	0	0	0	$\cdots$	0	0	0	0	0
R_1	0	0	0	0	0	0	0	0	0	0	$\cdots$	0	0	0	0	0
R_2	0	0	0	0	0	0	0	0	0	0	$\cdots$	0	0	0	0	0
R_3	0	0	0	0	0	0	0	0	0	0	$\cdots$	0	1	0	0	0
R_4	0	0	0	0	0	0	0	0	0	0	$\cdots$	0	1	0	0	0
R_5	0	0	0	0	0	0	0	0	0	0	$\cdots$	0	0	0	0	0
R_6	0	0	0	0	0	0	0	0	0	0	$\cdots$	0	0	0	0	0
R_7	0	0	0	0	0	0	0	0	0	0	$\cdots$	0	1	0	0	0
$\cdots$											$\cdots$					
R_{151}	0	0	0	0	0	0	0	0	0	0	$\cdots$	0	0	0	0	0
R_{152}	0	0	0	0	1	0	0	0	0	1	$\cdots$	0	0	0	0	0
R_{153}	0	0	0	0	1	0	0	0	0	1	$\cdots$	0	0	0	0	0
R_{154}	0	0	0	0	0	0	0	0	0	1	$\cdots$	0	0	0	0	1
R_{155}	0	0	0	0	1	0	0	0	0	0	$\cdots$	0	0	0	0	0
R_{156}	0	0	0	0	1	0	0	0	0	0	$\cdots$	0	0	0	0	0
R_{157}	0	0	0	0	1	0	0	0	0	0	$\cdots$	0	0	0	0	0
R_{158}	0	0	0	0	1	0	0	0	0	1	$\cdots$	0	0	0	0	0

corresponds to an inequality $z_5 + z_9 \geq 1$. The objective function of new MILP is minimization of $\sum z_j$ subject to these constraints. We use Gurobi solver [8] to solve this MILP problem and it provides the 21 linear inequalities by removing the redundant inequalities. The set of 21 linear inequalities (Table 6) is used in the first module of MILP problem to minimize the number of active S-boxes.

3.2.3 Linear Inequalities for Optimizing the Probability of Differential Characteristic

We optimize the probability of differential characteristics in this module of MILP problem. This module utilizes the position of active S-boxes obtained in the first module. In the DDT of WARP S-box, the possible difference propagations are obtained with three different probabilities i.e. 1, 2^{-2}, 2^{-3}. Therefore, we use two extra variables (p_0,p_1) to encode these possible differential patterns. These patterns, with two extra bits, need to satisfy the Eq. 1.

$$
\begin{aligned}
(p_0, p_1) &= (0,0), \text{if } \Pr[(x_0, x_1, x_2, x_3) \rightarrow (y_0, y_1, y_2, y_3)] = 1 = 2^{-0} \\
(p_0, p_1) &= (0,1), \text{if } \Pr[(x_0, x_1, x_2, x_3) \rightarrow (y_0, y_1, y_2, y_3)] = 4/16 = 2^{-2} \\
(p_0, p_1) &= (1,0), \text{if } \Pr[(x_0, x_1, x_2, x_3) \rightarrow (y_0, y_1, y_2, y_3)] = 2/16 = 2^{-3}
\end{aligned} \tag{1}
$$

Further, by using the differential distribution probabilities of the S-box, 1304 inequalities are generated using the SageMath tool. We apply the similar proce-

Table 6. Linear inequalities for minimizing number of active S-boxes

No.	Linear inequalities
1	$-1 * x_3 - 1 * x_2 + 0 * x_1 - 1 * x_0 + 0 * y_3 + 0 * y_2 + 1 * y_1 + 0 * y_0 \geq -2$
2	$-2 * x_3 - 1 * x_2 - 1 * x_1 - 1 * x_0 + 1 * y_3 - 1 * y_2 + 1 * y_1 - 1 * y_0 \geq -5$
3	$0 * x_3 + 0 * x_2 + 1 * x_1 + 0 * x_0 - 1 * y_3 - 1 * y_2 + 0 * y_1 - 1 * y_0 \geq -2$
4	$0 * x_3 - 1 * x_2 - 2 * x_1 + 2 * x_0 - 2 * y_3 + 2 * y_2 - 1 * y_1 - 1 * y_0 \geq -5$
5	$-2 * x_3 - 2 * x_2 - 1 * x_1 + 3 * x_0 - 1 * y_3 + 3 * y_2 - 2 * y_1 - 1 * y_0 \geq -6$
6	$0 * x_3 + 1 * x_2 + 1 * x_1 + 1 * x_0 + 1 * y_3 - 2 * y_2 - 1 * y_1 - 2 * y_0 \geq -3$
7	$0 * x_3 - 1 * x_2 + 1 * x_1 - 1 * x_0 + 0 * y_3 - 1 * y_2 + 1 * y_1 - 1 * y_0 \geq -3$
8	$1 * x_3 + 1 * x_2 - 1 * x_1 - 2 * x_0 - 2 * y_3 - 2 * y_2 + 1 * y_1 + 2 * y_0 \geq -5$
9	$0 * x_3 + 1 * x_2 - 2 * x_1 - 2 * x_0 + 2 * y_3 + 1 * y_2 + 1 * y_1 - 1 * y_0 \geq -3$
10	$-1 * x_3 + 1 * x_2 - 2 * x_1 + 1 * x_0 + 3 * y_3 + 1 * y_2 - 1 * y_1 + 1 * y_0 \geq -1$
11	$-2 * x_3 + 3 * x_2 - 1 * x_1 - 2 * x_0 - 1 * y_3 - 1 * y_2 - 2 * y_1 + 3 * y_0 \geq -6$
12	$0 * x_3 - 2 * x_2 - 2 * x_1 + 1 * x_0 + 2 * y_3 - 1 * y_2 + 1 * y_1 + 1 * y_0 \geq -3$
13	$3 * x_3 + 3 * x_2 + 1 * x_1 + 2 * x_0 - 2 * y_3 + 2 * y_2 - 2 * y_1 + 1 * y_0 \geq 0$
14	$3 * x_3 - 2 * x_2 + 2 * x_1 + 1 * x_0 - 1 * y_3 - 2 * y_2 - 2 * y_1 + 1 * y_0 \geq -4$
15	$1 * x_3 - 2 * x_2 - 1 * x_1 + 1 * x_0 - 2 * y_3 + 2 * y_2 + 1 * y_1 - 2 * y_0 \geq -5$
16	$1 * x_3 + 2 * x_2 + 1 * x_1 + 2 * x_0 + 0 * y_3 - 1 * y_2 + 0 * y_1 - 1 * y_0 \geq 0$
17	$1 * x_3 - 2 * x_2 - 1 * x_1 - 2 * x_0 + 2 * y_3 + 3 * y_2 + 1 * y_1 + 3 * y_0 \geq -1$
18	$3 * x_3 + 1 * x_2 + 2 * x_1 - 2 * x_0 - 1 * y_3 + 1 * y_2 - 2 * y_1 - 2 * y_0 \geq -4$
19	$-2 * x_3 - 1 * x_2 + 1 * x_1 - 1 * x_0 + 3 * y_3 + 2 * y_2 + 3 * y_1 + 2 * y_0 \geq 0$
20	$-1 * x_3 + 2 * x_2 - 1 * x_1 + 2 * x_0 + 0 * y_3 + 1 * y_2 + 2 * y_1 + 1 * y_0 \geq 0$
21	$1 * x_3 - 1 * x_2 - 1 * x_1 - 1 * x_0 + 0 * y_3 - 1 * y_2 - 1 * y_1 - 1 * y_0 \geq -5$

Table 7. Linear inequalities for optimizing the probability

No	Linear inequalities
1	$0 * x_3 + 0 * x_2 + 0 * x_1 + 0 * x_0 + 0 * y_3 + 0 * y_2 + 0 * y_1 + 0 * y_0 - 1 * p0 - 1 * p1 \geq -1$
2	$0 * x_3 - 1 * x_2 + 0 * x_1 - 1 * x_0 + 0 * y_3 - 1 * y_2 + 0 * y_1 - 1 * y_0 + 4 * p0 + 3 * p1 \geq 0$
3	$0 * x_3 + 0 * x_2 + 0 * x_1 + 0 * x_0 + 0 * y_3 + 1 * y_2 - 1 * y_1 + 1 * y_0 + 1 * p0 + 0 * p1 \geq 0$
4	$-1 * x_3 - 1 * x_2 + 1 * x_1 + 2 * x_0 + 0 * y_3 + 0 * y_2 - 1 * y_1 - 2 * y_0 + 3 * p0 + 4 * p1 \geq 0$
5	$0 * x_3 - 3 * x_2 - 2 * x_1 - 3 * x_0 + 0 * y_3 + 1 * y_2 + 2 * y_1 + 1 * y_0 + 6 * p0 + 5 * p1 \geq 0$
6	$0 * x_3 + 2 * x_2 - 2 * x_1 - 2 * x_0 - 3 * y_3 - 1 * y_2 - 1 * y_1 + 2 * y_0 + 6 * p0 + 7 * p1 \geq 0$
7	$7 * x_3 + 4 * x_2 + 2 * x_1 - 2 * x_0 - 1 * y_3 + 4 * y_2 - 5 * y_1 - 8 * y_0 + 7 * p0 + 10 * p1 \geq 0$
8	$-4 * x_3 + 3 * x_2 - 1 * x_1 - 2 * x_0 - 1 * y_3 - 3 * y_2 - 2 * y_1 + 3 * y_0 + 8 * p0 + 10 * p1 \geq 0$
9	$1 * x_3 + 5 * x_2 + 2 * x_1 + 0 * x_0 + 2 * y_3 - 1 * y_2 - 2 * y_1 - 4 * y_0 + 2 * p0 + 5 * p1 \geq 0$
10	$0 * x_3 + 1 * x_2 - 3 * x_1 + 2 * x_0 + 1 * y_3 + 0 * y_2 - 1 * y_1 + 2 * y_0 + 3 * p0 + 1 * p1 \geq 0$
11	$-4 * x_3 - 2 * x_2 + 1 * x_1 - 2 * x_0 + 2 * y_3 + 1 * y_2 + 5 * y_1 + 1 * y_0 + 1 * p0 + 4 * p1 \geq 0$
12	$0 * x_3 + 2 * x_2 + 3 * x_1 - 1 * x_0 - 2 * y_3 - 1 * y_2 + 0 * y_1 - 1 * y_0 + 1 * p0 + 4 * p1 \geq 0$
13	$0 * x_3 + 1 * x_2 - 1 * x_1 + 1 * x_0 + 1 * y_3 - 1 * y_2 + 1 * y_1 - 1 * y_0 + 3 * p0 + 1 * p1 \geq 0$
14	$7 * x_3 - 2 * x_2 + 2 * x_1 + 4 * x_0 - 1 * y_3 - 8 * y_2 - 5 * y_1 + 4 * y_0 + 7 * p0 + 10 * p1 \geq 0$
15	$2 * x_3 + 1 * x_2 + 5 * x_1 + 1 * x_0 - 4 * y_3 - 2 * y_2 + 1 * y_1 - 2 * y_0 + 1 * p0 + 4 * p1 \geq 0$
16	$1 * x_3 + 2 * x_2 + 0 * x_1 + 2 * x_0 + 1 * y_3 + 2 * y_2 + 0 * y_1 + 2 * y_0 - 2 * p0 - 3 * p1 \geq 0$
17	$-2 * x_3 + 2 * x_2 - 4 * x_1 - 4 * x_0 + 5 * y_3 + 2 * y_2 + 1 * y_1 - 1 * y_0 + 5 * p0 + 8 * p1 \geq 0$
18	$0 * x_3 + 1 * x_2 - 3 * x_1 + 2 * x_0 - 1 * y_3 + 2 * y_2 - 1 * y_1 - 1 * y_0 + 5 * p0 + 3 * p1 \geq 0$
19	$-2 * x_3 - 4 * x_2 - 1 * x_1 + 2 * x_0 - 1 * y_3 + 2 * y_2 + 3 * y_1 - 1 * y_0 + 3 * p0 + 8 * p1 \geq 0$
20	$2 * x_3 - 4 * x_2 - 2 * x_1 - 1 * x_0 + 1 * y_3 - 1 * y_2 - 2 * y_1 + 2 * y_0 + 6 * p0 + 10 * p1 \geq 0$

dure as in previous section to reduce the number of inequalities and get a set of 20 linear inequalities (Table 7) to represent the DDT of S-box.

3.2.4 Modeling Linear Layers

In the round function, nibble-permutation and XOR are the linear operations. The permutation operation can be easily represented by renaming the variables only. To convert the XOR operation into linear inequalities, for each bit of U and V (Algorithm 1), we follow the conditions on bit variables to exclude the impossible patterns (Eq. 2). Here, u and v refer to the input bits and bit variable w is used to refer the output of XOR operation *i.e.* $w = u \oplus v$.

$$\begin{aligned} u + v - w &\geq 0 \\ u - v + w &\geq 0 \\ -u + v + w &\geq 0 \\ u + v + w &\leq 2 \end{aligned} \tag{2}$$

3.2.5 MILP Model

The linear inequalities for substitution and permutation layers are used to model an MILP problem and this MILP problem is solved to optimize the probability of differential characteristic. In this process, we first minimize the number of S-boxes and then by minimizing the probabilities, we get the desired differential characteristics. The objective function is the optimization of probability of differential characteristics as given in Eq. 3. The source code for MILP model of WARP is available on the GitHub[2].

$$Min \sum (3 \times p_0 + 2 \times p_1) \tag{3}$$

We use Gurobi to solve this MILP problem for WARP and construct the 18-round and 19-round differential characteristics with optimal probability. The differential characteristics for the 18-round and 19-round of WARP are presented in Sects. 3.3 and 3.4. We have also constructed 108 differential characteristics for 18-round WARP with the probability of 2^{-122} (Appendix A).

3.3 Differential Characteristics for 18-Round WARP

We solve the MILP problems for 17 and 18 rounds of WARP using Gurobi solver. The optimal solution for the 17-round problem is obtained with 57 active S-boxes and 2^{-114} probability. To extend the 17-round characteristic, one round MILP problem is modelled by fixing its output difference equal to the input difference of the 17-round characteristic. This one round MILP problem is solved to construct the 18-round characteristic by adding one round at the head of the 17-round characteristic. The extended 18-round differential characteristic is constructed with 61 active S-boxes and 2^{-122} probability as described in Table 8.

[2] https://github.com/tarunyadav/WARP-MILP.

Table 8. 18-round differential characteristics (extended from 17-round)

Round (r)	Input difference $\Delta_r = (x_{31}^r, x_{30}^r, \cdots, x_0^r)$	Probability (p)
1	0007a000fa7000000a000000d5f000d0	1
2	00700d00a0000000aa00000050000000	2^{-8}
3	0000d50000000000a000000000000a00	2^{-12}
4	000050000000000a000000000000aa00	2^{-16}
5	00000000000000a0000000000000a000	2^{-20}
6	000000000a00000000000000000a0000	2^{-20}
7	0000000aa0000000000a000000a00000	2^{-24}
8	000000aa00000a0000a00a00000a0000	2^{-28}
9	0a0000a00000af000000a00000a00000	2^{-36}
10	a0000f0a0000f000000a00000a000000	2^{-40}
11	0000f0a00000000a00a0000aaf0f0000	2^{-48}
12	00000a000a0000a00f0500aaf0f00a0a	2^{-56}
13	000aaf0aa000000afa500aa00500ada0	2^{-70}
14	00aaf0a000000aaaa000a00a5000df00	2^{-86}
15	00a00500000fa0aa000a00a0000af000	2^{-96}
16	000050000af000a000a500000aa00000	2^{-106}
17	00000000a000000055000000a000000a	2^{-112}
18	00000a0000000000500000000a0000a5	2^{-116}
19	0000a000000a000f0000000fa7000550	2^{-122}

Table 9. 18-round differential characteristics

Round (r)	Input difference $\Delta_r = (x_{31}^r, x_{30}^r, \cdots, x_0^r)$	Probability (p)
1	000af000faf000000a0000005f500050	1
2	00a00500a0000000af000000f0000000	2^{-8}
3	00005f0000000000f000000000000a00	2^{-12}
4	0000f0000000000a000000000000af00	2^{-16}
5	00000000000000a0000000000000f000	2^{-20}
6	000000000f00000000000000000a0000	2^{-20}
7	0000000ff0000000000a000000a00000	2^{-24}
8	000000fa00000a0000a00f00000a0000	2^{-28}
9	0a0000a00000aa000000f00000a00000	2^{-36}
10	a0000f0a0000a000000a00000a000000	2^{-40}
11	0000f0a00000000a00a0000aaa050000	2^{-48}
12	00000a000f0000a00f0d00aaa0500a0a	2^{-56}
13	000aaa0af000000affd00aa00d00ada0	2^{-70}
14	00aaa0a0000005aaf000a00ad000df00	2^{-86}
15	00a00d00000a50aa000a00a0000af000	2^{-96}
16	0000d0000aa000a000ad000005a00000	2^{-106}
17	00000000a00000000dd000005000000a	2^{-112}
18	0000500000000000d00000000a0000ad	2^{-116}
19	00005000000a00070000000da7000dd0	2^{-122}

We solve the MILP problem for 18-round WARP and construct 18-round differential characteristics without extending a lower round characteristic. Although, the patterns of active S-boxes and differential probabilities are similar to the characteristics described in Table 8. This 18-round differential characteristic with 61 active S-boxes and 2^{-122} probability is described in Table 9.

3.4 Differential Characteristics for 19-Round WARP

We solve the MILP problem for 19-round WARP and construct the differential characteristics with the least number of active S-boxes. We present the 19-round characteristic by extending the 18-round differential characteristics (Table 10).

We did not find any 19-round differential characteristics consisting of 65 or less active S-boxes. The best differential characteristic for 19-round WARP consists of 66 active S-boxes with the probability of 2^{-132}.

Table 10. 19-round differential characteristics

Round (r)	Input difference $\Delta_r = (x^r_{31}, x^r_{30}, \cdots, x^r_0)$	Probability (p)
1	0007a000fa7000000a000000d5f000d0	1
2	00700d00a0000000aa00000050000000	2^{-8}
3	0000d50000000000a000000000000a00	2^{-12}
4	0000500000000000a00000000000aa00	2^{-16}
5	0000000000000000a00000000000a000	2^{-20}
6	000000000a00000000000000000a0000	2^{-20}
7	0000000aa0000000000a000000a00000	2^{-24}
8	000000aa00000a0000a00a00000a0000	2^{-28}
9	0a0000a00000af000000a00000a00000	2^{-36}
10	a0000f0a0000f000000a00000a000000	2^{-40}
11	0000f0a00000000a00a0000aaf0f0000	2^{-48}
12	00000a000a0000a00f0500aaf0f00a0a	2^{-56}
13	000aaf0aa000000afa500aa00500ada0	2^{-70}
14	00aaf0a000000aaaa000a00a5000df00	2^{-86}
15	00a00500000fa0aa000a00a0000af000	2^{-96}
16	000050000af000a000a500000aa00000	2^{-106}
17	00000000a00000000550000a000000a	2^{-112}
18	00000a000000000005000000a0000a5	2^{-116}
19	0000a000000a000f0000000fa7000550	2^{-122}
20	000f0a000aa500f00d0000fd70005a00	2^{-132}

4 Key Recovery Attack on 21-Round WARP

We select the 16-round differential characteristic ($\Delta_2 \rightarrow \Delta_{18}$) from the 18-round differential characteristic (Table 9). The probability of the 16-round differential characteristic is 2^{-108}. We add two rounds at the beginning and three rounds at the end of the 16-round differential characteristic as shown in Table 12. Using the 16-round differential characteristic, we can launch a key recovery attack on the 21-round WARP. The 16-round characteristic is chosen in particular because the number of active bits in the head and tail of this characteristic are lesser. In each round, 64-bit round key is required and it is extracted directly from the 128-bit key K = (K_0, K_1). The key K_0 is used for the odd numbered rounds while the even numbered rounds use the key K_1 (Table 11). We need to guess the round keys which correspond to the actives S-boxes. The round keys used in 1st, 19th and 21st rounds are $(K_0^0, K_0^1, K_0^2, K_0^3, K_0^4, K_0^7, K_0^{10}, K_0^{11}, K_0^{13}, K_0^{14})$ and the keys $(K_1^1, K_1^3, K_1^4, K_1^7, K_1^8, K_1^{10}, K_1^{11}, K_1^{14})$ are used in 2nd and 20th rounds. In total, 72 bits (18 nibbles) of the round keys are used in these rounds.

Table 11. Round keys used in differential attack on WARP

Round	Subkeys
1	$K_0^0, K_0^1, K_0^2, K_0^3, K_0^4, K_0^5, K_0^6, K_0^7, K_0^8, K_0^9, K_0^{10}, K_0^{11}, K_0^{12}, K_0^{13}, K_0^{14}, K_0^{15}$
2	$K_1^0, K_1^1, K_1^2, K_1^3, K_1^4, K_1^5, K_1^6, K_1^7, K_1^8, K_1^9, K_1^{10}, K_1^{11}, K_1^{12}, K_1^{13}, K_1^{14}, K_1^{15}$
19	$K_0^0, K_0^1, K_0^2, K_0^3, K_0^4, K_0^5, K_0^6, K_0^7, K_0^8, K_0^9, K_0^{10}, K_0^{11}, K_0^{12}, K_0^{13}, K_0^{14}, K_0^{15}$
20	$K_1^0, K_1^1, K_1^2, K_1^3, K_1^4, K_1^5, K_1^6, K_1^7, K_1^8, K_1^9, K_1^{10}, K_1^{11}, K_1^{12}, K_1^{13}, K_1^{14}, K_1^{15}$
21	$K_0^0, K_0^1, K_0^2, K_0^3, K_0^4, K_0^5, K_0^6, K_0^7, K_0^8, K_0^9, K_0^{10}, K_0^{11}, K_0^{12}, K_0^{13}, K_0^{14}, K_0^{15}$

Table 12. Differential attack on 21-round WARP

Round (r)	Input difference $\Delta_r = (x_{31}^r, x_{30}^r, \cdots, x_0^r)$
1	00?0af?00????000000000?005??a00?
2	000af000?a?000000a0000005f?000?0
3	00a00500a0000000af000000f0000000
.	.
.	.
.	.
19	000005000000000d00000000a0000ad
20	00005000000a000?0000000?a?000dd0
21	000?0a000?ad00?00?0000???000d?00
22	00??a?0??dd?000???000??a000???00

4.1 Data Collection

We can build $2^n (n \leq 88)$ structures corresponding to fixed bits in the input difference (Δ_1). The objective is to minimize the value of n such that sufficient number of right pairs are left for key guessing phase. Each structure traverses the 40 undetermined (?) bits in Δ_1 (Table 12). Thus, each structure generates $2^{40*2-1} (= 2^{79})$ pairs[3] satisfying the differential. Therefore, the total number of pairs generated by the 2^n structures are 2^{n+79}. Such a pair will meet the third round differential in Table 12 with an average probability of 2^{-40}. The probability of obeying the differential after 19th round for the pair encrypted with the right key is 2^{-108}. Therefore, the number of pairs satisfying the differential with a right key guess after 19th round will be $2^{n+79} \times 2^{-40} \times 2^{-108} (= 2^{n-69})$. Hence, we choose n = 73 so that we could get at least $2^4 (= 16)$ right pairs under the correct key guessing.

4.2 Key Recovery

In this phase, we guess the key bits corresponding to the 4-bit key nibbles. This guess includes $K_0^0, K_0^2, K_0^3, K_0^{10}, K_0^{11}, K_0^{13}$ in 1st round, $K_1^3, K_1^7, K_1^{11}, K_1^{14}$ in 2nd round, K_0^0, K_0^3, K_0^{13} in 19th round, $K_1^1, K_1^3, K_1^4, K_1^8, K_1^{10}$ in 20th round and $K_0^1, K_0^4, K_0^7, K_0^{10}, K_0^{11}, K_0^{13}, K_0^{14}$ in 21st round.

Since K_0^0, K_0^3 are involved in 1st and 19th round, K_1^3 is involved in 2nd and 20th round, K_0^{10}, K_0^{11} are involved in 1st and 21st round, and K_0^{13} is involved in 1st, 19th and 21st round. Therefore, total 18(=25-7) unique 4-bit nibbles are involved in the key recovery phase. Hence, we construct $2^{18*4} (= 2^{72})$ counters for the possible values of the 72 key bits.

With n = 73, we repeat the key guessing procedure for each of the 2^{73+79} pairs. We are left with $2^{73+79-72} (= 2^{80})$ pairs after filtered by 72 fixed bits in Δ_{22}. Therefore, the expected counter value for a wrong key guess is $2^{73+79-72-40-56} (= 2^{-16})$ after filtered by undetermined bits in Δ_1 and Δ_{22}. As discussed in Subsect. 4.1, there are at least 16 right pairs remaining after 19th round. The right pairs will be used for key guessing and a key with the highest counter value will be the correct key.

4.3 Complexity

There are 2^n structures and 2^{40} pairs can be generated in each structure. With n = 73, the data complexity of the 21-round differential attack on WARP becomes $2^{73+40} (= 2^{113})$. We need to store the counter corresponding to 72 bits of the key, so the memory complexity of the attack becomes 2^{72}. In the first round, for each of the 2^{80} pairs, we need to guess the 24 key bits corresponding to the six active S-boxes. Therefore, time complexity of the first round becomes $2^{80+24} (= 2^{104})$. Similarly the time complexities for 2nd, 21st, 20th and 19th rounds are $2^{56+16} (= 2^{72})$, $2^{80+16} (= 2^{96})$, $2^{56+16} (= 2^{72})$ and $2^{36+0} (= 2^{36})$ respectively. There is no

[3] In this calculation, we consider a pair (a, b) same as (b, a).

need to guess the key bits for 19th round because these have been already guessed in the first round. Hence, the time complexity of the whole attack is bounded by the 2^{113} chosen plaintexts.

5 Conclusion

In this paper, we presented a 21-round key recovery attack and detailed differential characteristics for 18-round and 19-round WARP. We used MILP aided search to construct the differential characteristic for 18 rounds with the probability of 2^{-122} and the best differential characteristic for 19 rounds exists with a probability of 2^{-132}. We used the 16-round differential characteristic to mount a key recovery attack on 21 rounds by adding two rounds on the head and three rounds on the tail of this differential characteristic. The data complexity of the 21-round key recovery differential attack is 2^{113}. This paper presented the first key recovery attack on 21-round WARP. However, the attack does not pose any threat to the security of full round WARP against differential attack.

Appendix

A Differential Characteristics (108) of 18-Round WARP with Probability of 2^{-122}

No.	Input difference	Output difference
1	0x000af000faf000000a0000005f500050	0x00005000000a00070000000da7000dd0
2	0x00055000a75000000a000000aad00070	0x0000a000000f00050000000afd000aa0
3	0x000da000a5a000000a000000a5a00070	0x0000a000000f000f0000000fad0005a0
4	0x0005a000a5a0000005000000aa7000a0	0x00005000000a000a0000000a55000aa0
5	0x000aa000aa50000005000000aaa00050	0x00005000000a000a0000000aaf000ff0
6	0x000aa000aa5000000a000000daf00050	0x0000a000000a000500000005a5000da0
7	0x000ad000fa5000000a0000005ad000a0	0x0000a000000f000a0000000af7000a50
8	0x000aa000a5d000000a000000faa000d0	0x0000a000000f00050000000ff5000da0
9	0x0005a000aa70000005000000a55000a0	0x0000a0000005000a0000000faf000af0
10	0x000da000a5f00000050000007aa00070	0x0000a0000005000a000000057a000ff0
11	0x000da000a5a000000a000000a5a00070	0x0000a000000500050000000daf0005a0
12	0x0005a0005fa000000a000000adf000a0	0x0000a000000500050000000d750005a0
13	0x0005d000faa000000a000000aad00070	0x0000a000000a00050000000da5000aa0
14	0x0005a000ad50000005000000aa7000a0	0x0000a000000a000d0000000aaf000af0
15	0x000da000f5d000000a000000aaa00070	0x00005000000a00070000000dad000da0
16	0x0005f0007ad000000d000000aa5000a0	0x0000d000000a00070000000aa5000aa0
17	0x0005a000757000000d000000a57000a0	0x0000a000000a00050000000faf000da0
18	0x000aa000aaa000000a0000005a5000f0	0x0000a0000005000500000005aa000da0
19	0x0007d000a7a000000a000000dad00050	0x0000a000000a000a00000007da000aa0
20	0x000aa0005a5000000a000000aa5000f0	0x0000a000000a000500000005ad0005a0

(*continued*)

(*continued*)

No.	Input difference	Output difference
21	0x000da000a5a000000d000000aaa000a0	0x0000a000000f00050000000ffa000ad0
22	0x000aa000a57000000d000000a5a000f0	0x0000a000000f000a00000005aa000da0
23	0x0005a000ad7000000d000000ad7000a0	0x000070000005000d0000000faa000da0
24	0x000aa000555000000a000000daa000a0	0x0000a000000d000500000005aa000ad0
25	0x000da000a5a000000a000000ada000a0	0x0000a000000f000500000005a5000aa0
26	0x000aa000aa7000000a000000dd500050	0x0000a000000d00050000000fad000aa0
27	0x000aa0007d70000005000000a5a00050	0x0000a000000a000f0000000da5000aa0
28	0x0005a000757000000d000000a5a000a0	0x0000a000000a000a00000005ad000aa0
29	0x000aa000aa70000005000000ad5000a0	0x0000f000000a000f00000007dd0005a0
30	0x0005a000daa000000a000000a55000a0	0x0000a000000f000d0000000daf000af0
31	0x000aa000dda000000a000000aa700050	0x0000a000000d000a0000000d7f000af0
32	0x000aa000a5a000000a000000daa000f0	0x0000a000000f00050000000fff000af0
33	0x000af0005aa000000a0000005a500050	0x0000a000000d000500000005a7000a50
34	0x000da000755000000d0000007aa00070	0x0000a0000005000f0000000aad000aa0
35	0x000aa000ada0000005000000aa700050	0x0000a000000a00050000000dad000aa0
36	0x0005a000ad50000005000000aaa000a0	0x0000a0000005000d0000000aaf000ff0
37	0x0005a0007da000000d000000ad7000a0	0x0000a000000f000a0000000aad000da0
38	0x000aa000aa70000005000000add00050	0x0000a0000005000500000005aa000aa0
39	0x000aa0007df0000005000000af7000a0	0x0000f000000f000a00000005aa000aa0
40	0x000aa000adf000000a0000005a700050	0x0000a000000a00050000000a5a000aa0
41	0x000aa000aaa000000a0000005f500050	0x0000a000000a000f00000005a50005a0
42	0x0007a000d5a000000700000005a700050	0x000050000007000a00000007dd000aa0
43	0x000aa000fa7000000a000000ddd00050	0x0000a000000a000500000005aa0005a0
44	0x000da0005aa000000a000000aa500070	0x0000a000000f000500000005aa000aa0
45	0x000a5000da5000000a000000aa500050	0x0000a0000005000d0000000fa7000ad0
46	0x000aa0005a7000000a0000005d500050	0x00007000000500050000000057f000af0
47	0x000aa000d5f000000a0000005aa00050	0x0000a000000f000500000005af000aa0
48	0x000aa000ada000000f000000f5a00050	0x0000f000000f000a0000000afd000aa0
49	0x000aa0005aa000000a000000a5a00050	0x0000a0000005000a0000000d7f000aa0
50	0x0005a000a5a000000d000000ada000a0	0x0000a0000005000d0000000d7d000d70
51	0x0005a000aa5000000f000000aad000a0	0x0000a000000a000a0000000daa000a50
52	0x000ad000da5000000a0000005aa00050	0x0000a000000a000a0000000af7000ad0
53	0x000da000a5f00000050000007a700070	0x0000a000000f000a00000005af000af0
54	0x000aa00055a000000a0000005a700050	0x0000a000000f000d0000000ff5000da0
55	0x000aa000aa5000000f000000fad000a0	0x0000f000000a000f0000000a55000aa0
56	0x000fa000a570000005000000ad7000f0	0x0000d000000a00070000000a57000a50
57	0x0005a000aff000000a000000aaa000a0	0x0000a000000d000f0000000d75000aa0
58	0x000aa000a550000005000000aaa000d0	0x0000a000000a000d0000000ad50005a0
59	0x0005a000a57000000a000000ad7000a0	0x0000a0000005000f0000000d77000ad0
60	0x0005a0005aa000000a000000aa5000a0	0x0000a000000d000a0000000d77000ad0
61	0x0005a000a5a000000f000000afa000a0	0x0000a0000005000d0000000daa000fd0
62	0x0005a00075a000000d000000aaa000a0	0x0000a00000050005000000fa70005d0
63	0x000aa000a5d000000a0000005aa00050	0x0000a000000d000d0000000d7a000a50
64	0x000aa000d5d0000007000000daa00050	0x0000f000000a000a0000000aaa000a50

(*continued*)

(*continued*)

No.	Input difference	Output difference
65	0x000fa000aa7000000d000000ada000f0	0x0000a0000005000d00000005ad0005a0
66	0x000aa000f57000000a0000005da00050	0x0000d000000a00070000000755000fa0
67	0x000dd000aaa000000a000000aaa000a0	0x0000a000000f000d0000000daa000a50
68	0x000a5000a7a000000d000000aad000f0	0x00005000000a000a0000000aaa000a50
69	0x0005a000a5700000050000000ada000a0	0x0000a00000005000500000000faf000aa0
70	0x000aa000ffa000000a000000d5f00050	0x00005000000a000a0000000a5a000a50
71	0x000a5000aa5000000a000000da500050	0x0000f000000f000a0000000da7000ad0
72	0x0005a000f5a000000a000000a5a000a0	0x0000a000000a00050000000a5a000a50
73	0x0005a000ad5000000a000000aa7000a0	0x0000a000000f000d00000005aa000aa0
74	0x000aa00055a000000a000000dda00050	0x00005000000a00070000000add000aa0
75	0x000aa000a57000000a0000005da00050	0x0000a0000005000f00000005af000af0
76	0x000aa000d57000000a000000a5a000a0	0x0000a000000a000f00000005a7000f50
77	0x0005f000afa0000005000000aff000a0	0x00005000000a000a00000005aa000ad0
78	0x000aa000aaa000000a000000d5a00050	0x0000a00000050005000000057a000aa0
79	0x000aa000aa5000000f000000fa500050	0x0000a0000005000d0000000faf000af0
80	0x000aa00055a000000a0000005da00050	0x0000f000000f000a0000000daa0005d0
81	0x000aa000ad7000000d000000ad700050	0x000070000005000d0000000d7a0005a0
82	0x000aa0007aa0000005000000a5500050	0x0000a000000f000f00000005aa000da0
83	0x000aa000aaa000000a0000005a500050	0x0000a000000a000a0000000daa000ad0
84	0x000aa000d5a000000a000000daa000f0	0x0000d000000a00070000000ad7000a50
85	0x000aa0005aa000000a000000d5500050	0x0000a00000050005000000005ad000fa0
86	0x000aa0005aa000000a000000d5500050	0x0000a000000f000a0000000aaf0005a0
87	0x0005a000aaa0000005000000a55000a0	0x0000a0000005000a00000005af000aa0
88	0x000aa000ada000000d000000a57000d0	0x0000a0000005000f00000005aa000da0
89	0x0005a000aaa0000005000000a5d000a0	0x0000a000000a00050000000a5a000aa0
90	0x000aa000dd5000000a000000daa000d0	0x0000f000000a000a00000005ad000aa0
91	0x000aa000a5a000000a000000aaa00050	0x0000a000000a000f00000007d5000aa0
92	0x000aa0005f7000000a00000055a00050	0x0000a00000050005000000000d77000fd0
93	0x0007a000dff000000a000000daa000d0	0x0000a0000005000d0000000aa7000a50
94	0x000aa000dda000000a000000fa700050	0x0000a000000a000a0000000fa5000da0
95	0x000ad000aa50000005000000aa500050	0x0000a000000a00050000000a5d0005a0
96	0x0005a0007d700000050000007d7000a0	0x0000a0000005000a00000005a50005a0
97	0x000aa000ad5000000a0000005aa00050	0x0000a000000a000a0000000a5a000aa0
98	0x000df000aaf000000d000000afd00070	0x0000a00000050005000000000d75000aa0
99	0x000aa000a57000000a000000dda00050	0x0000a000000a000a0000000ada000af0
100	0x0005a000a57000000d000000a5a00070	0x00005000000a000a0000000a5a000aa0
101	0x000da000a5a000000a000000afa000a0	0x0000a0000005000f00000005ad000aa0
102	0x000a500057a000000a000000aad000a0	0x0000a000000a000f0000000aa5000aa0
103	0x00055000aaa000000d0000007af000a0	0x0000a000000a00050000000a55000fa0
104	0x0005f000aaf000000a000000af5000a0	0x0000a0000005000d0000000faa000aa0
105	0x0005a000a5f000000a000000afa000a0	0x00005000000a000a00000007da000aa0
106	0x000aa000aaa000000a00000055500050	0x0000a000000a000a0000000a55000aa0
107	0x0005a00075a000000d000000ada000a0	0x0000a000000f00050000000af5000aa0
108	0x000aa000a5a000000a0000005aa00050	0x0000a000000a00050000000755000aa0

References

1. Abdelkhalek, A., Sasaki, Y., Todo, Y., Tolba, M., Youssef, A.M.: MILP modeling for (large) S-boxes to optimize probability of differential characteristics. IACR Trans. Symmetr. Cryptol. **2017**(4), 99–129 (2017). https://doi.org/10.13154/tosc.v2017.i4.99-129. ISSN 2519-173X
2. Banik, S., et al.: WARP: revisiting GFN for lightweight 128-bit block cipher. In: Dunkelman, O., Jacobson, Jr., M.J., O'Flynn, C. (eds.) SAC 2020. LNCS, vol. 12804, pp. 535–564. Springer, Cham (2021). https://doi.org/10.1007/978-3-030-81652-0_21
3. Biham, E., Shamir, A.: Differential cryptanalysis of the full 16-round DES. In: Brickell, E.F. (ed.) CRYPTO 1992. LNCS, vol. 740, pp. 487–496. Springer, Heidelberg (1993). https://doi.org/10.1007/3-540-48071-4_34
4. Bogdanov, A., et al.: PRESENT: an ultra-lightweight block cipher. In: Paillier, P., Verbauwhede, I. (eds.) CHES 2007. LNCS, vol. 4727, pp. 450–466. Springer, Heidelberg (2007). https://doi.org/10.1007/978-3-540-74735-2_31
5. CPLEX. https://www.ibm.com/analytics/cplex-optimizer
6. Daemen, J., Rijmen, V.: The Design of Rijndael. Springer, Heidelberg (2002). https://doi.org/10.1007/978-3-662-04722-4
7. Gohr, A.: Improving attacks on round-reduced Speck32/64 using deep learning. In: Boldyreva, A., Micciancio, D. (eds.) CRYPTO 2019. LNCS, vol. 11693, pp. 150–179. Springer, Cham (2019). https://doi.org/10.1007/978-3-030-26951-7_6
8. Gurobi Optimizer. http://www.gurobi.com
9. Knudsen, L., Robshaw, M.J.B.: Block Cipher Companion. Springer, Heidelberg (2011). https://doi.org/10.1007/978-3-642-17342-4. ISBN 978-3-642-17341-7
10. Kumar, M., Suresh, T.S., Pal, S.K., Panigrahi, A.: Optimal Differential Trails in Lightweight Block Ciphers ANU and PICO. Cryptologia **44**(1), 68–78 (2020)
11. Logic Friday. http://sontrak.com/
12. Matsui, M.: On correlation between the order of S-boxes and the strength of DES. In: De Santis, A. (ed.) EUROCRYPT 1994. LNCS, vol. 950, pp. 366–375. Springer, Heidelberg (1995). https://doi.org/10.1007/BFb0053451
13. Mouha, N., Wang, Q., Gu, D., Preneel, B.: Differential and linear cryptanalysis using mixed-integer linear programming. In: Wu, C.-K., Yung, M., Lin, D. (eds.) Inscrypt 2011. LNCS, vol. 7537, pp. 57–76. Springer, Heidelberg (2012). https://doi.org/10.1007/978-3-642-34704-7_5
14. National Institute of Standards and Technology: Lightweight Cryptography, Finalists, NIST (2021)
15. SAGE. http://www.sagemath.org/index.html
16. Sun, S., Hu, L., Wang, P., Qiao, K., Ma, X., Song, L.: Automatic security evaluation and (related-key) differential characteristic search: application to SIMON, PRESENT, LBlock, DES(L) and other bit-oriented block ciphers. In: Sarkar, P., Iwata, T. (eds.) ASIACRYPT 2014, Part I. LNCS, vol. 8873, pp. 158–178. Springer, Heidelberg (2014). https://doi.org/10.1007/978-3-662-45611-8_9
17. Sun, S., et al.: Towards finding the best characteristics of some bit-oriented block ciphers and automatic enumeration of (related-key) differential and linear characteristics with predefined properties. Cryptology ePrint Archive, Report 2014/747 (2014)
18. Sasaki, Yu., Todo, Y.: New impossible differential search tool from design and cryptanalysis aspects. In: Coron, J.-S., Nielsen, J.B. (eds.) EUROCRYPT 2017, Part III. LNCS, vol. 10212, pp. 185–215. Springer, Cham (2017). https://doi.org/10.1007/978-3-319-56617-7_7

19. Sasaki, Yu., Todo, Y.: New algorithm for modeling S-box in MILP based differential and division trail search. In: Farshim, P., Simion, E. (eds.) SecITC 2017. LNCS, vol. 10543, pp. 150–165. Springer, Cham (2017). https://doi.org/10.1007/978-3-319-69284-5_11
20. Yadav, T., Kumar, M.: Differential-ML distinguisher: machine learning based generic extension for differential cryptanalysis. In: Longa, P., Ràfols, C. (eds.) LATINCRYPT 2021. LNCS, vol. 12912, pp. 191–212. Springer, Cham (2021). https://doi.org/10.1007/978-3-030-88238-9_10
21. Zhu, B., Dong, X., Yu, H.: MILP-based differential attack on round-reduced GIFT. In: Matsui, M. (ed.) CT-RSA 2019. LNCS, vol. 11405, pp. 372–390. Springer, Cham (2019). https://doi.org/10.1007/978-3-030-12612-4_19

Post-Quantum Cryptography and Homomorphic Encryption

SHELBRS: Location-Based Recommendation Services Using Switchable Homomorphic Encryption

Mishel Jain[1(✉)], Priyanka Singh[1(✉)], and Balasubramanian Raman[2(✉)]

[1] Dhirubhai Ambani Institute of Information and Communication Technology, Gandhinagar, Gujarat, India
{201911052,priyanka_singh}@daiict.ac.in

[2] Indian Institute of Technology, Roorkee, Roorkee, Utharakhand, India
bala@cs.iitr.ac.in

Abstract. Location-Based Recommendation Services (LBRS) has seen an unprecedented rise in its usage in recent years. LBRS facilitates a user by recommending services based on his location and past preferences. However, leveraging such services comes at a cost of compromising one's sensitive information like their shopping preferences, lodging places, food habits, recently visited places, etc. to the third-party servers. Losing such information could be crucial and threatens one's privacy. Nowadays, the privacy-aware society seeks solutions that can provide such services, with minimized risks. Recently, a few privacy-preserving recommendation services have been proposed that exploit the fully homomorphic encryption (FHE) properties to address the issue. Though, it reduced privacy risks but suffered from heavy computational overheads that ruled out their commercial applications. Here, we propose SHELBRS, a lightweight LBRS that is based on switchable homomorphic encryption (SHE), which will benefit the users as well as the service providers. A SHE exploits both the additive as well as the multiplicative homomorphic properties but with comparatively much lesser processing time as it's FHE counterpart. We evaluate the performance of our proposed scheme with the other state-of-the-art approaches without compromising security.

Keywords: Homomorphic encryption · Location-Based Recommendation Services (LBRS) · Co-occurrence Matrix (CM)

1 Introduction

Location-Based Recommendation Services (LBRS) grant users access to relevant information about their surroundings based on their location and history. For instance, a person searching for a coffee shop nearby his/her location. The service providers would provide the best search results considering his/her present location and previous history. However, availing of such services risks the user's privacy as the shared sensitive information could be misused by these third-party servers to their advantage, causing serious losses to the user [15]. This fact

L. Batina et al. (Eds.): SPACE 2021, LNCS 13162, pp. 63–80, 2022.
https://doi.org/10.1007/978-3-030-95085-9_4

kind of delimits the privacy-aware society rushing to leverage such services and creates an urgent need for privacy-preserving recommendation services.

The real-time location information of the user is handled by location based services (LBS). It also provides recommendation over encrypted history preferences which ensures the user's privacy. Lyu et al. proposed one such state-of-the-art protocol. They adopt the Hilbert curve [16] as a mapping tool, collaborative filtering recommender based on the co-occurrence matrix as a recommendation technique [11,17], and Brakerski-Gentry-Vaikuntanathan (BGV) fully homomorphic encryption (FHE) as an encryption scheme [2]. However, it is still infeasible for the use of commercial recommendation services due to the high processing time.

In this paper, we propose SHELBRS, a lightweight LBRS that will benefit the users as well as the service providers. Instead of FHE, we employ switchable homomorphic encryption (SHE) that securely switches between partially homomorphic encryption (PHE) schemes. Specifically, Paillier Homomorphic Encryption and ElGamal Homomorphic Encryption for performing additions and multiplications on the encrypted data. PHE evaluates arithmetic operations more efficiently at least 2–3 order of magnitude compared to FHE. SHE supports an arbitrary number of additions and multiplications over encrypted data and serves the principle of FHE with better efficiency. The overall computation and communication cost required in switching between the PHE's is reasonable for real-life applications. It overall reduces the processing time without compromising the security.

The remainder of this paper is structured as follows: Sect. 2 discusses some of the related works. Section 3 gives an overview of the Hilbert curve, collaborative filtering based on Co-occurrence Matrix (CM), PHE, and the SHE schemes. Section 4 presents the LBRS using FHE [9] while Sect. 5 details the proposed SHELBRS scheme. Section 6 discusses the experimental results and the security analysis of the proposed scheme. Section 7 concludes the work along with some future directions.

2 Related Work

Lattice-based FHE scheme introduced by Craig Gentry in 2009, is a milestone research that opened doors for proposing possible solutions for encrypted data. It was made possible as this scheme supported computation of arbitrary functions and operations on the ciphertext, without the need of actually decrypting it [3].

Many LBS were proposed in the literature to search nearest Point of Interests (POI)'s to the user's private location. In 2003, K-anonymous based technique was introduced which adopts temporal and spatial cloaking [4]. It acquires accuracy but requires a trusted third party to hide the user's location. Private Information Retrieval (PIR) [10], Private Circular Query Protocol (PCQP) [6] and Lightweight Private Circular Query Protocol (LPCQP) [19] are the LBS based on the cryptography methods. In PIR scheme, the user receives POI from the server's database based on Quadratic Residuosity Assumption (QRA) without server's knowledge of which POI a user is interested in. It provides security but takes high execution time for searching POIs. PCQP proposed by Lien et al. is an effective k-NN search algorithm based on Paillier cryptosystem and Hilbert curve. It secretly shifts the POI-info circularly which is stored on the server. LPCQP, proposed by Utsunomiya et al. is a lightweight protocol that removes unnecessary POI information from the requesting user to reduce computational cost. PIR, PCQP, and LPCQP are secure against single point failures and Denial of Service (DOS) attacks. In 2012, Pingley et al. proposed a context-aware scheme for privacy-preserving LBS [13]. It projects the user's location on various-grid-length Hilbert curve and uses location perturbation technique to prevent user's privacy from the LBS server. Gang et al. proposed location-based social network (LBSN) towards privacy preservation for "check-in" services in 2019 [18]. It designs the framework using k-anonymity based algorithms without using a trusted third-party server. It guarantees secure access and preserves user's location privacy.

The detail of recommender systems and discussion about different recommendation algorithms based on traditional and network approaches was studied by Lu et al. in 2012 [8]. It compares the performance of different recommendation algorithms. Badsha et al. introduced an Elgamal cryptosystem based privacy-preserving item-based Collaborative Filtering (CF) in 2016 [1]. It provides recommendations based on the user's average ratings and the similarities between the items. Zhang et al. proposed Factorization Machines (FM) based recommendation algorithm for Rural Tourism in 2018 [20]. It provides recommendations based on geographical distribution and seasonal features such as the user's best suitable season for traveling, how many kilometers is the traveling spot away from the city, and other user's reviews or comments for the particular location. In 2018, Horowitz et al. proposed a mobile recommender system named "EventAware" for the events [5]. It provides recommendations on the basis of both context-aware and tag-based algorithms. In 2019, Qi et al. proposed a time-aware and privacy-preserving distributed recommendation service based on a locality-sensitive hashing (LSH) to provide most accurate recommended results [14]. Papakyriakopoulos et al. analyzed the political networks based on hybrid collaborative filtering and deep learning recommender algorithms in 2020 [12]. It shows how hyperactive users influence recommendations. It also compares the results based on likes and comments with and without the inclusion of the hyperactive users along with the rest of the users in the datasets.

Combining both location privacy and privacy-preserving recommendations, Lyu et al. proposed privacy-preserving recommendations for LBS in 2019 [9]. It provides suggestions over encrypted previous histories considering user's live location data. This protocol uses one trusted third party server where sensitive data such as crypto keys are stored and one honest but curious server where all the computations are performed. Compared to Lyu et al. protocol, the proposed SHELBRS protocol requires less computation cost as it uses SHE instead of FHE and maintains security while sharing sensitive data between the servers.

3 Preliminaries

3.1 Hilbert Curve

Hilbert curve is a mapping tool that is used to transform 2-D space into 1-D space. It preserves the adjacency of the neighboring points and has best clustering properties. In order to preserve the adjacency property, the orientation is not retained [11,16]. As we increase the order of a pseudo-Hilbert curve, a given point on the line converges to a specific point. The two data points which are close to each other in 2-D space are also close to each other after mapping into 1-D space.

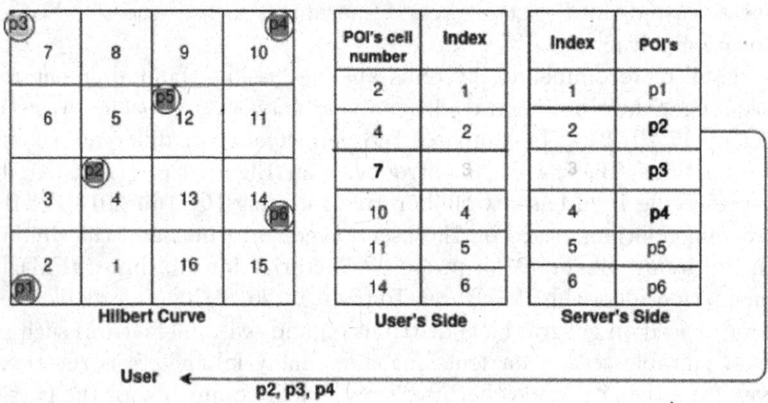

Fig. 1. The combination of continuous Hilbert space-filling curve and location-based services

Figure 1 shows a Hilbert curve over the landscape, storing the POI look-up table at the user end and the POI information table at the server end. The user *p*3 is located on cell 7 and he/she is requesting POIs from the server. At the user's side, p3 is located at Index-3 and after sending index information to the server, the server sends nearby POIs i.e. p2, p3, p4 corresponding to the current index back to the user. This is how the nearest POIs to the user's location is suggested when the landscape is mapped on the Hilbert curve. However, sending such information in plaintext does not ensure the user's privacy.

3.2 Collaborative Filtering (CF) Recommender Based on Co-occurrence Matrix (CM)

CF Recommender consists of two well-known algorithms: user-based CF and item-based CF. We used an item-based CF recommender as similarities between items are more stable than that of users. It finds the similarity between items and provides the best recommendation. Some E-commerce websites such as Amazon provide recommendations such as "A person that bought product A also bought product B" or "A person that liked the cafe A also liked cafe B".

CM contains the visited POIs information. It computes the number of times each pair of items occurs together in the user-item inversion list. To generate CM, the first step is to generate a user-item inversion list and the second step is to traverse the list and follow the algorithm as described:

- $CM[i][j](i! = j)$ is increased by 1 if item i and the item j are in the same user's inversion list.
- $CM[i][j](i == j)$ is increased by 1 for every item i.

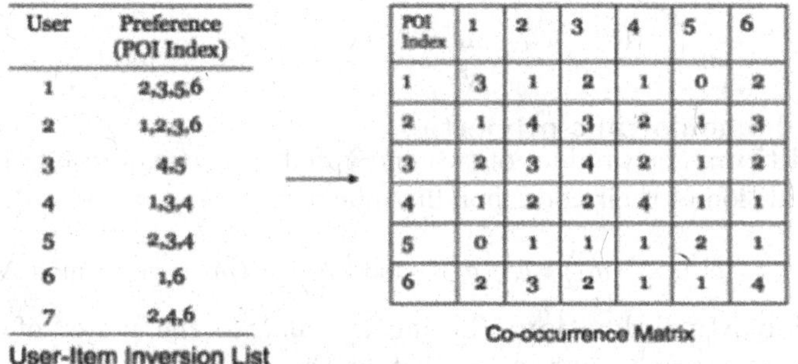

User	Preference (POI Index)
1	2,3,5,6
2	1,2,3,6
3	4,5
4	1,3,4
5	2,3,4
6	1,6
7	2,4,6

User-Item Inversion List

POI Index	1	2	3	4	5	6
1	3	1	2	1	0	2
2	1	4	3	2	1	3
3	2	3	4	2	1	2
4	1	2	2	4	1	1
5	0	1	1	1	2	1
6	2	3	2	1	1	4

Co-occurrence Matrix

Fig. 2. Formation of the final CM [9]

Figure 2 shows the formation of CM based on the user-item inversion list. According to the user-item inversion list, $User_1$ has the preference for indices 2, 3, 5, 6. The value at all possible pairs of indices in CM such as $CM[2][3]$, $CM[2][5]$, $CM[2][6]$, $CM[3][2]$, $CM[3][5]$, $CM[3][6]$, $CM[5][2]$, $CM[5][3]$, $CM[5][6]$, $CM[6][2]$, $CM[6][3]$, $CM[6][5]$ is incremented by 1. Every time an item occurs in the list, the value in CM such as $CM[2][2]$, $CM[3][3]$, $CM[5][5]$, and $CM[6][6]$ is incremented by 1. Likewise for all the users, the above algorithm is performed to get the final CM.

3.3 Partially Homomorphic Encryption (PHE)

PHE schemes are a kind of encryption schemes that allow only certain types of operations on the encrypted data. If we decrypt the processed encrypted data, the results would be the same as if calculated over the corresponding plaintext values. Based on the type of operations supported, it can be categorized as additive PHE or multiplicative PHE. For instance, Paillier is an example of additive PHE and ElGamal, an example of multiplicative PHE. We will briefly describe each of them along with their homomorphic properties.

Paillier Encryption as Additive PHE

- **KeyGen(1^n, +):** On input a security parameter 1^n, the algorithm chooses (N, p, q) where $N = p * q$, p and q are n bit primes, and $\phi(N) = (p - 1) * (q - 1)$. The Paillier ADD scheme public-private key pair:
$$\langle pk^+, sk^+\rangle = \langle N, (N, \phi(N))\rangle \tag{1}$$
- **Enc(pk^+, m):** The algorithm takes a plaintext m and a public key N as input. It chooses a random $r \in Z_N^*$ and outputs the ciphertext:
$$c^+ = (1 + N)^m.(r)^N \mod N^2 \tag{2}$$
- **Dec(sk^+, c^+):** The algorithm takes a ciphertext c^+ and a private key $(N, \phi(N))$ as input and outputs the message:
$$m = \frac{((c^+)^{\phi(N)} \mod N^2) - 1}{N}.\phi(N)^{-1} \mod N \tag{3}$$
- **Paillier homomorphic properties:**
  1. **Addition:** The product of two encrypted ciphertexts results in the sum or addition of their corresponding plaintexts:
$$Dec(E^+(m_1) * E^+(m_2) \mod N^2) = (m_1 + m_2) \mod N \tag{4}$$
  2. **Scalar Multiplication:** Raising a scalar to the power of encrypted ciphertext results in the product of the scalar and the corresponding plaintext:
$$Dec(E^+(m_1)^k) \mod N^2) = (k * m_1) \mod N \tag{5}$$

ElGamal Encryption as multiplicative PHE

- **KeyGen(1^n, ∗):** On input a security parameter 1^n, the algorithm chooses (N, p, q) where $N = p * q$, p and q are n bit primes, considers g as square value and sets $g = 16$. It also chooses a random odd number x, and sets $h = g^x \mod N$. The ElGamal MUL scheme public-private key pair:
$$\langle pk^*, sk^*\rangle = \langle (N, g, h), (N, g, x)\rangle \tag{6}$$
- **Enc(pk^*, m):** The algorithm takes a plaintext m and a public key (N, g, h) as input. It chooses a random $r \in Z_N^*$ and outputs the ciphertext:
$$c^* = \langle c_1^*, c_2^*\rangle = \langle mh^r, g^r \mod N\rangle \tag{7}$$
- **Dec(sk^*, c^*):** The algorithm takes a ciphertext c^* and a private key (N, g, x) as input and outputs the message:
$$m = \frac{c_1^*}{(c_2^*)^x} \mod N \tag{8}$$
- **ElGamal homomorphic properties:**
  1. **Multiplication:** The product of two encrypted ciphertexts results in the multiplication of their corresponding plaintexts:
$$Dec(E^*(m_1) * E^*(m_2) \mod N^2) = (m_1 * m_2) \mod N \tag{9}$$

3.4 Switchable Homomorphic Encryption (SHE)

We work with a variant of ElGamal MUL scheme E^* and Paillier ADD scheme E^+. ElGamal MUL scheme uses a large composite modulus i.e., $N = p * q$, where p and q are large primes. Both the partially homomorphic schemes share the same modulus. We consider two servers, say a server and a proxy. The algorithms used in the SHE scheme are described as follows:

- **KeyGen**(1^n): On input a security parameter 1^n, the algorithm outputs (N, p, q), where $N = p * q$, p and q are n bit primes, and $\phi(N) = (p-1)(q-1)$. The Paillier ADD scheme public-private key pair:
$$\langle pk^+, sk^+ \rangle = \langle N, (N, \phi(N), p, q) \rangle \tag{10}$$
It also chooses the generator $g = 16$, two random odd numbers $x_0, x_1 \in Z_N^*$ where $|x_0| \approx |x_1| < 1/2\,|N|$. It sets $x = x_0 x_1$ and $h = g^x$. The ElGamal MUL scheme public-private key pair:
$$\langle pk^*, sk^* \rangle = \langle (N, g, h), (N, g, x_0, x_1) \rangle \tag{11}$$
- **Enc**(pk^o, m): The algorithm runs E^+ encryption scheme if o is '+' else runs E^* encryption scheme.
- **Dec**(sk^o, c^o): The algorithm runs E^+ decryption scheme if o is '+' else runs E^* decryption scheme.
- **KeyShaGen**(sk^+): The algorithm sets both the secret key shares k_0^+ (proxy) and k_1^+ (server) to NULL.
- **KeyShaGen**(sk^*): The algorithm sets both the secret key shares k_0^* (proxy) and k_1^* (server) to x_0 and x_1 respectively.
- **AddToMul**(c^+, pk^*): The algorithm is run locally by the server. Given an ADD ciphertext of the form:
$$E^+(m) = (1+N)^m.(r')^N \mod N^2 \tag{12}$$
and the MUL public key $pk^* = (N, g, h)$, the algorithm chooses a random $r \in Z_N^*$ and outputs the encrypted MUL ciphertext:
$$E^+(E^*(m)) = \left\langle (1+N)^{mh^r}.(r')^{Nh^r} \mod N^2, g^r \right\rangle \tag{13}$$
- **MulToAdd**(c^+, k_0^*, k_1^*): The algorithm is jointly run by a server and a proxy. On input an encrypted MUL ciphertext of the form (13) the server chooses a random $s \in Z_N^*$, computes
$$c' = (g^{r+s})^{k_1^*}, R = g^s \tag{14}$$
and forwards (13) and (14) to the proxy.
The proxy then using its key shares k_0^*, computes $(c')^{k_0^*} = h^{r+s}$ and finds its inverse $(h^{r+s})^{-1}$. It also computes and returns
$$\begin{aligned} c'' &= ((1+N)^{mh^r}.(r')^{Nh^r})^{h^{r+s-1}} \mod N^2 \\ &= (1+N)^{mh^{-s}}.(r')^{Nh^{-s}} \mod N^2 \\ &= E^+(mh^{-s}) \end{aligned} \tag{15}$$

and $R' := R^{k_0^*}$ to the server.
Finally, the server computes $(R')^{k_1^*} = h^s$ and recovers the corresponding ADD ciphertext $E^+(m)$ by homomorphically removing h^{-s} from c''.

4 Lyu et al.'s Protocol

In this section, we give an overview of Lyu et al. protocol which was meant to recommend services based on the current location of a user and his past behavior without compromising his privacy [9]. It solved the problems existing in the state-of-the-art privacy-preserving algorithms that were based on k-NN technique for searching POI's [6]. The major bottleneck was that the recommendation service didn't consider the user's past behavior while recommending any services that ultimately resulted in failing to attract the user's usage of the recommendation system. Another major demerit was it lacked any benefits for the service providers facilitating such services as the private keys were available only to the user and hence, the service providers could not extract any information from the user's data towards making their profits.

Lyu et al. resolved the aforementioned issues using collaborative filtering technique that works on top of database encrypted using FHE, besides encrypting the user's location and preferences. Also, it allowed the service providers to extract some aggregate information based on the user's data via an introduction of a Privacy Service Provider (PSP) that generates and holds the private keys. This increased the commercial value of the recommendation service but still the need of heavy computational resources required for FHE restricts the usage.

4.1 System Model

An overview of the protocol is shown in Fig. 3. It involves three main components:

- **Privacy-Preserving Recommendation Server (PPRS):** PPRS is a semi-trusted i.e. honest but curious entity that is responsible for finding the nearest POIs to the user, by considering the similarity between the POIs near the user and his current location. It performs two main tasks: The first task is to calculate the recommendation list based on preference vector PV and co-occurrence matrix CM. Here, PV provides a rating of a user for a particular item and CM describes the similarities between the items. The second task is to calculate the aggregated user behavior over the encrypted database (ED).
- **Privacy Service Provider (PSP):** PSP is a trusted third party which makes a profit from user's behavior statistics. It holds and generates the private and public key pairs. It is responsible for providing public keys to users, ED and PPRS whenever the requests arrive. It generates partial recommendation list based on user's location information.
- **Encrypted Database (ED):** It stores CM encrypted by FHE.

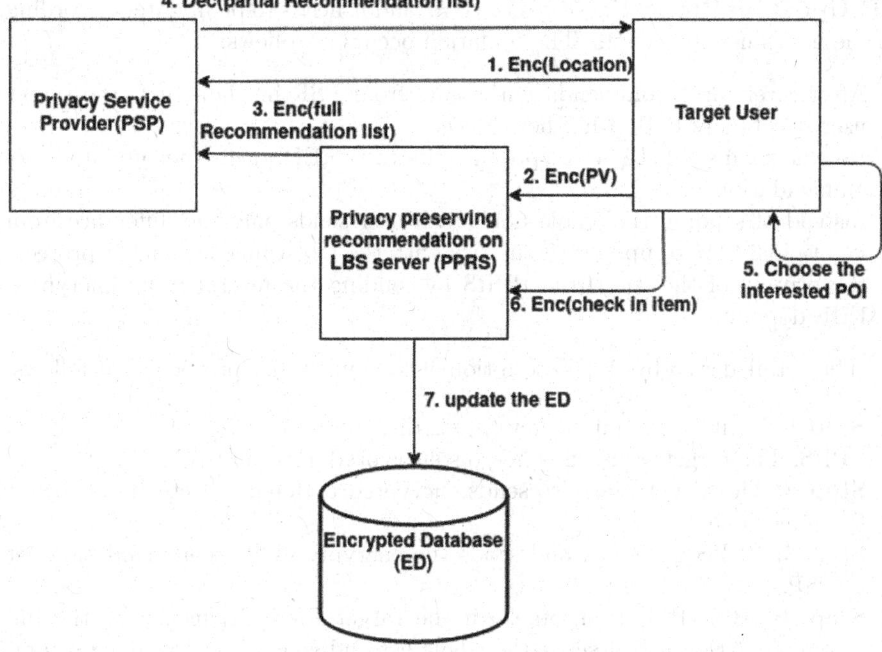

Fig. 3. An overview of Lyu et al.'s protocol

4.2 Description of Lyu et al.'s Protocol

This section describes Lyu et al.'s protocol. First, we describe briefly the three main phases of the protocol and then go for a detailed step-by-step description. The three main phases are as follows:

Initialization Phase: Personal co-occurrence matrix (CM_u), which contains the information of visited POIs, is generated by the user on the basis of his/her preferences. Each user sends his/her encrypted CM_u to the PPRS. PPRS constructs the final CM by combining these $CM_u's$. The operation performed here is exploiting the homomorphic addition property of FHE operation. This combined matrix CM is stored in the ED.

Recommendation Phase: For computing full recommendation list for the user, each item's prediction value is computed by performing homomorphic addition and multiplication property of FHE. Prediction value is derived as

$$P_{u.i} = \sum_{j \in N(u)} (w_{ij} * r_{uj}) \tag{16}$$

where,

$N(u)$ denotes all the items, w_{ij} is the similarity item i and j, and r_{uj} is the rating of user u for item j.

ED Updation Phase: ED stores the CM and it needs to be updated according to the user's new behaviors. The updation occurs as follows:

- After receiving recommendation results from PSP in plain text, the target user selects any POI of his/her choice.
- He/She then sends the encrypted results to the ED for further updated recommendation.
- Instead of sending the whole CM, each user sends only the difference from its original CM to update the matrix with the latest information. It protects the privacy of the user from PPRS by sending the matrix in an encrypted FHE domain.

The detailed step-by-step description of the Lyu et al.'s protocol is as follows:

Step 1: Initially, the public key (p_k) is distributed by the PSP to a user and PPRS. The target user sends her/his encrypted location to PSP.
Step 2: The target user also sends encrypted preference vector to PPRS at the same time.
Step 3: PPRS generates and sends the encrypted full recommendation list to PSP.
Step 4: After PSP decrypts both the target user's location and the full recommendation list, it scans the whole list and generates the partial recommendation list according to the user's location information. It ensures user's privacy by sending it through an encrypted channel to the target user.
Step 5: The target user selects the POI from the partial recommendation list.
Step 6: She/he sends the encrypted result to the PPRS.
Step 7: PPRS then updates the ED for providing the best recommendation.

5 Proposed SHELBRS Protocol

In our proposed framework, we replace the FHE component with SHE to minimize the overall computational complexity and also, speed up the entire process so that it could be better suited for real-life scenarios. The security of the proposed protocol is kept at par with the corresponding FHE based protocol. Our protocol does not make use of any trusted third party server to store crypto keys. It simply sends the secret key shares between the servers so that an individual server cannot leak any user's sensitive information.

The details of each stage of SHELBRS protocol is discussed as follows:

5.1 Setup Stage

The setup of SHELBRS is based on a client-server architecture. We consider two servers, say server X and server Y, and the interaction between the servers or a server and a client is shown in Fig. 4. Security holds as long as at least one of the servers is honest i.e. they do not collude by sharing cryptographic keys.

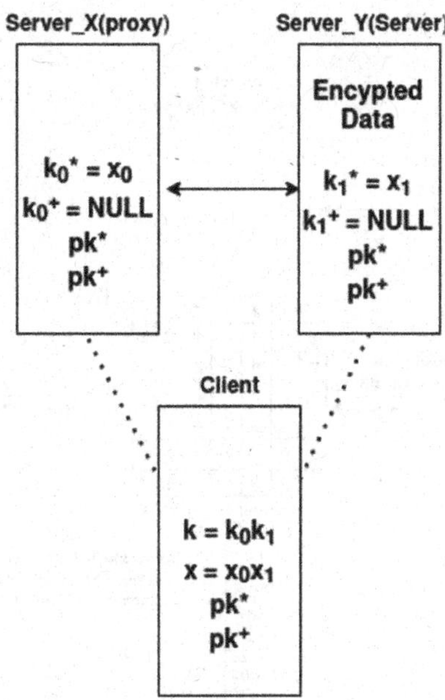

Fig. 4. Secure computation via two servers

Let us assume that the landscape I is mapped on a Hilbert curve and divided into indices $I_1, I_2, \ldots I_n$. Based on a client-server model, a client is located on one of the indices and has its own preference vector. The encrypted database of CM is already stored at server Y. A client generates a public-private key pairs using (10) (11) and sends public keys pk^+ and pk^* to both the servers. Clients uses KeyShaGen(sk^*) and KeyShaGen(sk^+) algorithms as described in Sect. 3.4 and sends k_0^* and k_0^+ to server X and k_1^* and k_1^+ to server Y. The POIs nearby user's location is recommended by the computations which are being performed on the servers.

5.2 Initialization Stage

This stage describes the steps which needs to be computed before the client starts executing his/her role.

- Personal co-occurrence matrix (CM_u) contains the information of visited POIs. During the initialization stage, each user generates his/her personal CM_u based on initial users' preference.
- An user u sends CM_u, which is encrypted by the public key pk^+, to the server Y.
- The end task is to merge all CM_u to generate the final CM. This requires paillier homomorphic Addition property as described in (4) and AddToMul algorithm as discussed in Sect. 3.4.

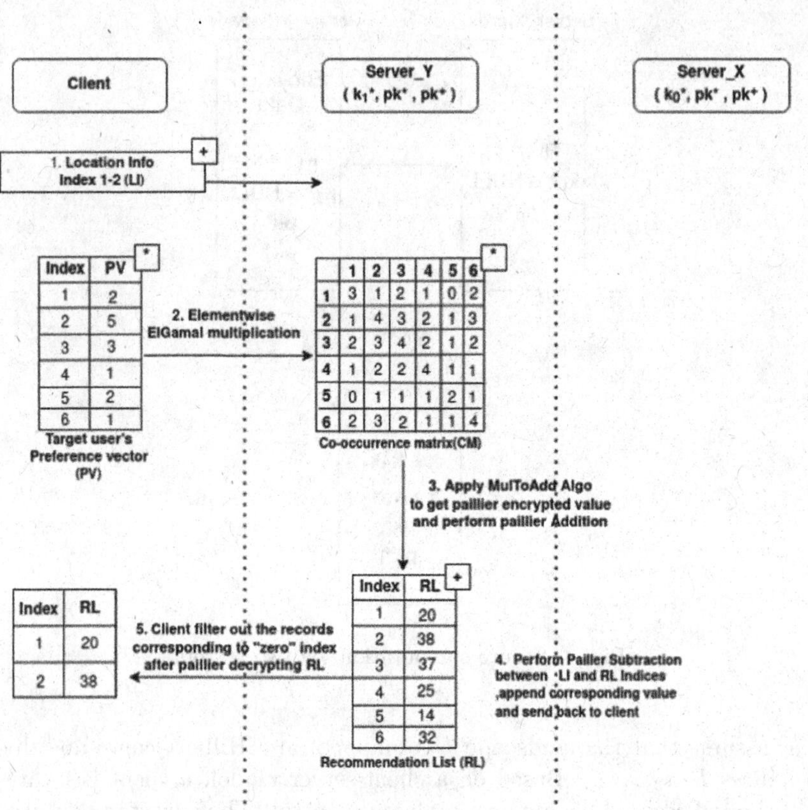

Index	PV
1	2
2	5
3	3
4	1
5	2
6	1

	1	2	3	4	5	6
1	3	1	2	1	0	2
2	1	4	3	2	1	3
3	2	3	4	2	1	2
4	1	2	2	4	1	1
5	0	1	1	1	2	1
6	2	3	2	1	1	4

Index	RL
1	20
2	38
3	37
4	25
5	14
6	32

Index	RL
1	20
2	38

Fig. 5. SHELBRS: proposed recommendation

– The encrypted CM is stored at server Y.

The computation of CM is considered as the initial setup required before client's experiment. So, the computation cost of CM is not considered in the total computation cost taken by the client.

5.3 Protocol Operation Stage

The detailed process of how the recommendation is being generated is shown in Fig. 5. The client and the servers interact in the following manner:

Step 1: The client encrypts history preference vector PV using $Enc(pk^*, PV)$ and location info using $Enc(pk^*, Location\_info)$ and sends it to server Y.
Step 2: The client computes each item's prediction value P using (16) to generate a recommendation list. The prediction is generated using Algorithm 1.

Algorithm 1. Recommendation

INPUT: CM^*, PV^*, Item Index set I^*

OUTPUT: Recommendation list RL for all items

Define: 1. CM^* is ElGamal encrypted co_occurrence matrix

2. PV^* is ElGamal encrypted history preference vector

3. RL[i] is item $i's$ recommendation score

procedure RECOMMEND(CM^* , PV^* , I^*, size)

  Assign $RL^+[1 \cdots size] = 0$

  for $i = 1;\ i <= size;\ i = i + 1$ **do**

    for $j = 1;\ j <= size;\ j = j + 1$ **do**

$$\begin{aligned} ctotal &= \textbf{ElGamalMultiplication}(CM[i][j]^*, PV[j]^*) \\ c1 &= \textbf{PallierEncryption}(pkadd, ctotal[0]) \\ temp &= \textbf{MulToAdd}([c1, ctotal[1]], k_1^*, k_0^*) \\ RL[i]^+ &= \textbf{PaillierAddition}(RL[i]^+, temp) \end{aligned}$$

    end for

  end for

  return RL^+

end procedure

To calculate each index's recommendation score, ElGamal encrypted CM^* and PV^* are elementwise multiplied using the multiplicative property of **ElGamal Encryption**. The corresponding result is transformed into encrypted ElGamal ciphertext using **Paillier Encryption** scheme in Sect. 3.3.

Step 3: It is further converted into Paillier encrypted ciphertext using **MulToAdd** algorithm in Sect. 3.4. The corresponding result is finally added using additive property of **Paillier Encryption** to generate the corresponding recommendation score.

Likewise, the above steps 2 and 3 are executed for each index to generate the final recommendation list.

Step 4: According to the target user's location, the final recommendation list is filtered out.

The server Y performs Paillier homomorphic subtraction property corresponding to the indices stored in the recommendation list and user's location. It appends the result to the recommendation list and the updated list is sent to the client.

Step 5: The client then decrypts it using Paillier decryption algorithm and filters out the records corresponding to the value '0'. The client chooses one of the locations (indices) from the recommendation list according to his/her choice and update his/her behavior in the inversion list. Each client sends only his/her new paillier encrypted CM_u to server Y which is the difference between the current CM_u and the client's original CM_u before the recommendations.

6 Experimental Results

To validate the proposed protocol based on SHE, the experiment is executed on Ubuntu 20.04.2 LTS powered by Intel® Core™ i5-6200U CPU @ 2.30 GHz × 4 processor and RAM 8 GB. We have considered a client and two servers on the same machine. In this experiment, we considered the artificial dataset with POIs in range {10, 20, 40, 80, 100, 1000}.

The CM is already stored on the server Y and then, the client starts executing his/her behavior. So, the execution time taken for the computations during initialization phase to generate CM is not considered in the total computation cost taken by the client. The time taken to generate public-private keypair is constant. The updation of ED can be performed even when a user is offline, so it does not affect the efficiency of the system.

Table 1. Computation cost

Total elements	Encryption time [s]	Recommendation time [s]	Decryption time [s]
10	0.001	0.022	0.001
20	0.001	0.081	0.001
40	0.001	0.299	0.002
80	0.003	1.142	0.004
100	0.004	1.923	0.006
1000	0.04	197.99	0.058

The total computation cost involves encryption of a client's preference vector, computation of recommendation list and decryption of recommendation list. In Table 1, we measured encryption time, recommendation time,and decryption time for the indices in an encrypted domain. We have run the experiment five times for each index and taken an average of it.

The experiment uses encryption which adds extra computation cost over plaintext. So, we calculated and compared the total computation cost for the plaintext and encrypted domain up to 1000 indices as shown in Table 2.

We also plotted the graph comparing the total execution time taken by SHELBRS scheme and Lyu et al. protocol in Fig. 6 and Table 3.

6.1 Security Analysis

Our protocol aims to provide data confidentiality. It does not leak any meaningful information throughout the protocol. The security of the scheme is based on the following assumptions:

- The ElGamal and Paillier schemes are secure.

Table 2. Comparison of total execution time in plaintext domain and encrypted domain

Total elements	Plaintext domain	Encrypted domain
10	0.001	0.024
20	0.001	0.083
40	0.002	0.302
80	0.005	1.149
100	0.007	1.933
1000	1.32	198.088

Table 3. Comparison of total execution time taken by proposed SHELBRS scheme and Lyu et al. [9]

Total elements	Proposed SHELBRS scheme	Lyu et al. [9]
10	0.024	2.79
20	0.083	5.48
40	0.302	11.13
80	1.149	22.32
100	1.933	28.03
1000	198.088	269.47

- At least one of the servers is honest i.e. if one of the servers is malicious, the other server remains honest.
- None of the servers collude.

Let us assume an Adversary A plays the role of either a malicious server Y or a malicious server X. Initially, A is given the public keys and private key shares to perform Paillier encryption E^+, ElGamal encryption E^*, AddToMul and MulToAdd algorithms. A is also given access to choose any arbitrary plaintext and can perform encryption to get the corresponding ciphertext. A user sends $E^*(m_0)$ to the server Y where m_0 is an integer except a value 0. Now, A's goal is to find a challenge m_0' such that $m_0' = m_0$. If A's goal is achieved, the security is broken. To prove $m_0's$ security, below mentioned lemmas are as follows.

Lemma 1: If Server Y is a malicious server and A chooses to attack AddToMul algorithm, it has access to $E^*(m_0)$, $E^+(m_0)$ and $E^+(E^*(m_0))$. Paillier encrypted $E^+(m_0)$ and $E^+(E^*(m_0))$ terms are semantically secure and no decryption key sk^+ is associated with any server, so, no information regarding m_0 is leaked through these terms. Server Y has key share $k_1^* = x_1$ and $E^*(m_0) = (m_0 h^r, g^r)$ where r is randomly chosen from the group Z_N^*. The security of $E^*(m_0)$ based

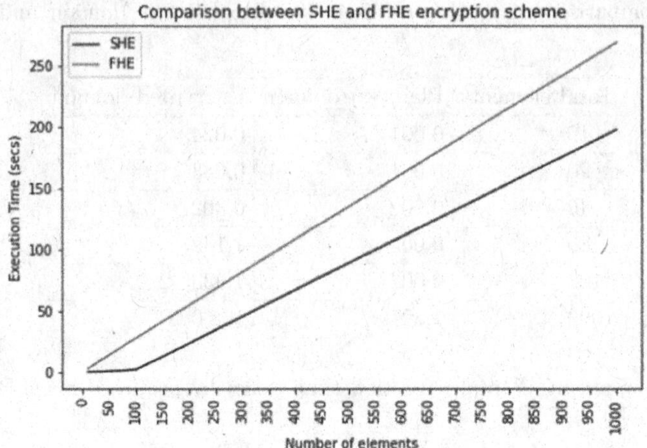

Fig. 6. Comparison of total execution time taken by proposed SHELBRS scheme and Lyu et al. [9]

on SHE security proof [7] is perfectly secure. So, A cannot learn anything about m_0 in the protocol.

Lemma 2: If Server Y is a malicious server and A chooses to attack MulToAdd algorithm, it has access to $k_1^* = x_1$. $E^*(m_0)$, $E^+(E^*(m_0))$, $R' = g^{sx_0}$ and $c'' = E^+(m_0 h^{-s})$. $E^*(m_0)$, $E^+(E^*(m_0))$ and c'' are secure according to Lemma 1. A cannot learn about secret key share x_0 from R' as s is randomly chosen from the group Z_N^*. Therefore, the proposed scheme is secure against the malicious activity performed by server Y itself.

Likewise, we can prove the data confidentiality using Lemma 1 and Lemma 2 when Server X acts as an adversary A.

Now, we will handle the case when the client performs elGamal encryption on a message m_0 where $m_0 = 0$. The ElGamal Encryption of m_0 plaintext results into one of the ciphertexts as "zero". This is not secure as it leaks information regarding plaintext data. To handle such problems, we can represent "zero" in the form

$$\textbf{MulToAdd}(E^+(E^*(n_1))) * \textbf{MulToAdd}(E^+(E^*(n_1)))^{-1} = E^+(0) \tag{17}$$

7 Conclusions and Future Work

A lightweight privacy-preserving recommendation protocol for LBS was proposed in this paper. It incorporated Hilbert curve, collaborative filtering recommender based on co-occurrence matrix and SHE to recommend the services. Based on the simulation and experiments, we found that the computation cost for 1000

POIs is 198.088 s. Compared with the state-of-the-art protocol, the proposed protocol takes less computation time and reduces complexity, providing at par security. As the future direction of the work, we would like to extend our protocol for the larger geographical area as we focused herein only on item-based filtering on a single geographical area.

References

1. Badsha, S., Yi, X., Khalil, I.: A practical privacy-preserving recommender system. Data Sci. Eng. **1**(3), 161–177 (2016)
2. Brakerski, Z., Gentry, C., Vaikuntanathan, V.: (Leveled) fully homomorphic encryption without bootstrapping. ACM Trans. Comput. Theory (TOCT) **6**(3), 1–36 (2014)
3. Gentry, C.: Fully homomorphic encryption using ideal lattices. In: Proceedings of the Forty-First Annual ACM Symposium on Theory of Computing, pp. 169–178 (2009)
4. Gruteser, M., Grunwald, D.: Anonymous usage of location-based services through spatial and temporal cloaking. In: Proceedings of the 1st International Conference on Mobile Systems, Applications and Services, pp. 31–42 (2003)
5. Horowitz, D., Contreras, D., Salamó, M.: EventAware: a mobile recommender system for events. Pattern Recogn. Lett. **105**, 121–134 (2018)
6. Lien, I.-T., Lin, Y.-H., Shieh, J.-R., Wu, J.-L.: A novel privacy preserving location-based service protocol with secret circular shift for k-NN search. IEEE Trans. Inf. Forensics Secur. **8**(6), 863–873 (2013)
7. Lim, H.W., Tople, S., Saxena, P., Chang, E.-C.: Faster secure arithmetic computation using switchable homomorphic encryption. IACR Cryptol. ePrint Arch., 2014:539 (2014)
8. Lü, L., Medo, M., Yeung, C.H., Zhang, Y.-C., Zhang, Z.-K., Zhou, T.: Recommender systems. Phys. Rep. **519**(1), 1–49 (2012)
9. Lyu, Q., Ishimaki, Y., Yamana, H.: Privacy-preserving recommendation for location-based services. In: 2019 IEEE 4th International Conference on Big Data Analytics (ICBDA), pp. 98–105. IEEE (2019)
10. Melchor, C.A., Gaborit, P.: A fast private information retrieval protocol. In: 2008 IEEE International Symposium on Information Theory, pp. 1848–1852. IEEE (2008)
11. Moon, B., Jagadish, H.V., Faloutsos, C., Saltz, J.H.: Analysis of the clustering properties of the Hilbert space-filling curve. IEEE Trans. Knowl. Data Eng. **13**(1), 124–141 (2001)
12. Papakyriakopoulos, O., Serrano, J.C.M., Hegelich, S.: Political communication on social media: a tale of hyperactive users and bias in recommender systems. Online Soc. Netw. Media **15**, 100058 (2020)
13. Pingley, A., Wei, Yu., Zhang, N., Xinwen, F., Zhao, W.: A context-aware scheme for privacy-preserving location-based services. Comput. Netw. **56**(11), 2551–2568 (2012)
14. Qi, L., Wang, R., Chunhua, H., Li, S., He, Q., Xiaolong, X.: Time-aware distributed service recommendation with privacy-preservation. Inf. Sci. **480**, 354–364 (2019)
15. Fenwick, M.I.R., Hittle, M., White, O.: Fitness app strava lights up staff at military bases. BBC Journal Archive (2018). https://www.bbc.com/news/technology-42853072

16. Sagan, H.: Space-Filling Curves. Springer, Heidelberg (2012)
17. Sarwar, B., Karypis, G., Konstan, J., Riedl, J.: Item-based collaborative filtering recommendation algorithms. In: Proceedings of the 10th International Conference on World Wide Web, pp. 285–295 (2001)
18. Sun, G., Song, L., Liao, D., Hongfang, Yu., Chang, V.: Towards privacy preservation for "check-in" services in location-based social networks. Inf. Sci. **481**, 616–634 (2019)
19. Utsunomiya, Y., Toyoda, K., Sasase, I.: LPCQP: lightweight private circular query protocol for privacy-preserving k-NN search. In 2015 12th Annual IEEE Consumer Communications and Networking Conference (CCNC), pp. 59–64. IEEE (2015)
20. Zhang, X., Yu, L., Wang, M., Gao, W.: FM-based: algorithm research on rural tourism recommendation combining seasonal and distribution features. Pattern Recogn. Lett. (2018)

On Threat of Hardware Trojan to Post-Quantum Lattice-Based Schemes: A Key Recovery Attack on SABER and Beyond

Prasanna Ravi[1,2,3(✉)], Suman Deb[1,3], Anubhab Baksi[1,2,3], Anupam Chattopadhyay[1,2,3], Shivam Bhasin[1,3], and Avi Mendelson[1,2,3]

[1] Temasek Laboratories, Nanyang Technological University, Singapore, Singapore
{prasanna.ravi,sumandeb,anubhab.baksi,anupam,sbhasin}@ntu.edu.sg

[2] School of Computer Science and Engineering, Nanyang Technological University, Singapore, Singapore

[3] Technion-Israel Institute of Technology, Haifa, Israel
mendlson@technion.ac.il

Abstract. Our work conducts the first study on analyzing the threat of Hardware Trojans (HT) for Post-Quantum Cryptographic (PQC) schemes in a 3rd Party IP setting. We propose novel HT-assisted chosen-ciphertext attacks for Key Encapsulation Mechanisms (KEM) based on the well known Learning With Error/Rounding (LWE/LWR) problem. Our proposed HT enables covert realization of a *Plaintext-Checking oracle* for attacker's carefully crafted ciphertexts, which leaks information about the long-term secret key through the corresponding session keys. We experimentally validate our attacks on Saber and Kyber (NIST finalist candidates for KEMs) and our attacks can recover the long-term secret key in a few hundred-thousand chosen-ciphertext queries (depending on the attack scenario). We also implemented different variants of the HT within open-source implementation of Saber (a NIST finalist candidate) for the Xilinx UltraScale+ FPGA, which incurs negligible area overhead of upto 0.98% more FFs and upto 0.03% more LUTs. Our proposed HT for Saber is carefully designed to increase its anti-detection capability, so as to pose a significant challenge to the state-of-the-art HT-detection techniques.

1 Introduction

The impending threat of large scale quantum computers to traditional RSA and ECC-based public-key cryptography prompted NIST to initiate a global level standardization process for quantum-attack resistant Public Key Encryption (PKE), Key Encapsulation Mechanisms (KEM) and Digital Signature Schemes (DSS). The *Post-Quantum Cryptography* (*PQC*) standardization process is currently in its third and final round with fifteen (15) candidates. The PQC research

L. Batina et al. (Eds.): SPACE 2021, LNCS 13162, pp. 81–103, 2022.
https://doi.org/10.1007/978-3-030-95085-9_5

community anticipate first draft standards for PQC in 2022 and a subset of the finalists will be standardized for wide-scale adoption.

NIST initially considered theoretical post-quantum security and implementation performance as key selection criteria for the standardization process [13]. However, several finalist candidates share very similar performance and security guarantees which prompted NIST to also consider other selection criteria. Among them, security of real-world implementations against attacks such as Side-Channel Analysis (SCA) and Fault Injection Analysis (FIA) emerged as an important factor in the standardization process [1]. This resulted in a large body of work on novel attack techniques [15,18] and efficient countermeasures [14,17] for SCA and FIA on practical implementations of PQC schemes.

Given the urgent need toward transitioning existing systems to PQC, we expect prominent and wide-spread use of 3rd Party IP (3PIP) cores for implementing PQC in real-world systems. Thus, apart from SCA and FIA, Hardware Trojans (HT) also form a very potent attack vector for practical PQC implementations, especially in a 3PIP setting. However to the best of our knowledge, there exists no work that has studied the possibility of HTs for PQC schemes.

In this respect, *we perform the first study on susceptibility of post-quantum Key Encapsulation Mechanisms (KEMs) to Hardware Trojans. We focus on 3PIP cores implementing schemes based on the well-known Learning With Error/Rounding (LWE/LWR) problem.* These schemes are provably secure in the *Indistinguishability Under Chosen-Ciphertext Attack* (IND-CCA) model, thereby resistant to Chosen-Ciphertext Attacks (CCAs) [1]. However, we identify vulnerable operations in LWE/LWR-based KEMs, which when minimally modified through Hardware Trojans (HTs) can subvert IND-CCA security in a chosen-ciphertext setting. The proposed HTs when activated through attacker's maliciously crafted ciphertexts, leak the long-term secret key, through the corresponding session keys. Our work highlights the ease of subverting IND-CCA security using a minuscule HT in 3PIP cores for LWE/LWR-based schemes for key recovery.

Contributions: The contributions of our work are summarized as follows

1. To the best of our knowledge, we propose the first Hardware Trojans for 3PIP cores implementing post-quantum KEMs and demonstrate novel HT-assisted CCAs for IND-CCA secure LWE/LWR-based KEMs.
2. Our proposed attacks build upon well-established Plaintext-Checking (PC) oracle-based CCAs for LWE/LWR-based schemes [7,18]. We propose a generic adaptation to *parallelize* the PC oracle-based CCA in a configurable manner for efficient key recovery in much fewer chosen-ciphertext queries[1].
3. Our proposed attacks rely on a trigger-based HT which exploits the inherent *ciphertext malleability* of LWE/LWR-based PKE schemes, to trigger under extremely rare conditions and recover full long-term secret key leaked through several session keys.

[1] As we show later in Sect. 4, the applicability of our parallelized PC oracle-based CCA depends on the utilization of KEM for key exchange within the protocol.

4. We validate our attack on two IND-CCA secure schemes, Saber [6] and Kyber [3], which are finalist candidates for KEMs in the ongoing NIST standardization process. We can fully recover the secret key in a few hundred to few thousand queries (depending on the setting) with a 100% success rate.
5. We implemented the HT on an open-source hardware implementation of Saber by Roy and Basso [19] for the Xilinx UltraScale+ FPGA, which incurs a negligible area overhead of upto 0.98% more FFs and upto 0.03% LUTs.
6. Our proposed HT has a few favourable charactersitics such as unified trigger and payload circuit and low-area footprint which argue well for its anti-detection capabilities. We therefore include an elaborate discussion on the applicability of well-known HT-detection techniques for 3PIP cores.

Availability of software. All softwares utilized for this work is placed into public domain. They are available at https://github.com/PRASANNA-RAVI/Hardware_Trojan_PQC.

2 Preliminaries

2.1 Notation

We denote the ring of integers modulo $q \in \mathbb{Z}^+$ as $\mathbb{Z}_q$ and $\mathbb{Z}_q^{\ell \times n}$ denotes matrices of size $(\ell \times n)$ with elements in $\mathbb{Z}_q$. An element $x \in \mathbb{Z}_q$ rounded to a lower modulus p as $\lfloor p/q \cdot x \rceil \in \mathbb{Z}_p$ is denoted as $\lfloor x \rceil_{q \to p}$. We denote the polynomial ring $\mathbb{Z}_q(x)/\phi(x)$ as R_q where all computations are performed modulo $\phi(x)$. If degree of $\phi(x)$ is n, then all elements in R_q are polynomials with degree $n-1$ (n coefficients). A matrix of polynomials in R_q is denoted as *module* (i.e.) $R_q^{k \times \ell}$. Elements in R_q and $R_q^{k \times \ell}$ are denoted in bold lower case letters. The ith coefficient of $\mathbf{a} \in R_q$ is denoted as $\mathbf{a}[i]$ and the ith polynomial of module $\mathbf{x}$ as $\mathbf{x}_i$.

2.2 Generic Framework for LWE/LWR-Based PKE

The generic framework to build LWE/LWR-based PKE schemes proposed by Lyubashevskey, Peikert and Regev [11] serves as the foundation for several NIST PQC candidates including the main finalists Saber (Module-LWR) and Kyber (Module-LWE), alternate finalist Frodo (Standard-LWE) and semi finalists NewHope (Ring-LWE), Round5 (Generalized-LWR) and LAC (Ring-LWE). The key differences between the schemes lie in aspects such as choice between LWE/LWR, polynomial ring R_q, span of secrets/errors etc. Without loss of generality, we describe the key-generation (KeyGen), encryption (Encrypt) and decryption (Decrypt) procedures of the PKE framework of Saber in Algorithm 1, which is based on the Module-LWR problem.

2.2.1 CCAs on LWE/LWR-Based PKE

The aforementioned PKE scheme is only secure in the *Indistinguishability under Chosen-Plaintext Attack* model (IND-CPA security), and thus susceptible to CCAs [7,18]. Their modus operandi is given as follows: The attacker queries the decryption device with malicious handcrafted ciphertexts ($\mathbf{c_{att}}$). These ciphertexts are built such that their corresponding decrypted messages (m') contain information about the secret key sk. When the PKE is used within protocols such as TLS, an attacker can guess m' for his/her chosen-ciphertexts, based on information about protocol success/failure. This is referred to as a *Plaintext-Checking* (PC) oracle which can be exploited by an attacker for key recovery. Thus, the decrypted message is a sensitive variable which needs to be concealed from an attacker to prevent key recovery.

2.2.2 Security Against CCAs

Most LWE/LWR-based schemes, including the NIST candidates, utilize the well known Fujisaki-Okamoto (FO) transform [8] to achieve security in the *Indistinguishability under Chosen-Ciphertext Attack* model (IND-CCA security). It

---

Algorithm 1: Generic framework of LWE/LWR based PKE schemes

Procedure PKE.KeyGen()
- $publicseed \leftarrow \mathcal{U}(\mathcal{B}^{32})$
- $\mathbf{a} = \mathsf{gen}(publicseed) \in R_q^{k\times k}$
- $\mathbf{s} \leftarrow \chi_{\mathbf{s}}(R_q^k)$
- $\mathbf{t} = \lfloor \mathbf{a}^T \times \mathbf{s} \rceil_{q\to p} \in R_p^k$
- **return** $(pk = \mathsf{PackPK}(\mathbf{t}, publicseed), sk = \mathsf{PackSK}(\mathbf{s}))$

Procedure PKE.Encrypt$(pk, m \in \mathcal{B}^{32}, r \in \mathcal{B}^{32})$
- $(\mathbf{t}, publicseed) = \mathsf{UnpackPK}(pk)$
- $\mathbf{a} \leftarrow \mathsf{gen}(publicseed)$
- $\mathbf{s}' \leftarrow \chi_{\mathbf{s}'}(R_q^k)$
- $\mathbf{t}_r = \lfloor \mathbf{t} \rceil_{q\to p} \in R_p^k$
- $\mathbf{u} = \lfloor \mathbf{a}^T \times \mathbf{s}' \rceil_{q\to p} \in R_p^k$
- $\mathbf{v} = \lfloor \mathbf{t}_r^T \mathbf{s}' + \mathsf{Encode}(m) \rceil_{q\to t} \in R_t$
- **return** $ct = \mathsf{PackCT}(\mathbf{u}, \mathbf{v})$

Procedure PKE.Decrypt(ct, sk)
- $\mathbf{u}, \mathbf{v} = \mathsf{UnpackCT}(ct)$
- $\mathbf{s} = \mathsf{UnpackSK}(sk)$
- $\mathbf{u}' = \lfloor \mathbf{u} \rceil_{p\to q}$
- $\mathbf{v}' = \lfloor \mathbf{v} \rceil_{t\to q}$
- $\mathbf{r} = (\mathbf{v}' - (\mathbf{u}')^T \mathbf{s}) \in R_q$
- $m' = \mathsf{Decode}(\mathbf{r})$
- **return** m'

---

forms a wrapper around the encryption and decryption procedures and uses multiple instantiations of one-way functions $\mathcal{H}$ and $\mathcal{G}$ resulting in Encapsulation (KEM.Encaps) and Decapsulation KEM.Decaps procedures, which are shown in Algorithm 2.

The encapsulation procedure instantiates the encryption procedure to generate a ciphertext ct for a message m (Line 5) and also generates a key K (Line 6). The decapsulation procedure instantiates the decryption procedure to retrieve the message m' from ct (Line 2). Subsequently, m' is re-encrypted (Line 4) to compute ct', which is then compared with the received cipherext (Line 5). The comparison succeeds for valid ciphertexts ($\mathsf{verify} = 1$) and a valid session key $K = \mathsf{KDF}(m', pk, ct)$ is generated (Line 7) which is dependent on m' and also matches with the session key generated by the encapsulator. But, the comparison fails for invalid ciphertexts and a pseudo-random key is generated (Line 10) which neither matches with the key of the encapsulator, nor depends on m'.

Thus, the IND-CCA secure decapsulation procedure has the ability to detect the validity of a ciphertext. An attacker cannot obtain any information about the decrypted message m' for malicious ciphertexts, *concretely removing the presence of the PC oracle.* This provides strong theoretical security guarantees against CCAs. Within a protocol such as TLS, IND-CCA secure KEMs are used for secure key-exchange where the long-term secret key sk (used by Alice) can be used to generate multiple session keys K for several TLS handshakes.

Algorithm 2: FO transform of a IND-CPA secure PKE into a IND-CCA secure KEM

```
1 Procedure KEM.Encaps(pk)
2     ρ ← U(B^32)
3     m = H(ρ)
4     r = G(m, pk)
5     ct = PKE.Encrypt(pk, m, r)
6     K = H(r, ct)
7     return ct, K
8 ____________________________________________
1 Procedure KEM.Decaps(sk, pk, ct)
2     m' = PKE.Decrypt(sk, ct)
3     r' = G(m', pk)
4     ct' = PKE.Encrypt(pk, m', r')
5     verify = Compare(ct, ct')
6     if verify = 1 then
7         return K = H(r', ct')
8     else
9         return K = H(z, ct')
          /* z ∈ B^32 is pseudo-random */
```

2.3 Practical CCAs on IND-CCA Secure KEMs

Though IND-CCA security provides theoretical security guarantees against CCAs, several works have shown that side-channel leakage from attack vectors such as timing, power consumption and Electromagnetic Emanation (EM) can be used to realize an artificial PC oracle for key recovery [7,18]. D'Anvers *et al.* [7] exploited variable run-time of error correcting codes in the decryption procedure to recover binary information about the decrypted message (i.e.) ($m' = m_0/m_1$) for chosen-ciphertexts, leading to full key recovery in a few thousand queries. Ravi *et al.* [18] then generalized the attack to constant-time implementations using the EM side-channel to multiple LWE/LWR-based PKE/KEMs.

More recently, Amiet *et al.* [2], Sim *et al.* [21] and Ravi *et al.* [16] identified deeper side-channel leakage in LWE/LWR-based schemes which simultaneously leak the complete decrypted message. Xu *et al.* [24] showed that these vulnerabilities can be exploited to recover the full decrypted message for chosen-ciphertexts. Their improved attack could recover the full secret key in just 8 chosen-ciphertext queries in the Kyber512 variant of Kyber KEM. Ngo *et al.* [12] subsequently extended the same attack to Saber KEM. The aforementioned attacks exploit varying amount of side-channel information about the decrypted message m' from practical implementations of LWE/LWR-based schemes for key recovery. However, these attacks assume the presence of a side-channel adversary who has direct physical access to the device and can obtain side-channel measurements with a reasonably high SNR [12,16].

In this work, we analyze the feasibility of mounting key recovery attacks on practical implementations of LWE/LWR-based schemes using Hardware Trojans (HTs). We propose novel HTs within the decapsulation procedure which enables realization of a stealthy PC oracle, that leaks information about the decrypted message for attacker's chosen-ciphertexts through the session keys. While known implementation attacks rely on side-channels, we propose the first HT-assisted key recovery attack for LWE/LWR-based schemes. *Thus, our attacks do not rely on side-channels and hence, can be carried out by a remote attacker without any physical access to the target device.*

3 PC Oracle-Based CCA on LWE/LWR-Based KEMs

Our HT-assisted key recovery attacks build upon PC oracle-based CCA on LWE/LWR-based KEMs. We validate our proposed attacks on two schemes - Saber KEM [6] based on Module-LWR (MLWR) and Kyber KEM [3] based on the Module-LWE (MLWE) problem. Our choice is motivated by two reasons: 1) They are finalists of the NIST process. 2) The MLWE/MLWR problem is a generalization of the standard LWE/LWR and the RLWE/RLWR problem. Thus, our attacks on the MLWR-based scheme can be adapted to other variants of the LWE/LWR problem. We primarily use Saber to describe our attack and the same analysis easily extends to Kyber.

3.1 PC Oracle-Based CCA

We utilize the PC oracle-based CCA proposed by Ravi *et al.* [18] and adapt it to Saber. Refer to the decryption procedure of Saber in Algorithm 1, the ciphertext consists of two components: $\mathbf{u} \in R_q^k$ (k polynomials in R_q) and $\mathbf{v} \in R_q$ and the secret key is the module $\mathbf{s} \in R_q^k$ with $R_q = \mathbb{Z}_q(x)/(x^n + 1)$. The attack works by recovering one coefficient at a time, and we thus describe recovery of the first secret coefficient $\mathbf{s}_0[0]$ and extend the same technique for full key recovery. For brevity, we denote the first secret polynomial $\mathbf{s}_0$ as $\mathbf{s}$. The attacker chooses the ciphertext $(\mathbf{u}, \mathbf{v})$ as follows:

$$\mathbf{u}_i = \begin{cases} U \cdot x^0 & \text{if } i = 0, \\ 0 & \text{if } 1 \leq i \leq k-1 \end{cases} \tag{1}$$

$$\mathbf{v} = V \cdot x^0 \tag{2}$$

where $(U, V) \in \mathbb{Z}^+$. For this chosen-ciphertext, each bit of the decrypted message m' (i.e.) m'_i for $i \in [0, n-1]$ is given as:

$$m'_i = \begin{cases} \mathsf{Decode}(V - U \cdot \mathbf{s}[0]), & \text{if } i = 0 \\ \mathsf{Decode}(-U \cdot \mathbf{s}[i]), & \text{for } 1 \leq i \leq n-1 \end{cases} \tag{3}$$

Thus, every bit m'_i is only dependent on the corresponding secret coefficient $\mathbf{s}[i]$. For a given tuple (U, V), the decrypted message m' is given as:

$$m'_i = \begin{cases} \mathcal{F}(\mathbf{s}[0]), & \text{if } i = 0 \\ 0, & \text{for } 1 \leq i \leq n-1 \end{cases} \tag{4}$$

Thus, m' can only take two possible values (i.e.) $m' = 0$ (all bits zero - Class O) or $m' = 1$ (all bits except LSB have a value of 0 - Class X) and its value solely depends upon the coefficient $\mathbf{s}[0]$. We choose values for (U, V) such that m' (O/X) can act as a binary distinguisher for every candidate of $\mathbf{s}[0]$. If an attacker has access to a binary PC oracle that responds if a given ciphertext decrypts to O/X, he/she can uniquely recover $\mathbf{s}[0]$. For the recommended parameters of Saber, the secret coefficients lie in the range $[-4, 4]$. Refer to Fig. 1 for the binary tree whose traversal based on the binary PC oracle's response can uniquely identify $\mathbf{s}[0]$ in not more than 5 queries. The same approach can also be adapted to Kyber KEM and refer to Fig. 5 in Appendix A for the corresponding binary tree of Kyber768 (recommended parameters).

3.1.1 Recovering Other Secret Coefficients

Similar to recovery of $\mathbf{s}[0]$, other secret coefficients can be recovered by exploiting the property of polynomial multiplication in the ring $R_q = \mathbb{Z}_q[x]/(x^n + 1)$. The product of a polynomial $\mathbf{r} \in R_q$ with x^p rotates the polynomial by p positions in an anti-cyclic fashion (i.e.) $\mathbf{r} \cdot x^p \in R_q = \mathsf{AntiRotr}(\mathbf{r}, p)$ where

$$\mathsf{AntiRotr}(\mathbf{s}, p) = \begin{cases} -\mathbf{r}[n - p + i], & \text{for } 0 \leq i < p \\ \mathbf{r}[i - p], & \text{for } p \leq i \leq n-1 \end{cases} \tag{5}$$

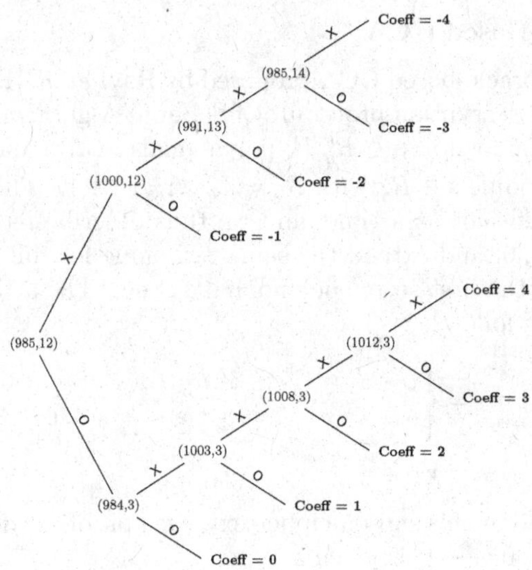

Fig. 1. Binary decision tree based on the decrypted message m' ($m' = 0$ - Class O vs $m' = 1$ - Class X) to uniquely distinguish every candidate for secret coefficient of Saber (recommended parameters). Each node corresponds to the tuple (U, V) and each edge denotes the PC oracle's response (O/X)

Thus, for $\mathbf{u}_0 = U \cdot x^p$ and $\mathbf{v} = V$, the first message bit m'_0 is given as:

$$m'_0 = \begin{cases} V - U \cdot \mathbf{s}[0], & \text{if } p = 0 \\ V - U \cdot (-\mathbf{s}[n-p]), & \text{for } 1 \leq p \leq n-1 \end{cases} \tag{6}$$

Thus, changing the rotation constant p between 0 to $n-1$ ensures that m'_0 depends upon different secret coefficients, which can be recovered in a similar manner as $\mathbf{s}[0]$. While the first secret polynomial $\mathbf{s}_0$ is recovered using the first polynomial of $\mathbf{u}$ (i.e.) $\mathbf{u}_0$, other secret polynomials (i.e.) $\mathbf{s}_i$ for $i \in [1, k-1]$ can be similarly recovered using the corresponding polynomial $\mathbf{u}_i$. We refer to the attacker's chosen-ciphertexts as $\mathsf{ct}_{\mathsf{attack}}$ throughout the paper.

We successfully validated the binary PC oracle-based CCA through simulations on the recommended parameter set of Saber KEM and Kyber KEM (768 secret coefficients). We assumed the presence of a binary oracle which provides information about whether $m' =$ O/X. For Saber, we could recover the full secret key in approximately $2.09k$ chosen-ciphertext queries over 1000 trials with a 100% success rate. For Kyber, full key recovery was possible in approximately $1.76k$ chosen-ciphertext queries with a 100% success rate.

3.2 Parallelized PC Oracle-Based CCA

A close observation of the binary PC oracle-based attack shows that m' for the chosen-ciphertexts only contains a single bit information about the secret key, since all but one bit of m' are fixed to 0. We propose a parallelized version of the

PC oracle-based CCA such that m' carries information about multiple secret coefficients. We demonstrate our approach with simultaneous recovery of two secret coefficients $(\mathbf{s}[0], \mathbf{s}[1])$ while the same can be extended to any number of coefficients. We choose $\mathbf{u} = U \cdot x^0$ and $\mathbf{v} = V \cdot (1 + x)$. Thus, the decrypted message m' is given as:

$$m'_i = \begin{cases} \mathsf{Decode}(V - U \cdot \mathbf{s}[i]), & \text{if } i = \{0, 1\} \\ \mathsf{Decode}(-U \cdot \mathbf{s}[i]), & \text{for } 2 \le i \le n - 1 \end{cases} \tag{7}$$

For the same choice of tuples (U, V) used for the binary distinguisher for the binary PC oracle attack (Fig. 1), each message bit is given as:

$$m'_i = \begin{cases} \mathcal{D}(\mathbf{s}[i]), & \text{if } i = \{0, 1\} \\ 0, & \text{for } 2 \le i \le n - 1 \end{cases} \tag{8}$$

Thus, m' now depends on two secret coefficients $(\mathbf{s}[0], \mathbf{s}[1])$ in two corresponding message bits (m'_0, m'_1), while all other bits are fixed to 0. In fact, the number of secret dependent message bits in m' denoted as b_{sec} can be chosen by the attacker based on the chosen ciphertexts $(\mathbf{u}, \mathbf{v})$. More concretely, b_{sec} is equal to the number of non-zero coefficients of the ciphertext polynomial $\mathbf{v}$.

For the binary PC oracle-based CCA ($b_{sec} = 1$), 8 chosen-ciphertexts are required in total for unique distinguishability in Saber (Refer Fig. 1). If there exists a more informative oracle which provides information about a generic b_{sec} bits of m', then full key recovery is possible in $(768 \times 8)/b_{sec} = (6144/b_{sec})$ queries using our parallelized attack approach. For Kyber768, full key recovery is possible in $(768 \times 4)/b_{sec} = 3072/b_{sec}$ queries (Refer Fig. 5 in Appendix A).

Recently, Xu *et al.*[24] and Ngo *et al.* [12] also proposed parallelized PC oracle-based CCA on Kyber and Saber KEMs respectively. However, our attack approach is subtly different from the aforementioned attacks in the following manner. The chosen-ciphertexts used in [24] and [12] ensure that all bits of the decrypted message m' depend upon the corresponding secret coefficients. However, our approach is more generic which allows the attacker to configure the number of secret dependent bits (b_{sec}) in m', while the remaining message bits are fixed to 0. Though it might appear to be inefficient to not utilize all the message bits for key recovery, we will later show that the unused 0 bits of the decrypted message can be efficiently used to embed the trigger activation pattern for the HT. This is however not possible using the approach of [24] and [12].

While the PC oracle facilitates key recovery, it is clearly non-existent in IND-CCA secure KEMs due to the use of FO transform. In the following, we show that a minicule HT within the decapsulation procedure can be used to realize an artificial PC oracle which facilitates key recovery using the proposed binary and parallelized CCAs for LWE/LWR-based schemes.

4 HT-Assisted Key Recovery Attack

4.1 Adversary Model

Our attacker is an IP developer who distributes malicious hardware designs of Saber as either soft (RTL-level), firm (netlist-level) or hard (GDSII-level) IP cores to potential SoC vendors (Alice). The attacker only inserts HT in the decapsulation procedure while the key generation and encapsulation procedures are HT-free. The Saber IP uses a long-term secret key sk to generate multiple session keys K. The secret key sk used by the target device could either be generated at a secure offline facility or generated online directly on the target device. The long-term secret key is periodically refreshed and the lifetime of the secret key depends upon the application use-case, ranging from a few hours to a few days/months.

The attacker's motive is to recover the long-term secret key sk, since it can be used to recover all the corresponding session keys K used for encrypted communication. The HT-infested IP does not contain any additional I/O ports apart from the valid I/O ports. The attacker does not require any physical access to the target, but only requires to communicate with the target (i.e.) attacker is an encapsulator in a TLS session with the target device prompting decapsulation of chosen ciphertexts using the secret key sk.

4.2 Intuition

Referring to the IND-CCA secure decapsulation procedure in Algorithm 2, a given ciphertext ct is labelled valid or invalid by the verify signal, the output of ciphertext comparison (Line 5 of $\mathsf{KEM.Decaps}$). While $\mathsf{verify} = 1$ denotes a valid ciphertext, $\mathsf{verify} = 0$ denotes an invalid ciphertext. Thus, decapsulation of $\mathsf{ct}_{\mathsf{attack}}$ results in $\mathsf{verify} = 0$, which generates a pseudo-random key. Lets say, we design a HT which always sets $\mathsf{verify} = 1$ irrespective of the validity of the ciphertext (i.e.) all ciphertexts (valid/invalid) are labelled valid.

If we query the HT-infested decapsulation procedure with chosen-ciphertexts of the binary PC oracle-based CCA, then the session key K generated for $\mathsf{ct}_{\mathsf{attack}}$ is not pseudo-random, but dependent upon the decrypted message m' where $K = \mathcal{F}(m', pk, ct)$. It can only assume two values (i.e.) $K_0 = \mathcal{F}(0, pk, ct)$ or $K_1 = \mathcal{F}(1, pk, ct)$ where (pk, ct) is public. Thus, the session key K serves as the PC oracle's responses which can be used for key recovery. In essence, the HT downgrades the security from being IND-CCA secure to IND-CPA secure thereby allowing CCAs.

However, this HT is easy to detect since invalid ciphertexts always return a wrong key, thereby allowing trivial detection of the inserted HT during functional testing. *Thus, we propose to design a stealthier HT which only downgrades the security for attacker's chosen-ciphertexts* $\mathsf{ct}_{\mathsf{attack}}$*, while demonstrating normal behaviour for all other ciphertexts (valid/invalid).* This ensures that the session key K leaks the long-term secret key only for $\mathsf{ct}_{\mathsf{attack}}$.

4.3 Applicability of Binary/Parallel Oracle-Based CCA

When Saber is used in a protocol such as TLS 1.3, the protocol mandates the encapsulator to first send data encrypted using the session key K (typically certificates and other protocol associated data). However, the attacker does not know the value of K (K_0/K_1). Thus, he/she generates encrypted data for a random choice of $K = K_0/K_1$ based on the success/failure of the protocol, deduces the value of K and thereby m'. Here, the target device only provides binary information (success/failure) and thus, there is no advantage for an attacker in utilizing the parallelized PC oracle-based CCA compared to its binary counterpart for key recovery.

However, it is possible that other protocols (custom) mandate the decapsulator (target) to first generate encrypted data using the key K. In this case, the attacker can use the encrypted data to recover the the session key K containing b_{sec} number of secret dependent bits in a single query, thereby realizing a parallelized PC oracle. But, for each query the attacker needs to perform $2^{b_{sec}}$ offline computations to recover the correct value of m'. For Saber, $b_{sec} = 32$ results in only 192 queries and $2^{32} \cdot 192 \approx 2^{39}$ offline computations for full key recovery. Similarly for Kyber (Kyber768), only 96 online queries and 2^{38} offline computations are required for full key recovery. Thus, there exists a well defined trade-off between the number of chosen-ciphertext queries (online) and offline computational complexity for key recovery. The number of secret dependent bits used for message recovery can be chosen based on the attack setting (if parallel PC oracle is present) as well as the attacker's ability to perform offline computations.

5 HT Design Methodology

A typical HT is composed of two parts: 1) Trigger and 2) Payload. The trigger circuit activates the HT upon satisfaction of a special activation condition. Upon activation, the payload circuit modifies the targeted signal/s which elicits malicious behaviour, exploitable by an attacker.

5.1 Design of HT Trigger Mechanism

Our proposed HT should be activated only for the attacker's chosen-ciphertexts, while it should remain dormant for other ciphertexts (valid/invalid). Typical HT for crypto IP cores use an attacker defined input pattern for HT activation [4]. However, the malicious ciphertexts (Sect. 3) used for the PC oracle-based CCA have a very low entropy with many 0 coefficients. Thus, triggering based on the input could lead to easy detection during functional testing.

We therefore propose to use the decrypted message m' to activate the HT. However, m' for the attacker's chosen ciphertexts also have a very low entropy since most of their bits are 0. These 0 bits are unused by an attacker and thus do not contain any sensitive information. We show that *ciphertext malleability* property of LWE/LWR-based schemes can be used to embed a trigger activation pattern within these unused bits of m', which can be used for HT activation.

5.1.1 Exploiting Ciphertext Malleability for HT Trigger

Ciphertext malleability is a property of cryptographic algorithms which allows transformation of a ciphertext ct for an unknown message m into another ciphertext $\hat{ct}$ which decrypts to a variant of the message (i.e.) $\hat{m} = \mathcal{K}(m)$. Ciphertext malleability for LWE/LWR-based schemes has been used in the context of SCA for key recovery attacks [16].

Given a ciphertext $ct = (\mathbf{u}, \mathbf{v})$ of a message m (Refer to Algorithm 1), adding $\lceil q/2 \rfloor$ (center of the integer ring $\mathbb{Z}_q$) to a coefficient $\mathbf{v}[i]$ ($i \in [0, n-1]$) flips the corresponding message bit m'_i (i.e.) $(0 \to 1)/(1 \to 0)$. We denote $m'_i = \mathsf{Flip}(m, i)$ whose i^{th} bit has been flipped compared to m. More concretely,

$$\begin{aligned} \mathsf{PKE.Decrypt}(ct = (\mathbf{u}, \mathbf{v})) &= m \\ \mathsf{PKE.Decrypt}(\hat{ct} = (\mathbf{u}, \mathbf{v} + 1 \cdot x^i)) &= \mathsf{Flip}(m, i) \end{aligned} \tag{9}$$

Any number of bits of the decrypted message m' can be simultaneously flipped by adding $\lceil q/2 \rfloor$ to the corresponding coefficients of $\mathbf{v}$. We exploit this property to embed a trigger activation pattern in b_{act} number of these unused 0 bits. We denote the trigger activation pattern as $\mathsf{trig\_pattern}$ whose value lies in the range $[0, 2^{b_{act}} - 1]$. We now simply add $\lceil q/2 \rfloor$ to the appropriate coefficients of $\mathbf{v}$ based on the value of $\mathsf{trig\_pattern}$. Thus, the unused 0 bits in the decrypted message m now have a value equal to $\mathsf{trig\_pattern}$. Thus, we are able to use ciphertext malleability to embed the trigger activation pattern within the decrypted message, without disturbing the segment containing the secret dependent message bits (denoted as sec), which are used for key recovery.

The HT trigger is thus a simple *comparator* which compares the act segment of the decrypted message to $\mathsf{trig\_pattern}$ and activates the HT if comparison succeeds. We denote the output of trigger circuit (trigger signal) as $\mathsf{trig\_signal}$. Larger the number of bits in act (b_{act}), smaller is the activation probability (i.e.) $p_{act} = 2^{-b_{act}}$ (e.g.) $b_{act} = 128$ implies $p_{act} = 2^{-128}$. Thus, b_{act} is chosen to attain a negligible activation probability. The trigger activation pattern $\mathsf{trig\_pattern}$ is only known to the IP vendor/author who implanted the HT. Thus, the HT can only be activated by ciphertexts constructed by the attacker. For all other ciphertexts, it activates with a negligible probability of p_{act}.

The decrypted message m' of the attacker's chosen-ciphertexts can thus be partitioned into the following three segments:

$$m' = (\mathsf{act}|\mathsf{sec}|\mathsf{zero}) \tag{10}$$

where act denotes the trigger activation pattern, sec denotes the segment of secret dependent message bits and zero denotes the segment of the remaining unused 0 bits. The width of each of these segments as well as their order within the message are free to be chosen by the attacker during design time. The attacker constructs ciphertexts so that the act segment of the decrypted message has the value of $\mathsf{trig\_pattern}$.

5.2 Design of HT Payload

Upon activation, the HT payload should tamper the output of ciphertext comparator so that the malicious ciphertexts are marked as valid (i.e.) verify = 1 (Line 5 of KEM.Decaps in Algorithm 2). The original output of ciphertext comparison is verify, while the tampered output (trojan payload) is denoted as verify′. The HT payload circuit is thus a simple 2-input multiplexer with trig_signal as its select input. For random valid/invalid ciphertexts (trig_signal = 0), the valid verify signal is simply passed to the output (i.e.) verify′ = $verify$. However, for the attacker's malicious ciphertexts corresponding to the trigger activation pattern (trig_signal = 1), verify′ is set to 1 indicating a valid ciphertext. The HT payload signal verify′ is fed to the final key derivation function (KDF) which generates the session key K.

The value of session key K for the attacker's chosen-ciphertexts act as response of the PC oracle for the attacker's chosen ciphertexts. This can be used to retrieve the value of the sec segment of the decrypted message, which subsequently leads to key recovery. Refer to Fig. 2 for a pictorial illustration of our HT-assisted CCA on the HT-infested decapsulation procedure where the signals and blocks associated with our proposed HT are marked in red. We validated our attack methodology through attack simulations on the recommended parameter sets of both Saber and Kyber. Our attacks were expectedly able to recover the full secret key in a few hundred to few thousand queries (depending on binary/parallelized PC oracle-based CCA) with a 100% success rate. In the following, we discuss the concrete implementation details of our proposed HT within the decapsulation hardware of Saber.

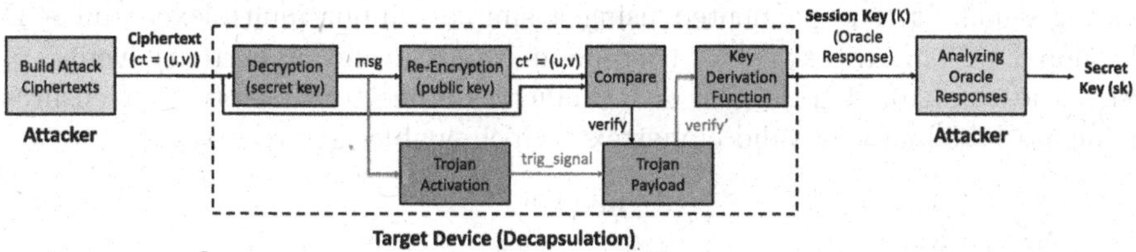

Fig. 2. Attack Flow of our HT-assisted CCA targeting Decapsulation procedure of LWE/LWR-based Schemes

6 Implementation Details

We implemented our HT on the publicly available hardware implementation of the high-speed instruction set co-processor for Saber by Roy and Basso [19]. Refer to Fig. 2 of [19] for the top-level schematic of this co-processor which can implement all the three procedures (i.e.) key generation, encapsulation and decapsulation of Saber. It contains a data memory implemented using Block RAM tiles and a small program memory implemented in LUTs. There are dedicated computation blocks for polynomial multiplication, binomial sampling, Keccak-based hash functions and other low-level arithmetic and data handling operations. For more details, we refer the reader to [19].

6.1 Implementing HT Trigger

We observe that the decrypted message m' in the Saber hardware is generated *four* (4) bits at a time. The complete message (256 bits) is aggregated in an internal buffer over several clock cycles before being written to the data memory. Thus, we implement a sequential comparator which compares the act segment of m' with the trigger activation pattern trig_pattern, 4 bits at a time. The pattern can either be stored in an internal buffer or in the data memory along with other constants used for normal operation. For the sequential message comparator, we implement using a simple 4-bit combinational logic based on a tree of *xor* and *or* gates and a simple sequential control logic.

Refer to Fig. 3(a) for the HT trigger circuit whose output is the trigger activation signal trig_signal (output of D flip-flop DFF1). This signal tracks the output signal of the 4-bit combinational comparator (out) and stops updating as soon as a 4-bit comparison fails (i.e.) out = 0 results in trig_signal = 0. The use of a sequential message comparator (instead of a parallel comparator) significantly reduces area consumption.

6.2 Implementing HT Payload

Refer to Fig. 3(b) for the HT payload circuit which takes as input the original ciphertext comparison output verify and generates the HT payload verify′ based on trig_signal. It is implemented using a simple 2-input multiplexer and a D flip-flop DFF2. If trig_signal = 0 (random valid/invalid ciphertext), verify′ = verify (no change). If trig_signal = 1 (malicious ciphertext), verify′ = 1 ensures malicious labelling as a valid ciphertext, which enables key recovery.

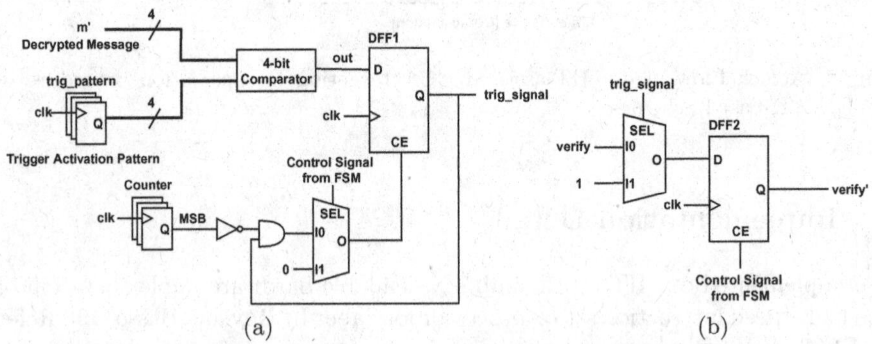

Fig. 3. Schematic of HT Trigger and Payload

6.2.1 Analysing the Operation of HT-infested Target

We classify the ciphertext inputs to the decapsulation procedure into three types:

- *Valid Ciphertexts*: Ciphertexts generated according to valid encapsulation procedure (KEM.Decaps in Algorithm 2)
- *Invalid Ciphertexts*: Randomly generated data or valid ciphertexts with at least one bit error. The errors in ciphertext could either be generated by the attacker or due to noise in the communication channel.
- *Malicious Ciphertexts*: Specially crafted ciphertexts by the attacker.

Table 1. Value of different signals within the HT-infested target for different types of input ciphertexts. The number in parantheses denotes probability of attaining the denoted value. p_{act} denotes probability of HT activation.

Type of ciphertext	trig_signal (prob.)	verify	verify′ (prob.)
Valid	$0\ (1-p_{act})$	1	$1\ (1)$
Invalid	$0\ (1-p_{act})$	0	$0\ (1-p_{act})$
Malicious	$1\ (1)$	0	$1\ (1)$

Table 1 illustrates operation of the HT-infested target for different types of input ciphertexts. A close observation reveals that *the HT payload signal* verify′ *takes the same value for both the malicious ciphertexts as well as valid ciphertexts.* Both malicious and valid ciphertexts are labelled as valid (i.e.) verify′ $= 1$. Moreover, our HT payload is only a single bit. We will now use these features to propose an improved HT design which has a unified payload and trigger circuit and a reduced area footprint, with the goal of increasing the stealthiness of the HT.

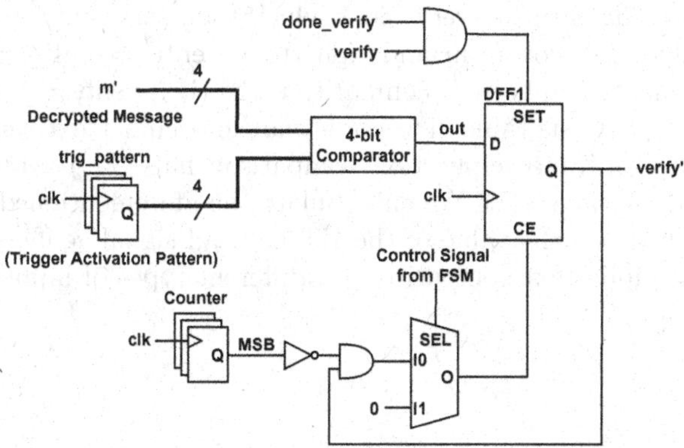

Fig. 4. Improved HT design with unified trigger and payload circuit

Table 2. The HT payload verify′ of our improved HT circuit (Fig. 4) after message comparison (m_{cmp}) and ciphertext comparison (ct_{cmp}) for different types of input ciphertexts. We ignore the negligible probabilities of HT activation for valid/invalid ciphertexts for ease of explanation.

Type of ciphertext	Value of verify signal after	
	m_{cmp}	ct_{cmp}
Valid	0	1
Invalid	0	0
Malicious	1	1

6.3 Improved HT Design

Given that the HT payload is the same for both malicious as well as valid ciphertexts, we propose to activate the HT for valid ciphertexts (i.e.) explicitly set trig_signal to 1 for a valid ciphertext. This also ensures that verify′ = 1 which is the expected output for a valid ciphertext. To realize this, we use the valid verify signal (i.e.) output of ciphertext comparison as a feedback to the HT trigger circuit. This signal is connected to the *SET* input of the D flip-flop DFF1 of the HT trigger circuit. With this simple modification, we observe that the trig_signal can be directly used as the HT payload. Thus, our HT has a unified trigger and payload circuit, which results in a compact design and lower area footprint. Refer to Fig. 4 for the improved HT design whose output is nothing but the HT payload verify′. The verify signal is gated using the done_verify control signal (from original design) which indicates completion of the ciphertext comparison operation.

Let us now analyze the operation of the improved HT. For simplicity, we assume no accidental HT activation for random valid/invalid ciphertexts. For a valid ciphertext, verify′ = 0 after message comparison. Subsequently, ciphertext comparison succeeds ensuring verify to 1 which then sets verify′ to 1 overriding its previous value of 0. For an invalid ciphertext, verify′ = 0 after message comparison. Subsequently, ciphertext comparison fails (i.e.) verify = 1 which ensures verify′ retains its previous value of 0. For a malicious ciphertext, verify′ = 1 after message comparison. Since ciphertext comparison fails (i.e.) verify = 0, verify′ retains its previous value of 1. We encapsulate the aforementioned observations in Table 2 which shows the value of the HT payload signal verify′ after message comparison and ciphertext comparison for different types of input ciphertexts.

6.4 Implementation Results

We implemented the original (HT-free) and HT-infested implementations of Saber for the Zynq UltraScale *xczu9eg-ffvb1156-2-e* FPGA using Xilinx Vivado v.2018.3. We present the post-implementation (place and route) area utilization results in Table 3 for three different activation probabilities p_{act} (i.e.) number of bits compared for HT activation (32, 64 and 128 bits). For the different variants, we only observe a negligible increase of 0.98% more FFs and upto 0.03% more LUTs. We observe that the 128-bit variant consumes 6 extra LUTRAMs due to the use of a large 128-bit buffer to store the trigger activation pattern, while the other variants do not utilize any LUTRAMs. Moreover, there is no increase in the the numbers of Block RAMs, IOs and global buffers (BUFGs). We expect a similar area overhead for our proposed HT for other LWE/LWR-based schemes. We also successfully verified our attack on the HT-infested hardware implementation of Saber resulting in a 100% success rate in recovering the long-term secret key.

Our improved HT design has two advantages. Firstly, the unification of the payload and trigger circuit results in a compact design with a very low area footprint. Secondly, the unified design is very different compared to most HTs which have a separate payload and trigger circuit and therefore argues well for its anti-detection capability. In the following section, we discuss the applicability of well-known HT-detection techniques for 3PIP cores. In this respect, we identify a few favourable characteristics which could provide strong resistance against several detection techniques.

7 On the Applicability of HT Detection Techniques

There are several HT detection techniques applicable in a 3PIP setting and their applicability depends on several factors such as:

1. *Type of IP*: Soft-IP/Firm-IP/Hard-IP
2. *Access Rights to IP User*: Ability to view internals, make modifications, insert debug probes etc.

Table 3. Area utilization results for variants of the HT-infested hardware of Saber. The overheads compared to the original design are denoted in %.

Implementation	No. (Overhead in %)					
	FFs	LUTs	LUTRAMs	BRAMs	IOs	BUFGs
HT-Free	9747 (–)	24103 (–)	0	2	189	7
128-bit HT	9843 (0.98%)	24111 (0.03%)	6	2	189	7
64-bit HT	9797 (0.51%)	24110 (0.03%)	0	2	189	7
32-bit HT	9766 (0.19%)	24096 (−0.03%)	0	2	189	7

We restrict ourselves to techniques for Soft-IPs and Firm IPs, while focussing on two common scenarios, based on access privilege provided to the IP user: 1) Black Box IP and 2) White Box IP. We note that only reference-free (golden model-free) detection techniques are applicable in the 3PIP setting.

In a black box IP setting, the user cannot access any internal nets within the IP. He/she can only control the primary inputs and observe the primary outputs. The HT-infested target provably demonstrates normal behaviour with a very high probability for both valid/invalid ciphertexts (Sect. 5). Thus, faulty behaviour is not observed during functional verification with a very high probability, which makes detection of our proposed HT very challenging in a black-box IP.

7.1 White Box IP

The user has complete access to the internals of the design, either the RTL code or synthesized gate-level netlist. There are expensive techniques like complete reverse engineering which can potentially identify the HT. We however highlight how some commonly used methods stand against our proposed HT. Existing approaches can be broadly classified into two categories:

7.1.1 Dynamic Detection

These techniques rely on logic simulation and monitor the activity of internal signals/nets of the IP for the verifier's chosen inputs. We expect that the following properties of our proposed HT (Fig. 4) might offer a significant challenge or at best resist common dynamic detection methods.

a) High Switching Activity: There are a few well-known techniques such as UCI [9] (Unused Circuit Identification) and VeriTrust [25] which identify dormant or redundant circuits that do not have any observable effect on the normal operation of the device. These techniques work on the premise that HT-related signals are mostly dormant during normal operation or at least retain the same value for a very long time. We observe that our HT uses a sequential comparator that compares 4-bits at a time. Thus, its output has a high switching probability of 1/16. Therefore, all nets in the comparator also have a reasonably high switching activity. We observe (through simulations) that all HT-related signals at least have a single transition for any input ciphertext. Moreover, the Saber hardware is significantly larger compared to simpler ciphers such as AES and thus employs a complex FSM with a high number of control signals which also have a low switching activity. This raises the difficulty in distinguishing valid signals with low switching activity from HT-related signals.

b) Participation of HT in Normal Operation: Cakır and Malik [5] propose to check HT-related signals that have weak statistical correlation with the circuit's valid functional signals. The switching activity of all internal nets is used to compute a certain similarity weight for each net. A significant divergence in the similarity weights is expected for HT-related nets.

We observe that the output of 4-bit combinational comparator denoted as out (within the HT) which carries the trojan value, affects the HT payload verify′ even during normal operation. In fact, verify′ = out for most of the time during normal operation. Only for valid ciphertexts, its value is overriden by verify much later, after ciphertext comparison. For invalid ciphertexts, out is directly used as input to the KDF function (no overriding), thereby participating in normal operation even without HT activation. This is unlike typical HTs where the trojan value is carried to the payload only upon HT activation. This poses a strong challenge for techniques relying on signal correlation analysis. In fact, a similar approach of combining the HT trigger with the valid blocks was used by DeTrust [26] to defeat Veritrust [25], a well-known dynamic detection technique.

7.1.2 Static Detection

Unlike dynamic techniques, static techniques do not rely on logic simulation but analyze the circuit's structure using well-defined metrics such as testability (controllability and observability) and statement hardness, for HT detection [20, 23]. The following properties of our proposed HT might offer resistance against common static techniques.

a) HT-related nets with Similar Controllability and Observability as Valid Signals: Salmani *et al.* [20] proposed *COTD* which utilizes testability of signals as a metric for HT detection, and flags nets with low controllability or observability. We argue that HT-related signals have equivalent controllability and observability as a few other valid signals in the circuit.

In particular, the valid signal verify and the trojan signal out have very similar characteristics. Both signals are related to sequential comparators, with verify related to the sequential ciphertext comparator and out being part of the sequential message comparator. Moreover, the number of bytes compared in the ciphertext comparator (1088 bytes) is much higher than the message comparator (< 16 bytes). Thus, it is possible that the trojan signal out has better controllability than the valid signal verify. Secondly, the valid signal verify is fed back to the HT circuit and is connected to the same D flip-flop DFF1 as out, which is connected to the KDF block. Thus, we expect both signals to have similar observability at the primary outputs. This could therefore provide increased resistance to techniques relying on testability analysis for HT detection.

b) Sequential Arrival of Trigger Vector: Waksman *et al.* [23] proposed FANCI, a framework which identifies signals with weakly affecting inputs using static Boolean function analysis. It relies on the premise that HT trigger input has a weak impact on the output signals. However, DeTrust [26] defeated FANCI using trojans whose trigger pattern arrives over several clock cycles. Along the same lines, our HT also utilizes a sequential comparator since the decrypted message containing the trigger vector arrives 4-bits at a time. Thus, we expect our HT to likewise defeat FANCI and similar detection methods.

b) Non-Trivial Leakage of Secret Key: Formal verification techniques have been demonstrated for successful HT detection in a number of works [10, 22]. The IP vendor and IP user agree upon a set of pre-defined security properties to be satisfied by the IP. Subsequently, proof-checking tools are used to verify adherence to agreed-upon security properties as well as detect unintended functionalities. However, it is difficult to predefine rules to cover all possible risks. Moreover, existing works have only demonstrated detection of trivial trojans in ciphers which directly leak the secret key through the output [10,22]. However, our HT does not involve such trivial leakage of the secret key, but relies on indirect secret key leakage through a sensitive internal variable (i.e.) decrypted message for malicious ciphertexts. However, defining such security properties for LWE/LWR-based schemes is non-trivial and thus warrants future study.

We clarify that we do not claim/prove concrete resistance against HT detection techniques, but only show that our proposed HT has a number of interesting properties which could either pose a strong challenge or at best potentially defeat existing HT detection techniques.

8 Conclusion

We propose novel HT-assisted CCAs for 3PIP cores implementing IND-CCA secure KEMs based on the LWE/LWR problem. We experimentally validated our attack on Saber and Kyber which works with a 100% success rate, and also practically implemented our HT within the open-source implementation of Saber, which incurs a negligible area overhead. We also demonstrated that our proposed HT might pose a significant challenge to state-of-the-art HT-detection techniques. Similar HTs are also possible for post-quantum schemes based on a different paradigm but we leave that possibility for future work.

Acknowledgment. The authors would like to acknowledge the financial support received from the Singapore National Research Foundation under the SoCure NRF2018NCR-NCR002-0001 grant (www.green-ic.org/socure) for carrying out this research.

A Chosen Ciphertexts for Key Recovery in Kyber

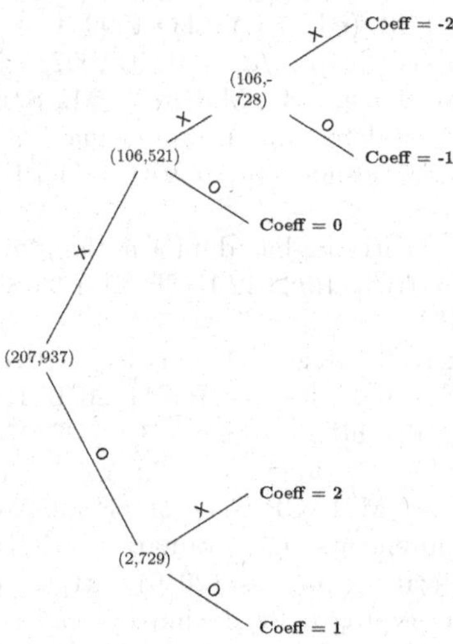

Fig. 5. Binary decision tree based on the decrypted message m' ($m' = 0$ - Class O vs $m' = 1$ - Class X) to uniquely distinguish every candidate for secret coefficient of Kyber (recommended parameters). Each node corresponds to the tuple (U, V) and each edge denotes the PC oracle's response (O/X)

References

1. Alagic, G., et al.: Status report on the second round of the NIST PQC standardization process. Technical report, July, NIST (2020)
2. Amiet, D., Curiger, A., Leuenberger, L., Zbinden, P.: Defeating NewHope with a single trace. In: Ding, J., Tillich, J.-P. (eds.) PQCrypto 2020. LNCS, vol. 12100, pp. 189–205. Springer, Cham (2020). https://doi.org/10.1007/978-3-030-44223-1_11
3. Avanzi, R., et al.: CRYSTALS-Kyber (version 2.0) - Algorithm Specifications And Supporting Documentation, 1 April 2019. Submission to the NIST post-quantum project
4. Bhasin, S., Danger, J.L., Guilley, S., Ngo, X.T., Sauvage, L.: Hardware trojan horses in cryptographic IP cores. In: 2013 Workshop on Fault Diagnosis and Tolerance in Cryptography, pp. 15–29. IEEE (2013)
5. Cakır, B., Malik, S.: Hardware trojan detection for gate-level ICS using signal correlation based clustering. In: 2015 Design, Automation & Test in Europe Conference & Exhibition (DATE), pp. 471–476. IEEE (2015)
6. D'Anvers, J.P., Karmakar, A., Sinha Roy, S., Vercauteren, F.: Saber: Algorithm Specifications And Supporting Documentation (Round 2). Submission to the NIST post-quantum project

7. D'Anvers, J.P., Tiepelt, M., Vercauteren, F., Verbauwhede, I.: Timing attacks on error correcting codes in post-quantum secure schemes. IACR Cryptology ePrint Archive **2019**, 292 (2019)
8. Fujisaki, E., Okamoto, T.: Secure integration of asymmetric and symmetric encryption schemes. In: Wiener, M. (ed.) CRYPTO 1999. LNCS, vol. 1666, pp. 537–554. Springer, Heidelberg (1999). https://doi.org/10.1007/3-540-48405-1_34
9. Hicks, M., Finnicum, M., King, S.T., Martin, M.M., Smith, J.M.: Overcoming an untrusted computing base: detecting and removing malicious hardware automatically. In: 2010 IEEE Symposium on Security and Privacy, pp. 159–172. IEEE (2010)
10. Jin, Y., Makris, Y.: Proof carrying-based information flow tracking for data secrecy protection and hardware trust. In: 2012 IEEE 30th VLSI Test Symposium (VTS), pp. 252–257. IEEE (2012)
11. Lyubashevsky, V., Peikert, C., Regev, O.: On ideal lattices and learning with errors over rings. In: Gilbert, H. (ed.) EUROCRYPT 2010. LNCS, vol. 6110, pp. 1–23. Springer, Heidelberg (2010). https://doi.org/10.1007/978-3-642-13190-5_1
12. Ngo, K., Dubrova, E., Guo, Q., Johansson, T.: A side-channel attack on a masked IND-CCA secure Saber KEM. IACR Cryptol. ePrint Arch. **2021**, 79 (2021)
13. NIST: Submission requirements and evaluation criteria for the post-quantum cryptography standardization process (2016). https://csrc.nist.gov/csrc/media/projects/post-quantum-cryptography/documents/call-for-proposals-final-dec-2016.pdf
14. Oder, T., Schneider, T., Pöppelmann, T., Güneysu, T.: Practical CCA2-secure and masked ring-LWE implementation. IACR Transactions on Cryptographic Hardware and Embedded Systems **2018**(1), 142–174 (2018)
15. Pessl, P., Primas, R.: More practical single-trace attacks on the number theoretic transform. In: Schwabe, P., Thériault, N. (eds.) LATINCRYPT 2019. LNCS, vol. 11774, pp. 130–149. Springer, Cham (2019). https://doi.org/10.1007/978-3-030-30530-7_7
16. Ravi, P., Bhasin, S., Roy, S.S., Chattopadhyay, A.: On exploiting message leakage in (few) NIST PQC candidates for practical message recovery and key recovery attacks. IACR Cryptology ePrint Archive **2020**, 1559 (2020)
17. Ravi, P., Poussier, R., Bhasin, S., Chattopadhyay, A.: On configurable SCA countermeasures against single trace attacks for the NTT. IACR Cryptology ePrint Archive **2020**, 1038
18. Ravi, P., Roy, S.S., Chattopadhyay, A., Bhasin, S.: Generic side-channel attacks on CCA-secure lattice-based PKE and KEMs. IACR Transactions on Cryptographic Hardware and Embedded Systems, pp. 307–335 (2020)
19. Roy, S.S., Basso, A.: High-speed instruction-set coprocessor for lattice-based key encapsulation mechanism: saber in hardware. IACR Transactions on Cryptographic Hardware and Embedded Systems, pp. 443–466 (2020)
20. Salmani, H.: COTD: reference-free hardware trojan detection and recovery based on controllability and observability in gate-level netlist. IEEE Trans. Inf. Forensics Secur. **12**(2), 338–350 (2016)
21. Sim, B.Y., et al.: Single-trace attacks on message encoding in lattice-based KEMs. IEEE Access **8**, 183175–183191 (2020)
22. Vedula, V., Rajendran, J., Murugadhandayuthapany, A., Karri, R.: Security verification of 3rd party intellectual property cores for information leakage. In: Proceedings of the GOMACTECH (2015)

23. Waksman, A., Suozzo, M., Sethumadhavan, S.: FANCI: identification of stealthy malicious logic using Boolean functional analysis. In: Proceedings of the 2013 ACM SIGSAC Conference on Computer & Communications Security, pp. 697–708 (2013)
24. Xu, Z., Pemberton, O., Roy, S.S., Oswald, D.: Magnifying side-channel leakage of lattice-based cryptosystems with chosen ciphertexts: the case study of kyber. Technical report (2020). https://eprint.iacr.org/2020/912
25. Zhang, J., Yuan, F., Wei, L., Liu, Y., Xu, Q.: VeriTrust: verification for hardware trust. IEEE Trans. Comput. Aided Des. Integr. Circuits Syst. **34**(7), 1148–1161 (2015)
26. Zhang, J., Yuan, F., Xu, Q.: DeTrust: defeating hardware trust verification with stealthy implicitly-triggered hardware trojans. In: Proceedings of the 2014 ACM SIGSAC Conference on Computer and Communications Security, pp. 153–166 (2014)

Safe-Error Attacks on SIKE and CSIDH

Fabio Campos[1(✉)], Juliane Krämer[2(✉)], and Marcel Müller[2(✉)]

[1] Max Planck Institute for Security and Privacy, Bochum, Germany
campos@sopmac.de

[2] Technische Universität Darmstadt, Darmstadt, Germany
juliane@qpc.tu-darmstadt.de, neikos@neikos.email

Abstract. The isogeny-based post-quantum schemes SIKE (NIST PQC round 3 alternate candidate) and CSIDH (Asiacrypt 2018) have received only little attention with respect to their fault attack resilience so far. We aim to fill this gap and provide a better understanding of their vulnerability by analyzing their resistance towards safe-error attacks. We present four safe-error attacks, two against SIKE and two against a constant-time implementation of CSIDH that uses dummy isogenies. The attacks use targeted bitflips during the respective isogeny-graph traversals. All four attacks lead to full key recovery. By using voltage and clock glitching, we physically carried out two of the attacks - one against each scheme -, thus demonstrate that full key recovery is also possible in practice.

Keywords: Post-quantum cryptography · Isogeny-based cryptography · Fault attacks

1 Introduction

The youngest field of post-quantum cryptography that is studied within NIST's standardization process is isogeny-based cryptography, which was first described in 2006 [1,2]. Some years later, in 2011, De Feo et al. presented a fast cryptographic scheme based on isogenies, named SIDH (Supersingular Isogeny Diffie-Hellman) [3]. SIDH was used to create the key encapsulation mechanism SIKE (Supersingular Isogeny Key Encapsulation) [4], which was submitted to NIST's standardization process and selected as round 3 alternate candidate, i.e., SIKE is considered promising, but needs to be further studied before being considered for standardization. In 2018, Castryck et al. presented another isogeny-based system, called CSIDH (Commutative Supersingular Isogeny Diffie-Hellman) [5]. Unlike SIKE, CSIDH is non-interactive, making it a potential drop-in replacement for current Diffie-Hellman schemes. CSIDH has not been submitted to NIST's standardization process because it was designed only after the submission deadline had passed. Although the actual security of the suggested CSIDH parameters against quantum attacks was recently questioned [6,7], CSIDH is still a promising and widely discussed isogeny-based scheme. However, the recent

Author list in alphabetical order; see https://www.ams.org/profession/leaders/culture/CultureStatement04.pdf.

L. Batina et al. (Eds.): SPACE 2021, LNCS 13162, pp. 104–125, 2022.
https://doi.org/10.1007/978-3-030-95085-9_6

quantum attacks show that the young field of isogeny-based cryptography has not been sufficiently studied with respect to (quantum) cryptanalysis yet. Also, the physical security of isogeny-based schemes has not been sufficiently studied yet.

In this work, we analyze the physical security of SIKE and CSIDH. Physical attacks allow attackers to deduce secret information of an algorithm by observing or modifying the platform it operates on. In a passive (or side-channel) attack, the attacker analyzes physical information that they can measure while cryptographic operations are computed. In an active attack, on the other hand, the attacker directly interacts with the running algorithm, causing a change in its operations through which information can be extracted. Hence, active attacks are also called fault attacks.

Analyzing SIKE and CSIDH with respect to a specific fault attack is the focus of this work. We analyze both schemes regarding their vulnerability towards *safe-error attacks*. Safe-error attacks have been first published by Yen and Joye in 2000 [8]. They suggested that by inducing transient faults, an implementation leaks one bit of information depending on whether the algorithm results in an error or not. Yen and Joye first described attacks on smart cards using a square-and-multiply algorithm and later applied safe-error attacks on the Montgomery ladder, showing that by perturbing memory during computation, one can deduce one bit of secret information [9]. Safe-error attacks are particularly interesting because even if the algorithm were to detect a fault in its operation, it will still leak information. Hence, standard countermeasures, like checking for faults and outputting a random value in case a fault was detected, still provide the attacker with information and therefore are not sufficient to protect an implementation against safe-error attacks.

Safe-error attack mitigations usually do not feature in current implementations, rendering them vulnerable against these attacks, see, e.g., [10]. Also our work shows that recent implementations of isogeny-based schemes do not provide explicit protection against safe-error attacks. This is concerning especially since some of our attacks are similar to attacks that have long been known in the ECC community, e.g., [8,9].

Our Contribution. The focus of this work is to analyze SIKE and CSIDH with respect to safe-error attacks. To the best of our knowledge, SIKE has not been studied with respect to these attacks before.

We develop attack scenarios for SIKE and CSIDH and demonstrate the feasibility of the presented safe-error attacks by performing practical experiments. The experiments were performed against C implementations of SIKE and CSIDH on a ChipWhisperer board with an ARM Cortex-M4 processor as target core. The implementation of CSIDH that we attacked is a constant-time implementation based on dummy isogenies. We achieve full key recovery of all n bits of the secret key within $O(n)$ interactions for two of the four attacks laid out in this paper. We discuss possible countermeasures and their performance impact. The code used for this work is available[1] in the public domain, which includes the modified CSIDH and SIKE Cortex-M4 implementation and all attack scripts.

[1] https://github.com/Safe-Error-Attacks-on-SIKE-and-CSIDH/SEAoSaC.

The attack against SIKE that we carried out practically can analogously be applied to B-SIDH [11].

Related Work. Although isogeny-based cryptography provides promising candidates for quantum-resistant public-key schemes, only few results regarding the physical security of isogeny-based cryptography in general and SIDH [12–15], SIKE [16], and CSIDH [17–19] in particular exist. Galbraith et al. presented the first fault attack on SIDH, together with corresponding countermeasures [13]. In [12], Koziel et al. propose different zero-value attacks on SIDH. Based on loop-abort fault injection, Gélin and Wesolowski presented side-channel and fault attacks against isogeny-based primitives [14]. The first published physical attack on SIKE was a power side-channel attack exploiting differences in calculations depending on the secret key [16]. Ti proposed in [15] a fault attack on SIDH by changing the base point to a random point via fault injection. In [20], Tasso et al. presented the first experimental realization of Ti's theoretical fault attack and proposed countermeasures against this attack. Cervantes-Vázquez et al. [18] analyzed CSIDH for potential attacks by reviewing and improving the constant-time implementations of [21] and [22]. Furthermore, they proposed a dummy-free CSIDH algorithm. A recent work [17] presents safe-error and further fault attacks, together with countermeasures, on a constant-time CSIDH implementation with dummy isogenies. The attack against CSIDH that we carried out practically attacks the resulting implementation of [17]. LeGrow and Hutchinson [19] suggest to randomize the order of execution of isogenies to increase the number of attacks required when attacking dummy-based constant-time implementations of CSIDH.

Concurrently to our work, several PQC schemes have been analyzed with respect to safe-error attacks [10]. However, isogeny-based schemes are not covered in this work.

Organization. In Sect. 2, we present necessary background on SIKE, CSIDH, and safe-error attacks. In Sects. 3 and 4, we present safe-error attacks on SIKE and CSIDH, respectively. In Sect. 5, we explain how to perform the described safe-error attacks on a real device and present full key recovery. We discuss possible countermeasures in Sect. 6 and conclude this work in Sect. 7.

2 Background

We first discuss implementation details of SIKE and CSIDH. For readers not familiar with isogenies, we refer to [23]. Afterwards, the introduction to safe-errors shows the pattern common to the attacks and how they work.

2.1 SIKE

SIKE (Supersingular Isogeny Key Encapsulation) is an interactive key encapsulation using supersingular elliptic curves [4]. SIKE has passed into the third round of the NIST process[2] as alternate candidate for future standardization.

[2] https://doi.org/10.6028/NIST.IR.8309.

```
// Main loop
for (i = 0; i < nbits; i++) {
    bit = (m[i >> LOG2RADIX] >> (i & (RADIX-1))) & 1;
    swap = bit ^ prevbit;
    prevbit = bit;
    mask = 0 - (digit_t)swap;

    swap_points(R, R2, mask);
    xDBLADD(R0, R2, R->X, A24);
    fp2mul_mont(R2->X, R->Z, R2->X);
}
```

Listing 1: LADDER3PT – SIKE

To achieve the goal of becoming standardized it will need to be studied further, especially with respect to efficiency improvements and all aspects of misuse resistance. SIKE uses SIDH internally, and SIDH will be the main target of the attacks presented in the following section. For a detailed overview of SIDH as used in SIKE, we refer to [4].

SIDH is constructed as follows: A public prime $p = 2^{e_2}3^{e_3} - 1$ such that $2^{e_2} \approx 3^{e_3}$ is chosen, as well as two points on the torsion group associated to their base: $P, Q \in E_0[2^{e_2}]$ or $E_0[3^{e_3}]$. These represent the respective public generators. The rest of the algorithm is computed over $\mathbb{F}_{p^2}$. At the start of the exchange, each party agrees on picking a base of either 2 or 3 as long as they differ between them. Afterwards, each party generates a private key $\mathrm{sk} \in \mathbb{F}_{p^2}$. Of note here is that in the efficient implementation of [4], three points are used. The third point is $R = P - Q$ and is used to speedup the computation through a three-point ladder [24](cf. Algorithms 1 and 4, and Listing 1). Using these generators as well as their private key, each party then computes their public curve E_2 or E_3. This curve is calculated through a chain of e_2 2-isogenies, or e_3 3-isogenies respectively. Each isogeny uses a generator of the form $\langle P + [\mathrm{sk}]Q\rangle$ as the kernel. The projection of the other party basis point and this curve are then sent to the other party, where the same procedure is repeated to arrive at the curve $E_{2/3}$ and $E_{3/2}$. These two curves are isomorphic to each other and thus the parties have arrived at a shared secret: the j-invariant of $E_{2/3}$ and $E_{3/2}$, respectively.

The submitted implementation from round 3 is constant-time and already includes several countermeasures against fault attacks. The implementation is secure against the attack presented in Sect. 3.1, but vulnerable to the second one as presented in Sect. 3.2.

2.2 CSIDH

CSIDH (Commutative Supersingular Isogeny Diffie-Hellman) describes a non-interactive key exchange using supersingular elliptic curves [5]. For a more detailed overview of the key exchange, we refer to [5].

CSIDH is constructed as follows: A prime p is chosen of the form $p = 4 \cdot \ell_1 \cdots \ell_n - 1$, where the ℓ_i are small pairwise distinct odd primes. The rest

Algorithm 1: xDBLADD

function xDBLADD

Input: $(X_P : Z_P), (X_Q, Z_Q), (X_{Q-P} : Z_{Q-P})$, and $(a_{24}^{+} : 1)$ $(A + 2C : 4C)$

Output: $(X_{[2]P} : Z_{[2]P}), (X_{P+Q}, Z_{P+Q})$

$t_0 \leftarrow X_P + Z_P$

$t_1 \leftarrow X_P - Z_P$

$X_{[2]P} \leftarrow t_0^2$

$t_2 \leftarrow X_Q - Z_Q$

$x_{P+Q} \leftarrow X_Q + Z_Q$

$Z_{[2]P} \leftarrow t_1^2$

$t_1 \leftarrow t_1 \cdot X_{P+Q}$

$t_2 \leftarrow X_{[2]P} \cdot -Z_{[2]P}$

$X_{[2]P} \leftarrow X_{[2]P} \cdot Z_{[2]P}$

$X_{P+Q} \leftarrow a_{24}^{+} \cdot t_2$

$Z_{P+Q} \leftarrow t_0 - t_1$

$Z_{[2]P} \leftarrow X_{P+Q} + Z_{[2]P}$

$X_{P+Q} \leftarrow t_0 + t_1$

$Z_{[2]P} \leftarrow Z_{[2]P} \cdot t_2$

$Z_{P+Q} \leftarrow Z_{P+Q}^2$

$X_{P+Q} \leftarrow X_{P+Q}^2$

$Z_{P+Q} \leftarrow X_{Q-P} \cdot Z_{P+Q}$

$X_{P+Q} \leftarrow Z_{Q-P} \cdot X_{P+Q}$

return $(X_{[2]P} : Z_{[2]P}), (X_{P+Q}, Z_{P+Q})$

of the algorithm is computed in $\mathbb{F}_p$. The algorithm uses elliptic curves in Montgomery form: $E_0 : y^2 = x^3 + Ax^2 + x$. To begin, each party generates a secret key $(e_1, \ldots, e_n)$, where each e_i is sampled uniformly random from the interval $[-m, m]$ with $m \in \mathbb{N}$. The key exchange is then prepared by calculating the elliptic curve associated with the secret key: For each e_i a total of $abs(e_i)$ ℓ_i-isogenies have to be calculated. The sign of e_i represents the direction taken in the respective ℓ_i-isogeny graph. As the composition of isogenies is commutative, each computed curve will be isomorphic no matter in which order they are calculated. The isognies are then chained to compute the public curve associated to the secret key: $E_0 \xrightarrow{(e_1,\ldots,e_n)} E_A$. Bob does the same to calculate E_B. The parameter of the curves E_A and E_B correspond to the public keys and are then exchanged and each party repeats their isogeny calculation using the other's public key as the starting curve: Alice calculates $E_B \xrightarrow{(e_1,\ldots,e_n)} E_{BA}$ and Bob calculates E_{AB} in a similar fashion. The final curves E_{BA} and E_{AB} are the same, and the shared secret is the A parameter of this curve in Montgomery form.

The straightforward implementation of the algorithm would be highly variable in time, since different amounts of isogenies need to computed, depending on the secret key. It would be easy for an attacker to trace the amount of isogenies calculated and their degree as isogenies with a larger degree require more computational effort. In 2019 Meyer et al. have presented a constant-time implementation of CSIDH [21]. The authors tackle this issue by making the amount of isogeny evaluations constant, thus only leaking the degree of the isogenies themselves and not the exact number of them. This follows from the aforementioned fact that higher degree isogenies take longer to construct and, e.g., could be recovered through a timing attack. They achieve this by calculating "dummy" isogenies which serve as extra computational time to thwart timing attacks from finding the real amount of isogenies of a given degree. Further, they change the interval from which the secret key parts are sampled from $[-m, m]$ to $[0, 2m]$ so that an attacker cannot tell apart secret keys with unbalanced positive and negative parts. Unfortunately, these dummy calculations have added a new attack vector: loop-abort attacks. Such an attack was first described in passing by Cervantes-Vázquez et al. in [18]. In [17] the approach using dummy isogenies has been further refined. Campos et al. analyzed the constant-time implementation for fault-injection attacks. This resulted, among others, in added safeguards to the point evaluation and codomain curve algorithm. However, these safeguards do not protect against the attack described in Sect. 4.1, as the attacker assumed in this paper has a different threat model.

Following [21] Onuki et al. proposed to speed-up the implementation by reverting the secret key part interval to $[-m, m]$ and guarding against unbalanced keys by using two points instead of one [22]. This change, however, has introduced a possible new attack vector as described in Sect. 4.2.

2.3 Safe-Error Attacks

In [8], Yen and Joye introduce a new category of active attacks, so called safe-error attacks. In this kind of attacks, the adversary uses fault injections to perturb a specific memory location with the intent of not modifying the final result of the computation: the algorithm may overwrite or throw away modified values, making them "safe errors". The presence or absence of an error then gives insight into which codepath the algorithm executed. Two kinds of safe-error attacks exist: in a memory safe-error (M safe-error) attack, the attacker modifies the memory, i.e., in general these attacks focus on specific implementations [9,25,26]. In a computational safe-error (C safe-error) attack, however, the computation itself is attacked through, e.g., skipping instructions. Hence, C safe-error attacks rather target algorithmic vulnerabilities [9,26].

The general construction of a safe-error attack is as follows:

Suppose an algorithm iterates over secret data. It then branches and does slightly different calculations depending on whether a given bit in the secret data is equal to 0 or 1. The algorithm presented in Algorithm 3 has been secured against timing side-channel attacks by consuming the same time in each branch. Precisely this predictability, enforced to thwart timing attacks, makes safe-error attacks easier to carry out, as these attacks require timed fault-injections. When implementing countermeasures, implementers thus have to investigate all implications that these countermeasures have. However, since some side-channel attacks, e.g., timing attacks, are generally easier to carry out than other physical attacks, e.g., safe-error attacks, it can still be the right decision to fix a specific

Algorithm 2: CSIDH Algorithm by Onuki et al.

Input: $A \in \mathbb{F}_p, m \in \mathbb{N}$, a list of integers $(e_1, \ldots, e_n) \in [-m, m]^n$ and n distinct odd primes $\ell_1, \ldots, \ell_n$ s.t. $p = 4\prod_i \ell_i - 1$.
Output: $B \in \mathbb{F}_p, m \in \mathbb{N}$ s.t. $E_B = (\mathfrak{l}_1^{e1} \cdots \mathfrak{l}_n^{e2}) * E_A$, where $\mathfrak{l}_i = (\ell_i, \pi - 1)$ for $i = 1, \ldots, n$, and π is the p-th power Frobenius endomorphism of E_A.

Set $e_i' = m - |e_i|$ for $i = 1, \ldots, n$
while *some* $e_i \neq 0$ *or* $e_i' \neq 0$ **do**
  Set $S = \{i | e_i \neq 0 \text{ or } e_i' \neq 0\}$
  Set $k = \prod_{i \in S} \ell_i$
  Generate points $P_0 \in E_A[\pi + 1]$ and $P_1 \in E_A[\pi - 1]$ by Elligator
  Let $P_0 \leftarrow [(p+1)/k]P_0$ and $P_1 \leftarrow [(p+1)/k]P_1$
  for $i \in S$ **do**
    Set s the sign bit of e_i
    Set $Q = [k/\ell_i]P_s$
    Let $P_{1-s} \leftarrow [\ell_i]P_{1-s}$.
    if $Q \neq \infty$ **then**
      if $e_i \neq 0$ **then**
        Compute an isogeny $\phi : E_A \to E_B$ with $\ker \phi = \langle Q \rangle$
        Let $A \leftarrow B, P_0 \leftarrow \phi(P_0), P_1 \leftarrow \phi(P_1)$, and $e_i \leftarrow e_i - 1 + 2s$
      else
        Dummy computation
        Let $A \leftarrow A, P_s \leftarrow [\ell_i]P_s$, and $e_i' \leftarrow e_i' - 1$.
    Let $k \leftarrow k/\ell_i$
return A

Algorithm 3: A toy algorithm vulnerable to a variable-access attack

Input: S the n-bit secret key
Output: a public message M

$M \leftarrow 1$
$K \leftarrow 0$
$P \leftarrow 0$
for $i \in 0..n$ **do**
  if $S_i = 0$ **then**
    $K \leftarrow \text{calculate}(S_i, P, K)$
  else
    $P \leftarrow \text{calculate}(S_i, K, P)$
  $M \leftarrow M + K * P$
return M

vulnerability by enabling other, practically less relevant attacks. In application-related implementations, explicit branching on secret data is usually avoided. However, the different memory access patterns still occur due to the structure of the respective algorithm. As we show in Sect. 3.1, using a constant time swap

Table 1. Access patterns depending on the i-th bit of the secret key

Condition	Read variables	Written variables
$S_i = 0$	P, K	K
$S_i = 1$	P, K	P

algorithm instead of condition branching is not sufficient and may even provide an additional attack vector.

Analyzing the read and write patterns of Algorithm 3 and classing them according to the state that they occur in allows to look for differences that could be exploitable. These differences can be rendered in a table, such as Table 1. This allows for visual inspection of differences.

This representation makes it immediately clear that even though the same method is being called, it affects different data. This allows an attacker to exploit the difference between the two branches by modifying one memory location and checking whether a safe-error occurred.

Example: Let's assume we try to attack the first branch, when $S_i = 0$. During the calculate routine, we modify the memory used by the variable K in such a way that it does not change the result of the computation. This is done by perturbing the memory once the given memory location is not read anymore, but before it is being potentially written to. After the calculate routine has executed, either K or P has been overwritten. If our guess of $S_i = 0$ was correct, due to being overwritten after being perturbed by the fault, K now holds again correct information in context of the algorithm. Letting the algorithm finish leaks the information whether our guess was correct: If it finishes normally, S_i was indeed 0. If we assume that M is known and verifiable, we can check to see if the outcome was wrong, or, simpler, an error occurred. If either happened, then S_i was 1, as the faulted K did not get overwritten and subsequently changed the calculation. This attack needs to be then repeated n times to fully recover the secret key S.

3 Attacks on SIKE

In this section, we analyze the implementation of SIKE submitted to round 3 of NIST's standardization process [4] in the context of safe-error attacks. First, we describe a memory safe-error attack in Sect. 3.1, then we describe a computational safe-error attack in Sect. 3.2. For both attacks, we assume that the victim has a static secret key. Both the encapsulator and the decapsulator can be the victim of this attack.

3.1 M-Safe Attack on SIKE

We first give a high-level overview on how the attack is constructed. Then, we give a more detailed analysis of the individual steps of the attack.

Algorithm 4: The 3-Point Ladder

function LADDER3PT

  Input: $m = (m_{l-1}, ..., m_0)_2 \in \mathbb{Z}, (x_P, x_Q, x_{Q-P})$, and $(A : 1)$

  Output: $(X_{P+[m]Q} : Z_{P+[m]Q})$

  $((X_0 : Z_0), (X_1 : Z_1), (X_2 : Z_2)) \leftarrow ((x_Q : 1), (x_P : 1), (x_{Q-P} : 1))$

  $a_{24}^{+} \leftarrow (A + 2)/4$

  for $i = 0$ **to** $l - 1$ **do**

    if $m_i = 1$ **then**

      $((X_0 : Z_0), (X_1 : Z_1)) \leftarrow$ **xDBLADD**$((X_0 : Z_0), (X_1 : Z_1), (X_2 : Z_2), (a_{24}^{+} : 1))$

    else

      $((X_0 : Z_0), (X_2 : Z_2)) \leftarrow$ **xDBLADD**$((X_0 : Z_0), (X_2 : Z_2), (X_1 : Z_1), (a_{24}^{+} : 1))$

  return (X_1, Z_1)

Table 2. Access patterns depending on the ith-bit of the secret key

Condition	Read variables	Written variables
$m[i] = 0$	$(X_0, Z_0), (X_1, Z_1), (X_2, Z_2)$	$(X_0, Z_0), (X_2, Z_2)$
$m[i] = 1$	$(X_0, Z_0), (X_1, Z_1), (X_2, Z_2)$	$(X_0, Z_0), (X_1, Z_1)$

As shown in Sect. 2.1 each SIKE participant has their own secret key $m \in \mathbb{F}_{p^2}$. This key is used to calculate the subgroup $\langle P, [m]Q \rangle$ representing the kernel of their secret isogeny. The point multiplication $[m]Q$ is performed through a three-point ladder algorithm as seen in Algorithm 4. Important here is that the **LADDER3PT** function is called with the secret key m as the first argument. The attacker requires the following capabilities: They need to be able to introduce a memory fault during a specific point of execution, as well as be able to verify the result of a given SIKE run. Both the shared secret as well as any execution errors need to be known afterwards. The attack proposed in this section then follows three parts:

With the goal of extracting an n-bit secret key, the attacker

1. initiates a SIKE key agreement,
2. introduces a memory fault of any kind (bit-flip, scrambling,...) during the i-th iteration of **LADDER3PT**, and
3. uses the result of the SIKE run to obtain the value of the i-th bit of the secret key.

Steps 1 to 3 have to be repeated n times to reconstruct the complete secret key.

In detail, this means that the attack on this three-point ladder algorithm follows the schema as described in Sect. 2.3. Depending on a given bit of the secret key, different variables are modified. This can be seen in Table 2. In this case either (X_1, Z_1) or (X_2, Z_2) are passed to **xDBLADD**. Without loss of generality, let's assume for the rest of this section that we attack m and that the guess for the i-th bit is $m[i] = 1$. By following the general outlines of a safe-error attack one needs to modify (X_1, Z_1) between its last use and the moment it gets written to. Such a moment exists in Algorithm 4 Line 6 (cf. Sect. 2.1): (X_1, Z_1) is passed to the **xDBLADD** subroutine as the *second* argument, thus $(X_Q, Z_Q) = (X_1, Z_1)$ in Algorithm 1 (cf. Sect. 2.1). (X_1, Z_1) is passed as the *third* argument in Line 8, this difference is dependent on the secret key. The **xDBLADD** method (as seen in Line 6 in Algorithm 1) then returns two values, one of which is assigned to (X_1, Z_1) in Algorithm 4. In the **xDBLADD** routine from Line 6 onwards, (X_Q, Z_Q) is no longer read, and thus the value of (X_1, Z_1) stays unused until the function returns. This is where the attacker executes the active attack, by scrambling the values backing (X_Q, Z_Q), i.e., (X_1, Z_1). If the attack on the memory location of (X_1, Z_1) was successful and our guess was correct, the algorithm will, upon return, overwrite our modification and finish without encountering an error. One can thus conclude that $m[i] = 1$. Should our guess of $m[i] = 1$ be incorrect, then the algorithm computes a mismatching shared secret or raises an error. In this case, $m[i] = 0$. Either way, a single bit of information is gained of the secret key. Consequently, all n bits of the static secret key m can be read by this method and the full key can be recovered through n runs of this attack. The complete attack thus consists of these steps:

1. The attacker observes a normal SIKE key agreement.
2. As **xDBLADD** gets called during **LADDER3PT**, overwrite (X_1, Z_1) on the i-th iteration and observe the final result.
3. If the SIKE de/encapsulation fails, we know that (X_1, Z_1) did *not* get overridden. Thus $m[i] = 0$ otherwise $m[i] = 1$.

Repeat steps 1 to 3 n times to recover the complete n-bit secret key.

The SIKE implementation in [4] has several parameter sets, each influencing the range of possible values of the secret key. For example, SIKEp610 has an exponent $e_2 = 305$ with an estimated NIST security level 3 [4]. The private key m is thus sampled from $\{0, ..., 2^{305} - 1\}$, giving the private key 305 bits of total length. Therefore an attacker, trying to attack a SIKEp610 instantiation, would need to repeat the attack at least 305 times to achieve full key recovery.

In the latest version of **xDBLADD**, as published for the third NIST PQC process round [4], the authors have chosen to use a simultaneous double-and-add algorithm. This implementation prevents this particular attack as there is no moment during execution that P or Q is written before it is potientially read. This is also true during compilation: the order of operations in the assembly stays the same. Nonetheless, future implementations have to make sure that they are not vulnerable when using a different algorithm.

3.2 C-Safe Attack on SIKE

Similar to the M safe-error attack on SIKE described in the previous section, the attack described in this section exploits the difference in memory accesses depending on a bit of the secret key. Again, each party generates their own private key m, used to generate the subgroup $\langle P + [m]Q \rangle$ of their private isogeny (cf. Sect. 2.1). This point multiplication $P + [m]Q$ is done through a three-point ladder as seen in Algorithm 4 and Listing 1 (cf. Sect. 2.1). In the C implementation, published in [4], the authors use a constant-time swapping algorithm to exchange the points R and $R2$ depending on the i-th bit of the secret key (see Line 359 of Listing 1). The function is called `swap_points` and accepts both points and a mask as input. We denote the i-th bit of the secret key as $m[i]$. The mask of the swapping function is calculated as $\text{xor}(m[i], m[i-1])$, with a starting value of 0 for $m[i-1]$ if $i = 0$. If the mask is 1 the points are exchanged, otherwise they are left as is. This behavior can be exploited by meddling with this function call. It could for example simply be skipped, or the computation of the mask be perturbed such that on a 0 mask it stays 0, but on a 1 mask the value is randomized. Assuming $\text{xor}(m[i], m[i-1])$ and an attacker skips this function call using an active attack on the i-th loop, the end result will be unchanged. If the value had been $\text{xor}(m[i], m[i-1])$, then the end result would be wrong, as the wrong point would have been used for the rest of the calculation.[3] Since we know that in the first iteration $m[i-1]$ is forced to 0, the mask is simply set to the value of $\text{xor}(m[0], 0) = m[0]$. The second iteration of attack then knows the value of $m[0]$ and so on. Thus, in general the bit $m[i]$ is leaked through a C safe-error. As the keyspace for m is equal to $[0, ..., 2^{e_2} - 1]$, similar to the attack in Sect. 3.1, the attack needs to be repeated at least 305 times to achieve full key recovery when the parameter set SIKEp610 is used.

4 Attacks on CSIDH

In this section, we analyse CSIDH with respect to safe-error attacks. We analyse two recent implementations of CSIDH [17,22]. Both implementations are constant-time implementations, and both implementations achieve this kind of timing attack resistance through dummy isogeny computations. The main difference between both implementations is that in [17], computations are done on one point only, while in [22], two points are used. The analysis of both implementations with respect to safe-error attacks is presented in Sect. 4.1 and Sect. 4.2, respectively. For both of the presented attacks, it is assumed that the victim uses a static secret key.

4.1 M Safe-Error Attack on an Implementation Using One Point

In [17] Campos et al. have evaluated possible physical attack vectors for CSIDH implementations using dummy isogenies. One threat model they did not consider, is one that can introduce memory faults. This will be the focus of the attack in this section. The attacker only needs to be able to change a single bit in a certain byte range. In [17], during the execution of a dummy isogeny, the curve parameter A is not modified. If however a non-dummy isogeny is calculated, then the A parameter is changed corresponding to the newly calculated

[3] Wrong shared secret or an error raised from the algorithm.

Table 3. Access pattern depending on the secret key e during the key exchange

Condition	Read variables	Written variables
$e_i \neq 0$	P_0, P_1	P_0, P_1
$e_i = 0$	P_s where s is the sign bit of e_i	P_s

curve. This leads to a possible attack vector: assume without loss of generality that the algorithm is currently calculating isogenies of degree ℓ_i. If it is currently calculating a dummy isogeny, a new parameter A is computed, but *directly discarded.* If a real isogeny is calculated, that result is then used further. A fault injected with the intent of modifying the parameter A can now discern if a real or dummy isogeny is being calculated: if one attacks a real isogeny, the modified value will be propagated and cause a mismatch of the final shared secret. If it was a dummy isogeny however, the modified A was discarded and the shared secret is not impacted. This is now repeated for each possible value of e_i, so as to find out the first time a dummy isogeny is calculated. The value of e_i is then the amount of real isogenies that have been calculated for ℓ_i. In the implementation in [17] e_i is sampled from the range $[0, 10]$, therefore one needs on average 5 attacks per e_i to recover its value. In CSIDH-512 of [17] the secret key has 74 components, thus on average, an attacker would need to run $5 \times 74 = 370$ attacks to recover the full key.

4.2 M Safe-Error Attacks on an Implementation Using Two Points

In [22], Onuki et al. have introduced a new algorithm that uses two points to calculate the CSIDH action. This version has an issue similar to the one described in Sect. 4.1, where the parameter A is discarded when calculating a dummy isogeny. Thus it has also the potential for an M safe-error attack by attacking the A parameter assignment. Unlike the implementation in [17], in [22] the range $[-5, 5]$ is used for each e_i. Even though an attacker additionally needs to recover the sign of e_i now, this reduces the amount of overall attacks required to recover a single e_i.

Further, the CSIDH action as described in [22] has another M safe-error attack vector that will be explained in this section. Table 3 shows the access patterns of two different variables depending on a part of the secret key: only one point is overwritten when e_i equals 0 during the CSIDH action calculation at Line 17 in Algorithm 2 (cf. Sect. 2.2). This opens up the potential of perturbing a given P_0 or P_1 and finding out if this had any effect on the calculation. If there was no effect, then the sign of e_i is equal to the index of the point that was overwritten: 0 if positive, 1 if negative. This allows the attacker to find the sign of a specific e_i since the dependency between isogenies of degree ℓ_i and its running allows for attacking a specific degree ℓ_i [5]. Now let s_i be the sign of e_i. In total, Algorithm 2 does e_i calculations of isogenies of order ℓ_i. After each calculation, it decrements e_i to keep track of how many more real isogenies need to be computed. Once $e_i = 0$, only dummy operations are executed. The task is thus, to find out how many real isogenies are calculated. One can run the following procedure to find the value of e_i: Start with $n = 0$. Modify P_{s_i} after n iterations just before it is potentially overwritten, and check the final result. If the shared secret is correct or n is larger than the maximal possible value for e_i, we know $e_i < n$ at that point and we can stop the process, otherwise $e_i > n$, increment n and retry. Once this procedure terminates, e_i equals the amount of calculated real isogenies. Applying this procedure repeatedly, one can deduce the whole secret key $(e_1, ..., e_n)$. As [22] uses an instantiation where the private key elements can range from -5 to 5, in total $2.5 + 1 = 3.5$ attacks are required per e_i, as well as finding s_i. In that instantiation, 74 elements are used per secret key, therefore an attacker would need to run $74 \times 3.5 = 259$ attacks on average for the signs and the full key recovery in total. The attack can be summarised as follows:

1. Reveal which ℓ_i is currently being computed from the length of computation.
2. On Line 17 in Algorithm 2 only P_{s_i} is being assigned. Thus, perturbing the memory of P_{s_i} while $[\ell_i]P_{s_i}$ is being calculated will allow to deduce whether $i = 0$, or $i = 1$. From now on, we assume that s_i is known for each e_i.
3. Knowing the sign allows us to now explicitly attack either P_0 or P_1 and thus find out whether a real or dummy isogeny is being calculated.

If the final shared secret is correct, it was a real isogeny, otherwise it was a dummy. The value of e_i is equal to the count of real isogenies. Once all e_i and their signs s_i have been recovered, the full private key $(e_1, ..., e_n)$ can be reconstructed.

5 Practical Experiments

In this section, we explain how to perform the described attacks on a ChipWhisperer board and present the achieved security impact. In the case of SIKE, we present full key recovery. In the case of CSIDH, due to the relatively long runtime on the target architecture ($\approx$7 s for the reduced version of CSIDH), we calculated the maximum number of possible runs in advance and determined further attack parameters accordingly.

All practical attacks were implemented using the ChipWhisperer tool chain[4] (version 5.3.0) in Python (version 3.8.2) and performed on a ChipWhisperer-Lite board with a 32-bit STM32F303 ARM Cortex-M4 processor as target core. Based on available implementations, we wrote slightly modified ARM implementations of SIKEp434 and CSIDH512 to make them suitable for our setup. Security-critical spots remained unchanged. All binaries were build using the GNU Tools for ARM Embedded Processors 9-2019-q4-major[5] (gcc version 9.2.1 20191025 (release) [ARM/arm-9-branch revision 277599]) using the flags: `-Os -mthumb -mcpu=cortex-m4 -mfloat-abi=soft`.

[4] https://github.com/newaetech/chipwhisperer, commit fa00c1f.
[5] https://developer.arm.com/.

In all attack models the adversary aims to attack the calculation of the shared secret in order to learn parts of the private key. The shared secrets are calculated without randomness, i.e., points and private keys used were computed in advance. Both in the case of SIKE and CSIDH, the adversary is able to randomise variables or skip instructions by injecting one fault per run. Furthermore, we assume that the attacker is able to trigger and attack the computation of the shared secret multiple times using the same pre-computed private keys. However, in a real environment the attacker is limited to observe the impact of a fault injection (whether both shared secrets are equal or not), by noticing possible unexpected behaviour in the protocol. Although static keys are mostly used in server environments where such invasive fault attacks are not feasible, Noack et al. [27] described exemplary environments and challenge-response scenarios where such static-key attacks can be deployed. Furthermore, CSIDH provides a non-interactive (static-static) key exchange with full public-key validation.

5.1 Attacks on SIKE

Since the current implementation [4] is immune to the attack described in Sect. 3.1, we focus on the attack explained in Sect. 3.2. As described, the adversary deploys safe-error analysis to recover the private key during the computation of the three-point ladder. Since the attacked algorithm runs in constant time, an attacker can easily locate the critical spot, which in our case represents the main loop within the ladder computation. Thus, an attacker who can accurately induce any kind of computational fault inside that spot at the i-th iteration, may be able to deduce if the i-th bit of the private key is set or not, i.e., $\mathrm{sk}_i = 0$ or $\mathrm{sk}_i = 1$ according to whether the resulting shared secret is incorrect or not. Thus, in this model the required number of injections for a full key recovery only depends on the length of the private key. In this setup, the fault is injected by suddenly modifying the clock (clock glitching), thus, forcing the target core to skip an instruction.

The SIKEp434 Cortex-M4 implementation[6] from [28] available at the pqm4 project [29] provided the basis for our implementation. However, this attack can be applied to all available software implementations of SIKE[7] including the round-3 submission [4] to NIST's standardisation process. More precisely, the code part that represents this vulnerability remains the same across all available implementations.

Results. We assume that the attacker knows critical spots within the attacked loop (cf. Listing 1) which reveal one bit of the private key after a single fault injection with high accuracy. As shown in this work, such spots and the corresponding suitable parameters for the injection (e.g., width and internal offset of the clock glitch) can be empirically determined in advance with manageable effort.

---

[6] https://github.com/mupq/pqm4, commit 20bcf68.

[7] https://sike.org/#implementation.

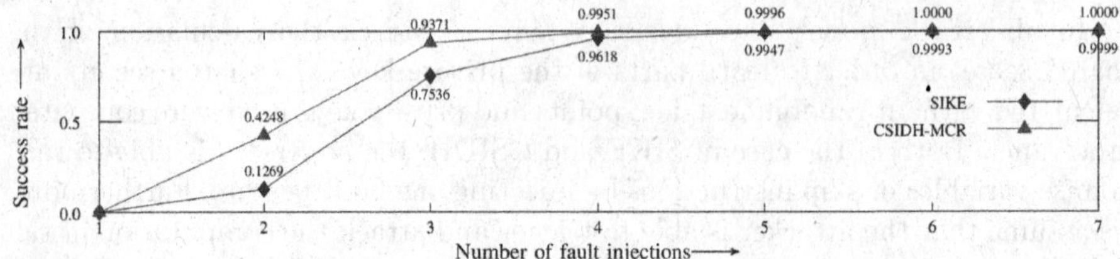

Fig. 1. Success rate for full key recovery as a function of the number of fault injections per bit (SIKE) or isogeny (CSIDH), respectively. Let α be the number of injections for each bit/isogeny. Since a single faulty shared secret is sufficient to distinguish the cases, the success rate for full key recovery can be calculated by $P(\alpha) = [(0.5 \cdot (1 - B(0, \alpha, p_1))) + (0.5 \cdot B(0, \alpha, p_0)))]^\lambda$, where λ equals the number of bits in the case of SIKE and equals $\sum_{i=1}^{n} \lceil \log_2(m_i) \rceil$ for all m_i of the corresponding bound vector $\mathtt{m} = (m_1, m_2, \ldots, m_n)$ in the case of CSIDH, $B(k, n, p) = \binom{n}{k} \cdot p^k (1-p)^{n-k}$, and p_0, p_1 correspond to the respective probabilities.

In order to determine the success rate for each individual of the 218 bits of the private key, we performed 21,800 fault injections (100 injections for each bit) and achieved a relatively high accuracy. More precisely, we obtained on average over all bits 100% (leading to an error probability $p_0 = 0$, as denoted in Fig. 1) accuracy for the case $\text{sk}_i = 0$ and an accuracy of over 86% (denoted as p_1 in Fig. 1) for the case $\text{sk}_i = 1$. As shown in Fig. 1, only 5 fault injections are required for each bit, thus 1,090 injections in total to achieve a success rate above 99% for full key recovery. Since in our inexpensive setup a single run takes about 12 s, full key recovery requires about 4 h.

5.2 Attacks on CSIDH

Since the practical implementation is similar for both attacks, we show without loss of generality how we realised the attack described in Sect. 4.1. The attacker aims to distinguish a real from a dummy isogeny. For this, they inject a fault during the computation of an isogeny and observe if it impacts the resulting shared secret. In this attacker model the adversary can target isogeny computations at positions of their choice and is further able to trace the faulty isogeny computation to determine its degree. Due to non-constant time computation within the calculation of the isogeny (e.g., a square-and-multiply exponentiation based on the degree [17,21,22]), the degree of a given isogeny might be recovered with manageable effort, e.g., using Simple Power Analysis [30].

In our setup, the fault is injected by temporarily under-powering the target core, i.e., by reducing for some clock cycles the value of the supply voltage of the attacked device below the minimum value the device is specified for. Such an attack might lead to an unpredictable state in the target variable during an assignment and can therefore be applied to attack the vulnerable spot regarding the co-domain curve A, as defined in Sect. 4.2. For illustration, the attacks occur

Table 4. Results for CSIDH attacking the first isogeny

Key	# of trials	Faulty shared secret	Accuracy
$S_1 = (-1, 1)$	2500	0.0%	100.0%
$S_2 = (0, 1)$	2500	92.4%	92.4%

during the calculation of the first isogeny, but the other isogenies can be attacked similarly. The implemented attacks are based on the implementation from [17].

Results. As suggested in [17], in order to increase the number of attempts by reducing the time required for a single run, we reduced the key space in CSIDH512 from 11^{74} to 3^2. Further, all required values, e.g. points of corresponding order, were calculated in advance, leading in total to a reduction from 15,721M to 115M clock cycles for a single run. Due to the reduced key space, private keys are of the form $S = (e_0, e_1)$, where $e_i \in [-1, 1]$. To obtain results for both cases (dummy and real), we performed experiments using different private keys. In the first case, the private key $S_1 = (-1, 1)$ consists of real isogenies only. Thus, attacks should not impact the computation of the shared secret. As expected, after 2,500 attempts, there is no faulty shared secret, achieving an accuracy of 100% (leading to an error probability $p_0 = 0$, as denoted in Fig. 1). In the second case, however, the selected private key $S_2 = (0, 1)$ implies the calculation of a dummy isogeny since $e_0 = 0$. Hence, fault injections should lead to a faulty shared secret. Here, we achieved an accuracy of over 92% (denoted as p_1 in Fig. 1). Table 4 shows the achieved results of the applied attacks in our setup. Hence, based on these numbers, we assume an attacker can distinguish real from dummy isogenies with a single injection with high accuracy.

Since in dummy-based constant-time implementations of CSIDH (e.g., Meyer, Campos, and Reith (MCR) [21] or Onuki, Aikawa, Yamazaki, and Takagi (OAYT) [22]), the private key vector $(e_1, \ldots, e_n)$ is sampled from an interval defined by a bound vector $\mathtt{m} = (m_1, m_2, \ldots, m_n)$, the number of fault injections required to obtain the absolute value of a certain e_i strongly depends on the corresponding bound vector. More precisely, since the computation of a given degree ℓ_i occurs deterministically (real-then-dummy), the attacker performs a binary search through the corresponding m_i to identify the computation of the first dummy isogeny. Thus, the number of attacks required to obtain the absolute value of a certain e_i depends only on the corresponding bound m_i.

The achieved key space reductions are due to the fact that an attacker after a certain number of attacks knows the absolute values for the private key vector $(e_1, \ldots, e_n)$. In the case of the OAYT implementation of CSIDH512 (where $-m_i \leqslant e_i \leqslant m_i, m_i = 5$ for $i = 0, \ldots, 73$), our approach leads to a private key space reduction from 2^{256} to 2^{74} in the worst case ($e_i \neq 0$ for $i = 0, \ldots, 73$) and to $2^{67.06}$ in the average case after at least $222 \cdot 4 = 888$ fault injections for a success rate over 99%. The remaining key space can be further reduced by a meet-in-the-middle approach [5] to about $2^{34.5}$ in the average case. For achieving a success rate over 99%, when attacking the MCR implementation (where

$0 \leqslant e_i \leqslant m_i, m_i \in [1, 10]$ for $i = 0, \ldots, 73$), at least $296 \cdot 4 = 1184$ injections are required for full key recovery (cf. Fig. 1) since only positive values are allowed for the private key vector. Considering the running time of the non-optimised implementation of CSIDH512 of about 5 min for a single run in our setup, full key recovery would require about 98 h in the case of the MCR implementation and about 74 h to achieve the mentioned key space reduction in the case of the OAYT version.

Since recent works [6,7] suggests that CSIDH-512 may not reach the post-quantum security as initially considered [5], some works recommend to increase the size of the CSIDH prime p [6,7,31]. However, from a classical perspective, since the classical security only depends on the size of the private key space, the number of prime factors ℓ_i remains unchanged. Thus, apart from the longer running time due to possibly larger prime factors, increasing the quantum security has no further influence on the effectiveness of the presented attack.

6 Countermeasures

In this section we discuss general countermeasures against safe-error attacks and then present concrete countermeasures for SIKE and CSIDH.

In safe-error attacks, a simple check of the final result before transmitting can still leak one bit. This can be easily seen in the attack on SIKE in Sect. 3.2. If the attacker successfully executes an attack, even if the result is checked for correctness, the implementation will leak one bit: either the algorithm fails or it returns an unusable result, or the induced error is overwritten, both of which represent a successful attack. This makes efficient generic countermeasures hard to design, as, for instance, simply repeating a calculation after a fault has been detected can be detected, too: an algorithm that suddenly takes twice as long shows that the attack was successful.

Using infective computation [32], a succesfully induced fault directly, i.e., without the necessity of checking, modifies the output value such that the faulty output does not allow to reveal secret values. In case of safe-error attacks, this is also not a solution, since any faulty output shows that the fault was successful. This is all an attacker needs to know in case of safe-error attacks.

An effective countermeasure consists in redundant computation with consistency check, i.e., calculating the susceptible operations repeatedly and then choose the value to be output by majority vote. However, this is costly, since, assuming that an attacker can realize a fault n times within a single computation of the algorithm, the susceptible operations have to be computed $2 \cdot n + 1$ times. Since second-order faults, i.e., two faults within one computation, are practical [33], this would require at least a fivefold repetition of the susceptible operations.

Another route, which is not in the hands of the implementer, is the selection of hardware the algorithm executes on. Hardware-based detection of fault attacks through, for instance, voltage sensing or intrusion detection, are possible ways of shutting down the execution - independent of the effect of the fault on the computation - before any information could have been leaked [34].

It is important to note that the attacks presented in this paper exploit secret-dependent memory access. Implementations and future optimizations should thus take special care to eliminate any such occurrence and treat them with the same rigour as secret-depending timings. This also extends to "branch-less" versions of algorithms, where, for instance, a pointer is swapped depending on the bit of a secret key; this does not remove the secret dependence of the underlying memory.

The discussion shows that to prevent safe-error attacks, the susceptible functions have to be adjusted, as in [8].

6.1 Securing SIKE

As explained in Sect. 3.1, by using a simultaneous double-and-add algorithm within **xDBLADD** [4], the particular M safe-error attack on SIKE can be prevented.

A possible countermeasure against the key recovery presented in Sect. 3.2 is to add an additional check to the **LADDER3PT** algorithm. The attack relies on skipping the `swap_points` method. Hence, a relatively inexpensive way of detecting an attack is to verify whether the swap actually took place. Thus, in each loop the implementation would save the current points, run the swap operation, and eventually check if the calculated mask had the intended effect.

Although the proposed countermeasure to conditional point swaps from [17] could be adapted to SIKE, the described approach (cf. [17], section VI, paragraph C, point 1) represents no real countermeasure. An attack in the case where no swap takes place (decision bit = 0) does not lead to a false result (wrong point order), while attacking the conditional swap in the case of a swap (decision bit = 1) the order check of the resulting point should fail.

6.2 Securing CSIDH

Since the current CSIDH action algorithms branch on the secret key, it is a prime target for exploitation. One possible way of making attacks more difficult is shown in [19]. Here, LeGrow and Hutchinson show that using a binary decision vector to interleave the different ℓ_i-isogenies, an attacker has to do more than 8x as many attacks to gain the same amount of information.

Another approach is to choose an implementation that is dummy-free. So far however, dummy-free implementations have come at the cost of being twice as slow [18]. Further research might be able to close this performance gap and thereby completely eliminate attacks based on dummy isogenies.

Securing CSIDH against physical attacks is clearly difficult and care has to be taken to not accidentally enable another attack by fixing a specific vunerability. One such occurrence are dummy isogenies, introduced as timing attack countermeasures in [21], which allow an attacker to learn secret information through fault injections. Although in this specific situation using dummy isogenies might be reasonable as timing attacks are in general easier to carry out than fault injections, all implications a countermeasure can have have always to be considered so that implementers can consciously reason about trade-offs.

7 Conclusion

This work shows how safe-error attacks can be applied to recent isogeny-based cryptographic schemes. We presented four different attacks on the SIKE and CSIDH cryptosystems. It is important to note that the resilience of SIKE against the attack described in Sect. 3.1 solely depends on the structure of the actual implementation. As such, any further implementententations need to make sure to not introduce the possibility of this safe-error attack. We have shown how to practically realize two of these attacks and how to achieve full key recovery in a static key context on both SIKE and CSIDH.

We discussed that securing cryptosystems against safe-error attacks is non-trivial. This also partially explains why some of the attacks that we applied to isogeny-based cryptographic schemes have similarly been known in the ECC community for a long time, and yet have not been prevented in current implementations of SIKE and CSIDH. As safe-errors exploit differences of computation and memory access depending on the secret key, a simple check is not sufficient. It is equally important, that countermeasures against certain attacks do not open ways for further safe-error attacks [25]. This can be the case for example when implementing a simple consistency check, which might not trigger on all injections, thus inadvertently leaking data. The same holds true for constant-time implementations, which are designed to thwart timing attacks. The implementations of CSIDH that we attacked in this work are constant-time, but based on dummy isogenies, which enable our attack. CTIDH [35], a recent faster constant-time algorithm for CSIDH, is also vulnerable to safe-error attacks. In this case, the attacks should occur during the dummy operations within the *MatryoshkaIsogeny* (cf. [35], Sect. 5.2.2). Dummy-free implementations, which do also exist, are probably not vulnerable to the attacks presented in this paper; however, they are prone to timing attacks. Future research therefore needs to find a way to secure CSIDH at the same time against timing and safe-error attacks.

Acknowledgments. JK acknowledges funding by the Deutsche Forschungsgemeinschaft (DFG) - SFB 1119 - 236615297, and JK and MM acknowledge funding by the German Federal Ministry of Education and Research (BMBF) under the project QuantumRISC.

References

1. Couveignes, J.M.: Hard homogeneous spaces. IACR Cryptology ePrint Archive, p. 291 (2006). http://eprint.iacr.org/2006/291
2. Rostovtsev, A., Stolbunov, A.: Public-key cryptosystem based on isogenies. IACR Cryptology ePrint Archive, p. 145 (2006). http://eprint.iacr.org/2006/145

3. Feo, L.D., Jao, D., Plût, J.: Towards quantum-resistant cryptosystems from supersingular elliptic curve isogenies. J. Math. Cryptol. **8**(3), 209–247 (2014). https://doi.org/10.1515/jmc-2012-0015
4. Jao, D., et al.: "SIKE," National Institute of Standards and Technology, Technical report (2020). https://csrc.nist.gov/projects/post-quantum-cryptography/round-3-submissions
5. Castryck, W., Lange, T., Martindale, C., Panny, L., Renes, J.: CSIDH: an efficient post-quantum commutative group action. In: Peyrin, T., Galbraith, S. (eds.) ASIACRYPT 2018. LNCS, vol. 11274, pp. 395–427. Springer, Cham (2018). https://doi.org/10.1007/978-3-030-03332-3_15
6. Peikert, C.: He gives C-sieves on the CSIDH. In: Canteaut, A., Ishai, Y. (eds.) EUROCRYPT 2020. LNCS, vol. 12106, pp. 463–492. Springer, Cham (2020). https://doi.org/10.1007/978-3-030-45724-2_16
7. Bonnetain, X., Schrottenloher, A.: Quantum security analysis of CSIDH. In: Canteaut, A., Ishai, Y. (eds.) EUROCRYPT 2020. LNCS, vol. 12106, pp. 493–522. Springer, Cham (2020). https://doi.org/10.1007/978-3-030-45724-2_17
8. Yen, S.-M., Joye, M.: Checking before output may not be enough against fault-based cryptanalysis. IEEE Trans. Comput. **49**(9), 967–970 (2000). https://doi.org/10.1109/12.869328
9. Joye, M., Yen, S.-M.: The Montgomery powering ladder. In: Kaliski, B.S., Koç, K., Paar, C. (eds.) CHES 2002. LNCS, vol. 2523, pp. 291–302. Springer, Heidelberg (2003). https://doi.org/10.1007/3-540-36400-5_22
10. Bettale, L., Montoya, S., Renault, G.: Safe-error analysis of post-quantum cryptography mechanisms - short paper. In: 18th Workshop on Fault Detection and Tolerance in Cryptography, FDTC 2021, Milan, Italy, 17 September 2021, pp. 39–44. IEEE (2021). https://doi.org/10.1109/FDTC53659.2021.00015
11. Costello, C.: B-SIDH: supersingular isogeny Diffie-Hellman using twisted torsion. In: Moriai, S., Wang, H. (eds.) ASIACRYPT 2020. LNCS, vol. 12492, pp. 440–463. Springer, Cham (2020). https://doi.org/10.1007/978-3-030-64834-3_15
12. Koziel, B., Azarderakhsh, R., Jao, D.: Side-channel attacks on quantum-resistant supersingular isogeny Diffie-Hellman. In: Adams, C., Camenisch, J. (eds.) SAC 2017. LNCS, vol. 10719, pp. 64–81. Springer, Cham (2018). https://doi.org/10.1007/978-3-319-72565-9_4
13. Galbraith, S.D., Petit, C., Shani, B., Ti, Y.B.: On the security of supersingular isogeny cryptosystems. In: Cheon, J.H., Takagi, T. (eds.) ASIACRYPT 2016. LNCS, vol. 10031, pp. 63–91. Springer, Heidelberg (2016). https://doi.org/10.1007/978-3-662-53887-6_3
14. Gélin, A., Wesolowski, B.: Loop-abort faults on supersingular isogeny cryptosystems. In: Lange, T., Takagi, T. (eds.) PQCrypto 2017. LNCS, vol. 10346, pp. 93–106. Springer, Cham (2017). https://doi.org/10.1007/978-3-319-59879-6_6
15. Ti, Y.B.: Fault attack on supersingular isogeny cryptosystems. In: Lange, T., Takagi, T. (eds.) PQCrypto 2017. LNCS, vol. 10346, pp. 107–122. Springer, Cham (2017). https://doi.org/10.1007/978-3-319-59879-6_7
16. Zhang, F., et al.: Side-channel analysis and countermeasure design on ARM-based quantum-resistant SIKE. IEEE Trans. Comput. **69**(11), 1681–1693 (2020). https://doi.org/10.1109/TC.2020.3020407
17. Campos, F., Kannwischer, M.J., Meyer, M., Onuki, H., Stöttinger, M.: Trouble at the CSIDH: protecting CSIDH with dummy-operations against fault injection attacks. In: 17th Workshop on Fault Detection and Tolerance in Cryptography, FDTC 2020, Milan, Italy, 13 September 2020, pp. 57–65. IEEE (2020). https://doi.org/10.1109/FDTC51366.2020.00015

18. Cervantes-Vázquez, D., Chenu, M., Chi-Domínguez, J.-J., De Feo, L., Rodríguez-Henríquez, F., Smith, B.: Stronger and faster side-channel protections for CSIDH. In: Schwabe, P., Thériault, N. (eds.) LATINCRYPT 2019. LNCS, vol. 11774, pp. 173–193. Springer, Cham (2019). https://doi.org/10.1007/978-3-030-30530-7_9
19. LeGrow, J.T., Hutchinson, A.: An analysis of fault attacks on CSIDH. IACR Cryptology ePrint Archive, p. 1006 (2020). https://eprint.iacr.org/2020/1006
20. Tasso, É., De Feo, L., El Mrabet, N., Pontié, S.: Resistance of isogeny-based cryptographic implementations to a fault attack. In: Bhasin, S., De Santis, F. (eds.) COSADE 2021. LNCS, vol. 12910, pp. 255–276. Springer, Cham (2021). https://doi.org/10.1007/978-3-030-89915-8_12
21. Meyer, M., Campos, F., Reith, S.: On lions and elligators: an efficient constant-time implementation of CSIDH. In: Ding, J., Steinwandt, R. (eds.) PQCrypto 2019. LNCS, vol. 11505, pp. 307–325. Springer, Cham (2019). https://doi.org/10.1007/978-3-030-25510-7_17
22. Onuki, H., Aikawa, Y., Yamazaki, T., Takagi, T.: (Short Paper) A faster constant-time algorithm of CSIDH keeping two points. In: Attrapadung, N., Yagi, T. (eds.) IWSEC 2019. LNCS, vol. 11689, pp. 23–33. Springer, Cham (2019). https://doi.org/10.1007/978-3-030-26834-3_2
23. Costello, C.: Supersingular isogeny key exchange for beginners. In: Paterson, K.G., Stebila, D. (eds.) SAC 2019. LNCS, vol. 11959, pp. 21–50. Springer, Cham (2020). https://doi.org/10.1007/978-3-030-38471-5_2
24. Faz-Hernández, A., López-Hernández, J.C., Ochoa-Jiménez, E., Rodríguez-Henríquez, F.: A faster software implementation of the supersingular isogeny Diffie-Hellman key exchange protocol. IEEE Trans. Comput. **67**(11), 1622–1636 (2018). https://doi.org/10.1109/TC.2017.2771535
25. Sung-Ming, Y., Kim, S., Lim, S., Moon, S.: A countermeasure against one physical cryptanalysis may benefit another attack. In: Kim, K. (ed.) ICISC 2001. LNCS, vol. 2288, pp. 414–427. Springer, Heidelberg (2002). https://doi.org/10.1007/3-540-45861-1_31
26. Yen, S.-M., Kim, S., Lim, S., Moon, S.-J.: RSA speedup with Chinese remainder theorem immune against hardware fault cryptanalysis. IEEE Trans. Comput. **52**(4), 461–472 (2003). https://doi.org/10.1109/TC.2003.1190587
27. Noack, D., et al.: Industrial use cases and requirements for the deployment of post-quantum cryptography (2020). https://www.quantumrisc.de/results/quantumrisc-wp1-report.pdf
28. Seo, H., Anastasova, M., Jalali, A., Azarderakhsh, R.: Supersingular Isogeny Key Encapsulation (SIKE) round 2 on ARM cortex-M4. IEEE Trans. Comput. **70**(10), 1705–1718 (2021). https://doi.org/10.1109/TC.2020.3023045
29. Kannwischer, M.J., Rijneveld, J., Schwabe, P., Stoffelen, K.: pqm4: testing and benchmarking NIST PQC on ARM cortex-M4. IACR Cryptology ePrint Archive, p. 844 (2019). https://eprint.iacr.org/2019/844
30. Kocher, P., Jaffe, J., Jun, B.: Differential power analysis. In: Wiener, M. (ed.) CRYPTO 1999. LNCS, vol. 1666, pp. 388–397. Springer, Heidelberg (1999). https://doi.org/10.1007/3-540-48405-1_25
31. Chávez-Saab, J., Chi-Domínguez, J., Jaques, S., Rodríguez-Henríquez, F.: The SQALE of CSIDH: square-root vélu quantum-resistant isogeny action with low exponents. IACR Cryptology ePrint Archive, p. 1520 (2020). https://eprint.iacr.org/2020/1520
32. Gierlichs, B., Schmidt, J.-M., Tunstall, M.: Infective computation and dummy rounds: fault protection for block ciphers without check-before-output. In: Hevia,

A., Neven, G. (eds.) LATINCRYPT 2012. LNCS, vol. 7533, pp. 305–321. Springer, Heidelberg (2012). https://doi.org/10.1007/978-3-642-33481-8_17

33. Blömer, J., da Silva, R.G., Günther, P., Krämer, J., Seifert, J.: A practical second-order fault attack against a real-world pairing implementation. In: Tria, A., Choi, D. (eds.) 2014 Workshop on Fault Diagnosis and Tolerance in Cryptography, FDTC 2014, Busan, South Korea, 23 September 2014, pp. 123–136. IEEE Computer Society (2014). https://doi.org/10.1109/FDTC.2014.22
34. Yuce, B., Ghalaty, N.F., Deshpande, C., Patrick, C., Nazhandali, L., Schaumont, P.: FAME: fault-attack aware microprocessor extensions for hardware fault detection and software fault response. In: Proceedings of the Hardware and Architectural Support for Security and Privacy 2016, HASP@ICSA 2016, Seoul, Republic of Korea, 18 June 2016, pp. 8:1–8:8. ACM (2016). https://doi.org/10.1145/2948618.2948626
35. Banegas, G., et al.: CTIDH: faster constant-time CSIDH. IACR Transactions on Cryptographic Hardware and Embedded Systems, vol. 2021, no. 4, pp. 351–387 (2021). https://doi.org/10.46586/tches.v2021.i4.351-387

Hardware Security and Side-Channel Attacks

Network Data Remanence Side Channel Attack on SPREAD, H-SPREAD and Reverse AODV

Pushpraj Naik(✉) and Urbi Chatterjee

Department of Computer Science and Engineering, Indian Institute of Technology Kanpur, Kanpur, India
{pushpraj,urbic}@cse.iitk.ac.in

Abstract. Side Channel Attacks (SCAs) was first introduced by Paul Kocher in 1996 to break the secret key of cryptographic algorithms using the inherent property of the implementation along with the mathematical structure of the cipher. These categories of attacks become more robust as they do not require any mathematical cryptanalysis to retrieve the key. Instead, they exploit the timing measurements, power consumption, leaked electromagnetic radiation of the software/hardware platforms to execute key-dependent operations for the cipher. This, in turn, aids the adversary to gather some additional information about the computation. The overall concept of leaking secrets through side channel has been extended for Wireless Sensor Networks (WSNs) that implements Secret Sharing (SS) Scheme to exchange secrets between two nodes across multiple paths. Now in the idealized network model, it is assumed that for such SS schemes, all the paths between the two communicating nodes are atomic and have the same propagation delay. However, in the real implementation of TCP/IP networks, the shares propagate through every link and switch sequentially. Hence the attacker can probe any number of paths or switches to get the residual shares from previous messages that still exist in the network even when a new message is being sent. This kind of side channel vulnerability is known as Network Data Remanence (NDR) attacks. In this paper, we specifically target two SS schemes named Secure Protocol for Reliable Data Delivery (SPREAD) and Hybrid-Secure Protocol for Reliable Data Delivery (H-SPREAD), and an on-demand routing protocol named Path Hopping Based on Reverse AODV (PHR-AODV) to launch NDR based side channel attacks on the WSNs. We then show two specific categories of NDR attacks; a) *NDR Blind* and b) *NDR Planned* on the schemes mentioned above. We use an in-house C++ library to simulate our proposed attacks, and the experimental results reveal that the impact of *NDR Blind* attacks is negligible for these schemes, whereas the probability of data recovery for *NDR Planned* attacker proportionally increases with the path length.

Keywords: Side channel attack · Network data remanence · Secret sharing scheme · Wireless sensor networks

L. Batina et al. (Eds.): SPACE 2021, LNCS 13162, pp. 129–147, 2022.
https://doi.org/10.1007/978-3-030-95085-9_7

1 Introduction

For more than last two decades, Side Channel Attacks (SCAs) have been rigorously analyzed and successfully launched on hardware and embedded systems to leak the secret key while running the cryptographic algorithms. These channels bring forth crucial state information about the implementation that is not generally available to the classical adversaries. To briefly highlight, implementations of crypto processors often incur variable execution time to process the data-dependent operations due to performance optimization. Using *timing side channel*, an adversary can carefully measure the time required for the secret key operation of the cipher and derive some additional information about the secret key that would help the attacker to launch SCA successfully. In [1], it was shown that the timing information with known ciphertext, the adversary can extract secret exponent of RSA [2] and Diffie-Hellman [3] key exchange. Similarly, in *power side channel* [4], the adversary measures the power consumption of a hardware platform while running the cryptographic algorithms and try to relate it with either the secret key, typically known as Simple Power attacks (SPAs) or the differential of an intermediate state in two consecutive rounds of the cipher depending on the secret key, known as Differential Power Attacks (DPAs) [4]. The attacker can also collect the *electromagnetic radiation* (EM) of an embedded system during the execution of the cipher using an EM probe and optionally with a low-noise amplifier. Then similar to SPAs and DPAs, the secret key can be extracted using the EM side channel traces. Finally, an adversary can manipulate a hardware device using abrupt changes in voltage or clock in order to generate glitches in the circuit. This is otherwise called *fault attacks* and would eventually lead to temporary changes in the intermediate states of the cipher implementation and produce faulty ciphertexts. The pair of correct and faulty ciphertext then can expose the secret key of the cipher using some statistical analysis.

In recent years, the concept of side-channel has not been limited to hardware platforms or even cryptographic algorithms. The very basic idea of leaking side-channel information during an operation can also be easily extended for wireless sensor networks (WSNs), where an extensive collection of low-cost sensor nodes work collectively to carry out some real-time sensing and monitoring tasks within a designated area, such as military sensing and tracking hostile ground [5]. Since the sensor nodes are resource-constrained, it is difficult to deploy the traditional cryptographic algorithms for privacy and security purposes. Hence, several WSN applications and even software-defined networks (SDN) tend to adapt secret sharing (SS) schemes to exchange secrets between two communicating nodes. The SS schemes take advantage of the fact that the sender and the receiver (of the secret) are connected through multiple paths. It divides the secret S into n pieces so that S can be reconstructed from any k shares, but even the complete knowledge of $(k-1)$ shares can not reveal any information about S. It provides robust key construction even when $(n-k)$ shares are lost or dropped, and security breaches expose all but one of the remaining shares. However, the ideal assumption in SS schemes is that *the paths between the sender and the receiver are atomic, and all paths have an identical delay;* in other words, the attacker has only one chance of capturing the packets. Unfortunately, these assumptions are far from reality; in any realistic network, various networking devices such as routers, switches, hubs, bridges, etc., constitute the paths. Every component that is added to the path induces some propagation delay while transferring a network packet, making the idealized assumptions of the SS schemes inaccurate. Due to this reason, the network has residual shares of a secret for more than one-time quanta, thus giving the attacker more than one chance to probe the path and capture the packets. This makes SS schemes vulnerable to a new family of side channel attacks named Network Data Remanence (NDR).

Based on the attack strategy, we can classify the NDR attacker into two categories as follows:

1. *NDR Blind*: This attacker randomly picks a set of nodes out of all the intermediate nodes available between the sender and the receiver and captures the shares. It can also update the chosen nodes with time.
2. *NDR Planned*: Here, the attacker is moderately more intelligent than *NDR Blind* as in the first tick, it selects a set of intermediate nodes which are at a distance one from the sender. On the next tick, it listens to the nodes at a distance of two from the sender to capture the shares it missed during the first tick. The attacker goes one link away from the sender at every tick until all the shares of the first message are delivered to the receiver. The attacker then proceeds to the nodes at a distance one from the sender to capture the shares of the second message.

In [6], the first SS scheme that was shown to be vulnerable to NDR side-channel attack was Multipath Switching Secret Sharing (MSSS) scheme [7]. It was also mentioned in [6], the other SS schemes and routing protocols [5,8–13] can be also vulnerable against NDR. But it was a challenge to select the suitable adversarial model and attack methods that were not mentioned in [6]. This motivated us to investigate the impact of NDR attack on SPREAD, H-SPREAD, and PHR-AODV schemes.

In summary, the major contributions of our work are as follows:

1. We have formed the appropriate adversarial model and attack methodology for the SPREAD scheme and applied NDR Blind and NDR Planned attack on it.
2. Extending the concept of SPREAD, we have successfully shown the NDR attack also in the H-SPARED scheme.
3. Additionally, to show the extensibility of the NDR attack in applications other than the SS schemes, we have shown how to launch the NDR Blind, and NDR Planned attacks on PHR-AODV, which is an on-demand routing protocol.
4. Finally, we have implemented a simulation of NDR attacks using an in-house C++ library. The experimental results reveal that the probability of data recovery for NDR Planned attacker proportionally increases with the path length, hence can be suitably applied to real WSN and SDN scenarios.

Paper Organisation. The rest of the paper is arranged as follows. In Sect. 2 we give the background about the working principle of Secret Sharing (SS) Schemes, MSSS, NDR side channel, NDR Attack on MSSS. In Sect. 3 we give the working principle of SPREAD and H-SPREAD. In Sect. 4 we elaborate how NDR attack is launched in SPREAD and H-SPREAD. In Sect. 5 we describe the working principle of PHR-AODV. In Sect. 6 we describe how NDR Attacks are launched in PHR-AODV. In Sect. 7 we give experimental setup, results and plots corresponding to NDR attack on SPREAD, H-SPREAD, and PHR-AODV. In Sect. 8 we conclude our paper.

2 Background

In this section, we provide the basics of SS Schemes, MSSS, NDR side channel, NDR Attack on MSSS and the working principle of Secure Protocol for Reliable Data Delivery (SPREAD), Hybrid-Secure Protocol for Reliable Data Delivery(H-SPREAD) and Path Hopping Based on Reverse AODV (PHR-AODV).

2.1 Working Principle of Secret Sharing (SS) Scheme

First proposed by Shamir [14] and independently by Blakely [15], the secret sharing scheme is the building block for secure multiparty communication and distributed storage.

To better understand the scheme, we briefly discuss the threshold SS Scheme next [16]. Let K, N be positive integers, such that $K \leq N$. A (K, N)-threshold SS Scheme is a method of sharing a secret T among a finite set P of N participants, in such a way that any K participants can compute the value of T, but no group of $K-1$ participants can do so. The value of T is chosen by a special participant called dealer denoted by D, and it is assumed that $D \notin P$. D gives each participant some partial information called *shares*. The shares are distributed in secrecy, so no one knows what each other's portion is.

We represent Shamir's scheme, that is based on polynomial interpolation constructed over a finite field. Let $P = \{p_i : 1 \leq i \leq N\}$ be the set of N participants, S is the set of *shares* and $\mathcal{K} = GF(q)$, where $q \geq N+1$ i.e. q be a prime number that is greater than the total number of potential shares and the largest possible secret. Let $S = GF(q)$, implying that each share belongs to the field.

Next, D picks distinct non-zero value of $GF(q)$ denoted by $x_i, 1 \leq i \leq N$ in the initialization phase and gives the value x_i to p_i. The values x_i can be made public since these are not the actual shares. Now to send a secret T, D performs the following three steps:

1. First, it independently and randomly chooses $(K-1)$ elements of $GF(q)$ denoted as $a_1, a_2, \ldots, a_{K-1}$.
2. Then it computes $y_i = a(x_i)$ for $1 \leq i \leq N$, where

$$a(x) = T + \sum_{j=1}^{K-1} a_j x^j.$$

3. Finally it distributes the shares y_i to p_i.

Next we discuss how K participants can figure out the secret. Suppose participants $p_1, p_2, \ldots, p_K$ want to figure out T. It is known that $y_i = a(x_i)$ for $1 \le i \le N$ where $a(x)$ is the polynomial chosen by D. $a(x)$ can be expressed in the following way:

$$a(x) = a_0 + a_1 x + \cdots + a_{K-1} x^{K-1},$$

where coefficients $a_0, \ldots, a_{K-1}$ are unknown and $a_0 = T$ is the secret. K linear equations with K unknowns can be obtained by participants. There will be a unique solution if the equations are linearly independent, and a_0, i.e. the secret, will be disclosed.

A simplified version of (K, N)-threshold SS Scheme is (K, K)-threshold scheme, here $N = K$. This scheme work for any set $\mathbf{Z}_m$ with $S = \mathbf{Z}_m$. It is *not* necessary that m is prime and $m \ge N + 1$.

D performs the following steps to send the secret.

1. It independently and randomly chooses $K - 1$ elements of $\mathbf{Z}_m$, let's denote them by $y_1, y_2, \ldots, y_{K-1}$.
2. Then it computes, $y_K = T - \sum_{i=1}^{K-1} y_i \bmod m$.
3. And then it distributes y_i to p_i, where $1 \le i \le K$.

K participants can compute secret T by simply adding their secrets as follows:

$$T = \sum_{i=1}^{K} y_i \bmod m,$$

It may be demonstrated that less than K participants are incapable of discovering the secret. If we assume that the first $(K - 1)$ participants can sum their secrets to reveal the secret, they must get $T - y_i$. However, they do not know the value of y_i. Hence the secret remains hidden.

Next we illustrate the MSSS and applicability of this threshold secret sharing scheme on it.

2.2 Working Principle of MSSS

Secret sharing and multi-path routing are a perfect complement for ensuring secrecy. These systems employ (K, N) SS Schemes to generate message shares and send each share over node-disjoint routes. As long as the opponent may only access $(K - 1)$ routes, secrecy is ensured. Furthermore, as long as K routes supply the shares, these systems are reliable. In schemes like [8] and [5], there are N path accessible between the sender and the receiver. The sender chooses a set of paths to transfer the shares. In systems where a fixed set of routes are utilized, the adversary can deduce the set of paths chosen by the sender by monitoring the network.

Another method for maintaining secrecy is path switching. A random route is selected for each message in the scheme [9]. Because the chosen routes contain the entire message, they are unreliable.

To solve the shortcomings of the previous methods, path switching with multi-path routing and secret sharing are integrated, in which time is split into ticks, senders and receivers can switch among a set of paths, and transmit message shares on these paths in each tick.

MSSS enables the senders to send messages to the receivers with perfect information-theoretic security without using secret keys. It is assumed that the sender and the receiver are connected by N node-disjoint paths, K of which the adversary can observe at any time. To produce K shares for the message, the sender utilizes (K, K) secret sharing. It chooses K paths at random from a total of N paths and sends each share along a different path. The adversary has the ability to monitor K paths of their choosing. Time is divided into ticks, and during each tick, the sender and receiver might switch communication channels.

The adversarial model assumed over here is that the adversary is mobile and can change the paths that they are monitoring in each tick. The adversary's goal is to find all the K paths on which data are being transmitted in each tick. Using the (K, K) secret sharing implies that all the K shares must be captured to reconstruct the message. While the MSSS system provides information-theoretic security against adversaries who have access to a quantum computer, it does so at the expense of increased bandwidth. As a result, when bandwidth optimization is the primary issue, it is not appropriate.

Next we describe the Network Data Remanence side-channel and threat model.

2.3 Network Data Remanence Side-Channel

In this subsection, we introduce the side-channel created by the implementation of MSSS in the real network. We first describe how the data packet propagation in the network causes side-channel information to leak and then proceed with the attacks that actually exploit this information. In the design of MSSS, the network can be abstracted as a set of wires connecting the sender and the receiver over which all packets travel instantaneously. The security analysis of such an SS scheme is based on the above network abstraction. In real network, each path comprises links and switches. Hence the propagation of shares is not atomic; instead, shares travel through each link and switch sequentially following the *store and forward* design. To eavesdrop on a path, the attacker can probe any number of links and switches on a path depending on their capabilities. Probing does not always require physical access; it can be done remotely. In the case of an SDN, probing can be done by installing an appropriate forwarding rule on the chosen switch, and the attacker can receive a copy of any packet that matches the IP addresses of the sender and the receiver.

Since the paths are not atomic and each path has a different delay (the major two assumptions of an ideal network in a secret sharing scheme), the residual share of previous messages still exists in the network when a new message is being sent. This behavior is not specific to SDN-based implementation of MSSS; it can also be seen in real network implementation of MSSS. This is called as *Network Data Remanence* (NDR).

2.4 NDR Attacks on MSSS

Next, we show how MSSS is vulnerable against NDR Blind and NDR Planned attacks. As discussed earlier, to attack MSSS, the NDR adversary leverages the residual shares present in the network or devices such as routers, switches, and hubs, etc. Now, it can be classified into two categories: a) NDR Blind and b) NDR Planned, based on the way the adversary chooses the number of paths to probe for retrieving the secret. These two methodologies are described as follows:

Let N be the total number of paths available between the sender and the receiver. We assume that all the paths have the same length, denoted as L. The sender breaks the message into K shares $K < N$ and selects K random paths to deliver the shares at every tick.

- **NDR Blind:** As mentioned in Sect. 1, NDR Blind adversary picks a set of nodes from all the intermediate nodes available between the sender and the receiver at every tick to collect the shares of the secret. Let us assume that $P_{bln}(m,t)$ denotes the probability of capturing m shares until tick t. We can define $P_{bln}(m,1)$ as follows:

$$P_{bln}(m,1) = \begin{cases} \frac{\binom{K}{m} * \binom{(L-1)N-K}{K-m}}{\binom{(L-1)N}{K}}, & (L = 2 \text{ and } 0 < 2K - N \leq m \leq K) \\ & \text{or } 0 \leq m \leq K \leq \frac{N}{2} \\ 0, & \text{otherwise} \end{cases} \quad (1)$$

Here the term $(L-1)N$ denote the total number of intermediate nodes. We have only one tick to select m shares. NDR Blind attack's goal is to select K nodes out of all the intermediate nodes (denoted by the denominator). The first term in numerator, i.e., $\binom{K}{m}$ selects m nodes out of all the K data-carrying nodes. The second term selects the remaining $(K-m)$ nodes from the rest of the non-data-carrying nodes. Suppose $L = 2$, the probability of data recovery equals $P_{bln}(K,1)$ because the attacker has only one intermediate node (in other words, only one tick) to capture the shares. In the next tick, the shares will be delivered to the receiver. But when $t > 1$, $P_{bln}(m,t)$ can be computed as:

$$P_{bln}(m,t) = \sum_{x=0}^{K} P_{bln}(m-x, t-1) * D_{bln}(m,x) \quad (2)$$

where $D_{bln}(m,x)$ denote the probability of capturing x new shares by the NDR Blind attacker at tick t provided that $m-x$ shares were captured before tick t. The probability of $D_{bln}(m,x)$ is given by:

$$D_{bln}(m,x) = \frac{\binom{K-m+x}{x} * \binom{(L-1)N-K+m-x}{K-x}}{\binom{(L-1)N}{K}} \quad (3)$$

The probability of data recovery by NDR Blind is given by $P_{bln}(K, L-1)$.

- **NDR Planned:** On the other hand, NDR Planned attacker selects the nodes at a distance one from the sender in the first tick and gradually moves away from the sender to capture the missed shares in the previous ticks. Let $P_{pln}(m,t)$ denote the probability that NDR Planned attacker has captured exactly m shares by tick t. We define $P_{pln}(m,1)$ as follows:

$$P_{pln}(m,1) = \begin{cases} \frac{\binom{K}{m}*\binom{N-K}{K-m}}{\binom{N}{K}}, & 0 \leq m \leq K \leq \frac{N}{2} \text{ or} \\ & 0 < 2K - N \leq m \leq K \\ 0, & \text{otherwise} \end{cases} \tag{4}$$

Here NDR Planned attacker's goal is to capture K data-carrying paths out of all the paths available between the sender and the receiver (i.e., N). The first term in numerator selects m data-carrying paths out of K and second term selects remaining $(K-m)$ paths from non-data-carrying paths. For $1 < t < L$, $P_{pln}(m,t)$ can be computed using the following formula,

$$P_{pln}(m,t) = \sum_{x=0}^{f(m)} P_{pln}(m-x,t-1) * \frac{\binom{K-m+x}{x} * \binom{N-K+m-x}{K-x}}{\binom{N}{K}} \tag{5}$$

where

$$f(m) = \begin{cases} min(m-(2K-N),K), & 2K > N \\ min(m,K), & 2K \leq N. \end{cases} \tag{6}$$

The probability of message recovery by NDR Planned attacker is given by $P_{pln}(K, L-1)$.

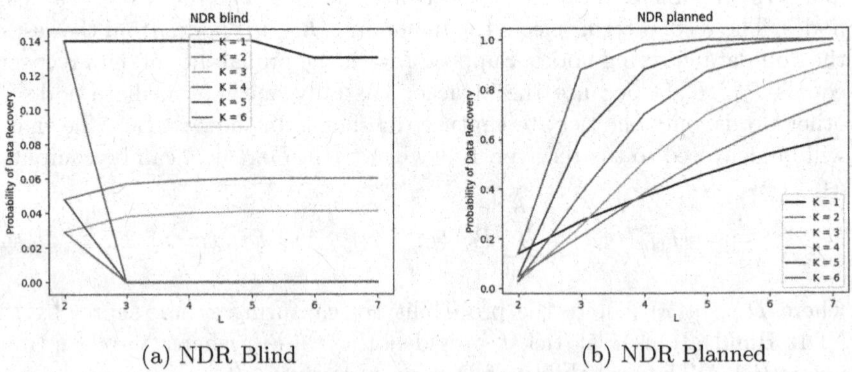

(a) NDR Blind (b) NDR Planned

Fig. 1. NDR Blind and NDR Planned probability of data recovery with seven node disjoint paths

Figure 1 shows the probability of data recovery when $N = 7$. First, we see that for $L = 2$ and $K = 1$ (i.e., SS scheme is not used), NDR Blind and NDR Planned attacker gives similar probability. First, look at NDR Blind. As the path length, L increases and the sender uses the SS scheme (i.e., $K > 1$), the probability of data recovery decreases. Second, NDR Planned attacker performs significantly better than NDR Blind. The probability of data recovery approaches one when the path length is sufficiently large.

3 Working Principle of SPREAD and H-SPREAD

In this section, we describe the working principle of SPREAD and H-SPREAD. *SPREAD* is a mechanism that enhances data confidentiality in a mobile ad-hoc network (MANET). In order to find the optimal path for secure communication, SPREAD utilizes a pathfinding algorithm that is based on a modified version of node disjoint shortest pair algorithm [17]. In addition, modified Dijkstra's algorithm is also used to allow negative links in the graph. Similar to traditional secret sharing schemes, SPREAD also splits the messages into multiple shares and sends them across various channels, requiring the adversary to capture all the shares from all the paths in order to compromise the message. A (K, N)-threshold secret sharing mechanism is utilized to partition the messages in SPREAD. The significant advantage of the N shares is that one cannot learn anything about the secret from any less than K shares, but one may rebuild the secret from any K out of N shares using an effective algorithm.

Next, to make it adaptable to MANET applications, it is further assumed that M node disjoint paths are available from the sender to the receiver in the network. Let $\underline{p} = [p_1, p_2, \ldots, p_M]$ be the vector to represent the path security, where p_i $(i = 1, 2, \ldots, M)$ is the probability that path i is compromised; p_i does not include the likelihood that source or destination nodes are compromised, i.e. source and destination nodes are considered to be trustworthy. We presume that if one node is compromised, all shares passing through that node are also compromised. As a result, if one or more nodes along a path are compromised, the path is considered compromised. Since the paths are node disjoint, the probability of one path being compromised is independent of the probability of other paths being compromised.

To assign the N shares to the M available paths, a share allocation mechanism is used. Let us denote the share allocation as $\underline{n} = [n_1, n_2, \ldots, n_M]$ where n_i denote the number of shares allocated to path i, $n_i \geq 0, \sum_{i=1}^{M} n_i = N$. We say that a message is compromised when K or more shares are compromised. Let us denote the probability of message being compromised in terms of share allocation $\underline{n}$ as $P_{msg}(\underline{n})$. We can now formulate the share allocation problem as constraint optimization problem:

$$minimize\ P_{msg}(\underline{n})$$

given that:

$$\sum_{i=1}^{M} n_i = N \text{ where } n_i \text{ is an integer}, n_i \geq 0$$

The SPREAD scheme can be classified into two categories based on redundancy introduced due to (K, N)-SS schemes. When $K \leq N$, we can define $r = 1 - T/N$ as the redundancy factor. Redundancy is a popular method of increasing reliability. Less redundancy makes a scheme more secure but less resistant to link failure, wireless signal fading, etc. On the other hand, a system with redundancy is always considered robust against the above-mentioned issues. We give the analysis of more secure SPREAD (i.e., with no redundancy) because the less secure SPREAD (i.e., with redundancy) will extrapolate the attack's success rate, so as the probability of data recovery.

Non-redundant SPREAD provides maximum security when at least one share or at most $T - 1$ are allocated to each path i.e.

$$1 \leq n_i \leq T - 1 \quad where\ i = 1, \cdots, M$$

$$and \sum_{i=1}^{M} n_i = N$$

This allocation forces the adversary to compromise all the paths. Given the scenario, the probability that whole secret message is compromised is given by $P_{msg}(\underline{n})$.

$$P_{msg}(\underline{n}) = \prod_{i=1}^{M} p_i$$

We can assume that the different paths have different probabilities of being compromised i.e. $p_1 \leq p_2 \ldots, \leq p_M$. So the security depends on the paths that are selected. The more paths we use to propagate the shares, the lesser the risk and the more secure the message is. As a result, if γ_{P_n} is the needed security level (in terms of message compromise probability), the SPREAD scheme should select the first m paths which satisfy

$$P_{msg}(\underline{n}) = \prod_{i=1}^{M} p_i \leq \gamma_{P_n}$$

to deliver the message.

H-SPREAD, on the other hand, is also reliability and security-enhancing technique but in WSN. It uses distributed N-to-1 multi-path discovery protocol to find multiple paths between each sensor and the base station (BS). The N-to-1 multi-path discovery protocol uses techniques based on simple flooding, which starts at the base station. It also uses two additional mechanisms for discovering multiple paths between the sensors and the BS. The first method is known as branch-aware flooding. It makes use of the flooding approach to identify a specific number of node disjoint routes based on the topology of the network. Multi-path extension of flooding is the second technique that is employed in H-SPREAD. It exchanges the node-disjoint paths found in phase one with the nodes on different branches. This method can enhance the number of routes identified at each node.

The security analysis of H-SPREAD is similar to that of SPREAD. H-SPREAD also considers (K, N)-threshold SS scheme. There are N node disjoint paths available between sensor and BS, M of which are carrying shares of the message. Vector $\underline{q} = [q_1, q_2, \ldots, q_M]$ denotes security characteristics of paths, where q_i is probability that ith path might be compromised. Vector $\underline{n} = [n_1, n_2, \ldots, n_M]$ denote the share allocation, where n_i is the number of packets assigned to ith path, and is positive integer such that $\sum_{i=1}^{M} n_i = N$.

Let $\psi(i)$ denote the indicator function on the i-th path. $\psi(i) = 1$ denotes that ith path is compromised with probability q_i, and $\psi(i) = 0$ denotes that i-th path is not compromised with probability $(1 - q_i)$. In order to compromise the message, the adversary needs to capture at least K shares.

The probability that the message might get compromised (P_C) is given by

$$P_C(\underline{n}) = Pr\{\sum_{i=1}^{M} \psi(i) \cdot n_i \geq K\} \tag{7}$$

where $\psi(i) \cdot n_i$ is the number of shares on the i-th path that are compromised. The calculation of P_C can be derived as follows. Without a loss of generality, we assume that $q_1 \leq q_2 \leq \ldots, \leq q_m$. Let $R(j, i)$ denote probability that minimum of j packets are compromised from first i paths.

$$\begin{aligned} R(j, i) &= q_i R(j - n_i, i - 1) + (1 - q_i) R(j, i - 1) \\ &\quad where\ R(j, i) = 1, \text{ for } j \leq 0, i \geq 0 \\ &\quad and\ R(j, 0) = 0, \text{ for } j > 0 \end{aligned} \tag{8}$$

Now, P_C can be simply calculated as:

$$P_C(\underline{n}) = R(K, M) = q_M R(K - n_M, M - 1) + (1 - q_M) R(K, M - 1) \tag{9}$$

To improve data confidentiality, we can reduce the probability P_C by sending more shares on more secure paths. Next, we show how NDR attacks are launched on the two schemes mentioned above.

4 Proposed NDR Side Channel on SPREAD and H-SPREAD

This section elaborates on how the NDR attack is launched in the SPREAD and H-SPREAD schemes. The main intuition of launching NDR attacks on SPREAD lies in the observation that: Once the sender selects a set of paths to send the shares of the first messages, the sender does not select new paths for the subsequent messages (refer to Sec. VIII of [6]). Instead, the sender uses the same set of paths for the entire communication, which makes the routing *static*.

The adversary can use this information while launching NDR attacks on SPREAD and capture all the remaining packet flows with a probability of 1. Now, it is assumed in [8] that after applying the pathfinding algorithm, the sender has N node disjoint paths. Each path at least has three hops, i.e., $(L \geq 3)$. The sender then uses the (K, N)-SS scheme to transform the message into K shares.

Now, the adversarial model that we assume here is that the attacker can monitor the nodes and capture the shares at switches. The attacker can also redirect a copy of shares flowing through the switches if the nodes/switches are vulnerable due to the weak password or software fault. We further assume that it takes one tick to travel from one hop to another. Since there are $(L-1)$ hops/intermediate nodes, the shares take a maximum of $(L-1)$ ticks to reach the receiver. The adversary also has the same amount of time, i.e., $(L-1)$ ticks to capture the shares of a message. Next, we illustrate how this setup can be exploited by both NDR blind, and NDR planned attackers as mentioned below:

- **NDR Blind:** In the attack setup, the attacker randomly selects K intermediate node in every tick expecting to get i shares (where $i \geq 0$). The adversary's goal is to capture K shares until all the shares of a message are delivered to the receiver. Let $P(m, t)$ be the probability of capturing m shares until t ticks. We can derive the probability $P(m, t)$ using the following recursive formula:

$$P(m,t) = \sum_{i=0}^{K} P(m-i, t-1) * \frac{\binom{K-m+i}{i} * \binom{(L-1)N-K+m-i}{K-i}}{\binom{(L-1)N}{K}} \tag{10}$$

  where $\frac{\binom{K-m+i}{i} * \binom{(L-1)N-K+m-i}{K-i}}{\binom{(L-1)N}{K}}$ factor gives the probability of capturing i $(i \geq 0)$ new shares in one tick, given $(m-i)$ shares are already captured before t ticks and $P(m-i, t-1)$ gives the probability of capturing $(m-i)$ shares in $(t-1)$ ticks.
  Equation 11 which is the base condition, occurs when the attacker has to capture m shares in a single tick.

$$P_{bln}(m,1) = \begin{cases} \frac{\binom{K}{m} * \binom{(L-1)N-K}{K-m}}{\binom{(L-1)N}{K}}, & (L = 2 \text{ and } 0 < 2K - N \leq m \leq K) \\ & \text{or } 0 \leq m \leq K \leq \frac{N}{2} \\ 0, & \text{otherwise} \end{cases} \tag{11}$$

- **NDR Planned** attacker, on the other hand, selects nodes smartly by choosing nodes at a distance of one in the first tick and gradually move away from the sender to capture the remaining shares.
  Let $P(m, t)$ denote the probability of capturing m shares until t ticks. The probability of recovering one message by NDR Planned is given as

$$P(m,t) = \sum_{i=0}^{K} P(m-i, t-1) * \frac{\binom{K-m+i}{i} * \binom{N-K+m-i}{K-i}}{\binom{N}{K}} \tag{12}$$

  Here also, the attacker has $L-1$ ticks to capture the shares. Every tick attacker probes K nodes at an appropriate distance from the sender to capture i $(i \geq 0)$

shares. The second term in Eq. 12 gives the probability of capturing i new shares, given $(m - i)$ shares have already been captured before t ticks. The base condition occurs when the attacker captures m shares at one tick, given as Eq. 13

$$P(m,1) = \begin{cases} \frac{\binom{K}{m} * \binom{N-K}{K-m}}{\binom{N}{K}}, & 0 \leq m \leq K \leq \frac{N}{2} \text{ or} \\ & 0 < 2K - N \leq m \leq K \\ 0, & \text{otherwise} \end{cases} \tag{13}$$

SPREAD and H-SPREAD schemes differ only in their *path-finding algorithm and their field of applicability.* SPREAD uses a modified version of the node disjoint shortest pair algorithm to find multiple paths between the sender and the receiver and is used in MANET. On the other hand, H-SPREAD uses N-to-1 multi-path discovery protocol to find multiple paths used in WSN. The rest of the mechanism used for message secrecy is identical. Therefore, the attack analysis and the results of both SPREAD and H-SPREAD are identical.

Equations 10 and 12 are similar to Eq. 2 and 5 respectively because these equations give the probability of data recovery for one message only. However, as discussed above, the SPREAD scheme does not change paths used for communication. In the worst case, the attacker can take $(L - 1)$ tick to capture the shares of the first message, but after the attacker has captured the shares of the first message, it knows the paths on which the shares of the next message will be delivered therefore if we consider the total M messages that the sender sends to the receiver. The adversary can spare $(L - 1)$ messages to capture shares of the first message with probability $P(K, L-1)$. While other $(M-L+1)$ messages can be captured with probability one. So, the overall percentage of message recovery is given by

$$P_{msg}(K, L, M) = \left(\frac{1 * P(K, L-1) + (M - L + 1) * 1}{M} \right) * 100\% \tag{14}$$

Our attack methodology uses Eq. 10 and 12 to show NDR attack on SPREAD and H-SPREAD. We give the plots related to the attacks in Sect. 7.

5 Working Principle of Path Hopping Based on Reverse AODV for Security (PHR-AODV)

R-AODV (Reverse-AODV) is a routing protocol with simple multi-path searching. The sender builds multiple partial node-disjoint paths from itself to the receiver by broadcasting *Route Request* (RREQ) message and initiating route discovery procedure. Upon receiving the RREQ message by the sender, the receiver also broadcasts its reply *Reverse Request* (R-RREQ). When the sender receives the R-RREQ message, it stores the path as multiple paths between itself and the receiver. In this way, the source node creates partial or complete non-disjoint multi-paths from the source to the destination. Each data packet is sent over a distinct path each time by the sender. This makes it difficult for an eavesdropper to obtain all of the data, and it also makes network penetration more difficult. In [9], the authors have provided an estimation for the total number of active malicious nodes present in the network and the malicious node intrusion rate.

Let us assume N_p is the number of nodes in the routing path, N_{all} is the number of all nodes in the network, M is the number of malicious nodes, S is the number of paths from source to a destination. Now, if we define ρ_m as the probability of active malicious nodes, then it can be represented as below:

$$\rho_m = (N_p * M)/N_{all}$$

whereas, ρ_i gives the malicious node intrusion rate and be represented as follows:

$$\rho_i = \rho_m/S \tag{15}$$

Equation 15 shows that if the number of paths increases, the intrusion rate decreases, given that the total number of malicious nodes is fixed. Keeping the basic system assumption of the R-AODV scheme, we next proceed to our proposed NDR attack on it.

6 Proposed NDR Side Channel Attack on PHR-AODV

As discussed in Sect. 5, the PHR-AODV scheme does not break the message into shares. Instead, it sends one complete message in one path and chooses a different path for the following message. In other words, PHR-AODV uses path hopping but not an SS scheme. We assume that the source node has already initiated the Reverse-AODV procedure, and it has N partially node disjoint paths to the destination. For the security analysis, we assume that L is the path length of each path discovered by the source node. Source node sends each message on a different path than the previous one. We further assume that it takes one tick to cover one hop. Therefore message will reach the destination by $(L - 1)$ ticks.

- **NDR Blind:** As we know, in PHR-AODV at any time, only one path carries data. Let $P(1, t)$ be the probability of capturing one data-carrying path out of all N paths present between the source and the destination by t ticks. It can be given by the recursive equation as below:

$$P(1, t) = P(1, t-1) * (1 - q) + P(0, t-1) * q \tag{16}$$

The attacker's goal is to capture a node carrying the message within t ticks. The attacker has two options in every tick. First is, the node selected is indeed carrying the message; the probability of this event is denoted by q. Then the adversary does not need to find any node, and the term $P(0, t-1)$ equals one. The second option is that the node in consideration at a particular tick is not carrying the message; the probability of this event is $(1 - q)$. In the second option, the adversary's task is reduced to find a node carrying the message in $(t-1)$ ticks, i.e., $P(1, t-1)$. Finally, as NDR Blind randomly selects one node out of all intermediate nodes, the value of q is defined as follows:

$$q = \frac{1}{(L-1) * N}$$

where the boundary condition of Eq. 16 is $P(0, t) = 1$.

- **NDR Planned:** The security analysis of NDR Planned is similar to that of NDR Blind, as, in PHR-AODV, there is no SS scheme used along with path hopping. In NDR Planned, the adversary initially chooses a node at a distance one from the sender and checks if that node is carrying the message or not. If the node is carrying the message with probability q, then the adversary does not need to find any node, i.e., $P(0, t-1)$ equals one, but if the node is not carrying the message with probability $(1-q)$, then the adversary needs to find a node at a distance of two from the sender given by $P(1, t-1)$. The adversary gradually moves away from the sender till the message is delivered to the receiver. Here q is equal to $\frac{1}{N}$ because, at any time, the adversary can consider N nodes.

Overall the analysis shows the attacker that systematically exploits the NDR side-channel given enough path length can reconstruct the message quickly, whereas the attacker who does not use a systematic approach finds it challenging to reconstruct the message.

7 Experimental Setup and Results

In this section we describe the experimental set up to launch the NDR attack and its impact on SPREAD, H-SPREAD and PHR-AODV. We have implemented the attack methodology using an in-house C++ library and executed it in Intel® Core^{TM} i5-1035G1 CPU @ 1.00 GHz × 8 machine. For the experimental setup, we have considered seven node disjoint paths between the sender and the receiver, path lengths in the range of (2–10), and the number of shares in the range of (1–7).

Let us first discuss the impact of NDR attacks on SPREAD and H-SPREAD. In Fig. 2(a), we plot the probability of *data recovery* with respect to *path length* for NDR Blind attackers for both SPREAD and H-SPREAD. For path length of two and without SS scheme (i.e., $K = 1$), the probability of data recovery is 0.14 for the NDR Blind attackers. Moreover, with the increase in path length and applied SS scheme, the probability for the data recovery either remains the same or goes down. As NDR blind attacker chooses the nodes in the path randomly for message recovery, it misses many shares of the secret. Hence the success rate of the attack also gets impacted.

On the other hand, the NDR Planned attacker well utilizes the side channel. The plot in Fig. 2(b) shows that when the *path length* increases for both SPREAD and H-SPREAD, the probability of data recovery also increases. With a sufficiently large path length (i.e., $L \geq 4$), the probability reaches one, i.e., with

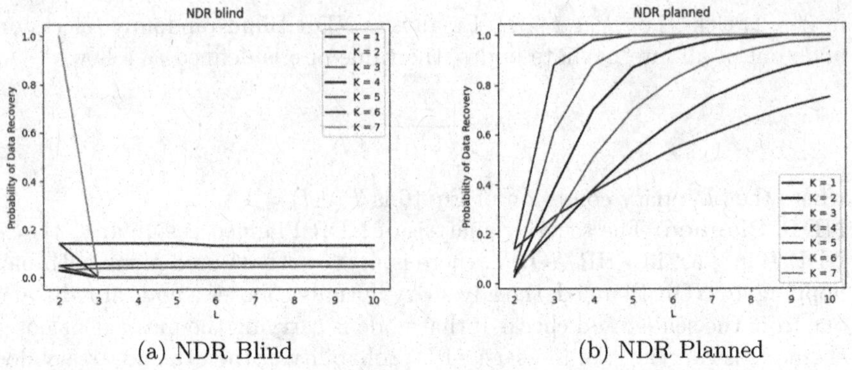

(a) NDR Blind (b) NDR Planned

Fig. 2. Probability of data recovery by NDR Blind and NDR Planned for SPREAD and H-SPREAD with seven node disjoint paths

a 100% success rate, an attacker can retrieve all shares of the secret. Hence we can conclude that in comparison to the NDR Blind attacker, the NDR Planned attacker performs better for both schemes.

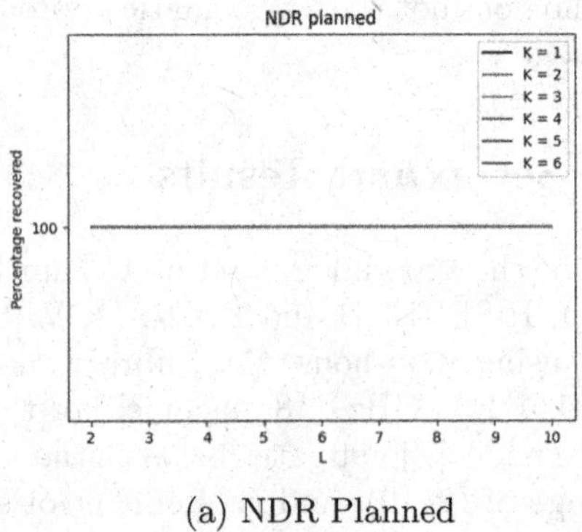

(a) NDR Planned

Fig. 3. NDR Planned attacker showing 100% data recovery percentage in SPREAD and H-SPREAD.

Next, we further elaborate on how NDR Planned attacker can capture all the messages after knowing the paths used by the sender for communication. We assume that the NDR attacker captures at least one share of the first message before all the shares of the first message are delivered to the receiver. Since the sender does not change the paths for communication in both SPREAD and H-SPREAD schemes, the adversary can quickly know the paths even if it manages to capture one share of the first message. We have assumed that path length is L. Hence there are $(L-1)$ intermediate nodes. So, in the worst case, the attacker captures only one share of the first message before it is delivered to the receiver.

When the attacker captures this share, the sender has already sent the rest of the $(L-2)$ message shares into the network. So attacker gets the first message share out of $(L-1)$ message shares, and after that, the attacker can capture all the shares because it knows the paths that the sender and the receiver are using. The same scenario has been shown in Fig. 3. Here irrespective of the *path length* and *number of shares*, the attacker can retrieve all the shares of the message with 100% probability.

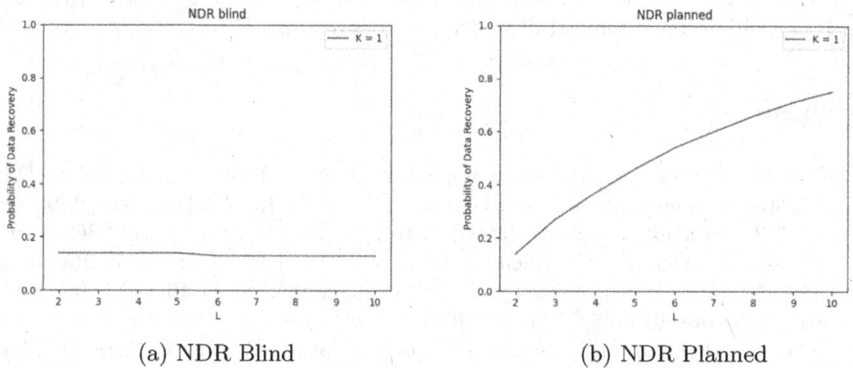

(a) NDR Blind (b) NDR Planned

Fig. 4. Probability of data recovery by NDR Blind and NDR Planned for PHR-AODV with seven node disjoint paths

Next we present the experimental results of applying NDR Blind and NDR Planned attack on PHR-AODV. As discussed in Sect. 5, the scheme chooses different paths to send different messages. But as it does not involve any SS scheme, the whole message from the sender to the receiver follow the same path. Figure 4(a) shows the probability of data recovery by NDR Blind and NDR Planned for the scheme. From the plot given in the figure, it can be seen that it has only one value of K. We have considered the *path length* ranging from 2–10 and NDR Blind, as expected, provides the data recovery probability as 0.14. Therefore, it misses most of the shares of the secret. On the other hand, NDR Planned gives a significantly better probability of data recovery than the NDR Blind attacker as shown in Fig. 4(a). The probability of data recovery increases from 0.14 to 0.75, when *path length* is increased across 2 to 10.

8 Conclusion

NDR side-channel attack has recently come up as a threat in WSN, MANET, and SDN applications as it can impact the data confidentiality of the given platform. In this work, we have considered two SS schemes, SPREAD and H-SPREAD and an On-demand routing protocol, PHR-AODV, and analyzed their vulnerability against NDR attacks. All three use cases are vulnerable against NDR Blind and NDR Planned attacks. Although NDR Blind attacker is less effective, NDR Planned attacker can be a great challenge for the network protocol designers as this attack methodology can recover the secret shares with the success rate of 75% to 100%. Introducing secret sharing schemes as a lightweight alternative to encryption schemes was a good starting point for resource-constraint devices. However, as shown in this work, keeping the ever-increasing size of wired/wireless networks in mind, this attack can be prevalent with the increased number of connecting paths between two communicating devices. Thus, designing a countermeasure against such side-channel attack would be equally challenging and can be considered a potential direction for future work.

References

1. Kocher, P.C.: Timing attacks on implementations of Diffie-Hellman, RSA, DSS, and other systems. In: Koblitz, N. (ed.) CRYPTO 1996. LNCS, vol. 1109, pp. 104–113. Springer, Heidelberg (1996). https://doi.org/10.1007/3-540-68697-5_9
2. Rivest, R.L., Shamir, A., Adleman, L.M.: A method for obtaining digital signatures and public-key cryptosystems (reprint). Commun. ACM **26**(1), 96–99 (1983). https://doi.org/10.1145/357980.358017
3. Diffie, W., Hellman, M.E.: New directions in cryptography. IEEE Trans. Inf. Theory **22**(6), 644–654 (1976). https://doi.org/10.1109/TIT.1976.1055638
4. Kocher, P., Jaffe, J., Jun, B.: Differential power analysis. In: Wiener, M. (ed.) CRYPTO 1999. LNCS, vol. 1666, pp. 388–397. Springer, Heidelberg (1999). https://doi.org/10.1007/3-540-48405-1_25
5. Lou, W., Kwon, Y.: H-SPREAD: a hybrid multipath scheme for secure and reliable data collection in wireless sensor networks. IEEE Trans. Veh. Technol. **55**(4), 1320–1330 (2006). https://doi.org/10.1109/TVT.2006.877707
6. Rashidi, L., et al.: More than a fair share: network data remanence attacks against secret sharing-based schemes. In: 28th Annual Network and Distributed System Security Symposium, NDSS 2021, virtually, 21–25 February 2021. The Internet Society (2021). https://www.ndsssymposium.org/ndss-paper/more-than-a-fair-share-network-data-remanence-attacks-against-secret-sharing-based-schemes/
7. Safavi-Naini, R., Poostindouz, A., Lisý, V.: Path hopping: an MTD strategy for quantum-safe communication. In: Okhravi, H., Ou, X. (eds.) Proceedings of the 2017 Workshop on Moving Target Defense, MTD@CCS 2017, Dallas, TX, USA, 30 October 2017, pp. 111–114. ACM (2017). https://doi.org/10.1145/3140549.3140560
8. Lou, W., Liu, W., Fang, Y.: SPREAD: enhancing data confidentiality in mobile ad hoc networks. In: Proceedings IEEE INFOCOM 2004, The 23rd Annual Joint Conference of the IEEE Computer and Communications Societies, Hong Kong, China, 7–11 March 2004, pp. 2404–2413. IEEE (2004). https://doi.org/10.1109/INFCOM.2004.1354662
9. Talipov, E., Jin, D., Jung, J., Ha, I., Choi, Y.J., Kim, C.: Path hopping based on reverse AODV for security. In: Kim, Y.-T., Takano, M. (eds.) APNOMS 2006. LNCS, vol. 4238, pp. 574–577. Springer, Heidelberg (2006). https://doi.org/10.1007/11876601_69
10. Lou, W., Fang, Y.: A multipath routing approach for secure data delivery. In: 2001 MILCOM Proceedings Communications for Network-Centric Operations: Creating

the Information Force (Cat. No.01CH37277), vol. 2, pp. 1467–1473 (2001). https://doi.org/10.1109/MILCOM.2001.986098
11. Jafarian, J.H., Al-Shaer, E., Duan, Q.: Formal approach for route agility against persistent attackers. In: Crampton, J., Jajodia, S., Mayes, K. (eds.) ESORICS 2013. LNCS, vol. 8134, pp. 237–254. Springer, Heidelberg (2013). https://doi.org/10.1007/978-3-642-40203-6_14
12. Duan, Q., Al-Shaer, E., Jafarian, H.: Efficient random route mutation considering flow and network constraints. In: IEEE Conference on Communications and Network Security, CNS 2013, National Harbor, MD, USA, 14–16 October 2013, pp. 260–268. IEEE (2013). https://doi.org/10.1109/CNS.2013.6682715
13. Zhang, L., et al.: Path hopping based SDN network defense technology. In: 12th International Conference on Natural Computation, Fuzzy Systems and Knowledge Discovery, ICNC-FSKD 2016, Changsha, China, 13–15 August 2016, pp. 2058–2063. IEEE (2016). https://doi.org/10.1109/FSKD.2016.7603498
14. Shamir, A.: How to share a secret. Commun. ACM **22**(11), 612–613 (1979). https://doi.org/10.1145/359168.359176
15. Blakley, G.R.: Safeguarding cryptographic keys. In: International Workshop on Managing Requirements Knowledge, pp. 313–313. IEEE Computer Society (1979)
16. Stinson, D.R.: An explication of secret sharing schemes. Des. Codes Cryptogr. **2**(4), 357–390 (1992). https://doi.org/10.1007/BF00125203
17. Bhandari, R.: Survivable Networks: Algorithms for Diverse Routing. Springer, Heidelberg (1999)

Parasite: Mitigating Physical Side-Channel Attacks Against Neural Networks

Hervé Chabanne[1,2], Jean-Luc Danger[2], Linda Guiga[1,2(✉)], and Ulrich Kühne[2]

[1] Idemia, Courbevoie, France
[2] Télécom Paris, Institut polytechnique de Paris, Paris, France
{herve.chabanne,linda.guiga,jean-luc.danger, ulrich.kuhne}@telecom-paris.fr

Abstract. Neural Networks (NNs) are now the target of various side-channel attacks whose aim is to recover the model's parameters and/or architecture. We focus our work on EM side-channel attacks for parameter extraction. We propose a novel approach to countering such side-channel attacks, based on the method introduced by Chabanne et al. in 2021, where parasitic convolutional models are dynamically applied to the input of the victim model. We validate this new idea in the side-channel field by simulation.

Keywords: Neural networks · Model confidentiality · Physical side-channel attacks · Reverse engineering

1 Introduction

Neural Networks (NNs) now form a major part of our daily lives. Most fields such as the medical or biometric ones rely on them to carry out a great variety of tasks. To achieve high accuracy in NNs, a careful selection of the architecture and a long and computationally intensive training of its parameters is however required. The architecture and parameters therefore constitute intellectual property.

Moreover, once the architecture and/or parameters of a certain NN are known, some attacks such as adversarial ones or membership inference ones are made easier. Unfortunately, several papers describe side-channel attacks (SCAs) aiming at reverse-engineering the architecture and/or the parameters of such NN models [1,3,13,16–18,28,32]. So far, few countermeasures have been proposed.

Electromagnetic (EM) and power SCAs are particularly powerful, as the attacker can extract both the architecture and the weights of the victim model [1,9,15,28]. Since EM-based attacks can, moreover, be carried out from a distance [5,29], we focus our work on EM-based SCAs. Even though SCAs are well-studied topic in the cryptography world, common protections are hard to apply to NNs, as there are too many parameters to protect [8] (most often over one million parameters [27]).

L. Batina et al. (Eds.): SPACE 2021, LNCS 13162, pp. 148–167, 2022.
https://doi.org/10.1007/978-3-030-95085-9_8

In cryptographic applications, exact outputs are required. This is not the case in Machine Learning, where the model's accuracy is the primary gauge. In this paper, we exploit this fact to introduce a novel approach to mitigating reverse-engineering attacks against CNNs. The authors of [7] add parasitic CNNs to protect NNs against equation-based attacks by changing their internal structure. We consider a novel way of thwarting SCAs using similar parasitic CNNs to hide the victim model's input without changing its accuracy. Thus, our contributions are:

- A novel way of countering side-channel based reverse-engineering attacks against CNNs
- An evaluation of our model by simulation, in terms of security and complexity.

1.1 Threat Scenario

We consider an attacker who:

- knows the target model's architecture
- knows the model's input
- aims at recovering the weights of the said model
- can monitor electromagnetic emanations

We mainly discuss EM traces in this paper, as CSI NN [1] manages to recover both the weights and architecture of NN models through them thanks to a probe. But even though CSI NN [1] only considers an EM physical attack using a probe, [5] shows that it is possible to carry out an EM analysis from a distance.

In what follows, we start by presenting related works in Sect. 2 and the necessary background on Neural Networks and SCAs, in Sect. 3. Then we detail our proposal in Sect. 4. We evaluate our protection in Sect. 5. After discussing the possible improvements in Sect. 6, we conclude in Sect. 7.

2 Related Works

NNs have been the target of reverse-engineering attacks of various types: some are based on mathematical aspects and systems of equations [6,19,20,23,26]. Others use Machine Learning to achieve their goal [25]. Several recent papers have also used SCAs to recover models' architectures and parameters [1,3,13,16–18,28,32]. The latter are the ones we focus on in this paper. Few countermeasures exist [11,12,24,30].

[30] proposes a physical protection through an NN accelerator that mitigates side-channel attacks. The authors of [24] claim to introduce the first physical side-channel countermeasure, through hardware masking and hiding. [12] improves on [24], ensuring that only masking is used. Finally, [24] tackles memory access pattern attacks, using common cryptographic tools to randomize memory accesses.

Contrary to [12,24,30], the countermeasure we propose is not a hardware one. Moreover, we only need to focus on the first layer of the NN models at hand to protect it in full, thus drastically limiting the number of parameters to hide.

Similarly to [7], we dynamically add parasitic models to counter mathematical attacks such as [6,23]. Thus, at each run, we select one parasitic model at random among the available pretrained ones, and add it at the entrance of the model to protect. However, more complex SCAs such as those of higher order require a more elaborate protection. The goal of the authors is to change the structure of NNs through CNNs containing *ReLU* activation functions that approximate a noisy identity. One or several such CNNs can be added at different locations in the model to achieve the said goal. Similarly, we consider adding one – or several – small CNNs that approximate a noisy identity function at the entrance of the model to hide the inputs. Thus, even though the method applied is similar, our aim is different. We use the same parasitic models to introduce a novel countermeasure to SCAs against NNs. The novelty of our approach comes from the fact that we do not wish our protected model to return the same results as the original one. While we keep the same accuracy for both models, we allow our protected model's outputs to deviate from the original ones. This is not possible in the cryptographic domain where cryptographic algorithms thwart SCAs, since the latter require exact outputs.

3 Background

3.1 Neural Networks

NNs are algorithms trained to carry out specific tasks. They are comprised of various layers, each containing several neurons. They can be represented as graphs, where the nodes are the neurons and the edges are the weights. The weights are values specifically trained over a dataset to enable the NN to accurately carry out the task at hand.

The layers that compose NNs can be of different types:

- In Fully connected (FC) layers, a neuron is computed as the sum of the previous layer's neurons multiplied by the associated weights. A *bias* is generally added to the value. For input $X = x_{1\leq i\leq m}$, weights $W = w_{1\leq i\leq n, 1\leq j\leq m}$ and biases $\beta = \beta_{1\leq i\leq n}$, this can therefore be written as:

$$O_i = \sum_{k=1}^{m} w_{i,k} \times x_k + \beta_i \implies O = W \cdot X + \beta$$

- In convolutional layers, a convolution is operated between one –or several – filter(s) and the input. For a given filter $F_{1\leq i\leq k, 1\leq j\leq k}$, input $X_{1\leq i\leq n, 1\leq j\leq n}$ and a bias β, the layer then computes:

$$O_{i,j} = \sum_{l=1}^{k} \sum_{h=1}^{k} X_{i+l,j+h} \times F_{l,h} + \beta$$

  If the layer's stride s – or step size – is different from 1, and there are c_{in} input and c_{out} output channels, then the operation becomes:

$$O_{i,j,c_o} = \sum_{c=1}^{c_{in}} \sum_{l=1}^{k} \sum_{h=1}^{k} X_{c,s\cdot i+l,s\cdot j+h} \times F_{c,l,h,c_o} + \beta_{c_o}$$

where β_{c_o} is the bias for the c_o output channel.
- In pooling layers, the output is considered by blocks. Only one significant value is selected per block. The goal of such layers is to reduce the dimensionality of the input. One common pooling layer is the max pooling, where only the maximum among all block values is kept.
- In Batch Normalization layers, the aim is to normalize the layer's input. The output is then computed as follows:

$$o_{i,j} = \gamma \times \frac{x_{i,j} - E}{\sqrt{V + \epsilon}} + \beta$$

where ϵ, γ and β are trained parameters. E and V are the learnt expected value and variance.

Each layer is followed by a nonlinear *activation* function. Two common ones are:

- For $x \in \mathbb{R}$, $ReLU(x) := \max(0, x)$
- For $x \in \mathbb{R}^n$, $Softmax(x) := \frac{e^x}{\sum_{i=0}^{n} e^{x_i}}$

An NN model only comprised of FC layers is called Fully Connected (FC), while a model with mainly convolutional layers is a Convolutional Neural Network (CNN).

Once an NN's parameters are trained, we define its accuracy over a dataset D as the percentage of correct predictions over D. In image processing, most standard NNs reach over 98% accuracy on the MNIST dataset. It is typical for modern NNs to reach over 90% on the CIFAR one [21]. Finally, the most recent models also achieve over 90% accuracy over the large ImageNet dataset [10].

3.2 Correlation Electromagnetic Analysis

Correlation Electromagnetic Analysis (CEMA) is a statistical side-channel attack where the attacker measures the EM emanations of a device during its operation in order to recover a secret [4]. The attack uses a leakage model, a function that makes a prediction on the EM radiation depending on a hypothesis on (parts of) the secret. Typical leakage models for instance for CMOS circuits use the Hamming distance to approximate the activity induced by a state change in the circcuit. In order to find the correct hypothesis – corresponding to the actual value of the secret – Pearson's correlation coefficient is used. In a nutshell, in order to extract the secret, the attacker proceeds as follows:

1. First, she establishes the leakage model.
2. She gathers EM traces for various inputs.
3. For each hypothesis on the secret and each known input, she computes the EM emanations predicted by the leakage model.
4. She computes the Pearson correlation coefficient between the above prediction and the observed (measured) EM consumption. This can be written as:

$$\rho(T, T') = \frac{cov(T, T')}{\sigma_T \cdot \sigma_{T'}}$$

where T and T' are the observed and predicted EM traces, respectively, and σ_T, σ'_T are their standard deviations.

5. Select the hypothesis that leads to the highest Pearson coefficient ρ.

Gathering EM traces can be achieved by placing a probe against the microprocessor of the attacked device [1]. If the traces need to be gathered from a distance, a software-defined radio may be used [5]. New methods relying on machine learning techniques allow the attacker to carry out side-channel analysis from a further distance (15 m) [29]. On unprotected implementations, CEMA attacks are very effective and can be carried out with inexpensive equipment [4].

3.3 Side-Channel Attacks on Neural Networks

Originally, CEMA (and its power equivalent, CPA) has been applied to cryptographic implementations of block ciphers such as AES or DES in order to extract the secret key. While there are no keys to protect within NNs, it has been shown that EM-based side-channel attacks can also be used to recover the parameters of Neural Networks. Let us describe one such attack, CSI NNs [1], on an FC model. The same procedure can also be adapted to CNNs.

The attacker proceeds layer by layer, with no prior knowledge about the model. The first step is to determine the total number of neurons. This only requires a Simple Electromagnetic Analysis (SEMA): the potential attacker observes the EM traces and can directly observe the number of neurons on the traces. Indeed, each neuron's multiplications with its associated weights appear as a block of spikes in the EM traces, as is shown in Fig. 8 of [1].

Then, they target each individual multiplication $w \cdot x$ where w is a weight and x is a neuron, and apply CEMA to determine w. For such an individual multiplication, they first identify the associated EM traces. Then, they consider all possible hypotheses w_h for the weight. They compute the theoretical EM trace – as described in Sect. 3.2 – of that multiplication, given w_h and x. They do so over several inputs, and compare the resulting theoretical and observed traces. The Pearson coefficient (see Sect. 3.2) of the two traces reveals the correct hypothesis.

This, however, does not provide the number of layers of the model. To achieve a full recovery of the model, another guess is required. Multiplications are computed layer by layer. Thus, a given multiplication either belongs to layer l or to layer $l + 1$. For each multiplication, the attacker needs to hypothesize the value for w_h as well as whether w belongs to l or to $l + 1$. Once again, a CEMA then provides the potential attacker with the correct hypothesis for the layer and value of w.

Finally, the activation functions are determined through a time analysis that we will not detail here. As is shown in [28], this step can also be achieved through an EM-based attack.

To summarise, the attacker proceeds as follows:

1. For the first layer, the attacker knows the input $X = \{x_1, ..., x_n\}$. Determine the weights for the connection between the input layer and the first layer.
2. Determine all of the weights as well as the number of neurons in the first layer through the double hypothesis, SEMA and CEMA described previously.
3. Determine the activation function through a time – or EM-based – analysis
4. Move to the next layer and repeat the extraction process (mix of SEMA, CEMA with a double hypothesis and time analysis for the activation function) for each multiplication, until no neuron remains.

As stated in Sect. 1.1, we consider an attacker that already has access to the model's architecture. Thus, the layer guessing step can be skipped here: a mix of SEMA, CEMA and time analysis layer by layer should be enough to carry out the attack.

This is one example of an attack we could mitigate.

4 Adding Parasitic Layers

In the following section, we explain a novel approach to protecting against SCAs that target NN parameters.

4.1 Proposal Overview

Common cryptographic methods to tackle SCAs cannot be applied to protect millions of parameters, as they incur too much overhead [8]. It is therefore necessary to consider a new approach to the problem.

The first observation one can make is that since the attacker in [1] – described in Sect. 3.3 – proceeds layer by layer, protecting the first layer should be enough to protect the entire model. Indeed, the deduced weights from the first layer are used to compute the input to the following layer and proceed with the attack.

A second observation is that the attacker requires the input values to recover the first layer's weights. An intuitive countermeasure to this attack would therefore consist in hiding the said input values.

Third, contrary to common cryptographic problems, NNs' layers do not require exact responses. The output of each layer can be approximated as long as the model's accuracy is not affected.

Those three observations show that hiding the input values should mitigate the attack at hand. Hence, we propose to dynamically apply one or several CNN models approximating the identity to the entrance of the model. Our aim is to make sure the modified model's input is different from the original input, with only a slight drop in the accuracy. The extracted weights a potential attacker would get for the first layer are then only an approximation of the actual weights. Even if those first weights are still close to the original ones, the error propagates to the following layers, amplifying the noise and making the extracted model's accuracy much lower than the original one.

4.2 Proposal Description

Let us now detail our proposal.

As explained in Sect. 4.1, we aim at hiding a model's input values without decreasing its accuracy, by dynamically adding small CNNs approximating a noisy identity function. Our method is designed to limit the access to the correct input, which is required by the attacker of Sect. 3.3.

Adding layers dynamically means that at each run – or after a certain number of runs –, we consider parasitic CNNs with different weights and/or a different architecture. At each run – or after a certain number of runs –, we also select the said parasitic model at random among a set of small pretrained CNN models.

To carry out a CEMA, an attacker requires several traces. If the small CNN we add to the input changes from one run to the other, the attack becomes much harder. As explained in Sect. 3.3, CSI NN [1] enables an attacker to determine the architecture of a victim NN along with its parameters. But because in any case, several traces are required, the randomization in both the weights and architecture should still mitigate the attack.

Thus, our methodology is as follows:

- Train a set S of small CNNs that approximate a noisy identity. For x in the input space I and $s \in S$: $s(x) = x + \mathcal{N}_s(x)$ where $\mathcal{N}_s$ is a Gaussian distribution
- At each run, select $s \in S$. For $x \in I$, run $x' := s(x)$.
- Feed x' to the target model.

Figure 1 shows the location where we add the parasitic CNN $s \in S$, to an FC model with one hidden layer. Here, s is applied to the input x and the result x' is then fed to the model at hand.

Let us analyse the consequences of adding such CNNs at the entrance of the model. Let X be the model's input and X' be the noisy input. Let $x_{i,j} \in X$. To recover the weight w in each multiplication $x_{i,j} \cdot w$, the attacker requires several power or EM traces for that operation. She also needs to know $x_{i,j}$. But the input of the target model is $s(X) = X'$, and the attacker does not have access to X'. Furthermore, given she requires several traces and the parasitic CNN changes from one run to the next, the attack cannot be carried out on the parasitic layers directly, knowing input X. This is why we believe that our protection thwarts first-order physical side-channel attacks such as CSI NN [1] (see Sect. 5 for our results).

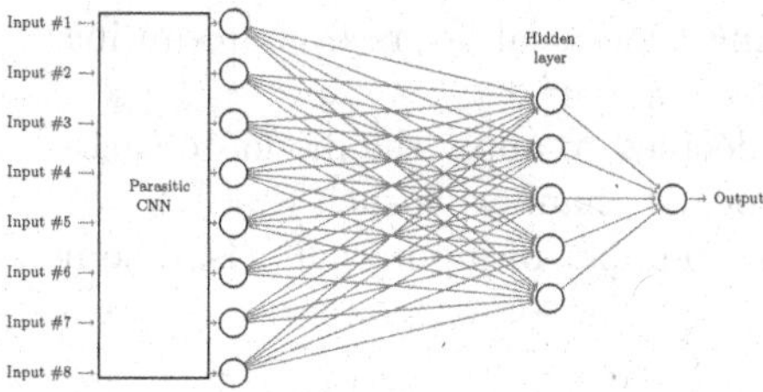

Fig. 1. Fully Connected Neural Network with one hidden layer where a parasitic CNN approximating the identity has been added to approximate the model's input.

4.3 Approximating the Identity Function

To prevent the attack, our goal is to add noise to the input without decreasing the model's accuracy.

One possible way to achieve this is to add CNNs approximating the identity to the entrance of the original model. If we denote M such a CNN model, then M is trained to reach $M(x) = x$. This yields the advantage of making the attack in [1] harder in the extended case where the attacker does not know the architecture.

Since NNs are designed to solve complex tasks, the identity is easily achievable for them. Thus, trying to approximate the identity through a CNN model M leads to practically no difference between the input x and the model's output $M(x)$. This is shown in [33], where the authors manage to approximate the identity function under major constraints.

Because of this, simply adding a CNN approximating the identity does not have any impact on the attack. Indeed, no noise is added to the input, therefore keeping the observed values unchanged to the attacker. Therefore, the parasitic models we add are trained to approximate the identity function to which we add noise. The goal when training a CNN model M then becomes $M(x) = x + \mathcal{N}$, where $\mathcal{N}$ is a given noise. We further detail our proposal in Sect. 4.2.

Let us now compute the complexity of adding such CNN models to the original model. Let us consider a convolutional layer with input shape (n, n, c_{in}), c_{out} output channels and a filter of shape $k \times k \times c_{out}$. Then the output of the layer has shape $(n' = n-k+1, n' = n-k+1, c_{out})$. Let us denote X the input of the layer, O its output and W its weights with shape (k, k, c_{in}, c_{out}). Then, as per Sect. 3.1, we have the following: $O_{i,j,q} = \sum_{c=1}^{c_{in}} \sum_{l=1}^{k} \sum_{h=1}^{k} X_{i+l,j+h,c} \cdot W_{l,h,c,q}$.

This implies that for each neuron, $k \times k \times c_{in}$ multiplications are required. Therefore, each output channel adds $k \times k \times c_{in} \times (n-k+1) \times (n-k+1)$ multiplications. Since we have c_{out} channels, the total number of additional multiplications for one convolutional layer is $c_{out} \times k \times k \times c_{in} \times (n-k+1) \times (n-k+1) = O(n^2)$. Generally, convolutional layers include some zero-padding to preserve the input and output sizes. This increases the necessary multiplications to:

$$M = c_{out} \times k \times k \times c_{in} \times n \times n$$

To conclude, adding l identical layers leads to an increase in the number of multiplications of $l \times k \times k \times n^2 \times c_{in} \times c_{out}$.

In this paper, we decided to apply the model to each channel independently. Thus, the input number of channels is such that $c_{in} = 1$ here, but we multiply the total by the actual number of input channels. The new formula for l layers is then:

$$M = c_{in}^{(1)} \times \left[c_{out}^{(1)} \times k^{(1)} \times k^{(1)} \times n^{(1)^2} + \sum_{i=2}^{l} c_{out}^{(i)} \times k^{(i)} \times k^{(i)} \times n^{(i)^2} \times c_{in}^{(i)}\right]$$

where $c_{in}^{(i)}$ is layer i's number of input channels, $c_{out}^{(i)}$ is layer i's number of output channels, $k^{(i)}$ is layer i's filter size and $n^{(i)}$ is the layer's input size.

The reason why we chose this approach is so that the parasitic CNNs can be adapted to inputs with any number of input channels. Moreover, this way, we can keep a low number of channels in the middle layers without fearing any loss of information.

5 Evaluation

5.1 Simulation

To comfort our idea, we simulate two attacks.

In the first simulation, we consider one fixed parasitic model at the entrance of the target model. The attacker does not know the parasite's architecture or weights, and her aim is to recover the target model's weights. We proceed layer by layer, as in CSI NN [1]. We suppose that the attacker knows all the outputs of intermediary multiplications in the first layer[1].

Let X^1, W^1 and O^1 denote, respectively, the input, the weights and the output of the model's first layer. For simplicity, let us only consider the case where the first layer is a convolutional one. We remind the reader in Sect. 3.1 that: $O_{i,j}^1 = \sum_{l=0}^{k} \sum_{h=0}^{k} X_{i+l,j+h}^1 \cdot W_{l,h}^1$.

Let X'^1 denote the input with added noise. The attacker only knows X'^1 and the values $o_{i,j,l,h}^1 := X_{i+l,j+h}^1 \cdot W_{l,h}^1$. She proceeds as follows:

1. For each output $O_{i,j}^1$, the attacker computes $W_{l,h}'^1 := \frac{o_{i,j,l,h}^1}{X_{i+l,j+h}'^1}$ if $X_{i+l,j+h}'^1 \neq 0$. Otherwise, the attacker finds a nonzero input neuron $X_{i'+l,j'+h}'^1$ to compute $W_{l,h}'^1$ in a similar fashion.
2. Once the first layer's weights are recovered, the attacker computes the second layer's weights, $W_{i,j}^2$. For this, she first computes $X'^2 := \sum_{h=0}^{k} X_{i+l,j+h}'^1 \cdot W_{l,h}'^1$. She takes X'^2 as the input of the second layer and extracts the second layer's weights as in the first step.

[1] This is an unrealistic assumption, but since we aim to demonstrate the effectiveness of our protection, we assume perfect conditions for the attacker. Real CEMA attacks are much harder.

3. The attacker repeats the previous step until all the layers' weights have been recovered.
4. If there is a bias, the attacker simply recovers it through: $\beta = X'^2 - O^1$.

In fact, to make sure we introduce as little noise as possible, we average the obtained weights over 64 inputs.

In a second simulation, we select a different pretrained parasite at each run. The attacker can therefore try to approximate the added layers. However, at each run, the parasitic CNN's weights – and possibly the architecture – change. Since, as mentioned in Sect. 4, the attacker requires several traces to recover the weights, this change of model at each run affects the results. We simulated this by averaging the various extracted weights over 64 inputs. This second simulated attack also proceeds one layer at a time, as follows:

1. Start with the first parasitic layer, and compute the weights as in the first simulation.
2. Repeat the operation over several inputs, and set the layer's weights to the average w_{av} of the extracted values.
3. The next layer's inputs is the output of the first layer with w_{av} as the weights.
4. For each remaining layer in the model at hand (including the parasitic layers), repeat the previous three steps.

Let us also note that in both simulations, we discard the weights that result in a division by 0 – meaning that no nonzero input value among the provided set can be found –, by setting the extracted weights to 0.

5.2 Models Considered

Since we are mostly interested in models that could be used on smartphones and embedded systems in general, we consider two small models: LeNet [31] and MobileNetV2 [27], that we trained on the CIFAR-10 dataset [21]. LeNet is only comprised of two convolutional layers followed by three dense layers. MobileNetV2's more complex architecture is detailed in Table 1.

Finally, the parasitic models we add are based on the ones used in [33], with various layer numbers and in some cases, an additional Batch Normalization layer after each convolutional one. We mainly focus on models with 1 or two convolutional layers, described in Fig. 2.

5.3 Results

The set of possible parasitic CNNs should be tailored to the user's requirements and tolerance: some tasks do not require as high an accuracy as more sensitive ones. In general, we here consider that a couple of percents drop can be acceptable. To select the architectures that can be added to the set of possible architectures, we can determine the accuracy of the protected model depending on the standard deviation of the noise of the parasitic models at hand. Figure 3 shows the impact of parasitic layers with various standard deviations

Table 1. Description of the MobileNetV2 architecture [27]. Each line corresponds to a group of layers, repeated n times. All layers in a given group have c output channels. The first layer of the group has stride s while the others have stride 1. t is the expansion factor: if there are c input channels and c' output channels in a block, there is an intermediary operation with $t \cdot c$ channels.

Input Shape	Operation	Expansion t	Channels c	Repetition n	Stride s
$224^2 \times 3$	Convolution (3×3)	–	32	1	2
$112^2 \times 32$	Bottleneck	1	16	1	1
$112^2 \times 16$	Bottleneck	6	24	2	2
$56^2 \times 24$	Bottleneck	6	32	3	2
$28^2 \times 32$	Bottleneck	6	64	4	2
$14^2 \times 64$	Bottleneck	6	96	3	1
$14^2 \times 96$	Bottleneck	6	160	3	2
$7^2 \times 160$	Bottleneck	6	320	1	1
$7^2 \times 320$	Convolution (1×1)	–	1,280	1	1
$7^2 \times 1,280$	Average Pooling (7×7)	–	–	1	–
$1 \times 1 \times 1,280$	Convolution (1×1)	–	k	–	–

on a MobileNetV2 architecture with a 71.44% accuracy on the CIFAR10 testing set (88.16% on the CIFAR10 training set). We see that the accuracy decreases with the standard deviation, but also depends on the training. In general, the drop in accuracy seems acceptable until around $\sigma = 0.2$.

We carry out the first simulated attack described in Sect. 5.1 on a LeNet architecture trained on the CIFAR10 architecture with a 70.69% accuracy on the testing set. The accuracy of the protected model depends on the parasitic model(s) added.

We also checked that when no parasite was added to the original model, our simulated attack did not result in a drop in the accuracy. We then added a parasitic model described in Sect. 5.2 approximating an identity function to which we added a Gaussian noise with a standard deviation of 0.2. The training and evaluation of the model at hand was performed on CIFAR10 images which have been normalized. Thus, the images with no protection have a mean of 0 and a standard deviation of 1. Thus, the ratio of standard deviations is: $SNR = \frac{1}{0.2} = 5$.

This led to an accuracy of 70.84%, which is very similar to the original model's accuracy. The first simulated attack described in Sect. 5.1 resulted in an extracted model with an accuracy of 12.66%.

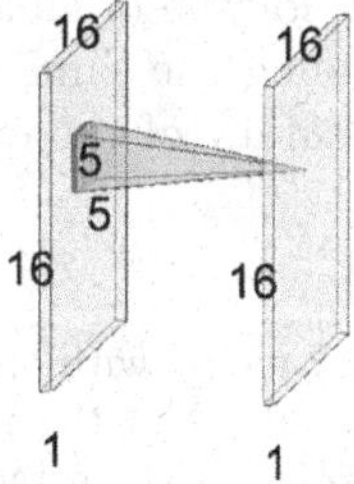

(a) Parasitic model with one convolutional layer. The input and output have shape (1, 16, 16). The filter shape is (5, 5).

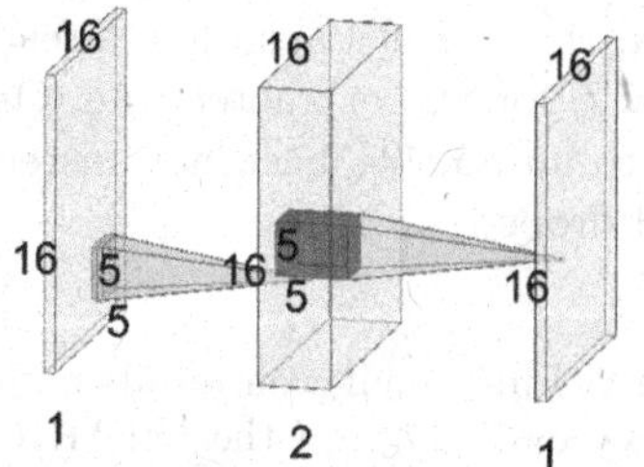

(b) Parasitic model with two convolutional layers. All inputs and output have shape (16, 16), but the middle layer has two channels. The filter shape is (5, 5).

Fig. 2. Parasitic CNN models with one (a) and two (b) convolutional layers. In both cases, the convolution is followed by a *ReLU* activation function and a Batch Normalization layer. (Images generated thanks to [22].)

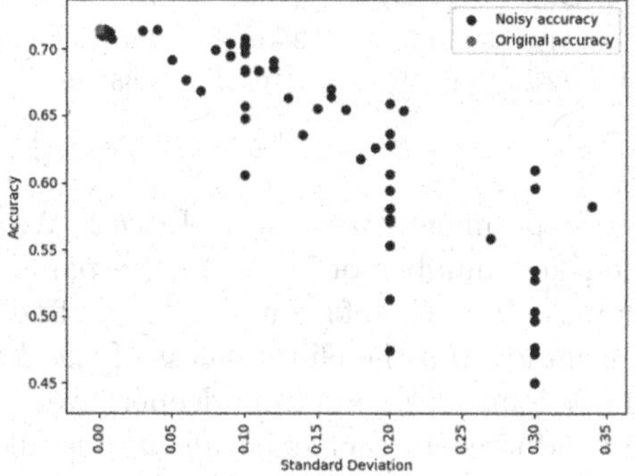

Fig. 3. Accuracy of a protected MobileNetV2 model with relation to the standard deviation of the parasitic models. The parasitic models P are trained to return $P(x) = x + \mathcal{N}_\sigma(x)$ where $\mathcal{N}_\sigma$ is a Gaussian noise with mean 0 and standard deviation σ.

In order to test our protection on a more representative NN model we applied this first simulated attack on the first twelve layers of MobileNetV2 trained on the CIFAR10 dataset. The original accuracy on CIFAR10's testing set is 71.41%. In this case, the preprocessing of the training images only consists in dividing by 255, making sure that the values are in the range [0, 1]. The standard deviation of the three input channels are, respectively: $0.25, 0.24$ and 0.26. We add a parasitic CNN approximating the identity function to which we added a Gaussian noise with a 0.2 standard deviation. We therefore have an SNR approximately equal to 1 for the three input channels. Adding a two-layer parasitic model with a 0.2 standard deviation leads to a 70.23% accuracy for the protected model. We observe that with only the first twelve layers considered for the first simulated attack, the model's accuracy already drops from 71.41% for the original model to 9.97% for the extracted one. On the training set, adding the same parasite leads to an 85.85% accuracy instead of 88.16%. The accuracy of the extracted model drops to 10.40%.

Table 2. First simulation results on a protected MobileNetV2 model with an original accuracy of 71.44% on the CIFAR10 testing set. The noise added in the protected case is a Gaussian distribution with various standard deviations σ. The attacker uses 128 inputs to extract the weights. We log the extracted accuracy, as well as the mean $d = \frac{E[\hat{W}-W]}{||W||_2}$ between extracted weights $\hat{W}$ and original ones W over the first four convolutions.

Number of parasitic layers	Standard deviation σ	New Accuracy	Extracted Accuracy	Mean Conv1	Mean Conv2	Mean Conv3	Mean Conv4
1	0.01	71.41%	71.21%	$1 \cdot 10^{-4}$	$2.1 \cdot 10^{-3}$	$5 \cdot 10^{-3}$	$3.3 \cdot 10^{-3}$
1	0.05	71.24%	69.54%	$3 \cdot 10^{-4}$	$4.9 \cdot 10^{-3}$	$6 \cdot 10^{-3}$	$2.9 \cdot 10^{-3}$
1	0.2	70.23%	18.17%	$3.1 \cdot 10^{-3}$	$1.33 \cdot 10^{-2}$	$1.79 \cdot 10^{-2}$	$1.29 \cdot 10^{-2}$
2	0.01	67.84%	11.74%	$1 \cdot 10^{-4}$	$1.7 \cdot 10^{-3}$	$6.9 \cdot 10^{-3}$	$2.3 \cdot 10^{-3}$
2	0.05	69.51%	10.15%	$3 \cdot 10^{-4}$	$4.8 \cdot 10^{-3}$	$9.5 \cdot 10^{-3}$	$7.6 \cdot 10^{-3}$
2	0.2	66.43%	9.97%	2.7054	$3.65 \cdot 10^{-2}$	$5.26 \cdot 10^{-2}$	$3.1 \cdot 10^{-2}$

We summarize our experimental results in Table 2. We see that increasing the standard deviation and number of layers in the parasite leads to a much lower extraction accuracy. It is therefore necessary to find a balance between a protected model's accuracy and the effectiveness of the defense. We also note that in most cases, the weights extracted from deeper layers are further from the original weights. We conducted further experiments, detailed in Appendices A (Pearson correlation in each layer) and B (distribution of the weight differences).

In Sect. 5.1, we described a second simulated attack, where the attacker also tried to approximate the added parasite, whose weights are modified at each run. On average, considering a set of 30 possible parasitic one-layer models, the model to which we add one parasitic layer at random has an accuracy of 70.61%. In this case, the attack on the aforementioned LeNet model leads to an extracted model with an accuracy of 11.18%.

Similarly, we apply this second simulated attack to the first 13 layers MobileNetV2 with an additional parasite. On average, this also leads to an extracted model with a very low accuracy: 10%.

Thus, in both simulations, the model extracted has a low accuracy, leading to a failed attack. This is the case even though we supposed the attacker had perfect traces and could average them over several inputs. We believe this proves the domino effect the weight extraction induces. Indeed, it does seem that the small error introduced in the first layer because of the small noise added to the inputs is transferred to the following layers and amplified by them.

Let us also compute the number of operations added through the parasitic models. As detailed in Sect. 4.2, one layer adds M multiplications:

$$M = c_{out} \times k \times k \times c_{in} \times n \times n$$

where c_{out}, c_{in} are the layer's number of output and input channels respectively, k is the filter size and (n, n) is the layer's input size. We also explained that here, we feed one channel at a time to the parasitic models.

In Sect. 5.1, we explain that, for the parasites, we consider models with various layer numbers.

The LeNet architecture can be considered small compared to the ones used nowadays in the image processing field. Adding one parasitic layer should therefore already be noticeable in the total number of multiplications. For the one-layer model described in Sect. 5.2, we have: $c_{out} = 1$, $c_{in} = 1$, $k = 5$ and $n = 32$. We also know that the inputs from the CIFAR10 dataset have 3 input channels. Ignoring the much less time consuming Batch Normalization layer, this amounts to: $M = nb\_input\_channels \times c_{in} \times c_{out} \times k \times k \times n \times n = 76,800$.

Thus, the one-layer model adds 76,800 multiplications to the original LeNet model. But for inputs of size $(32, 32, 3)$, LeNet requires 658,000 MAC (Multiply-Accumulate) operations. Thus, one such parasitic layer represents an 11.7% addition in the multiplications. Let us note that the tests carried out on LeNet were mainly for a proof-of-concept, as LeNet is no longer a standard model for image processing.

MobileNetV2 is much larger than LeNet, and we can therefore consider larger parasites. For the two-layer model described in Sect. 5.2, we have, for the first layer: $c_{out}^{(1)} = 2$,$c_{in}^{(1)} = 1$, $k^{(1)} = 5$ and $n^{(1)} = 32$. For the second layer, we have: $c_{out}^{(2)} = 1$,$c_{in}^{(2)} = 2$, $k^{(2)} = 5$ and $n^{(2)} = 32$. Ignoring the much less time consuming Batch Normalization layer, this amounts to : $M_{tot} = nb\_input\_channels \times (c_{out}^{(1)} \cdot k^{(1)} \cdot k^{(1)} \cdot c_{in}^{(1)} \cdot n^{(1)} \cdot n^{(1)} = 307,200$.

MobileNetV2 trained on the CIFAR10 dataset requires 6.32 millions MAC operations. Thus, the additional 307,200 multiplications only represent 4.9% of the original MAC operations.

One could argue that an attacker might proceed the same way as the defender, and also train CNNs on Gaussian noise to improve the extracted weights. However, when training the parasites several times, we noticed that the resulting weights were very different from one training to the next. Thus, the attacker would still need more work to extract the correct weights.

6 Discussions

6.1 Number of Traces to Recover the Weights

Since our protection consists in adding randomness, an attacker who gathers multiple traces should be able to approximate the correct weights. The question that remains is the number of traces necessary for an almost exact extraction.

For the first simulation, 1,024 traces already enable an attacker to increase the extracted model's accuracy from 11.74% with 128 traces to 71.19% for a model protected by a two-layer parasite with $\sigma = 0.01$. But increasing σ still enables a protection: for instance, with $\sigma = 0.05$, the extracted accuracy is 17.12% with only a slight drop in the original accuracy: 69.51% instead of 71.41%. It is therefore paramount to find a balance between the standard deviation, the number of parasitic layers, the drop in the model's accuracy and the effectiveness of the protection.

6.2 Increasing the Entropy of the Added Noise

To maximize the efficiency of the protection, it is important to have a large entropy in terms of the possible parasitic architectures. One way to increase the said entropy is to consider selecting either one or several CNNs at random instead of only one. These can then be applied to several parts of the input, as long as all the neurons are affected by at least one model.

Thanks to the randomness in the parasites' architectures, we believe that our protection would be particularly advantageous when extending it to the black box context – and [1]'s original threat model – where the attacker does not know the model's architecture, and which is enforced by [7]. This makes the parasitic set's entropy even more important.

6.3 Approximating the ReLU Activation Function

It is also possible to hide the activation functions by approximating them in a similar fashion. Further work could study the impact of training small CNNs that approximate the activation functions. Since CNNs contain nonlinear functions, they should be able to approximate any activation function. For instance, we could train a CNN (containing ReLU activation functions) to approximate a noisy ReLU instead of a noisy identity function. Because ReLUs are more complex than the identity, it would also be interesting to study whether ReLU is complex enough that a small CNN cannot very precisely approximate it – therefore introducing noise.

6.4 Improving the CNNs at Hand

Further work could also conduct a study on which architectures could best approximate a noisy identity while minimising the number of added parasitic operations. For instance, one could consider a smaller filter size: 3×3 instead of 5×5. One could also increase the stride of the introduced convolutional layers.

A balance between the number of added operations and a high entropy in the set of parasitic CNNs then needs to be reached. Indeed, the larger the filter and number of layers, the higher the number of operations. But limiting the possible filters and/or the number of layers decreases the set of possible CNNs. Hence, further testing needs to be carried out to determine the right balance.

6.5 Comparing to Common Countermeasures

The authors of CSI NN [1] consider two possible SCA countermeasures to thwart the parameter extraction: masking and shuffling independent operations. In both cases, they mention that these would lead to a large overhead.

According to the authors of [1], masking each neuron at each iteration should prevent the attack. However, masking a multiplication is expensive: it is at least twice the cost of the initial multiplication, as can be seen in Table 1 of [2]. Since masking needs to be applied to all the multiplications, the total number of multiplications in one run would double. In our case, our overhead only consisted in a small percentage of the original number of multiplications.

Shuffling is also an expensive operation. With the Fisher-Yates algorithm, if there are n elements to swap, then the algorithm runs in $O(n)$ but requires generating n truly random numbers [14]. Here, n is the number of operations which can be permuted. In an FC layer with n_x inputs and n_w weights, $n = n_x \times n_w$. In the convolutional case, supposing a stride of 1, an input shape (n_x, n_y, c_{in}) and a weight shape (k, k, c_{out}), there are $n = c_{out} * (n_x - k + 1) * (n_y - k + 1)$ convolutional operations to shuffle. Since random number generation is time consuming [1] and needs to be applied to all layers, we believe that our countermeasure should also generate less overhead.

7 Conclusion

In this paper, we propose a novel approach to protect against EM side-channel attacks targeting NN models, based on the technique introduced in [7]. Even though we mainly discussed CSI NN's [1] EM based attack, we believe that this protection should mitigate any statistical side-channel attack.

For a proof of concept, we simulated two attacks where we supposed the attacker had exact side-channel traces at her disposal. Sect. 5.3 shows that in both cases, the extracted model resulted in a very low accuracy on the CIFAR10 dataset. Moreover, in a realistic setting such as MobileNetV2, the added parasitic layers only incur a small increase in the number of multiplications, as detailed in Sect. 5.3.

Further work could, as stated in Sect. 5, increase the number of simulations and could also evaluate different noise parameters, as mentioned in Sect. 5.

Another possible consideration would be to have a more fine-grained evaluation that does not only take into account the accuracy of the extracted model. For instance, we could examine the distance between the extracted weights and the original ones, and carry out a layer by layer study.

Acknowledgements. We thank the reviewers for their very insightful inputs.

Appendix A Pearson Correlation

To further explain the way our countermeasure works, we measured the Pearson correlation coefficient ρ between the extracted weights and original ones, one output channel at a time. Figure 4 shows the coefficients for each extracted convolutional layer, for a 1-layer protected model with standard deviation $\sigma = 0.01$. Thanks to the plots, we can see that the correlation decreases for deeper layers.

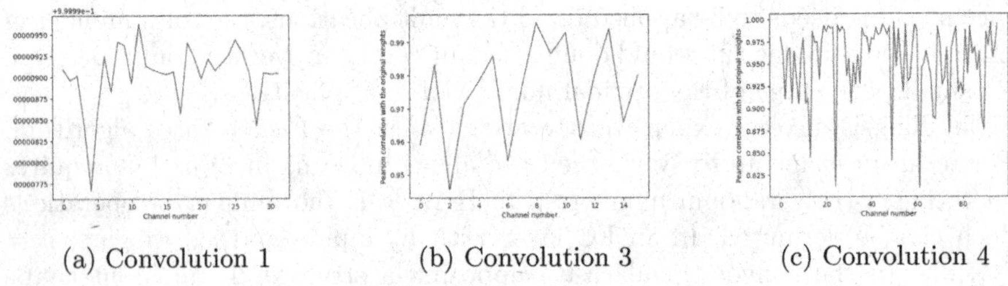

(a) Convolution 1 (b) Convolution 3 (c) Convolution 4

Fig. 4. Pearson correlation coefficient between the extracted weights and the original ones, for the first, third and fourth convolutions in MobileNetV2. Each point in the graph corresponds to the correlation coefficient for one output channel.

Appendix B Weight Distribution

In this appendix, we plot the distribution of weight differences $\delta = \frac{\hat{w}_i - w_i}{||W||_2}$ between the extracted and original weights, for each of the four recovered convolutional layers. We consider a MobileNetV2 model protected by a 1-layer parasite with standard deviation either $\sigma = 0.01$ in Fig. 5e or $\sigma = 0.1$ in Fig. 5j. As we reach deeper layers, recovered weights get further away from the original ones. Moreover, a higher σ leads to fewer correctly recovered weights. This also explains why the extracted accuracy for $\sigma = 0.1$ is so low: 12.9% when the original accuracy was 71.41% and the extracted accuracy for $\sigma = 0.01$ is 71.41%.

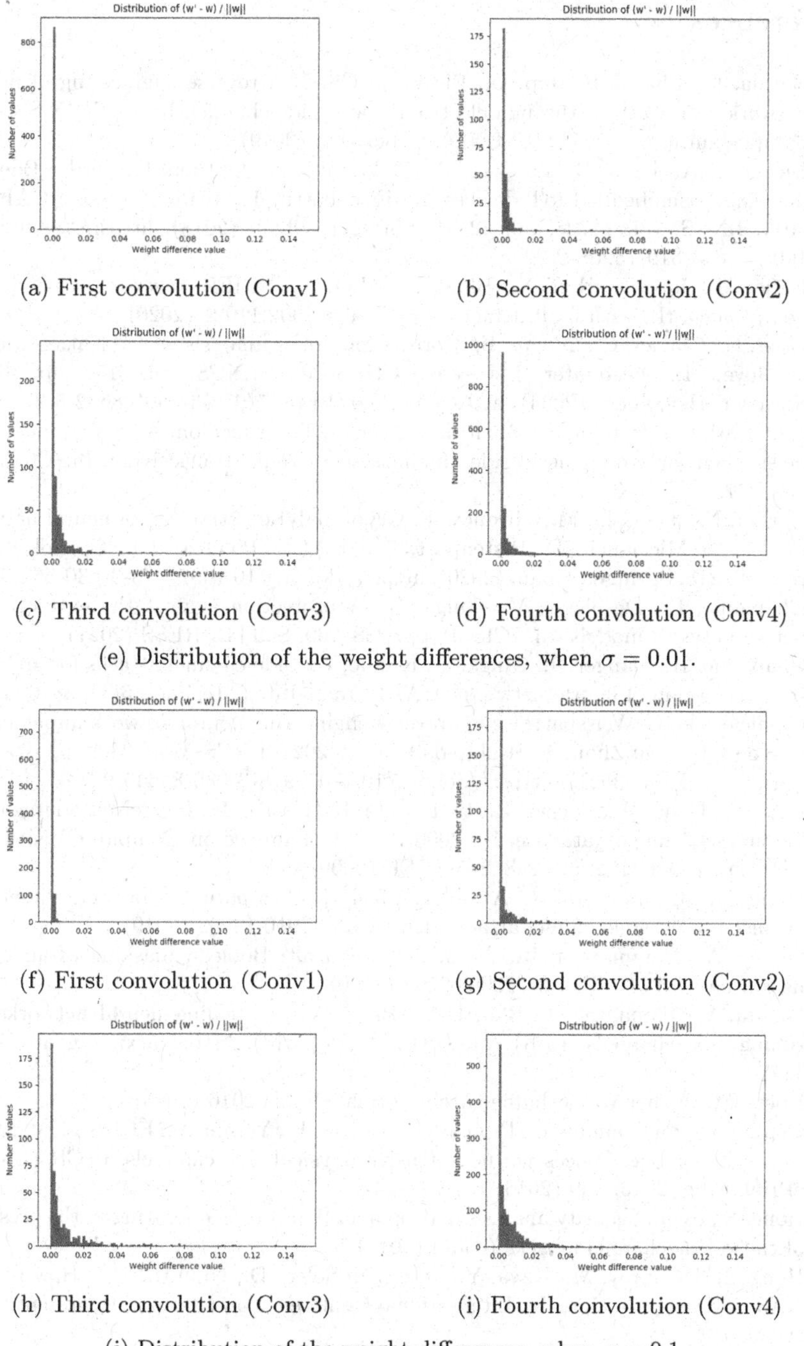

(a) First convolution (Conv1)

(b) Second convolution (Conv2)

(c) Third convolution (Conv3)

(d) Fourth convolution (Conv4)

(e) Distribution of the weight differences, when $\sigma = 0.01$.

(f) First convolution (Conv1)

(g) Second convolution (Conv2)

(h) Third convolution (Conv3)

(i) Fourth convolution (Conv4)

(j) Distribution of the weight differences, when $\sigma = 0.1$.

Fig. 5. Distribution of the weight differences $\frac{\hat{w}_i - w_i}{||W||_2}$ within each of the four MobileNetV2 convolutional layers extracted by the attacker, in the first simulation with 128 traces (see Sect. 5.1) and $\sigma = 0.01$ (e) or $\sigma = 0.1$ (j).

References

1. Batina, L., Bhasin, S., Jap, D., Picek, S.: CSI NN: reverse engineering of neural network architectures through electromagnetic side channel. In: USENIX Security Symposium, pp. 515–532. USENIX Association (2019)
2. Biryukov, A., Dinu, D., Le Corre, Y., Udovenko, A.: Optimal first-order Boolean masking for embedded IoT devices. In: Eisenbarth, T., Teglia, Y. (eds.) CARDIS 2017. LNCS, vol. 10728, pp. 22–41. Springer, Cham (2018). https://doi.org/10.1007/978-3-319-75208-2_2
3. Breier, J., Jap, D., Hou, X., Bhasin, S., Liu, Y.: SNIFF: reverse engineering of neural networks with fault attacks. CoRR abs/2002.11021 (2020)
4. Brier, E., Clavier, C., Olivier, F.: Correlation power analysis with a leakage model. In: Joye, M., Quisquater, J.-J. (eds.) CHES 2004. LNCS, vol. 3156, pp. 16–29. Springer, Heidelberg (2004). https://doi.org/10.1007/978-3-540-28632-5_2
5. Camurati, G., Poeplau, S., Muench, M., Hayes, T., Francillon, A.: Screaming channels: when electromagnetic side channels meet radio transceivers. In: CCS, pp. 163–177. ACM (2018)
6. Carlini, N., Jagielski, M., Mironov, I.: Cryptanalytic extraction of neural network models. In: Micciancio, D., Ristenpart, T. (eds.) CRYPTO 2020. LNCS, vol. 12172, pp. 189–218. Springer, Cham (2020). https://doi.org/10.1007/978-3-030-56877-1_7
7. Chabanne, H., Despiegel, V., Guiga, L.: A protection against the extraction of neural network models. In: ICISSP, pp. 258–269. SCITEPRESS (2021)
8. Chabanne, H., Danger, J., Guiga, L., Kühne, U.: Side channel attacks for architecture extraction of neural networks. CAAI Trans. Intell. Technol. **6**(1), 3–16 (2021)
9. Chmielewski, Ł, Weissbart, L.: On reverse engineering neural network implementation on GPU. In: Zhou, J., et al. (eds.) ACNS 2021. LNCS, vol. 12809, pp. 96–113. Springer, Cham (2021). https://doi.org/10.1007/978-3-030-81645-2_7
10. Deng, J., Dong, W., Socher, R., Li, L.J., Li, K., Fei-Fei, L.: ImageNet: a large-scale hierarchical image database. In: 2009 IEEE Conference on Computer Vision and Pattern Recognition, pp. 248–255. IEEE (2009)
11. Dubey, A., Cammarota, R., Aysu, A.: MaskedNet: a pathway for secure inference against power side-channel attacks. CoRR abs/1910.13063 (2019)
12. Dubey, A., Cammarota, R., Aysu, A.: BomaNet: Boolean masking of an entire neural network. CoRR abs/2006.09532 (2020)
13. Duddu, V., Samanta, D., Rao, D.V., Balas, V.E.: Stealing neural networks via timing side channels. CoRR abs/1812.11720 (2018). http://arxiv.org/abs/1812.11720
14. Eberl, M.: Fisher-yates shuffle. Arch. Formal Proofs 2016 (2016)
15. Genkin, D., Pachmanov, L., Pipman, I., Tromer, E., Yarom, Y.: ECDSA key extraction from mobile devices via nonintrusive physical side channels. IACR Cryptol. ePrint Arch. 2016, 230 (2016)
16. Hong, S., et al.: Security analysis of deep neural networks operating in the presence of cache side-channel attacks (code) (2017)
17. Hong, S., Davinroy, M., Kaya, Y., Dachman-Soled, D., Dumitras, T.: How to 0wn NAS in your spare time. In: International Conference on Learning Representations (2020)
18. Hua, W., Zhang, Z., Suh, G.E.: Reverse engineering convolutional neural networks through side-channel information leaks. In: DAC, pp. 4:1–4:6. ACM (2018)
19. Jagielski, M., Carlini, N., Berthelot, D., Kurakin, A., Papernot, N.: High-fidelity extraction of neural network models. CoRR abs/1909.01838 (2019)

20. Jagielski, M., Carlini, N., Berthelot, D., Kurakin, A., Papernot, N.: High accuracy and high fidelity extraction of neural networks. In: Capkun, S., Roesner, F. (eds.) 29th USENIX Security Symposium, USENIX Security 2020, 12–14 August 2020, pp. 1345–1362. USENIX Association (2020)
21. Krizhevsky, A.: Learning multiple layers of features from tiny images. Technical report (2009)
22. LeNail, A.: NN-SVG: publication-ready neural network architecture schematics. J. Open Source Softw. **4**(33), 747 (2019)
23. Milli, S., Schmidt, L., Dragan, A.D., Hardt, M.: Model reconstruction from model explanations, pp. 1–9. Association for Computing Machinery, New York (2019)
24. Mondal, A., Srivastava, A.: Energy-efficient design of MTJ-based neural networks with stochastic computing. ACM J. Emerg. Technol. Comput. Syst. **16**(1), 7:1–7:27 (2020)
25. Oh, S.J., Schiele, B., Fritz, M.: Towards reverse-engineering black-box neural networks. In: Samek, W., Montavon, G., Vedaldi, A., Hansen, L.K., Müller, K.-R. (eds.) Explainable AI: Interpreting, Explaining and Visualizing Deep Learning. LNCS (LNAI), vol. 11700, pp. 121–144. Springer, Cham (2019). https://doi.org/10.1007/978-3-030-28954-6_7
26. Rolnick, D., Kording, K.P.: Reverse-engineering deep Relu networks. In: Proceedings of the 37th International Conference on Machine Learning, ICML 2020, 13–18 July 2020, Virtual Event. Proceedings of Machine Learning Research, vol. 119, pp. 8178–8187. PMLR (2020)
27. Sandler, M., Howard, A.G., Zhu, M., Zhmoginov, A., Chen, L.: MobileNetV2: inverted residuals and linear bottlenecks. In: 2018 IEEE Conference on Computer Vision and Pattern Recognition, CVPR 2018, Salt Lake City, UT, USA, 18–22 June 2018, pp. 4510–4520. IEEE Computer Society (2018)
28. Takatoi, G., Sugawara, T., Sakiyama, K., Li, Y.: Simple electromagnetic analysis against activation functions of deep neural networks. In: Zhou, J., et al. (eds.) ACNS 2020. LNCS, vol. 12418, pp. 181–197. Springer, Cham (2020). https://doi.org/10.1007/978-3-030-61638-0_11
29. Wang, R., Wang, H., Dubrova, E.: Far field EM side-channel attack on AES using deep learning. In: ASHES@CCS, pp. 35–44. ACM (2020)
30. Wang, X., Hou, R., Zhu, Y., Zhang, J., Meng, D.: NPUFort: a secure architecture of DNN accelerator against model inversion attack. In: CF, pp. 190–196. ACM (2019)
31. Y. LeCun, L. Bottou, Y.B., Haffner, P.: Gradient-based learning applied to document recognition. In: Proceedings of IEEE (1998)
32. Yan, M., Fletcher, C.W., Torrellas, J.: Cache telepathy: leveraging shared resource attacks to learn DNN architectures. In: USENIX Security Symposium, pp. 2003–2020. USENIX Association (2020)
33. Zhang, C., Bengio, S., Hardt, M., Mozer, M.C., Singer, Y.: Identity crisis: memorization and generalization under extreme overparameterization. In: 8th International Conference on Learning Representations, ICLR 2020, Addis Ababa, Ethiopia, 26–30 April 2020. OpenReview.net (2020)

Reinforcement Learning-Based Design of Side-Channel Countermeasures

Jorai Rijsdijk, Lichao Wu(✉), and Guilherme Perin

Delft University of Technology, Delft, The Netherlands

Abstract. Deep learning-based side-channel attacks are capable of breaking targets protected with countermeasures. The constant progress in the last few years makes the attacks more powerful, requiring fewer traces to break a target. Unfortunately, to protect against such attacks, we still rely solely on methods developed to protect against generic attacks. The works considering the protection perspective are few and usually based on the adversarial examples concepts, which are not always easy to translate to real-world hardware implementations.

In this work, we ask whether we can develop combinations of countermeasures that protect against side-channel attacks. We consider several widely adopted hiding countermeasures and use the reinforcement learning paradigm to design specific countermeasures that show resilience against deep learning-based side-channel attacks. Our results show that it is possible to significantly enhance the target resilience to a point where deep learning-based attacks cannot obtain secret information. At the same time, we consider the cost of implementing such countermeasures to balance security and implementation costs. The optimal countermeasure combinations can serve as development guidelines for real-world hardware/software-based protection schemes.

Keywords: Side-channel analysis · Reinforcement learning · Countermeasures · Deep learning

1 Introduction

Deep learning is a very powerful option for profiling side-channel analysis (SCA). In profiling SCA, we assume an adversary with access to a clone device under attack. Using that clone device, the attacker builds a model that is used to attack the target. This scenario maps perfectly to supervised machine learning, where first, a model is trained (profiling phase) and then tested on previously unseen examples (attack phase). While other machine learning approaches also work well in profiling SCA (e.g., random forest or support vector machines), deep learning (deep neural networks) is commonly considered the most powerful direction. This is because deep neural networks 1) do not require feature engineering, which means we can use raw traces, and 2) can break protected implementations, which seems to be much more difficult with simpler machine learning techniques

L. Batina et al. (Eds.): SPACE 2021, LNCS 13162, pp. 168–??, 2022.
https://doi.org/10.1007/978-3-030-95085-9_9

or the template attack [17]. As such, the last few years brought several research works that report excellent attack performance and breaking of targets in a (commonly) few hundred attack traces. What is more, attack improvements are regularly appearing as many new results from the machine learning domain can be straightforwardly applied to improve the side-channel attacks, see, e.g., [16, 19,25]. Simultaneously, there are only sporadic improvements from the defense perspective, and almost no research aimed to protect against deep learning-based SCA.

We consider this an important research direction. If deep learning attacks are the most powerful ones, an intuitive direction should be to design countermeasures against such attacks. Unfortunately, this is also a much more difficult research perspective. We can find several reasons for it:

- As other domains do not consider countermeasures in the same shape as in SCA, it is not straightforward to use the knowledge from other domains.
- While adversarial machine learning is an active research direction and intuitively, adversarial examples are a good defense against deep learning-based SCA, it is far from trivial to envision how such defenses would be implemented in cryptographic hardware. Additionally, adversarial examples commonly work in the amplitude domain but not in the time domain.
- It can be easier to attack than to defend in the context of masking and hiding countermeasures. Validating that an attack is successful is straightforward as it requires assessing how many attack traces are needed to break the implementation. Unfortunately, confirming that a countermeasure works would, in an ideal case, require testing against all possible attacks (which is not possible).

There are only a few works considering countermeasures against machine learning-based SCA to the best of our knowledge. Inci et al. used adversarial learning as a defensive tool to obfuscate and mask side-channel information (concerning micro-architectural attacks) [9]. Picek et al. considered adversarial examples as a defense against power and EM side-channel attacks [18]. While they reported the defense works, how would such a countermeasure be implemented is still unknown. Gu et al. used an adversarial-based countermeasure that inserts noise instructions into code [7]. The authors report that their approach also works against classical side-channel attacks. However, such a countermeasure cannot be implemented at zero cost. From a designer's perspective, knowing the trade-off between the countermeasures' complexity and target's performance (i.e., running speed and power consumption), the countermeasure should be carefully selected and tuned. Finally, Van Ouytsel et al. recently proposed an approach they called cheating labels, which would be misleading labels that the device is trying to make obvious to the classifier [13]. Differing from the previous listed works, this work aimed at showing the limitations analysis in the SCA context, regardless of the specific technique.

In this work, we do not aim at finding a more powerful countermeasure with adversarial examples. Instead, with the help of the reinforcement learning paradigm, our goal is to find an optimal combination of hiding countermeasures that have the lowest performance cost but still ensure that the deep learning-based SCA is difficult to succeed. Although the random search can reach similar goals, we argue that our SCA-optimized reinforcement learning method can consistently evolve the countermeasure selection, thus outputs reliable results. We emphasize that we simulate the countermeasures to assess their influence on a dataset. This is why we concentrate on hiding countermeasures, as it is easier to simulate hiding than masking (and there are also more options, making the selection more challenging). As we attack datasets that are already protected with masking, we consider both countermeasure categories covered. What we provide is an additional layer of resilience besides the masking countermeasure. The optimized combinations of countermeasures work in both amplitude and time domains and could be easily implemented in real-world targets. From a developer's perspective, the optimized combination can become the development guideline of protection mechanisms. In this paper, we conduct experiments with results indicating the time-based countermeasures as the key ingredient of strong resilience against deep learning-based SCA. Our main contributions are:

1. We propose a novel reinforcement learning approach to construct low-cost hiding countermeasure combinations, making deep learning-based SCA difficult to succeed.
2. We motivate and develop custom reward functions for countermeasure selection to increase the SCA resilience.
3. We conduct extensive experimental analysis considering four countermeasures, two datasets, and two leakage models.
4. We report on a number of countermeasures that indicate strong resilience against the selected profiling SCAs.

2 Preliminaries

Calligraphic letters ($\mathcal{X}$) denote sets and the corresponding upper-case letters (X) random variables and random vectors $\mathbf{X}$ over $\mathcal{X}$. The corresponding lower-case letters x and $\mathbf{x}$ denote realizations of X and $\mathbf{X}$, respectively. A dataset $\mathbf{T}$ is a collection of traces (measurements). Each trace $\mathbf{t}_i$ is associated with an input value (plaintext or ciphertext) $\mathbf{d}_i$ and a key candidate $\mathbf{k}_i$. Here, $k \in \mathcal{K}$ and k^* represents the correct key. As common in profiling SCA, we divide the dataset into three parts: a profiling set of N traces, a validation set of V traces, and an attack set of Q traces.

2.1 Deep Learning and Profiling Side-Channel Analysis

We consider the supervised learning task where the goal is to learn a function f that maps an input to the output ($f : \mathcal{X} \rightarrow Y$)) based on examples of input-output pairs. There is a natural mapping between supervised learning and profiling SCA. Supervised learning has two phases: training and test. The training phase corresponds to the SCA profiling phase, and the testing phase corresponds to the side-channel attack phase. The profiling SCA runs under the following setup:

- The goal of the profiling phase is to learn the parameters of the profiling model minimizing the empirical risk represented by a loss function on a profiling set of size N.
- The goal of the attack phase is to make predictions about the classes $y(x_1, k^*), \ldots, y(x_Q, k^*)$, where k^* represents the secret (unknown) key on the device under the attack.

Probabilistic deep learning algorithms output a matrix that denotes the probability that a certain measurement should be classified into a specific class. Thus, the result is a matrix P with dimensions equal to $Q \times c$, where c denotes the number of output labels (classes). The probability $S(k)$ for any key candidate k is the maximum log-likelihood distinguisher:

$$S(k) = \sum_{i=1}^{Q} \log(\mathbf{p}_{i,v}). \tag{1}$$

The value $\mathbf{p}_{i,v}$ represents the probability that a specific class v is predicted. The class v is obtained from the key and input through a cryptographic function and a leakage model.

From the matrix P, it is straightforward to obtain the accuracy of the model f. Still, in SCA, an adversary is not interested in predicting the classes in the attack phase but in obtaining the secret key k^*. Thus, to estimate the difficulty of breaking the target, it is common to use metrics like guessing entropy (GE) [21].

Given Q traces in the attack phase, an attack outputs a key guessing vector $\mathbf{g} = [g_1, g_2, \ldots, g_{|\mathcal{K}|}]$ in decreasing order of probability (g_1 is the most likely key candidate and $g_{|\mathcal{K}|}$ the least likely key candidate). Guessing entropy represents the average position of k^* in $\mathbf{g}$.

2.2 Side-Channel Countermeasures

It is common to protect the implementation with countermeasures. Countermeasures aim to break the statistical link between intermediate values and traces (e.g., power consumption or EM emanation). There are two main categories of countermeasures for SCA: masking and hiding. In many cases, they will be both implemented in increase the security level of the product.

In masking, a random mask is generated to conceal every intermediate value. More precisely, random masks are used to remove the correlation between the measurements and the secret data. In general, there are two types of masking: Boolean masking and arithmetic masking.

On the other hand, the goal of hiding is to make measurements looking random or constant. Hiding decreases the signal-to-noise ratio (SNR) only. Hiding can happen in the amplitude (e.g., adding noise) and time (e.g., desynchronization, random delay interrupts, jitter) dimensions. In our work, we simulate only hiding countermeasures as masking is always active.

2.3 Datasets and Leakage Models

The two datasets we use are versions of the ASCAD database [2]. Both datasets contain the measurements from an 8-bit AVR microcontroller running a masked AES-128 implementation. We attack the first masked key byte (key byte three). The datasets are available at https://github.com/ANSSI-FR/ASCAD. The first dataset version has a fixed key (thus, the key is the same in the profiling and attack set). This dataset consists of 50 000 traces for profiling and 10 000 for the attack. From 50 000 traces in the profiling set, we use 45 000 traces for profiling and 5 000 for validation. Each trace has 700 features (preselected window). The second version has random keys, with 200 000 traces for profiling and 100 000 for the attack. We use 5 000 traces from the attack set for validation (note that the attack set has a fixed but a different key from the profiling set). Each trace has 1 400 features (preselected window).

We consider two leakage models:

- The Hamming weight (HW) leakage model - the attacker assumes the leakage proportional to the sensitive variable's Hamming weight. Considering the AES cipher with 8-bit S-boxes, this leakage model has nine classes for a single key byte (values from 0 to 8).
- The Identity (ID) leakage model - the attacker considers the leakage in the form of an intermediate value of the cipher. Considering the AES cipher with 8-bit S-boxes, this leakage model results in 256 classes for a single key byte (values from 0 to 255).

2.4 Reinforcement Learning

Reinforcement learning (RL) aims to teach an agent how to perform a task by letting the agent experiment and experience the environment. There are two main categories of reinforcement learning algorithms: policy-based algorithms and value-based algorithms. Policy-based algorithms directly try to find this optimal policy. Value-based algorithms, however, try to approximate or find the value function that assigns state-action pairs a reward value. Most reinforcement learning algorithms are centered around estimating value functions, but this is not a strict requirement for reinforcement learning. For example, methods such as genetic algorithms or simulated annealing can all be used for reinforcement learning without ever estimating value functions [22]. In this research, we only focus on Q-Learning, belonging to the value estimation category.

Reinforcement learning has fundamental differences compared with supervised and unsupervised machine learning, commonly adopted by the SCA community. Supervised machine learning learns from a set of examples (input-output pairs) labeled with the correct answers. A benefit of reinforcement learning over supervised machine learning is that the reward signal can be constructed without prior knowledge of the correct course of action, which is especially useful if such a dataset does not exist or is infeasible to obtain. In unsupervised machine learning, the algorithm attempts to find some (hidden) structure within a dataset, while reinforcement learning aims to teach an agent how to perform a task through rewards and experiments [22].

Q-Learning. Q-Learning was introduced in 1989 by Chris Watkins [23] with an aim not only to learn from the outcome of a set of state-action transitions but from each of them individually. Q-learning is a value-based algorithm that tries to estimate $q_*(s, a)$, the reward of taking action a in the state s under the optimal policy, by iteratively updating its stored q-value estimations using Eq. (2). The simplest form of Q-learning stores these q-value estimations as a simple lookup table and initializes them with some chosen value or method. This form of Q-learning is also called Tabular Q-learning.

Equation (2) is used to incorporate the obtained reward into the saved reward for the current state R_t. S_t and A_t are the state and action at time t, and $Q(S_t, A_t)$ is the current expected reward for taking action A_t in state S_t. α and γ are the q-learning rate and discount factor, which are hyperparameters of the Q-learning algorithm. The q-learning rate determines how quickly new information is learned, while the discount factor determines how much value to assign to short-term versus long-term rewards. R_{t+1} is the currently observed reward for having taken action A_t in state S_t. $max_a Q(S_{t+1}, a)$ is the maximum of the expected reward of all the actions a that can be taken in state S_{t+1}.

$$Q(S_t, A_t) \leftarrow Q(S_t, A_t) + \alpha \left[R_{t+1} + \gamma \max_a Q(S_{t+1}, a) - Q(S_t, A_t) \right]. \quad (2)$$

3 Related Works

We divide related works into two directions: improving deep learning-based SCA and improving the defenses against such attacks. In the first direction, from 2016 and the first paper using convolutional neural networks [11], there are continuous improvements in the attack performance. Commonly, such works investigate (note this is only a small selection of the papers):

- **the importance of hyperparameters and designing top-performing neural networks**. Benadjila et al. made an empirical evaluation of different CNN hyperparameters for the ASCAD dataset [2]. Perin and Picek explored the various optimizer choices for deep learning-based SCA [15]. Zaid et al. proposed a methodology to select hyperparameters related to the size of layers in CNNs [29]. To the best of our knowledge, this is the first methodology to build CNNs for SCA. Wouters et al. [24] improved upon the work from Zaid et al. [29] and showed it is possible to reach similar attack performance with significantly smaller neural network architectures. Wu et al. used Bayesian optimization to find optimal hyperparameters for multilayer perceptron and convolutional neural network architectures [25]. Rijsdijk et al. used reinforcement learning to design CNNs that exhibit strong attack performance and have a small number of trainable parameters [20]. Our reinforcement learning setup is inspired by the one presented here, especially the reward function part[1] To improve the attack performance, some authors also proposed custom elements for neural networks for SCA. For instance, Zaid et al. [28], and Zhang et al. [30] introduced new loss functions that improve the attack performance.

- **well-known techniques from the machine learning domain to improve the performance of deep learning-based attacks**. Cagli et al. showed how CNNs could defeat jitter countermeasure, and they used data augmentation to improve the attack process [3]. Kim et al. constructed VGG-like architecture that performs well over several datasets, and they use regularization in the form of noise added to the input [10]. Perin et al. showed how ensembles could improve the attack performance even when single models are only moderately successful [14]. Wu et al. used the denoising autoencoder to remove the countermeasures from measurements to improve the attack performance [26]. Perin et al. considered the pruning technique and the lottery ticket hypothesis to make small neural networks reach top attack performance [16].
- **explainability and interpretability of results**. Hettwer et al. investigated how to select points of interest for deep learning by using three deep neural network attribution methods [8]. Masure et al. used gradient visualization to discover where the sensitive information leaks [12].

On the other hand, the domain of countermeasures' design against machine learning-based SCA is much less explored[2]. Indeed, to the best of our knowledge, there are only a few works considering this perspective as briefly discussed in Sect. 1. At the same time, it is unclear how such countermeasures would be implemented or the implementation cost.

4 the RL-Based Countermeasure Selection Framework

4.1 General Setup

We propose a Tabular Q-Learning algorithm based on MetaQNN that can select countermeasures, including their parameters, to simulate their effectiveness on an existing dataset against an arbitrary neural network. To evaluate the effectiveness of the countermeasures, we use guessing entropy. There are several aspects to consider if using MetaQNN:

1. We need to develop an appropriate reward function that considers particularities of the SCA domain. Thus, considering only machine learning metrics would not suffice.
2. MetaQNN uses a fixed α (learning rate) for Q-Learning while using a learning rate schedule where α decreases either linearly or polynomially are the normal practice [6].

[1] The authors mention they conducted a large number of experiments to find a reward function that works well for different datasets and leakage models, so we decided to use the same reward function.

[2] Many works consider the development of SCA countermeasures, but not specifically against deep learning approaches.

3. One of the shortcomings of MetaQNN is that it requires significant computational power and time to explore the search space properly. As we consider several different countermeasures with its hyperparameters, this results in a very large search space.

We model the selection of the right countermeasures and their parameters as a Markov Decision Process (MDP). Specifically, each state has a transition towards an accepting state with the currently selected countermeasures. Each countermeasure can only be applied once per Q-Learning iteration, so the resulting set of chosen countermeasures can be empty (no countermeasure being added) or contain up to four different countermeasures in any order.[3] One may consider that with the larger number of countermeasures being added to the traces, the more difficult the secret information to be retrieved by the side-channel attacks. However, one should note that the implementation of the countermeasure is not without any cost. Indeed, some software-based countermeasures add overhead in the execution efficiency (i.e., dummy executions), while others add overhead in total power consumption (i.e., dedicated noise engine).

To select optimal countermeasure combinations with a limited burden on the device, a cost function that can approximate the implementation costs should balance the strength of the countermeasure implementation and the security of the device. Thus, such a function is also a perfect candidate as a reward function to guide the Q-learning process. While we try to base the costs on real-world implications of adding each of the countermeasures in a chosen configuration, translating the total cost back to a real-world metric is nontrivial. Therefore, we design a cost function associated with each countermeasure, where the value depends on the chosen countermeasure's configuration. The total cost of the countermeasure set, c_{total}, is defined as:

$$c_{total} = \sum_{i=1}^{|C|} c_i. \tag{3}$$

Here, C represents the set of applied countermeasures, and c_i is the cost of the individual countermeasure defined differently for each countermeasure. Based on the values chosen by Wu et al. [26] for the ASCAD fixed key dataset, we set the total cost budget c_{max} to five, but it can be easily adjusted for other implementations. c_{max} set the upper limit of the applied countermeasure so that the selected countermeasure is in a reasonable range and avoid the algorithm to 'cheat' by adding all possible countermeasures with the strongest settings. Only countermeasure configurations within the remaining budget are selectable by the Q-Learning agent. If the countermeasures successfully defeat the attack (GE does not reach 0 within the configured number of attack traces), any leftover budget is used as a component of the reward function. By evaluating the reward function, we can find the best budget-effective countermeasure combinations,

[3] The countermeasures set is an ordered set based on the order that the RL agent selected them. Since the countermeasures are applied in this order, sets with the same countermeasures but a different ordering are treated as disjoint.

together with their settings, to protect the device from the SCA with the lowest budget.

We evaluated four countermeasures: desynchronization, uniform noise, clock jitter, and random delay interrupt (RDI), and applied them to the original dataset. The performance of each countermeasure against deep learning-based SCA can be found in [26]. The countermeasures are all applied a-posteriori to the chosen dataset in our experiments. Note that the implementations of the countermeasure are based on the countermeasure designs from Wu *et al.* [26]. Already that work showed that a combination of countermeasures makes the attack more difficult to succeed.

Some of these countermeasures generate traces of varying length. To make them all of the same length, the traces shorter than the original are padded with zeroes, while any longer traces are truncated back to the original length. The detailed implementation and design of each countermeasure's cost function are discussed in the following sections. We emphasize that the following definitions of the countermeasure cost are customized for the selected attack datasets. They can be easily tuned and adjusted to other implementations based on the actual design specifications.

Desynchronization We draw a number uniformly between 0 and the chosen maximum desynchronization for each trace in the dataset and shift the trace by that number of features. In terms of the cost for desynchronization, Wu *et al.* showed that a maximum desynchronization of 50 greatly increases the attack's difficulty. This leads us to set the desynchronization level (*desync_level*) ranges from 5 to 50 in a step of 5 (thus, not allowing the desynchronization value so large that it will be trivial to defeat the deep learning attack). The cost calculation for desynchronization is defined in Eq. (4). Note that the maximum c_{desync} is five, which matches the c_{max} we defined as the total cost of countermeasures (which is why c_{desync} needs to be divided by ten).

$$c_{desync} = \frac{desync\_level}{10}. \tag{4}$$

Uniform Noise. Several sources, such as the transistor, data buses, the transmission line to the record devices such as oscilloscopes, or even the work environment, introduce noise to the amplitude domain. Adding uniform noise amounts to adding a uniformly distributed random value to each feature. To make sure the addition of the noise causes a similar effect on different datasets, we set the maximum *noise_level* based on the dataset variation defined by Eq. (5):

$$max\_noise\_level = \frac{\sqrt{Var(T)}}{2}. \tag{5}$$

Here, T denotes the measured leakage traces. Then, max_noise_level is multiplied with a $noise\_factor$ parameter, ranging from 0.1 to 1.0 with steps of 0.1, to control the actual noise level introduced to the traces. Since the $noise\_factor$

is the only adjustable parameter, we define the cost of the uniform noise in Eq. (6) to make sure that the maximum c_{noise} equals to c_{max}.

$$c_{noise} = noise\_factor \times 5. \tag{6}$$

Clock Jitter. One way of implementing clock jitters is by introducing the instability in the clock [3]. While desynchronization introduces randomness globally in the time domain, the introduction of clock jitters increases each sampling point's randomness, thus increasing the alignment difficulties. When applying the clock jitter countermeasure to the ASCAD dataset, Wu *et al.* chose eight as the jitter level, but none of the attacks managed to retrieve the key in 10 000 traces. Thus, we decide to tune the jitter level (*jitter_level*) with a maximum of eight. The corresponding cost function is defined in Eq. 7. In the following experiments, we set the *jitter_level* ranging from 2 to 8 in a step of 2. Again, maximum c_{jitter} value matches the c_{max} value we defined before.

$$c_{jitter} = jitter\_level \times 1.6. \tag{7}$$

Random Delay Interrupts (RDIs) Similar to clock jitter, RDIs introduce local desynchronization in the traces. We implement RDIs based on the floating mean method [5]. More specifically, we add RDI for each feature in each trace with a configurable probability. If an RDI occurs for a trace feature, we select the delay length based on the A and B parameters, where A is the maximum length of the delay and B is a number $\leqslant A$. Since RDIs in practice are implemented using instructions such as *nop*, we do not simply flatten the simulated power consumption but introduce peaks with a configurable amplitude. Since the RDI countermeasure has many adjustable parameters, it will, by far, have the most MDP paths dedicated to it, meaning that during random exploration, it is far more likely to select it as a countermeasure. To offset this, we reduce the number of configurable parameters by fixing the amplitude for RDIs based on the *max_noise_level* defined in Eq. 5 for each dataset. Furthermore, we add 1 to the cost of any random delay interrupt countermeasure, as shown in Eq. 8, defining the cost function for RDIs.

$$c_{rdi} = 1 + \frac{3 \times probability \times (A + B)}{2}, \tag{8}$$

where A ranges from 1 to 10, B ranges from 0 to 9, and *probability* ranges from 0.1 to 1 in a step of 1. We emphasize that we made sure the selected B value is never larger than A.

When looking at the parameters Wu *et al.* [26] used for random delay interrupts applied on the ASCAD fixed key dataset, $A = 5$, $B = 3$ and $probability = 0.5$, none of the chosen attack methods show any signs of converging on the correct key guess, even after 10 000 traces. With our chosen c_{rdi}, this configuration cost equals seven, which we consider appropriate.

We emphasize that we selected the ranges for each countermeasure based on the related works, while the cost of such countermeasures is adjusted based on the maximum allowed budget. While these values are indeed arbitrary, they can be easily adjusted for any real-world setting. We do not give to each countermeasure the same cost, but normalize it so that the highest value for each countermeasure represents a setting that is difficult to break and consumes the whole cost budget.

4.2 Reward Functions

To allow MetaQNN to be used for the countermeasure selection, we use a relatively complex reward function. This reward function incorporates the guessing entropy and is composed of four metrics: 1) t': the percentage of traces required to get the GE to 0 out of the fixed maximum attack set size; 2) GE'_{10}: the GE value using 10% of the attack traces; 3) GE'_{50}: the GE value using 50% of the attack traces and 4) c': the percentage of countermeasures budget left over out of the fixed maximum budget parameter. The formal definitions of the first three metrics are expressed in Eqs. (9), (10), (11), and (12). We note this is the same reward function as used in [20].

$$t' = \frac{t_{max} - min(t_{max}, \overline{Q}_{tGE})}{t_{max}}. \tag{9}$$

$$GE'_{10} = \frac{128 - min(GE_{10}, 128)}{128}. \tag{10}$$

$$GE'_{50} = \frac{128 - min(GE_{50}, 128)}{128}. \tag{11}$$

$$c' = \frac{c_{max} - c_{total}}{c_{max}}. \tag{12}$$

The first three metrics of the reward function are derived from the GE metric, aiming to reward neural network architectures based on their attack performance using the configured number of attack traces.[4] Since we reward countermeasure sets that manage to reduce the SCA performance, we incorporate the inverse of these metrics into our reward functions, as these metrics are appropriate in a similar setting [20]. Combining these three metrics allows us to assess the countermeasure set performance, even if the neural network model does not retrieve the secret key within the maximum number of attack traces. We incorporate these metrics inversely into our reward function by subtracting their value from their maximum value. Combined, the sum of the maximum values from which we subtract (multiplied by their weight in the reward function) equals 2.5, as

[4] Note that the misleading GE behavior as discussed in [27] may happen during the experiments. Although one could reverse the ranking provided by an attack to obtain the correct key, we argue it is not possible in reality as an attacker would always assume the correct key being the one with the lowest GE (most likely guess).

shown in Eq. (13). The weight of each metric is determined based on a large number of experiments.

In terms of the fourth metric c', recall C is the set of countermeasures chosen by the agent, and c_{total} equals five. We only apply this reward when the key retrieval is unsuccessful in t_{max} traces, as we do not want to reward small countermeasure sets for their size if they do not adequately decrease the attack performance. Combining these four metrics, we define the reward function as in Eq. (13), which gives us a total reward between 0 and 1. To better reward the countermeasure set performance, making the SCA neural networks require more traces for a successful break, a smaller weight is set on GE'_{50}.

$$R = \frac{1}{3} \times \begin{cases} 2.5 - t' - GE'_{10} - 0.5 \times GE'_{50}, & \text{if } t_{GE=0} < t_{max} \\ 2.5 - GE'_{10} - 0.5 \times GE'_{50} + 0.5 \times c', & \text{otherwise} \end{cases} \tag{13}$$

We multiply the entire set of metrics by $\frac{1}{3}$ to normalize our reward function between 0 and 1. While this reward function does look complicated, it is derived based on the results from [20] and our experimental tuning lasting several weeks. Still, we do not claim the presented reward function is optimal, but it gives good results. Further improvements are always possible, especially from the budget perspective or the cost of a specific countermeasure.

5 Experimental Results

To assess the performance of the selected set of countermeasures for each dataset and leakage model, we perform experiments with different CNN models (as those are reported to reach top results in SCA, see, e.g. [10,29]). Those models are tuned for each dataset and leakage model combination without considering hiding countermeasures that we simulate. One could consider this not to be fair as those architectures do not necessarily work well with countermeasures. Still, there are two reasons to follow this approach as we 1) do not know a priori the best set of countermeasures and we do not want to optimize both architectures and countermeasures at the same time, and 2) evaluate against state-of-the-art architectures that are not tuned against any of those countermeasures to allow a fair assessment of all architectures.

Specifically, we use reinforcement learning to select the model's hyperparameter [20]. We execute the search algorithm for every dataset and leakage model combination and select the top-performing models over 2 500 iterations. To assess the performance of the Q-Learning agent, we compare the average rewards per ε. For instance, a ε of 1.0 means the network was generated completely randomly, while an ε of 0.1 means that the network was generated while choosing random actions 10% of the time. For the test setup, we use an NVIDIA GTX 1080 Ti graphics processing unit (GPU) with 11 Gigabytes of GPU memory and 3 584 GPU cores. All of the experiments are implemented with the TensorFlow [1] computing framework and Keras deep learning framework [4].

The details about the specific architectures can be found in Table 1. Note that Rijsdijk *et al.* implemented two reward functions: one that only considers the attack performance, and the other that also considers the network size (small reward function) [20]. We consider both reward functions aligned with that paper, leading to two models used for testing; the one denoted with RS is the model optimized with the small reward function. For all models, we use $he\_uniform$ and $selu$ as kernel initializer and activation function.

Table 1. CNN architectures used in the experiments [20].

Test models	Convolution (filter_number, size)	Pooling (size, stride)	Fully-connected layer
$ASCAD_{HW}$	Conv(16, 100)	avg(25, 25)	15+4+4
$ASCAD_{HW\_RS}$	Conv(2, 25)	avg(4, 4)	15+10+4
$ASCAD_{ID}$	Conv(128, 25)	avg(25, 25)	20+15
$ASCAD_{ID\_RS}$	Conv(2+2+8, 75+3+2)	avg(25+4+2, 25+4+2)	10+4+2
$ASCAD\_R_{HW}$	Conv(4, 50)	avg(25, 25)	30+30+30
$ASCAD\_R_{HW\_RS}$	Conv(8, 3)	avg(25, 25)	30+30+20
$ASCAD\_R_{ID}$	Conv(128, 3)	avg(75, 75)	30+2
$ASCAD\_R_{ID\_RS}$	Conv(4, 1)	avg(100, 75)	30+10+2

5.1 ASCAD Fixed Key Dataset

Figure 1 shows the scatter plot results for the HW and ID leakage models for both the regular and RS CNN. The vertical red line indicates the highest Q-learning reward for the countermeasure set, which could not prevent the CNN from retrieving the key within the configured 2 000 attack traces. Notably, a sharp line can be found on the right side of the Q-Learning reward plots, which is solely due to the c' component of the reward function. Although the selected CNNs can retrieve the secret key when no countermeasures were applied ($c' = 0$) for all experiments with both HW and ID leakage models, as soon as any countermeasure is applied, the attack becomes unsuccessful with 2 000 attack traces. Indeed, we observe that only very few countermeasures seem inefficient in defeating the deep learning attacks from the result plots.

For the experiments presented, the top countermeasures for ASCAD using different profiling models are listed in Table 2. Notably, the best countermeasure set in terms of performance and cost for this CNN consists of desynchronization with a level equal to ten, which could be caused by the lack of sufficient convolution layers (only one) in countering such a countermeasure. The rest of the top 20 countermeasure sets include or solely consist of random delay interrupts. This observation is also applied to other profiling models and ID leakage models. The amplitude for RDI is fixed for each dataset, as explained in Sect. 4.1. In terms of the parameters of RDIs, B stays zero for all three profiling models, indicating that A solely determines the length of RDIs. Indeed, B varies the mean of the number of added RDIs and enhances the difficulties in learning from the data. However, a larger B value would also increase the countermeasure cost, which is against the reward function's principle. From Table 2, we can observe both low values of A and *probability* being applied to the RDIs countermeasure, indicating the success of our framework in finding countermeasure with high performance and low cost.

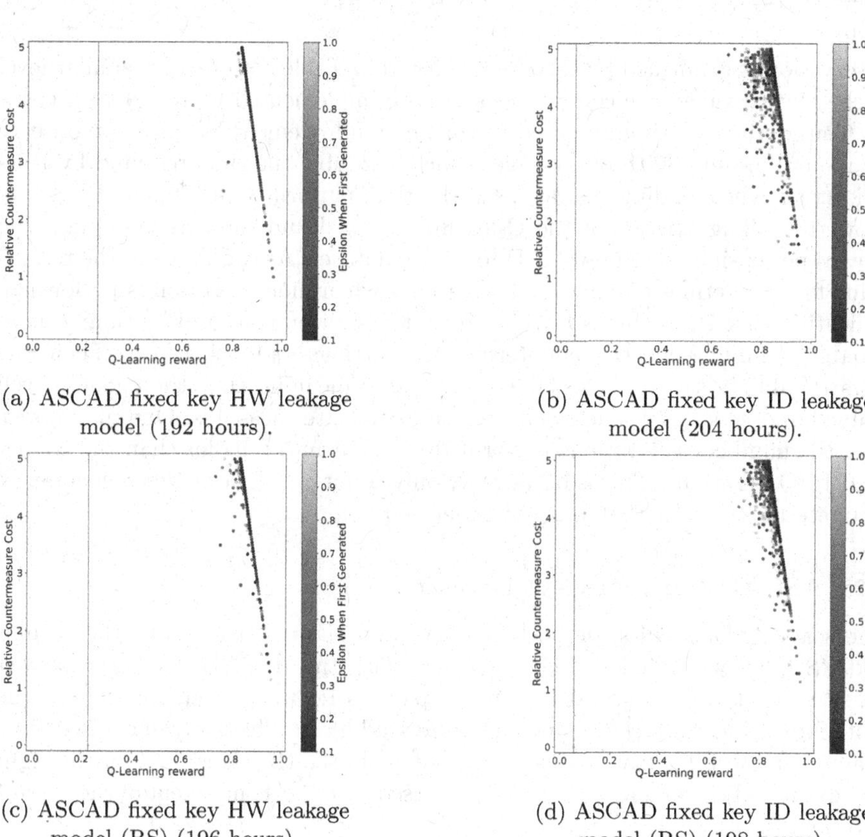

(a) ASCAD fixed key HW leakage model (192 hours).

(b) ASCAD fixed key ID leakage model (204 hours).

(c) ASCAD fixed key HW leakage model (RS) (196 hours).

(d) ASCAD fixed key ID leakage model (RS) (198 hours).

Fig. 1. An overview of the countermeasure cost, reward, and the ε value a countermeasure combination set was first generated for the ASCAD with fixed key dataset experiments. The red lines indicate the countermeasure set with the highest reward for that GE reached 0 within 2 000 traces. (Color figure online)

Next, we compare the general performance of the countermeasure sets between CNNs designed for the HW and ID leakage model. We observe that the ID model appears to be at least a little better at handling countermeasures. Specifically, for the ID leakage model CNNs, the countermeasures' Q-Learning reward variance is higher, indicating that the ID model CNNs can better handle countermeasures, making the countermeasure selection more important. This

Table 2. Best performing countermeasures for the ASCAD fixed key dataset.

Model	Reward	Countermeasures	c'
$ASCAD_{HW}$	0.967	Desync(desync_level = 10)	1.00
$ASCAD_{HW\_RS}$	0.962	RDI(A = 1, B = 0, probability = 0.10, amplitude = 12.88)	1.15
$ASCAD_{ID}$	0.957	RDI(A = 2, B = 0, probability = 0.10, amplitude = 12.88)	1.30
$ASCAD_{ID\_RS}$	0.962	RDI(A = 1, B = 0, probability = 0.10, amplitude = 12.88)	1.15

observation is confirmed by the c' value listed in Table 2: to reach a similar level of the reward value, the countermeasures are implemented with a greater cost.

Considering the time required to run the reinforcement learning, we observe we require around 200 h on average, which is double the time required by Rijsdijk et al. when finding neural networks that perform well [20]. In Fig. 2, we show the rolling average of the Q-learning reward and the average Q-learning reward per epsilon for the ASCAD fixed key dataset. As can be seen, the reward value for countermeasure gradually increases when more iteration is performed, indicating that the agent is learning from the environment and becoming more capable of finding effective countermeasure settings with a low cost. Then, the reward value is saturated when ε reaches 0.1, meaning that the agent is well trained and constantly finds well-performing countermeasures. One may notice that the number of iterations performed is significantly higher than the configured 1 700 iterations. This is because we only count an iteration when generating a countermeasure set that was not generated before.

5.2 ASCAD Random Keys Dataset

The scatter plot results for both the HW and ID model for both the regular and RS CNN are listed in Fig. 3. Aligned with the ASCAD fixed key dataset observation, the vertical red line in the plots is far away from the dots in the plot, indicating that the countermeasure's addition effectively increases side-channel attack difficulty. Furthermore, we again see the sharp line on the right side of the Q-Learning reward, which is caused by the c' component of the reward function.

Compared with the ASCAD results for both leakage models (Fig. 1), we see a greater variation of the individual countermeasure implementations: even with the same countermeasure cost, a different combination of countermeasures and their corresponding setting may lead to unpredictable reward values. Fortunately, we see this tendency with the RL-based countermeasure selection scheme and can better select the countermeasures' implementation with a limited budget. Finally, we observe that the later leakage model is more effective in defeating the countermeasure when comparing the HW and ID leakage models. In other words, to protect the essential execution that leaks the ID information, more effort may be required to implement countermeasures. The top-performing countermeasures for different profiling models are listed in Table 3. From the results, RDIs again become the most effective one among all of the considered countermeasures. The RDI amplitude is fixed at 16.95 for this dataset, as explained in Sect. 4.1.

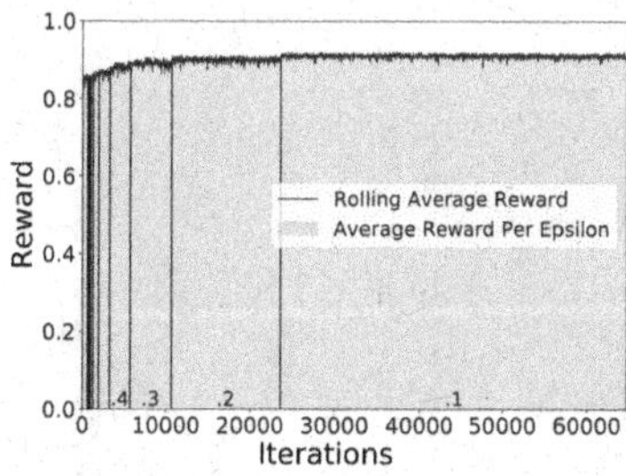

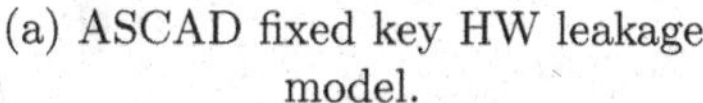
(a) ASCAD fixed key HW leakage model.

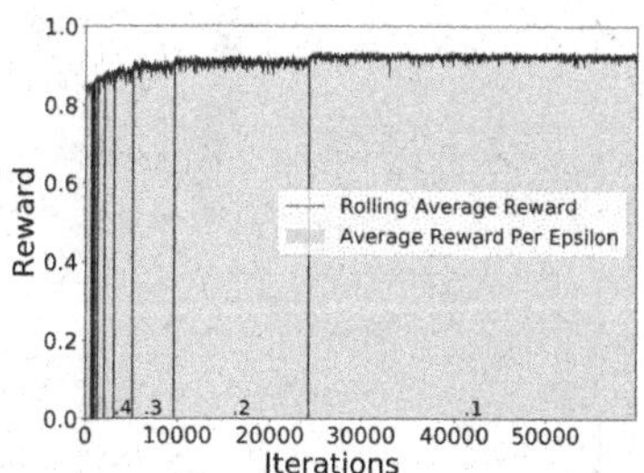

(b) ASCAD fixed key ID leakage model.

Fig. 2. An overview of the Q-Learning performance for the ASCAD with fixed key dataset experiments. The blue line indicates the rolling average of the Q-Learning reward for 50 iterations, where at each iteration, we generate and evaluate a countermeasure set. The bars in the graph indicate the average Q-Learning reward for all countermeasure sets generated during that ε. The results for RS experiments are similar. (Color figure online)

Interestingly, the countermeasures are implemented with higher costs when compared with the one used for ASCAD with a fixed key. The reason could be that training with random keys traces enhances the generalization of the profiling model. What is more, we also observe that we require significantly longer time to run the reinforcement learning framework: on average, 300 h, which is more than 12 days of computations. Interestingly, we see an outlier with the ASCAD random keys for the ID leakage model, where only 48 h were needed for the experiments.

Table 3. Best performing countermeasures for the ASCAD random keys dataset.

Model	Reward	Countermeasures	c'
$ASCAD\_R_{HW}$	0.940	RDI(A = 1, B = 0, probability = 0.20, amplitude = 16.95)	1.30
$ASCAD\_R_{HW\_RS}$	0.952	RDI(A = 2, B = 1, probability = 0.10, amplitude = 16.95)	1.45
$ASCAD\_R_{ID}$	0.942	RDI(A = 5, B = 0, probability = 0.10, amplitude = 16.95)	1.75
$ASCAD\_R_{ID\_RS}$	0.962	RDI(A = 1, B = 0, probability = 0.10, amplitude = 16.95)	1.15

The rolling average of the Q-learning reward and the average Q-learning reward per ε for the ASCAD random keys dataset are given in Fig. 4, Appendix A. Interestingly, at the beginning of Fig. 4a, there is a significant drop in Q-learning reward, followed by a rapid increase in the ε update from 0.4 to 0.3. A possible explanation could be that the model we used is powerful in defeating the selected countermeasures at the early learning stage. Still, the algorithm managed to learn from each interaction, finally selecting powerful countermeasures. In contrast, selecting countermeasure to defeat $ASCAD\_R_{ID}$ is an easy task: the reward value reaches above 0.8 at the very beginning, and it

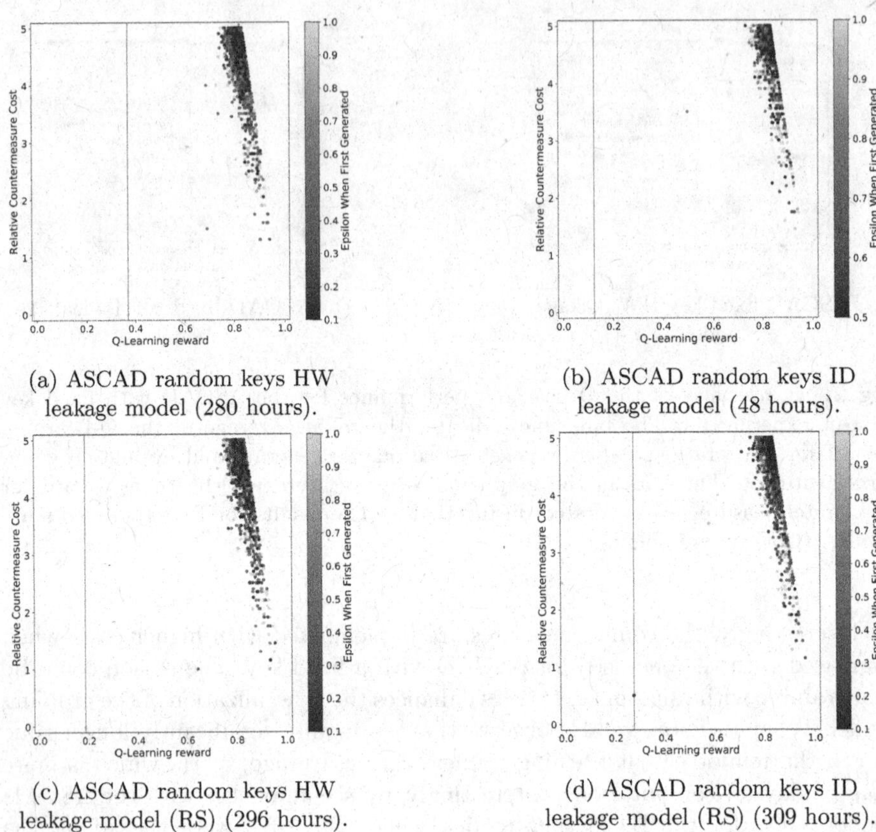

(a) ASCAD random keys HW leakage model (280 hours).

(b) ASCAD random keys ID leakage model (48 hours).

(c) ASCAD random keys HW leakage model (RS) (296 hours).

(d) ASCAD random keys ID leakage model (RS) (309 hours).

Fig. 3. An overview of the countermeasure cost, reward, and the ε value a countermeasure combination set was first generated for the ASCAD with random keys dataset experiments. The red lines indicates the countermeasure set with the highest reward for that GE reached 0 within 2 000 traces. (Color figure online)

stops increasing regardless of the number of iterations. Since each test consumes 300 h on average, we stopped the tests after around 3 000 iterations. There is a similar performance for settings with the RS objective in the ASCAD with the fixed key dataset: the RL algorithm is constantly learning. The highest reward value is obtained when ε reaches the minimum.

6 Conclusions and Future Work

This paper presents a novel approach to designing side-channel countermeasures based on reinforcement learning. We consider four well-known types of countermeasures (one in the amplitude domain and three in the time domain), and we aim to find the best combinations of countermeasures within a specific budget. We conduct experiments on two datasets and report a number of countermeasure combinations providing significantly improved resilience against deep learning-based SCA. Our experiments show that the best performing countermeasure combinations use the random delay interrupt countermeasure, making it a natural choice for real-world implementations. While the specific cost for each countermeasure was defined arbitrarily (as well as the total budget), we believe the whole approach is easily transferable to settings with real-world targets.

The experiments performed currently take significantly longer than might be necessary, as we generate a fixed number of unique countermeasure sets. In contrast, the chance to generate a unique countermeasure set towards the end of the experiments is significantly smaller (due to the lower ε). For future work, we plan to explore how to detect this behavior. Besides, it would be interesting to benchmark our method with Dynamic Programming or random solutions. We plan to consider multilayer perceptron architectures and sets of countermeasures that work well for different datasets and leakage models. Moreover, this work only evaluates existing countermeasures. It would also be interesting to investigate if reinforcement learning can be used to develop novel countermeasures.

A Q-Learning Performance for the ASCAD with Random Keys Dataset

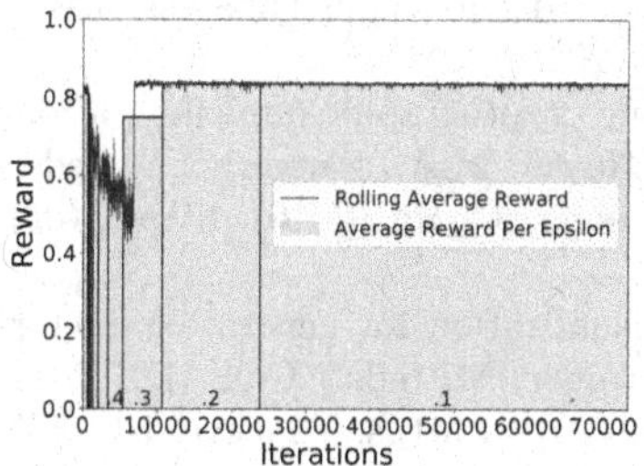

(a) ASCAD random keys HW leakage model.

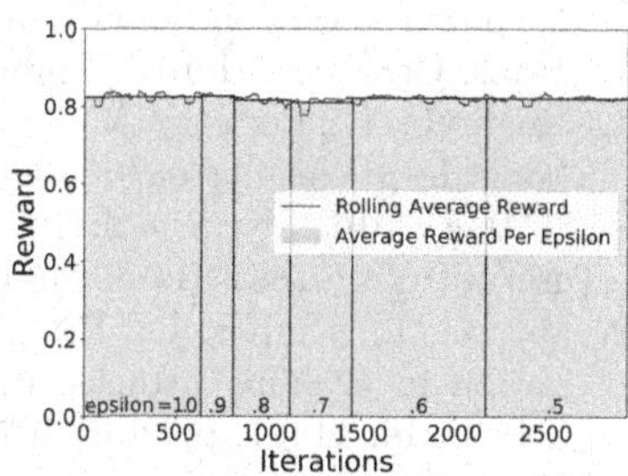

(b) ASCAD random keys ID leakage model.

Fig. 4. An overview of the Q-Learning performance for the ASCAD with the random keys dataset experiments. The blue line indicates the rolling average of the Q-Learning reward for 50 iterations, where at each iteration, we generate and evaluate a countermeasure set. The bars in the graph indicate the average Q-Learning reward for all countermeasure sets generated during that ε. The results for RS experiments are similar. (Color figure online)

References

1. Abadi, M., et al.: TensorFlow: large-scale machine learning on heterogeneous systems (2015). http://tensorflow.org/, software available from tensorflow.org

2. Benadjila, R., Prouff, E., Strullu, R., Cagli, E., Dumas, C.: Deep learning for side-channel analysis and introduction to ASCAD database. J. Cryptogr. Eng. **10**(2), 163–188 (2020). https://doi.org/10.1007/s13389-019-00220-8
3. Cagli, E., Dumas, C., Prouff, E.: Convolutional neural networks with data augmentation against jitter-based countermeasures. In: Fischer, W., Homma, N. (eds.) CHES 2017. LNCS, vol. 10529, pp. 45–68. Springer, Cham (2017). https://doi.org/10.1007/978-3-319-66787-4_3
4. Chollet, F., et al.: Keras (2015). https://github.com/fchollet/keras
5. Coron, J.-S., Kizhvatov, I.: An efficient method for random delay generation in embedded software. In: Clavier, C., Gaj, K. (eds.) CHES 2009. LNCS, vol. 5747, pp. 156–170. Springer, Heidelberg (2009). https://doi.org/10.1007/978-3-642-04138-9_12
6. Even-Dar, E., Mansour, Y.: Learning rates for q-learning. J. Mach. Learn. Res. **5**, 1–25 (2004)
7. Gu, R., Wang, P., Zheng, M., Hu, H., Yu, N.: Adversarial attack based countermeasures against deep learning side-channel attacks (2020)
8. Hettwer, B., Gehrer, S., Güneysu, T.: Deep neural network attribution methods for leakage analysis and symmetric key recovery. In: Paterson, K.G., Stebila, D. (eds.) SAC 2019. LNCS, vol. 11959, pp. 645–666. Springer, Cham (2020). https://doi.org/10.1007/978-3-030-38471-5_26
9. Inci, M.S., Eisenbarth, T., Sunar, B.: Deepcloak: Adversarial crafting as a defensive measure to cloak processes. CoRR abs/1808.01352 (2018). http://arxiv.org/abs/1808.01352
10. Kim, J., Picek, S., Heuser, A., Bhasin, S., Hanjalic, A.: Make some noise. unleashing the power of convolutional neural networks for profiled side-channel analysis. IACR Trans. Cryptogr. Hardw. Embed. Syst. 148–179 (2019)
11. Maghrebi, H., Portigliatti, T., Prouff, E.: Breaking cryptographic implementations using deep learning techniques. In: Carlet, C., Hasan, M.A., Saraswat, V. (eds.) SPACE 2016. LNCS, vol. 10076, pp. 3–26. Springer, Cham (2016). https://doi.org/10.1007/978-3-319-49445-6_1
12. Masure, L., Dumas, C., Prouff, E.: Gradient visualization for general characterization in profiling attacks. In: Polian, I., Stöttinger, M. (eds.) COSADE 2019. LNCS, vol. 11421, pp. 145–167. Springer, Cham (2019). https://doi.org/10.1007/978-3-030-16350-1_9
13. Ouytsel, C.B.V., Bronchain, O., Cassiers, G., Standaert, F.: How to fool a black box machine learning based side-channel security evaluation. Cryptogr. Commun. **13**(4), 573–585 (2021). https://doi.org/10.1007/s12095-021-00479-x
14. Perin, G., Chmielewski, L., Picek, S.: Strength in numbers: improving generalization with ensembles in machine learning-based profiled side-channel analysis. IACR Trans. Cryptogr. Hardw. Embed. Syst. **2020**(4), 337–364 (2020). https://doi.org/10.13154/tches.v2020.i4.337-364, https://tches.iacr.org/index.php/TCHES/article/view/8686
15. Perin, G., Picek, S.: On the influence of optimizers in deep learning-based side-channel analysis. In: Dunkelman, O., Jacobson, Jr., M.J., O'Flynn, C. (eds.) SAC 2020. LNCS, vol. 12804, pp. 615–636. Springer, Cham (2021). https://doi.org/10.1007/978-3-030-81652-0_24
16. Perin, G., Wu, L., Picek, S.: Gambling for success: The lottery ticket hypothesis in deep learning-based sca. Cryptology ePrint Archive, Report 2021/197 (2021). https://eprint.iacr.org/2021/197

17. Picek, S., Heuser, A., Jovic, A., Bhasin, S., Regazzoni, F.: The curse of class imbalance and conflicting metrics with machine learning for side-channel evaluations. IACR Trans. Cryptogr. Hardw. Embed. Syst. **2019**(1), 209–237 (2018). https://doi.org/10.13154/tches.v2019.i1.209-237, https://tches.iacr.org/index.php/TCHES/article/view/7339
18. Picek, S., Jap, D., Bhasin, S.: Poster: when adversary becomes the guardian - towards side-channel security with adversarial attacks. In: Proceedings of the 2019 ACM SIGSAC Conference on Computer and Communications Security, pp. 2673–2675. CCS 2019, Association for Computing Machinery, New York, NY, USA (2019). https://doi.org/10.1145/3319535.3363284
19. Ramezanpour, K., Ampadu, P., Diehl, W.: SCARL: side-channel analysis with reinforcement learning on the Ascon authenticated cipher (2020)
20. Rijsdijk, J., Wu, L., Perin, G., Picek, S.: Reinforcement learning for hyperparameter tuning in deep learning-based side-channel analysis. IACR Trans. Cryptogr. Hardw. Embed. Syst. **2021**(3), 677–707 (2021). https://doi.org/10.46586/tches.v2021.i3.677-707, https://tches.iacr.org/index.php/TCHES/article/view/8989
21. Standaert, F.-X., Malkin, T.G., Yung, M.: A unified framework for the analysis of side-channel key recovery attacks. In: Joux, A. (ed.) EUROCRYPT 2009. LNCS, vol. 5479, pp. 443–461. Springer, Heidelberg (2009). https://doi.org/10.1007/978-3-642-01001-9_26
22. Sutton, R.S., Barto, A.G.: Reinforcement Learning: An Introduction, 2 edn. MIT Press, Cambridge (2018). http://incompleteideas.net/book/the-book.html
23. Watkins, C.J.C.H.: Learning from delayed rewards. Phd thesis, University of Cambridge England (1989)
24. Wouters, L., Arribas, V., Gierlichs, B., Preneel, B.: Revisiting a methodology for efficient CNN architectures in profiling attacks. IACR Trans. Cryptogr. Hardw. Embed. Syst. **2020**(3), 147–168 (2020). https://doi.org/10.13154/tches.v2020.i3.147-168, https://tches.iacr.org/index.php/TCHES/article/view/8586
25. Wu, L., Perin, G., Picek, S.: I choose you: automated hyperparameter tuning for deep learning-based side-channel analysis. Cryptology ePrint Archive, Report 2020/1293 (2020). https://eprint.iacr.org/2020/1293
26. Wu, L., Picek, S.: Remove some noise: On pre-processing of side-channel measurements with autoencoders. IACR Trans. Cryptogr. Hardw. Embed. Syst. **2020**(4), 389–415 (2020). https://doi.org/10.13154/tches.v2020.i4.389-415, https://tches.iacr.org/index.php/TCHES/article/view/8688
27. Wu, L., et al.: On the attack evaluation and the generalization ability in profiling side-channel analysis. Cryptology ePrint Archive, Report 2020/899 (2020). https://eprint.iacr.org/2020/899
28. Zaid, G., Bossuet, L., Dassance, F., Habrard, A., Venelli, A.: Ranking loss: maximizing the success rate in deep learning side-channel analysis. IACR Trans. Cryptogr. Hardw. Embed. Syst. **2021**(1), 25–55 (2021). https://doi.org/10.46586/tches.v2021.i1.25-55
29. Zaid, G., Bossuet, L., Habrard, A., Venelli, A.: Methodology for efficient cnn architectures in profiling attacks. IACR Trans. Cryptogr. Hardw. Embed. Syst.**2020**(1), 1–36 (2019). https://doi.org/10.13154/tches.v2020.i1.1-36, https://tches.iacr.org/index.php/TCHES/article/view/8391
30. Zhang, J., Zheng, M., Nan, J., Hu, H., Yu, N.: A novel evaluation metric for deep learning-based side channel analysis and its extended application to imbalanced data. IACR Trans. Cryptogr. Hardw. Embed. Syst. **2020**(3), 73–96 (2020). https://doi.org/10.13154/tches.v2020.i3.73-96, https://tches.iacr.org/index.php/TCHES/article/view/8583

Deep Freezing Attacks on Capacitors and Electronic Circuits

Jalil Morris, Obi Nnorom Jr., Anisul Abedin, Ferhat Erata, and Jakub Szefer(✉)

Yale University, New Haven, CT 06511, USA
{jalil.morris,obi.nnorom,anisul.abedin,ferhat.erata, jakub.szefer}@yale.edu

Abstract. This paper introduces new deep freezing attacks on capacitors and electronic circuits that use them. The new attacks leverage liquid nitrogen to rapidly freeze electrolytic capacitors and supercapacitors to temperatures approaching −195 °C (−320 °F or 77 K). Due to the quick freezing to the extremely low temperatures, overall capacitance of the capacitors rapidly drops towards zero. Change of the capacitance can affect reliability and security of electronic circuits that these capacitors are used to build, and this work in particular evaluates electronic filters, as well as capacitor-powered microcontrollers, and their response to the deep freezing attacks. This work presents disruptive attacks that affect the operation of the target device, but then return device to normal operation after short amount of time when the components warm up. In addition to the disruptive attacks, this work also demonstrates destructive attacks where the target device is damaged due to the extreme freezing. Both types of attacks leave no trace as the liquid nitrogen evaporates after the attack is finished. This paper highlights new threats that designers should be aware of and defend against.

Keywords: Electrolytic capacitors · Supercapacitors · High-pass filters · Low-pass filters · Microcrontrollers · Liquid nitrogen · Freezing attacks · Security

1 Introduction

Computer and embedded systems depend on capacitors as the very basic building blocks of many electronic circuits that make them up. Two particular types of capacitors often used in electronic circuits are the electrolytic capacitors and supercapacitors. Electrolytic capacitors are polarized capacitors, which leverage wet or dry electrolytic, and can be made from aluminum, tantalum, or niobium. Wet aluminum capacitors tend to be widely used and are the focus of this work. Another type of widely used capacitors are supercapacitors, which have very high capacitance values, but tend to have lower voltage ratings compared to electrolytic capacitors. They can be polarized or non-polarized, although they are more commonly polarized, and use an electrolytic between the electrodes of the capacitor.

L. Batina et al. (Eds.): SPACE 2021, LNCS 13162, pp. 188–203, 2022.
https://doi.org/10.1007/978-3-030-95085-9_10

These capacitors are not entirely stable over all possible operating temperatures. Generally, Equivalent Series Resistance (ESR) increases as the temperature decreases, and this effect is particularly pronounced for aluminum electrolytic capacitors, "due to the limitation of wet electrolyte conductivity at low temperatures" [1]. Similar effects also exist in supercapacitors. Consequently, rapidly freezing such capacitors can have a significant effect on their capacitance, which is leveraged by our deep freezing attacks using liquid nitrogen (LN_2).

By using liquid nitrogen we can rapidly freeze electrolytic capacitors and supercapacitors to temperatures approaching −195 °C (−320 °F or 77 K). When the electrolyte in the capacitors freezes to these temperatures, the electrons or ions within the electrolyte no longer have much freedom to move, an electric field is not formed between the plates of the capacitor, and the overall capacitance of the capacitor rapidly drops towards zero. Rapid reduction of the capacitance has direct impact on the circuits that utilize these capacitors as we show in this work. This in particular leads to the new non-invasive and trace-free LN_2 attacks. LN_2can be obtained easily from chemical or scientific supply companies and, in small quantities, is easy to transport and deploy. The attacks are further very low-cost. Vendors such as Airgas charge about $0.28 per liter when LN_2 is purchased in bulk, while academic cleanroom at our institution charges about $0.10 per liter for bulk LN_2. Each individual attack instance uses no more than few liters, costing at most $0.50 per attack.

To evaluate the new physical LN_2 attacks, we investigate how the aluminum electrolytic capacitors respond to temperatures well below their operable range by dousing or dipping them in the liquid nitrogen. We also investigate how a capacitor's physical size, volume, composition, and electrical properties (i.e. capacitance and voltage rating) influence how effective liquid nitrogen is in changing a capacitor's characteristics. We further study the impact of the freezing duration on the measured capacitance changes. The main take-away is that even with short attack time on order of 10–30 s, a capacitor's capacitance drops towards zero. Further, capacitance quickly returns to normal when LN_2 is no-longer applied and the target allowed to warm up, leaving no trace of the attack. This is thus a new type of a disruptive attack, where device briefly operates abnormally during the attack, but then returns to normal operation when attack finishes. Although permanent damage was not observed when freezing individual capacitors, we did observe permanent damage of a microcontroller board when it was frozen while attacking on-board capacitors, leading to a possible new type of a destructive attack as well.

Many circuits' functionality depends on capacitors for their correct operation. A simple, but important class of circuits are electronic filters, such as high-pass and low-pass filters. Their cut-off frequency, i.e. frequency above which the high-pass filter passes signals or equivalently the frequency at which a low-pass filter attenuates signals, depends on the time constant, which is the product of the resistance (R) and capacitance (C). Affecting the capacitance of the capacitors in the filters, through the freezing attacks, directly affects the resistance and capacitance product, effectively changing the time constant and the behavior of the filter. Consequently, we investigate the deep freezing attacks and their effects on the cut-off frequency. We observe the high-pass filters begin to attenuate some signals that were passed before, and, conversely, low-pass filters allow some signals to pass which were attenuated before. This can in the least cause wrong sensor readings, or at worst cause unexpected faults in the system using the filters.

Capacitors are not only used in sensing circuits, but can also be used for energy storage. In particular electrolytic capacitors and supercapacitors can be used to power intermittent-computing devices, such as MSP430-class microcontrollers (MCUs). We evaluate how affecting the capacitance of these capacitors used to power microcontrollers can lead to a device crash or an inconsistent operation of the device.

For all the different types of devices and circuits that we consider, once the freezing effect wears off, the circuits usually return to their normal operation, without leaving any traces of the freezing attack. These are new types of disruptive attacks that temporarily modify behavior of the device, but then return the device to normal operation. In one case, a destructive attack was also observed, when a microcontroller board failed to operate after repeated freezing. The fact that circuits are not physically modified and that no easily observable traces persist after the freezing is finished (for the disruptive attacks) make these attacks very stealthy. For destructive attacks, even though the device is damaged, analyzing the source of the damage is difficult if all the traces of the LN_2 freezing are gone.

Based on our findings, we propose a set of defenses. Some of the different possible passive defenses can be easily deployed, such as switching away from using aluminum electrolytic capacitors or by adding insulation. In addition, active defenses can use temperature sensors deployed near critical capacitors or circuits to detect the freezing attack and take evasive action.

1.1 Paper Organization

The remainder of the paper is organized as follows. Section 2 presents background on capacitor temperature characteristics and cooling-related attacks. Section 3 gives the threat model. Section 4 overviews setup used for the experiments. Section 5 presents the evaluation results. Discussion of the results and potential defenses is given in Sect. 8 and the paper concludes in Sect. 9

2 Background

This section provides background on thermal characteristics of capacitors, and on existing work on security effects of cooling or freezing of electronic components.

2.1 Temperature Characteristics of Capacitors

Capacitors are passive electronic components that are used to store energy. Their capacitance is affected by temperature, and, for polarized aluminum electrolytic capacitors, the capacitance can decrease by almost 40% when exposed to low temperatures of −55 °C [1], [?]. Supercapacitors are also susceptible to temperature variations, and are typically not designed to work below −20 °C or −40 °C, as their capacitance is significantly reduced.

While the temperature effects on capacitors are known when the discrete capacitors are exposed to temperatures reaching −55 °C, how the capacitors behave when frozen by an attacker using liquid nitrogen and reaching −195 °C has not been evaluated from security perspective before. As will be explained in the threat model, Sect. 3, it is relatively easy to freeze the electronics with liquid nitrogen, without leaving a trace of an attack. It is in this context that we are especially interested in evaluating the impact of the freezing effects on different types of capacitors and circuits as a function of the freezing time of the capacitors.

2.2 Cold Boot and Chill Out Attacks

Security attacks based on rapidly cooling computer components are perhaps best exemplified by the Cold Boot attack [2], which focused on the internal capacitors found in the data cells of Dynamic Random Access Memory (DRAM) modules. The authors showed that by cooling DRAM chips (and thus the capacitors that they contain), the decay rate of the capacitors used to store data bits in DRAMs is reduced. This extends the time for which data persists in a powered-off chip, and allows malicious adversaries to transfer the cooled DRAM to a different computer to read the DRAM cells before the data is lost. The Cold Boot attacks focused on using up-side-down compressed air cans which leak compressed gas when used up-side-down and cool the DRAM. Authors also showed dipping DRAM chips in liquid nitrogen as a means to extend the time of the Cold Boot attack. Follow-up work, among others, showed similar security attacks by, for example, cooling smartphones in a refrigerator to extract keys stored in DRAM and break Android Full-Disk Encryption [4]. More recent work [6] showed that Cold Boot attacks still work in new DDR4 memories that use scrambling. The existing Cold Boot related work thus has focused on computer memories only, and did not consider electrolytic capacitors or supercapacitors, which we do in this work.

More recent work demonstrated the Chill Out attack [3], which focused on evaluation of behavior of capacitors and DC/DC converters when exposed to cooling sprays. The authors showed that there is a decrease in capacitance when electrolytic capacitors are cooled to about −55 °C, and that DC/DC converter behavior changes if the cooling is applied to the output electrolytic capacitors used in the converters. The authors used off-the-shelf electronic cooling sprays and, similar to prior work, up-side-down compressed air cans.

Our work differs from such prior research by considering the security implications of freezing capacitors individually, and also freezing capacitors inside electronic filters and energy-storage capacitors in microcontrollers. Neither did the existing work evaluate using liquid nitrogen to bring these devices to extreme temperatures approaching −195 °C.

3 Threat Model

This work assumes a malicious attacker who has physical access to the target device, but cannot modify or probe the target device, which could be easily noticed or detected by on-board circuitry. Instead, the attacker has a brief time window to make changes to the environment in which the device operates, such as by pouring liquid nitrogen or dipping it in liquid nitrogen. We assume the attacker can control the time of the LN_2 pouring or time of dipping in the LN_2. We assume the attacker has access to device for no more than about 30–60 s, making this a very fast attack.

While the attack could be detected by use of thermal sensors, to best of our knowledge, existing circuits targeted in this work do not contain thermal sensors or other defenses. Section 8 has a more detailed discussion of the potential defenses and other considerations. We further assume the defenders could analyze the device after the attack for any traces of the attack, but this type of attack leaves no trace of the freezing once the liquid nitrogen evaporates, allowing the attack to go undetected.

4 Experimental Setup

In this work, we use three basic setups: one to observe changes to capacitor behavior in response to freezing, one to test impact of capacitor freezing on a high-pass and low-pass filters, and one to test impact of capacitor freezing on capacitor-powered MCUs.

The *capacitor testing* setup uses the ADALM2000 power supply and oscilloscope module[1] to drive the capacitors with 3–5 V inputs by applying a step function input and captures the voltage across the capacitor as it is charging and discharging, under different freezing conditions. When step function is applied and input becomes one, the time to go from zero to full charge can be observed, and when the input goes to zero at the end of the step function, the time to go from full charge to zero can be observed. Both charging and discharging characteristics are measured using the ADALM2000 module.

The *high-pass and low-pass filter testing* setup uses a Keithley 2231A power supply to provide input voltages, the ADALM2000 to provide sine wave input to the filters with 5 V peak-to-peak voltage and frequency in the 1 kHz range, and captures the output of the high-pass filter and low-pass filter using a Tektronix MDO3104 Mixed Domain Oscilloscope with TPP1000 1 GHz passive probes.

The *microcontroller and supercapacitor testing* setup uses multiple MSP430-class microcontroller boards, especially `MSP430FR5994` and `MSP430FR5969` development boards. These can be powered through a USB cable, or a `P2110-EVB` harvester kit board can be used to power the microcontroller boards from an RF transmitter. All the boards are described in detail in Sect. 7. The capacitors on

[1] ADALM2000: Advanced Active Learning Module, https://www.analog.com/en/design-center/evaluation-hardware-and-software/evaluation-boards-kits/ADALM2000.html.

Table 1. Aluminum electrolytic capacitors of different types, physical dimensions, and voltage ratings used in the capacitor freezing tests. The capacitors are cylindrical in shape and their volume is $\pi(\frac{D}{2})^2 H$, where H is the height and D is the diameter. The times are rounded to the closest 15 second interval due to the experimental setup and the time measurement method.

Brand	Value	Rating	H	D	T_{zero}	T_{normal}
Capacitor freezing tests						
Panasonic	220 µF	6.3 V	11 mm	5 mm	15 s	120 s
Panasonic	220 µF	25.0 V	12 mm	8 mm	30 s	150 s
Panasonic	220 µF	63.0 V	22 mm	10 mm	45 s	210 s
Panasonic	470 µF	16.0 V	12 mm	8 mm	15 s	165 s
Panasonic	680 µF	35.0 V	20 mm	13 mm	45 s	210 s
Panasonic	1500 µF	50.0 V	36 mm	16 mm	120 s	360 s

these boards are subjected to the freezing attacks and the time before boards crash due to lack of stored energy as the capacitors are frozen is measured. Time is measured by observing an output LED which stops blinking when the test program crashes.

4.1 Liquid Nitrogen Freezing Approach

Liquid Nitrogen (LN_2) is used to gauge the effects of freezing the capacitors. When used to freeze a device, it is expected to freeze down to approximately −195 °C or −320 °F. To freeze the capacitors, they are either dipped or doused with LN_2. Liquid nitrogen is non-conducting, thus making it safe for pouring over electronics, or dipping electronics in it. For the capacitor-only tests, the capacitors are connected to the target circuit by long wires so that the capacitor is frozen, but the rest of the circuit is not affected. For dipping, the capacitors are lowered into a container filled with LN_2 and held inside LN_2 for the specified mount of time. For dousing, the capacitors are placed on a styrofoam surface and LN_2 is poured over for the specified amount of time. For other tests, if the capacitor is permanently attached to another device and cannot be removed, e.g., to the MCU board, the liquid nitrogen is poured on the capacitor for the specified amount of time, and it may also spill over onto adjacent components during pouring.

5 Capacitor Freezing Attacks

To understand impact of freezing on capacitors, we first perform a set of experiments to determine how the capacitance is affected by the freezing. This *capacitor testing* can give insights into attacks discussed in later sections. Table 1 shows capacitors of different types, physical dimensions, and voltage ratings used in the capacitor freezing tests.

Table 2. Aluminum electrolytic capacitors used in electronic filter tests. H is the height and D is the diameter of the cylindrical-shaped capacitors used in high-pass and low-pass filter tests.

Brand	Value	Rating	H	D
High-Pass filter tests				
Kemet	47 µF	25.0 V	13 mm	5 mm
Panasonic	220 µF	25.0 V	12 mm	8 mm
Nichicon	470 µF	16.0 V	13 mm	10 mm
Low-Pass filter tests				
Kemet	47 µF	25.0 V	13 mm	5 mm
Panasonic	220 µF	25.0 V	12 mm	8 mm
Nichicon	470 µF	16.0 V	13 mm	10 mm

The table in particular shows T_{zero} and T_{normal} which are the freezing time taken for freezing to cause an aluminum electrolytic capacitor's capacitance to approach zero and thawing time taken for capacitor to return to its normal capacitance, respectively. It can be seen from the table that in general T_{zero} is correlated with the physical volume of the capacitor. For same capacitance values, capacitors with bigger voltage rating in general have bigger volume. Thus for same capacitance values, capacitors with bigger voltage rating tend to take longer to cool down. T_{normal} is also related to the capacitor size and volume, and it can be seen that once frozen, the bigger the capacitor, the longer it takes for it to regain normal operation. For most of capacitors freezing of less than 60 s is sufficient to bring the aluminum electrolytic capacitors' capacitance down to zero, and these deep freezing times will be used to study effects on filters and capacitor-powered microcontrollers in the next sections.

6 Electronic Filter Freezing Attacks

In this section we evaluate effects of deep freezing on high-pass and low-pass filter circuits. Table 2 shows capacitors evaluated with these electronic filters. As we demonstrate in this section, the deep freezing is able to be used to non-invasively shift the cutoff frequency of these filters. We also call this a new Cutoff Frequency Shifting Attack (CFSA). By affecting the cutoff frequency, wrong operation of the filters can be induced.

6.1 Attacks on High-Pass Filters

The frequency above which the high-pass filter passes signals, i.e. the cutoff frequency, depends on the time constant $\frac{1}{RC}$, where R is the resistance and C is the capacitance. Freezing capacitors brings down value of C, effectively changing the time constant of the circuit, and increasing the cutoff frequency. For a fixed

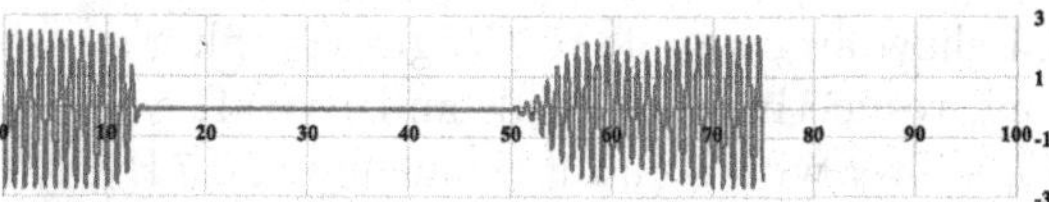

Fig. 1. Example of high-pass filter's response to 30 s of LN_2 pouring. The filter used 47 µF electrolytic capacitor. The x-axis is in seconds, and the y-axis is the output signal amplitude. The experiment was stopped at 75 s.

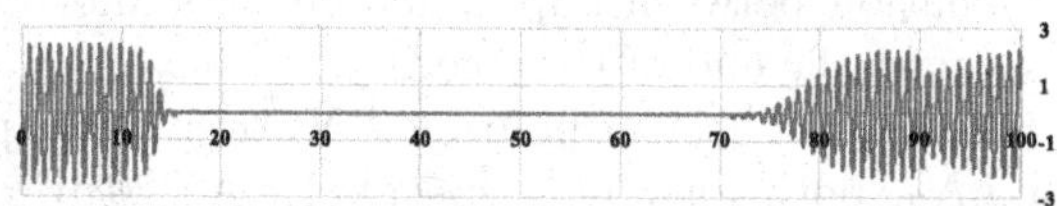

Fig. 2. Example of high-pass filter's response to 30 s of LN_2 pouring. The filter used 220 µF electrolytic capacitor. The x-axis is in seconds, and the y-axis is the output signal amplitude.

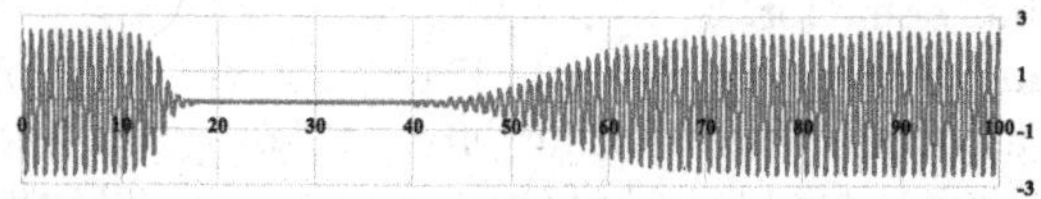

Fig. 3. Example of high-pass filter's response to 30 s of LN_2 pouring. The filter used 470 µF electrolytic capacitor. The x-axis is in seconds, and the y-axis is the output signal amplitude.

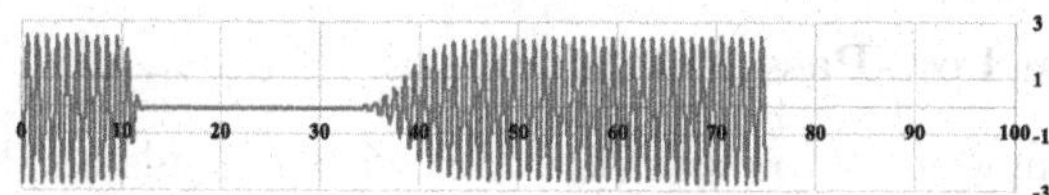

Fig. 4. Example of high-pass filter's response to 10 s of LN_2 pouring. The filter used 47 µF electrolytic capacitor. The x-axis is in seconds, and the y-axis is the output signal amplitude. The experiment was stopped at 75 s.

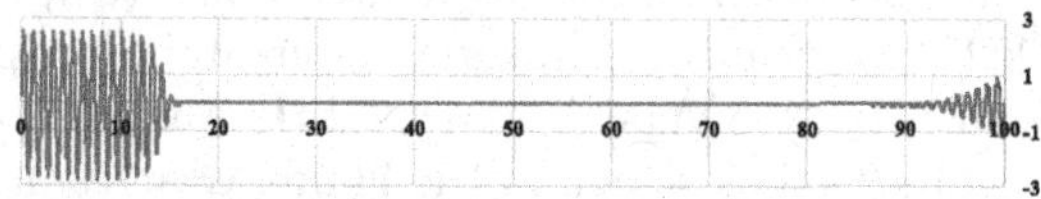

Fig. 5. Example of high-pass filter's response to 30 s of dipping in LN_2. The filter used 220 µF electrolytic capacitor. The x-axis is in seconds, and the y-axis is the output signal amplitude.

input frequency, as the capacitors freeze, the signal begins to be attenuated. For fixed size capacitor, this happens at approximately same time, regardless of the pouring duration. Once the pouring stops, the capacitors slowly start to warm up, which means the time constant changes back towards its original value, and the filter begins to pass the input signal again.

Figures 1 and 4 show an example of a high-pass filter's response to 30 s and 10 s of LN_2 pouring, respectively. A 47 µF and 15.6 kΩ were connected in series to create a high-pass filter with a cutoff frequency of 0.7 Hz. A 5 V peak-to-peak 1 Hz signal was passed through the filter and the output was observed as shown on the figures. The figures demonstrate that longer freezing results in longer time when filter attenuates frequency it should not. Figure 1 shows attenuation between approximately 10 s and 50 s marks, while Fig. 4, where freezing was shorter, shows attenuation between approximately 10 s and 35 s marks. In all cases the effect lasts past the end of the freezing.

Figures 2 and 5 compare effect of pouring LN_2 over the capacitors vs. dipping capacitors in LN_2, both for 30 s, respectively. A 220 µF and 3.3 kΩ were connected in series to create a high-pass filter with a cutoff frequency of 0.7 Hz. Again a 5 V peak-to-peak 1 Hz signal was passed through the filter and the output was observed as shown on the figures. It can be seen from the figures that dipping creates a longer-lasting freezing effect, and it takes longer for the filter to regain its original behavior.

Figures 1, 2, and 3 show filters with 47 µF, 220 µF, and 470 µF capacitors, respectively. For all three, the freezing effect takes place before the pouring finishes. The 47 µF capacitor recovers faster compared to 220 µF. For the 470 µF, although the input frequency is no-longer passed as seen from the figure, it may not be fully frozen, and starts to recover sooner. Due to biggest physical volume, the recovery rate is slowest as can be seen between 40 s and 80 s mark.

6.2 Attacks on Low-Pass Filters

The cutoff frequency of the low-pass filter likewise depends on the time constant of the circuit, which is the $\frac{1}{RC}$, where R is the resistance and C is the capacitance. As the capacitor freezes, the value of C is reduced, which increases the cutoff frequency. As a result, when low-pass filter is frozen, the previously attenuated signals begin to be passed through.

Figure 6 shows an example of low-pass filter's response to 30 s of LN_2 pouring. A 220 µF and 3.3 kΩ were connected in series to create a low-pass filter with a cutoff frequency of 0.7 Hz. A 5 V peak-to-peak 1 Hz was inputted to the filter, and the output was observed as shown in the figure. Our results indeed confirm the expectation that during the attack the input signal is not attenuated as much (between 20 s and 70 s mark), while once the capacitor begins to warm up the signal is again attenuated (after 70 s mark).

6.3 Attacks on Higher-Order Filters

Attacks in the previous section targeted first-order filters. In addition, we have tested second-order filters. We used same 47 µF, 220 µF, and 470 µF electrolytic capacitors. Each filter used only one type of capacitor. Since the higher-order filters use multiple capacitors, we tested LN_2 dipping attack on individual capacitors (where only one of the capacitors was frozen at a time), and on all capacitors (where all capacitors used in the filter were frozen at once). In particular, we

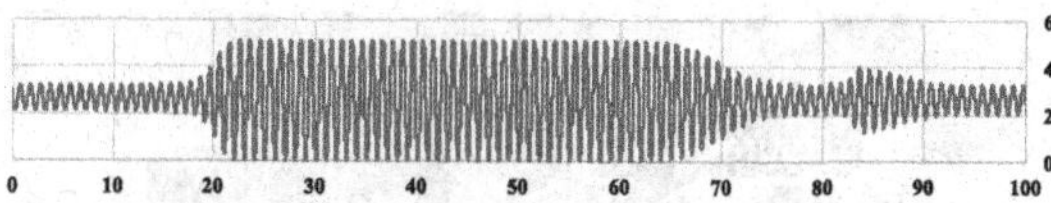

Fig. 6. Example of low-pass filter's response to 30 s of LN_2 pouring. The filter used 220 µF electrolytic capacitor. The x-axis is in seconds, and the y-axis is the output signal amplitude.

tested "Vin", "Vout," and a "Vin + Vout" capacitors. "Vin" indicates the test done on the capacitor closest to the input, "Vout" indicates the freezing test done on the capacitor closest to the output, and "Vin + Vout" indicates that both capacitors were dipped in LN_2 at the same time. The capacitors were dipped in LN_2 for 10 s, 30 s, and 60 s for different tests.

In all cases we observed similar results to the first-order filter tests. Regardless of which capacitor or capacitors were frozen, the filters behaved the same, e.g., high-pass filter is made to attenuate signals during freezing. Freezing the "Vin" capacitor causes high-pass filter to attenuate the inputs, and the second stage cannot recover this input. Freezing of the "Vout" capacitor attenuates the signal at the output, which unfrozen first stage cannot correct. Freezing of both capacitors simply combines the effects. Based on the results, we conclude that higher-order filters do not help mitigate the new freezing attacks.

6.4 Comparison to Freezing with Cooling Sprays

In addition to using liquid nitrogen, we used electronics cooling spray, similar to the Chill Out attack [3], but in our case we cooled the capacitors in the filters. The capacitors in the filters were sprayed for up to 30 s with the cooling spray. However, no significant effect was observed on the filters. This seems consistent with the existing work [3], where cooling capacitors with the cooling spray caused capacitance changes to be 10% or less. Thus, the time constant of the filter will be changed minimally when cooling spray is applied, while with the liquid nitrogen there is significant time constant change as the capacitance goes to zero.

7 Energy Storage Freezing Attacks

In addition to being able to modify behavior of circuits such as electronic filters, the freezing attacks can directly impact operation of devices that depend on them for energy storage. In particular, we have explored the MSP430-class microcontrollers (MCUs) which are a representative of transiently-powered computing devices, also called intermittent-computing devices. The intermittent-computing devices are used to run computations on limited amount of energy stored in the capacitors. The code running on intermittent-computing devices is designed to work with the specified capacitor by, for example, using checkpointing [5] to ensure forward progress between each discharge of the capacitor.

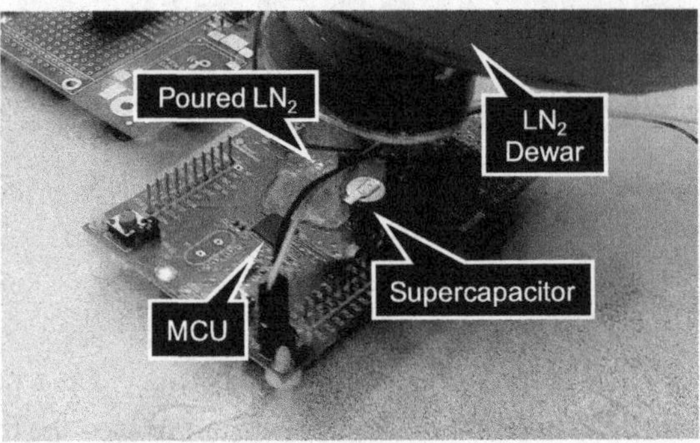

Fig. 7. Example of freezing attack via pouring LN_2 on the supercapacitor on the MSP430FR5994 board.

However, as we demonstrate in this section, freezing of the capacitors used for energy storage effectively cuts down, or even fully eliminates, the stored energy available to run computation. Freezing thus can be used to stop computation from progressing, or to introduce faults if the checkpoint is not reached. Because frozen capacitor stores less, or even zero, energy than what is assumed when selecting checkpoint locations, code that works correctly under normal conditions, will not work with frozen capacitors where energy storage is not sufficient to reach the checkpoints. The repeated deep freezing attacks may even permanently damage the boards, as we observe.

7.1 Capacitor-Powered MSP430-class MCUs

The freezing tests were conducted on the MSP430FR5994 development board with a 0.22 F supercapacitor and on the MSP430FR5969 development board with a 0.10 F supercapacitor. The boards can be powered via USB to charge the devices, and when USB cable is disconnected, they run on the energy stored in the on-board capacitors until the device runs out of energy.

In addition, a P2110-EVB harvester kit board was tested, which has a 0.05 F AVX BestCap supercapacitor, a 0.001 F electrolytic capacitor, or can be used with user-installed capacitor. The harvester kit board can be used to power the MPS430 boards, bypassing the capacitor on these boards. The harvester kit board is charged when a remote radio-frequency (RF) transmitter transmits power, when the transmitter is turned-off, or out of range, the harvester kit board powers the MSP430 boards from its capacitor. The P2110-EVB harvester kit board is optimized for operation in the 902–928 MHz band, but will operate outside this band with reduced efficiency. RF transmitter used transmits in at 915 MHz.

Table 3. MSP430-class MCUs and capacitors tested. FR5994 refers to the `MSP430FR5994` board, FR5969 refers to the `MSP430FR5969` board, and P2110 refers to the `P2110-EVB` harvester kit board. If harvester was used, the pre-installed or user-installed capacitor on the harvester was used, otherwise the MCU board's capacitor was used.

Board	Harvester Used?	Capacitor	Volt Rating	Type
Electrolytic capacitor tests				
FR5969	P2110	330 µF	25.0 V	Electrolytic
FR5969	P2110	470 µF	16.0 V	Electrolytic
FR5969	P2110	3300 µF	16.0 V	Electrolytic
Supercapacitor tests				
FR5994	P2110	0.05 F	—	Supercap.
FR5969	—	0.10 F	—	Supercap.
FR5994	—	0.22 F	—	Supercap

7.2 Setup for Microcrontroller Freezing Attacks

The freezing attacks on microcontrollers were done similar to attacks on capacitors and electronic filters discussed in prior sections: by dipping the capacitors in LN_2 or by pouring LN_2 over the capacitor. Figure 7 shows example of attack by pouring LN_2 over the supercapacitor on the `MSP430FR5994` board. Table 3 shows the boards and capacitors tested.

7.3 Freezing Attacks on Energy Storage in Electrolytic Capacitors

The `P2110-EVB` harvester kit board allows for installation of user-provided capacitor, and we tested three different types of electrolytic capacitors by installing them on the harvester kit board. The pre-installed 0.05 F AVX BestCap supercapacitor and 0.001 F electrolytic capacitor where both disabled by use of select jumpers. Auxiliary eZ-FET module on the `MSP430FR5994` board was disabled by removing jumpers to reduce energy consumption of the board.

The software running on the microcontroller was a simple code loop which is used to blink an LED following a predefined delay. Energy is consumed by the microcontroller as it is running the code as well as by the LED. Since the run-time on the electrolytic capacitors is very short, the oscilloscope was used to observe the VCC voltage and measure how long the device ran using the capacitor before energy ran out and VCC dropped below a threshold.

We evaluated effects of freezing before vs. after charging when dipping capacitors in LN_2. In the *freezing before and after charging* approach, the freezing starts before the energy-storage capacitor is charged. The total freezing time before device starts running in this approach is 50 s (20 s before charging plus 30 s while charging). In the *freezing after charging only* approach, the energy-storage capacitor is first charged, and freezing is then applied. The total freezing

Table 4. Freezing tests for 50 s of freezing of capacitors on MSP430-class MCUs tested on FR5969 with P2110 harvester for two freezing approaches. The run times are average of three runs. The control run time was measured when no freezing was performed. With freezing, the run time is indeed 0 s for both approaches.

Capacitor	Control	With freezing
Freezing before and after charging approach		
330 µF	0.009 s	0.000 s
470 µF	0.020 s	0.000 s
3300 µF	0.180 s	0.000 s
Freezing after charging only approach		
330 µF	0.009 s	0.000 s
470 µF	0.020 s	0.000 s
3300 µF	0.180 s	0.000 s

Table 5. Freezing test for checking varying amount of freezing of capacitors before charging on MSP430-class MCUs tested on FR5969 with P2110 harvester. The control run time was measured when no freezing was performed.

Capacitor	Control	10 s Freezing	20 s Freezing
Freezing before charging only approach			
330 µF	0.010 s	0.000 s	0.000 s
470 µF	0.020 s	0.000 s	0.000 s
3300 µF	0.160 s	0.080 s	0.016 s

time before device starts running in this approach is also 50 s (all after charging). In both approaches the total charging time is 30 s and on-board switches are used to enable or disable connection to the energy-storage capacitor to ensure fixed charging time and that device only starts running (and thus consuming energy) after the charging and 50 s of freezing are completed. For both approaches the capacitors were dipped in LN_2 and remained in LN_2 for the duration of the test. The results are shown in Table 4. As can be seen, with freezing the run time for both approaches is 0 s.

Since the extended freezing of the capacitors resulted in run time approaching zero, we also evaluated different freezing times. In a modified *freezing before charging only* approach, the capacitors are frozen for different amounts of time before they are charged, then they are removed from LN_2 and charged for 30 s and then the device is allowed to execute to measure run time. The results are shown in Table 5. As can be seen, for smallest capacitors, the devices still are not able to run. For largest capacitor, the run-time is cut by 50% with 10 s of freezing, and cut by almost 90% with 20 s of freezing.

Table 6. Example results of pouring LN_2 to perform a freezing attack on microcontroller when different supercapacitors were used for energy storage. The freezing time refers to how long the LN_2 was being poured over the supercapacitor.

Capacitor	Freezing time	Run-time before crash
0.22 F (FR5994 board)	0 s	204 s
	30 s	15 s
0.10 F (FR5969 board)	0 s	192 s
	30 s	27 s
0.05 F (P2110 board)	0 s	*device*
	30 s	*damaged*

7.4 Freezing Attacks on Energy Storage in Supercapacitors

In addition to electrolytic capacitors, we have evaluated three supercapacitors. The 0.22 F supercapacitor pre-installed on the `MSP430FR5994` development board, the 0.10 F supercapacitor pre-installed on the `MSP430FR5969` development board, and the 0.05 F AVX BestCap supercapacitor pre-installed on the `P2110-EVB` harvester kit board. For supercapacitor tests, the same testing software was used as in electrolytic capacitor tests. However, since the supercapacitors allow the device to run for hundreds of seconds, a stopwatch application was used to measure the run-time until the LED stopped blinking and device runs out of energy.

Table 6 shows the results of pouring LN_2 over the supercapacitors. It can be seen the freezing effect is also significant on the supercapacitors. Especially, with 30 s of pouring of LN_2, the code run-time before energy runs out is cut by over 85% for the capacitors. The exact run-time available depends on number of factors, such as how the LN_2 is poured. Also, note that the `MSP430FR5994` and `MSP430FR5969` boards have different power management circuitry and extensions (i.e. there are other differences than just the capacitor size), this can explain the similar run times, despite different capacitor values. However, the freezing effect has the same magnitude in stored energy reduction.

In addition to significantly reducing energy storage and causing premature crashes, we further observed that following multiple freezing attacks permanent damage can occur. In particular, the `P2110-EVB` harvester kit board was damaged following LN_2 pouring. While we leave analysis of destructive attacks as future work, one possible explanation of the damage are excess currents generated during the freezing that affected the harvester kit's logic and charging circuits. Thus deep freezing can not only produce transient effects, but also lasting device damage.

8 Discussion

To detect or defend the deep freezing attacks, different possible defenses can be deployed, as discussed below.

8.1 Alternative Polarized Capacitors

One potential passive defense for attacks on aluminum electrolytic capacitors includes switching to other types of capacitors, such as capacitors based on tantalum or niobium. Tantalum capacitors have added benefit of high capacitance per volume, but tend to be more expensive, about 4× more expensive compared to aluminum electrolytic capacitors. Niobium capacitors are an alternative to tantalum and have lower cost, but still are about 3× more expensive compared to aluminum electrolytic capacitors. Both types, however, are significantly less impacted by temperature changes.

8.2 Larger Capacitors

Based on our experiments, large capacitor sizes (larger volume) require longer freezing time for the attack to take effect. Consequently, a different passive mitigation, but not a full defense, is to use physically larger capacitors, e.g., use capacitors for larger voltage ratings, than what the target circuit requires.

8.3 Added Insulation

Alternatively, dedicated insulation can be added around capacitors or whole circuits as a passive defense. Freezing attacks would now require removal of the insulation, which would make the attack noticeable. However, insulation may cause circuits to overheat during normal operation.

8.4 Temperature Sensitive Packaging

Key to the attacks is that they are difficult to notice after the attack is finished since the packaging of the electronic components is mostly unchanged by the freezing. To allow for better detection of the attack after the attack has happened, temperature sensitive packaging or labeling could be used. Sample passive indicators could include labels that peel off due to extreme freezing, or paint that changes colors permanently after the freezing.

8.5 Temperature Sensors

As an active defense, temperature sensors can be deployed near critical electrolytic capacitors or circuits that use them, to detect the freezing attack. The system detection and response would have to happen within the short attack time, so that defensive action takes place before circuit is frozen. The filters could output an error signal if they detect unusual temperatures, or for the microcontroller scenario, additional checkpoints could be activated at run-time. However, in all cases, the freezing my affect the sensors themselves. Study of freezing impacts on sensors is orthogonal and future work.

9 Conclusion

This paper presented new deep freezing attacks on capacitors and electronic circuits that use them. This work demonstrated that liquid nitrogen can be leveraged to rapidly freeze electrolytic capacitors and supercapacitors to temperatures approaching −195 °C (−320 °F or 77 K). At these temperatures, electrolytic capacitors and supercapacitors cease to operate within their specification. As a proof-of-concept of real attacks, this work demonstrated that operation of electronic filters is affected by the freezing attacks and that filters can be made to attenuate (for high-pass filters) or pass (for low-pass filters) undesired frequencies when frozen. Meanwhile, for capacitor-power microcontrollers, this work demonstrated that the microcontrollers can be made to crash as energy storage is significantly reduced due to the deep freezing attacks. This paper thus highlighted a number of new threats that designers of electronic circuits should be aware of and also presented number of potential defenses that can be considered to mitigate the new threats.

Acknowledgment. This work was supported in part by NSF grant 1901901. The authors would like to thank Kelly Woods and the Yale University Cleanroom for assistance in obtaining liquid nitrogen used in the experiments.

References

1. Faltus, R., Flegr, Z., Šponar, R., Jáně, M., Zedníček, T.: DC/DC converter output capacitor benchmark. In: Annual Passive Components Symposium. CARTS Europe (2008)
2. Halderman, J.A., et al.: Lest we remember: cold-boot attacks on encryption keys. Commun. ACM **52**(5), 91–98 (2009)
3. Nnorom, Jr., O., Morris, J., Giechaskiel, I., Szefer, J.: Chill out: freezing attacks on capacitors and dc/dc converters. In: Proceedings of the European Test Symposium. ETS (2021)
4. Müller, T., Spreitzenbarth, M.: FROST: forensic recovery of scrambled telephones. In: International Conference on Applied Cryptography and Network Security. ACNS (2013)
5. Ransford, B., Sorber, J., Fu, K.: Mementos: system support for long-running computation on RFID-scale devices. In: International Conference on Architectural Support for Programming Languages and Operating Systems. ASPLOS (2011)
6. Yitbarek, S.F., Aga, M.T., Das, R., Austin, T.: Cold boot attacks are still hot: security analysis of memory scramblers in modern processors. In: International Symposium on High Performance Computer Architecture. HPCA (2017)

AI and Cloud Security

Encrypted SQL Arithmetic Functions Processing for Secure Cloud Database

Tanusree Parbat(✉) and Ayantika Chatterjee

Indian Instutite of Technology Kharagpur, Kharagpur, India

Abstract. With the growing opportunities in cloud computing, different types of databases are used for storing and managing heterogeneous data in the cloud. However, several reported data breaches show that data security promises as per cloud agreement are not adequate to move critical data to cloud. Homomorphic Encryption (HE) emerges as a security solution in this regard. However, it is a non-trivial task to realize any algorithm in circuit-based representation to be implemented in homomorphic domain. Moreover, existing encrypted databases are with limited features and still not fully able to perform SQL query processing along with complex mathematical operations in encrypted domain without any need of intermediate decryption. In this work, we explore implementing the encrypted counterparts of a few complex transaction-SQL related mathematical functions like ABS(), CEILING(), FLOOR(), SIGN(), SQUARE(), POWER(), and SQRT(), which are heavily used in cloud database queries. We have evaluated these mathematical operators without any intermediate decryption, considering the support of underlying fully homomorphic encryption (FHE). Though the usage of underlying FHE scheme incurs some performance bottleneck, our proposed designs are flexible enough to be realized on any leveled homomorphic encryption (LHE) scheme for performance improvement. Experimental results show FHE encrypted SQL conditional SELECT operations with complex mathematical functions can be performed within 48 min on a single processor for a dataset of 768 rows with 9 columns, and each data size of 16-bit. Performance can be further improved by suitable implementation platform translation from CPU to GPU or with the restrictions of leveled fully homomorphic encryption.

Keywords: Homomorphic Encryption · Cloud applications · SQL mathematical functions

1 Introduction

With the onset of Internet of Things (IoT), sensor-based devices contribute to increasing data generation rates day by day. To store and process such huge amount of data effortlessly, cloud computing is now a prominent platform. Several cloud databases like NoSQL, MongoDB, CouchDB have been reported [1] nowadays. However, storage data misuse, illegitimate outsourced data disclosure

L. Batina et al. (Eds.): SPACE 2021, LNCS 13162, pp. 207–225, 2022.
https://doi.org/10.1007/978-3-030-95085-9_11

are all incurring significant risks for the cloud applications with security critical data [2]. Therefore, data owners are no longer fully satisfied with cloud security agreements to preserve and operate critical data on the cloud. Traditional encrypted schemes confirm data security in storage. However, such encrypted data poses an extra challenge in case of cloud domain processing without an encryption key. Hence, previous IoT frameworks [3] support cloud processing only with insensitive data-part but, sensitive data is being computed locally on the user(edge) side to avoid critical information leakage. However, that incurs huge computation overhead at the edge site. Therefore, to process sensitive data inside the cloud directly maintaining data confidentiality, homomorphic encryption (HE) is a preferred choice [4].

HE enables a third party to conduct computations directly on encrypted data preserving the features of the function and format of the encrypted data [5]. Although this useful feature of HE was known for over 30 years, initial HE schemes were Partially Homomorphic Encryption(PHE), either additive or multiplicative. In additive HE, for sample messages m_1 and m_2, one can obtain $E(m_1+m_2)$ only with $E(m_1)$ and $E(m_2)$ without knowing m_1 and m_2 explicitly, where E denotes the encryption function. In 2009, first plausible construction of Fully Homomorphic Encryption (FHE) scheme was proposed. However, present research is still thriving to make FHE schemes performance practical. Hence, some less performance costly HE approaches with restricted features like Leveled Fully Homomorphic Encryption (LHE) or Somewhat homomorphic encryption (SHE) are mostly preferred over FHE while implementing practical applications on encrypted data.

There are multiple reported databases [6–10] in literature, encrypted with existing HE schemes. Some are based on partial HE [11–13] which supports either additive or multiplicative homomorphic operations. Some databases follow Somewhat homomorphic encryption (SHE) [14] which supports substantial arbitrary additions and few multiplication operations and Leveled Fully Homomorphic Encryption (LHE) [15], provides a certain level of homomorphic operations. Few other reported schemes [8] are deterministic which always generates the same ciphertext for a certain plaintext. However, all these reported databases have their inherent limitations either in terms of types of supporting queries or in case of preventing few known database attacks [16]. For this reason, complex mathematical functions (which are essential part of existing plaintext databases [10]) are either not supported or incorporated with the support of intermediate decryptions in existing encrypted SQL query processing [6–10].

In this work, we focus on designing encrypted counterparts of few complex mathematical operators [17] without any requirement of such intermediate decryption. For the implementation, we have considered fully homomorphic encryption (FHE) [18] as underlying scheme, which claims to support arbitrary bit-wise processing on encrypted data. Moreover, our proposed modules are flexible enough to be implemented over any LHE framework for better performance. But, in this work, we consider FHE to support unlimited SQL processing on encrypted data, which is not possible if the database is LHE encrypted. Few arithmetic functions such as ABS(), CEILING(), FLOOR(), SIGN(), SQUARE(), POWER(), and SQRT() are frequently used by Microsoft SQL Server [17] and Azure SQL database [10]. But, these operators are yet to be explored with encrypted SQL query processing. General SQL processing challenges in FHE domain with integer inputs already have been discussed in [19]. But, implementing these mathematical functions in homomorphic domain is significantly challenging as most of these functions receive floating-point numbers as inputs, which are not supported by existing FHE schemes. Another challenge in designing such mathematical operators is to realize all the algorithms in their respective circuit-based representations [20]. Moreover, many traditional concepts like looping, branch handling, etc., do not work directly on encrypted data considering our existing implementation platforms are unencrypted [21]. Considering all these aspects, we have revisited the algorithms related to these operators and implemented them with optimizations, which are suitable for FHE domain. Other trigonometry-related mathematical functions for instance, TAN(), COS(), SIN(), RADIAN(), COT(), etc., will be explored in our future work.

The rest of this paper is organized as follows: In Sect. 3, we discuss preliminary concepts of homomorphic encryption. Then, we describe FHE-based design implementation for encrypted SQL-related mathematical functions in Sect. 4. Next, we discuss the timing requirements in Sect. 5 followed by the conclusion in Sect. 6.

2 Prior Works

Recent studies report several databases (InfluxDB, CrateDB, MongoDB, RethinkDB, SQLite), which are well suited to store and process heterogeneous data [22]. One of them is InfluxDB [23], which efficiently handles single-node time-series data but does not support few database functions due to schemaless design. Like to similarly InfluxDB, MongoDB [24] is not efficiently scalable because of primary and secondary node configurations. It is mainly a single node database. On the contrary, CrateDB is highly scalable with the property of automatic rebalancing of data, and dynamic schema [24]. Another light-weight database is RethinkDB [25], which is an open-source, scalable, and with limited support of ACID (atomicity, consistency, isolation, and durability of transaction) property. In terms of IoT applications with the full support of SQL, SQLite [22] database is a perfect choice to reduce the query latency by caching the data locally. Unlike RDMS enterprise, SQLite keeps alive end application. However, all these mentioned databases are primarily designed for unencrypted data.

There are various reported encrypted databases in the literature supporting limited mathematical functions. In ZeroDB [7], all encrypted operations occur on the client-side after retrieving data from the server. In contrast, PHE based-CryptDB [8] supports only a limited number of queries, and complex mathematical functions are not addressed. In Stealthdb [6], decryption is required for computation on cloud side. Always Encrypted with secure enclave [10] requires a key to enable the enclave for computation. In [9], authors proposed few FHE-based secure cloud analytical solutions simply using encrypted addition and squaring operators. Kaiping et al. [26] proposed an efficient multiparty computational cloud framework under only partial HE [13]. In 2016, authors in [27] presented homomorphic arithmetic operations (like addition, subtraction, multiplication, and division) over encrypted integers applying BGV encrypted scheme under HElib library. Data processing frameworks reported based on this encrypted scheme are mostly limited with LHE.

In this context, we aim to design an encrypted counterpart of SQLite [28]. Though basic encrypted SQL query processing techniques with FHE are discussed in previous literature [19], encrypted transactional SQL queries with complex mathematical functions are not handled. Since such mathematical functions are supported by unencrypted SQLite and used in Azure databases, it is essential to explore such complex mathematical processing on encrypted data to get a complete encrypted SQLite framework (shown in Fig. 1). In the next section, we explain basics of HE, and in the subsequent sections, we discuss the steps to design such mathematical operators with underlying FHE support.

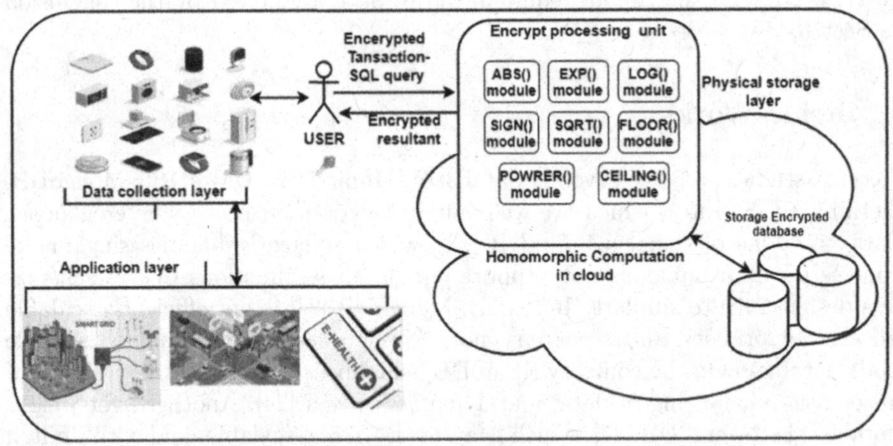

Fig. 1. Application framework with encrypted processing database

3 Preliminaries: Homomorphic Encryption(HE)

Homomorphic encryption [4] supports homomorphic evaluation of any arbitrary operation. It is a structure-preserving transformation between two sets (say P and C), where p_1, p_2 are members of P, and $c_1, c_2 \in C$. A transformation $T : P \to C$ is said to be homomorphic if transformation function with an operation $\oplus$ between two members of P i.e., $T(p_1 \oplus p_2)$ is equivalent to the transformation function over another operation $\ominus$ between individual members of C i.e., $T(c_1) \ominus T(c_2)$.

In general, a public-key homomorphic encryption technique ε integrates a series of polynomial-time procedures ($KeyGen_\varepsilon$, $Encrypt_\varepsilon$, $Decrypt_\varepsilon$), where $KeyGen_\varepsilon$, and $Encrypt_\varepsilon$ are probabilistic. HE incorporates a specific function $Evaluate_\varepsilon$ $(pk, f, c_1, ...c_t)$, which takes ciphertexts $c_1, ..., c_t$ as inputs and generates resultant ciphertext (corresponding to the computable result of plaintexts) by the public key pk with the help of function f, which can be evaluated in homomorphic way.

Due to this $Evaluate_\varepsilon()$, associated noise growth increases with multiplication and addition operation. Theoretically, this growth rate can be evaded if intermediate data decryption and reciphering are possible when growth rate rises beyond the threshold value. But a secret key is required to accomplish the task, which defeats the aim of FHE scheme. This problem is solved by **bootstrapping method** [18] which reduces the noise from ciphertext [5]. This method can evaluate the decryption circuit in homomorphic domain by an encrypted secret key. Later, different works have been proposed in literature to improve the performance of FHE scheme. We choose a non-deterministic FHE scheme mentioned in TFHE library [29] based on the work 'Fast Fully Homomorphic Encryption over the Torus'. TFHE supports faster bitwise homomorphism with bootstrapping in less than 0.1 s [29]. Another advantage of TFHE is that there is no limitation on number of gates and the bit-wise bootstrapping provides flexibility to develop operators as per application's operand bit-size requirement. In the succeeding section, we will realize few complex mathe-

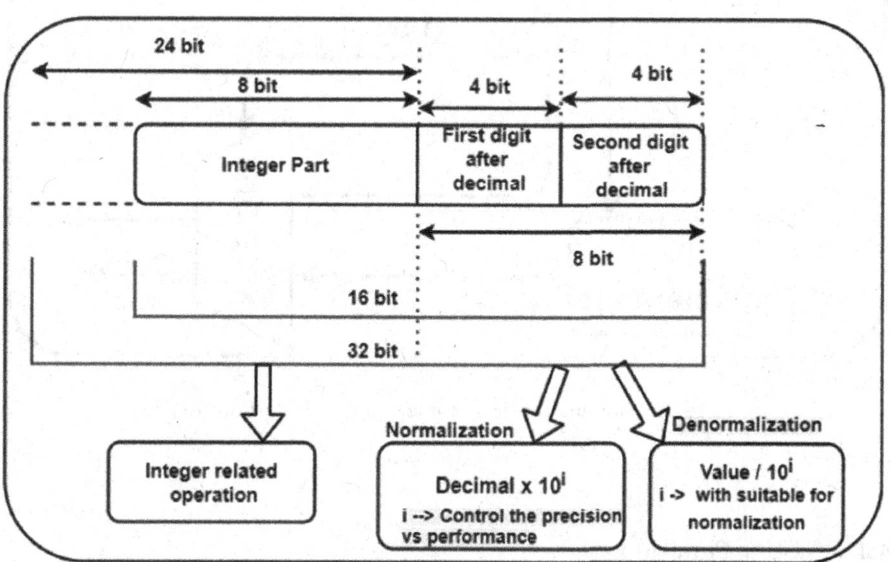

Fig. 2. Application specific floating point number representation

matical functions using basic FHE modules like **encrypted decision-making module (FHE MUX), encrypted comparison module (FHE_Is_Lesser, FHE_Is_Greater), FHE equality check module (FHE_Is_Equal), FHE arithmatic modules (FHE_Addition, FHE_Subtraction), etc.** as detailed in [21].

4 Designing SQL Associated Arithmetic Functions in Encrypted Domain

This section will explore encrypted counterpart design of few arithmetic functions to be executed with encrypted SQL queries. These mathematical functions should also handle floating-point numbers, which are impossible to handle with existing FHE libraries directly. Therefore, our solution in terms of floating-point number representation is shown in Fig. 2, which shows any floating-point number can be normalized by multiplying 10^i, where i is number of digits after decimal point taken into account. This i can be changed to control accuracy versus performance. After that, we FHE encrypt 'integer part' and 'after decimal part' and perform FHE processing on the whole or partial bits as and when required. After FHE processing, a suitable de-normalization module is applied just by discarding few bits, and that does not add any performance overhead.

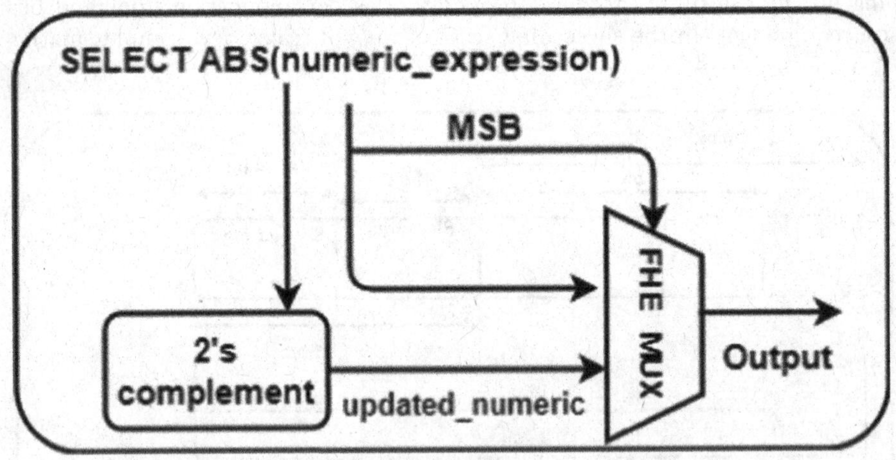

Fig. 3. Implementation of encrypted ABS() function

4.1 ABS() Function

ABS() function in SQL generates absolute value of a passed argument. If the argument is non-numeric, it is required to convert that into a numeric data-type.

Syntax of this function is **"SELECT ABS (Enc(numeric_expression));"** Fig. 3 shows implementation details, where FHE encrypted numeric_expression is passed as an argument in ABS(). In order to obtain the absolute value, most significant bit (MSB) of Enc(numeric_expression) is sent to an encrypted multiplexer (FHE MUX). Remaining two inputs of FHE MUX are encrypted updated_numeric(after performing 2's complement of Enc(numeric_expression) [21]) and Enc(numeric_expression). If the MSB is Enc(0), Enc(numeric _expression) is a positive numeric, and it will be selected as ABS_output; otherwise, output will be updated_numeric.

Algorithm 1: Algorithm for ceiling value

Input: *Enc(integer)*, *Enc(decimal)*
Output: CEILING(Enc(integer), Enc(decimal))
begin
  Eout= FHE_Is_Equal(Enc(0),Enc(decimal))
  updated Enc(integer part)= FHE_Addition(Enc(integer part),Enc(1))
  Ceiling_output= FHE MUX(Eout, Enc(integer part),updated Enc(integer part)
end

4.2 CEILING() and FLOOR() Function

Ceiling() function is used to evaluate any given numeric and return the nearest round figure value, which is greater or equal to the passing argument. General syntax of the Ceiling() is **"SELECT CEILING (Enc(numeric_expression));"** To implement this function, we follow our floating-point representation procedure. First, we normalize the decimal part of numeric expression with 10^i and store this *numeric_expression* in encrypted form as shown in Fig. 2. After that, according to the Algorithm 1, we compare (Enc(decimal)) with 4-bit Enc(0) with the help of FHE_Is_Equal module. If output of this module, *Eout* is *Enc*(1), it means decimal part is zero. Therefore, Enc(integer part) itself is ceiling value. If *Eout* = *Enc*(0), Enc(integer part) is incremented by *Enc*(1) using FHE_Addition. In order to get this decision, an FHE MUX is required where *Eout* is select input, and another two inputs are Enc(integer part) and updated Enc(integer part).

In FLOOR() function implementation, Enc(integer part) of *Enc(numeric_expression)* as shown in Fig. 2 is directly selected as output of Floor() function.

4.3 SIGN() Function

SIGN() function returns sign value of specified number passing as an argument. It will return 0 for positive number and 1 for the negative number. Syntax for encrypted SIGN() is given as **"SELECT**

SIGN(Enc(numeric_expression));" To implement this function, most significant bit (MSB) of *Enc*(*numeric_expression*) is sent as output. If this MSB is *Enc*(0), *Enc*(*numeric_expression*) is a positive numeric; otherwise, it is a negative number.

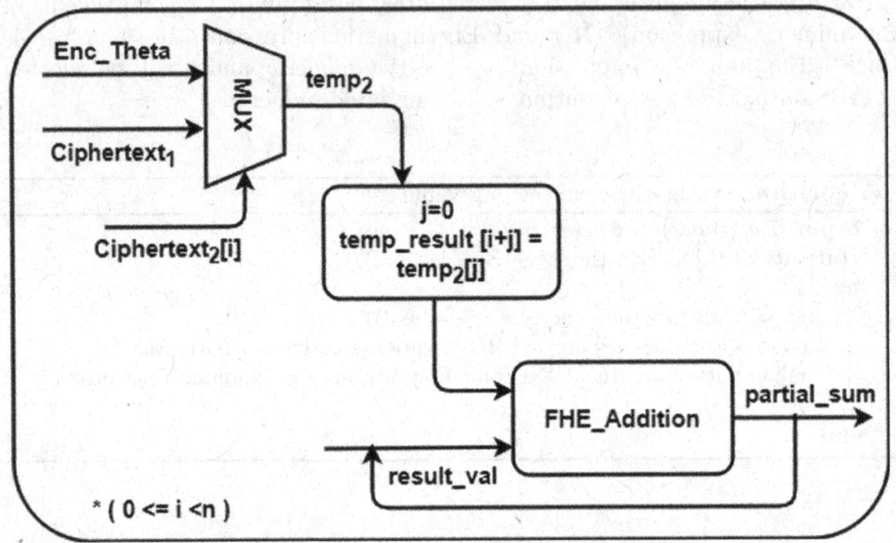

Fig. 4. Encrypted multiplication module

4.4 SQUARE() Function

SQL SQUARE() is used to compute square value of a numeric expression. SQL encrypted SQUARE() is as follows **"SELECT SQUARE(***Enc* (*numeric_expression*)**);"** In this experiment, we have used bit-wise multiplication using the shift-and-add method [30]. Figure 4 shows multiplication procedure, is used in our SQUARE() implementation, where one bit of the multiplier is multiplied with every bit of multiplicand. In our implementation, a multiplier is $ciphertex_2$, and $ciphertext_1$ is the multiplicand. These two ciphertexts and *Enc_Theta* (initialized to *Enc*(00)) send to the multiplexer (MUX) as a selector, second, and first inputs, respectively. Based on the selector bits, repetitive additions (FHE_Addition) are performed with *result_val* and right shifting of multiplexer output (shown in Fig. 4). In this way, we implement SQUARE() function.

4.5 EXP() and LOG() Function

To implement these two mathematical functions in a straightforward way, costly repetitive multiplications are required. However, a simple approach has been adopted by [31] to avoid such huge number of FHE multiplications for these functions. The general idea of this paper [31] is to preserve pre-computed function values within a specific integer range in encrypted form along with corresponding encrypted range values. In order to compute EXP() or LOG() for a particular encrypted integer, encrypted list search operation is performed over the preserved integer range.

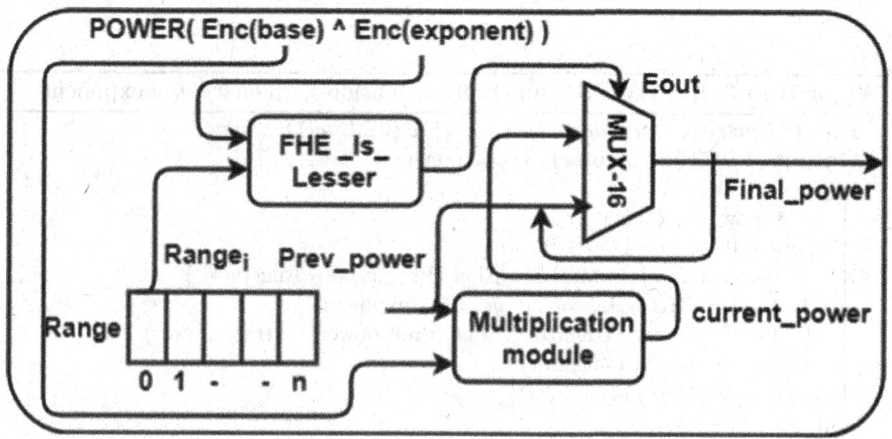

Fig. 5. Implementation of encrypted POWER() function

Algorithm 2: a) POWER() function calculation with unencrypted exponent

---

Input: *Enc*(*base*), *exponent*
Output: POWER(Enc(base), exponent)
begin
  power= Enc(1)
  for $i = 0$; $i < exponent$; $i = i++$ **do**
    power= Multiplication (power, Enc(base))
  end
end

4.6 POWER() Function

To compute POWER() function (b^e), we require two arguments base (b) and exponent (e), which is the power of base argument. The straightforward way to compute b^e is to compute $b * b$ within a loop of maximum loop count e. However, for encrypted e, the loop condition checking i < e (for loop index i) should generate encrypted result. This result cannot be processed by existing underlying processors to decide when to stop the iteration of the loop. That makes the encrypted loop handling infeasible. To implement an encrypted version of POWER() function, we consider the following two ways:

- **Case 1:** Only the base argument is encrypted for **POWER(Enc(base), exponent)**. According to Algorithm 2, *base* is initialized with $Enc(1)$. Then, considering unencrypted exponent we compute multiplication operations (shown in Fig. 4) inside a loop.

Algorithm 3: b) POWER() function calculation with encrypted exponent

```
Input: Enc(base), exponent, range = [Enc(0), Enc(1), ....Enc(n − 1)]
Output: POWER(Enc(base), Enc(exponent))
begin
    Prev_power= Enc(1)
    for i = 0; i < n; i = i + + do
        Current_power= Multiplication (Prev_power, Enc(Base))
        Eout= FHE_Is_Lesser(range_i, Enc(exponent))
        Final_power= FHE MUX(Eout, Prev_power, Current_power)
        Prev_power=Final_power
    end
end
```

- **Case 2:** Both base and exponent arguments are encrypted in FHE domain in this case. In this implementation, the main challenge is to decide an unencrypted value for loop iteration though the exponent value is encrypted. Figure 5 shows implementation details of POWER() with encrypted base and exponent. For k-bit exponent value, we consider $n = 2^k$ as the maximum loop count. However, for cases where the exponent value is less than n, we need to compute $b * b$ only up to e value is reached. In encrypted domain, we do that in the following way as shown in Algorithm 3: Initially, we set $Prev\_power = Enc(1)$. $Current\_power$ is calculated multiplying $Prev\_power$ and Enc(base) with the help of multiplication module (shown in Fig. 4) during each loop iteration. FHE_Is_Lesser module [21] is used to find whether value of encrypted loop count ($range_i$ computed as $Enc(0), Enc(1), Enc(2) \ldots Enc(n-1)$) and checked if it is lesser than $Enc(exponent)$ in each iteration ($range_i < Enc(exponent)$). In this condition checking , if $range_i < Enc(exponent)$, output $Eout$ will be $Enc(0)$; otherwise $Enc(1)$. According to this $Eout$ value, $Final\_power$ value will be selected through FHE MUX, where first and second inputs are $Current\_power$ and $Prev\_power$ respectively, and $Eout$ is used as select input. This encrypted decision-making will not allow to increase the final result further once encrypted loop count is equal to $Enc(exponent)$. Further, loop iterations will perform encrypted $b * b$ computations, but that will not contribute to the final result.

However, it is evident that Algorithm 3 is performance costly and includes some extra encrypted multiplications only to make the loop handling feasible.

Lower Range (LB)	Upper Range (UB)	Square root	Range offset
Enc(1)	Enc(4)	Enc(1)	Enc(0.4)
Enc(4)	Enc(9)	Enc(2)	Enc(0.2)
Enc(9)	Enc(16)	Enc(3)	Enc(0.1)
Enc(16)	Enc(25)	Enc(4)	Enc(0.1)
Enc(25)	Enc(36)	Enc(5)	Enc(0.1)
Enc(36)	Enc(49)	Enc(6)	Enc(0.1)
Enc(49)	Enc(64)	Enc(7)	Enc(0.1)
Enc(64)	Enc(81)	Enc(8)	Enc(0.1)
Enc(81)	Enc(100)	Enc(9)	Enc(0.1)
Enc(100)		Enc(10)	

Fig. 6. Approximate range offset of intermediate sub-ranges

4.7 SQRT() Function

Implementing SQRT() on FHE data is a challenging task, especially to calculate the square root value of a non-perfect square value. Here, we propose approximate square root computation steps for $Enc(numeric\_expression)$ (shown in algorithm 4) based on arithmetic estimates assuming input $numeric\_expression$ belongs to a particular range. We consider a few intermediate sub-ranges (such as $(1, 4)$, $(4, 9)$, $\ldots(81, 100)$) within the maximum range according to the Algorithm 4 and store lower range, upper range, square root, and range offset for each sub-range as shown in Fig. 6. Here, lower range contains encrypted perfect square numbers in the range, and upper range stores immediate next encrypted perfect square number. Square root column holds square root values of lower range numbers in increasing order, and the range offset (last column) holds average difference between each of the non-perfect square values within a specific upper and lower range i.e., $(\sum_{j=1}^{n}(lower\_range_i + j) - lower\_range_i)/(upper\_range_i - lower\_range_i)$, where $n = (upper\_range_i - 1)$.

For the sake of implementation simplicity, we assume maximum upper range value, $max\_Val = 100$ in this implementation. We also assume that values of square root column are multiplied by 100 to normalize the floating-point numbers. We follow Fig. 2 to normalize the floating-point range offset value. To compute SQRT() function for both perfect square and non-perfect square inputs, following steps are considered as detailed in Fig. 7:

Initially,we compare the given $Enc(numeric\_expression)$ with all encrypted lower range (LB) and upper range (UB) values from the range Table (Fig. 7) using FHE comparison modules FHE_Is_Greater and FHE_Is_Lesser [19]. Output of FHE_Is_Greater module, $Eout$ is fed into MUX_1 as select input. If

Algorithm 4: Square root finding algorithm

Input: LB={Enc(1),Enc(4),Enc(9)..Enc(100)},
UB={Enc(4),Enc(9),Enc(16)..Enc(100)},
root={Enc(100),Enc(200),Enc(300),..Enc(1000)},
offset={Enc(0),Enc(40),Enc(20),..Enc(10)}, Enc(numeric_expression)

Output: SQRT(Enc(numeric_expression))

begin
UB=upper range
LB=lower range
while *FHE_Is_Greater (Enc(numeric_expression),lower range$_i$)* **do**
find range offset
end
while *FHE_Is_Lesser (Enc(numeric_expression),lower range$_{n-i}$)* **do**
find nearest lower range
find nearest square root value
end
difference= FHE_Subtract (Enc(numeric_expression),nearest lower range)
SQRT_result=FHE_Addition (nearest square root value, Multiplication (range offset, ABS(difference)))
end

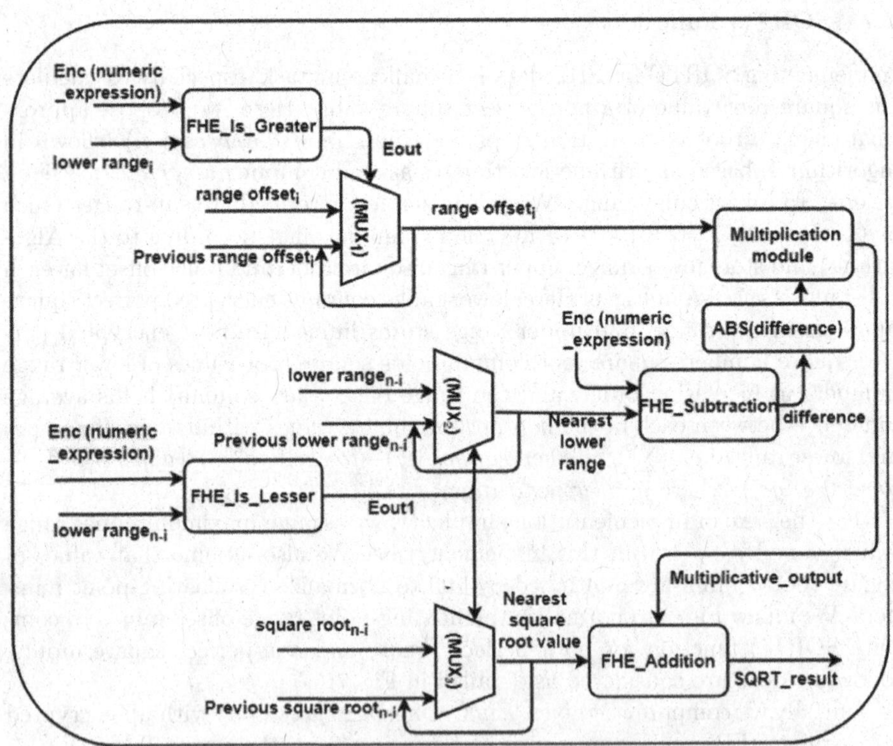

Fig. 7. Implementation of Encrypted SQRT()

$Eout = Enc(0)$, that indicates encrypted $Enc(numeric\_expression) > lower$ $range_i$. Then first input of MUX_1, range offset$_i$ comes to the output of MUX_1; otherwise, second input, 'previous range offset$_i$' will be selected as output. In general exact range offset can be computed as follows:

range offset $= (\sum_{j=1}^{n}(lower\_range_i + j) - lower\_range_i)/num$,
where $n = (upper\_range_i - 1)$ and num is total number of non-perfect square values within the bounded range values $(upper\_range_i - lower\_range_i)$.

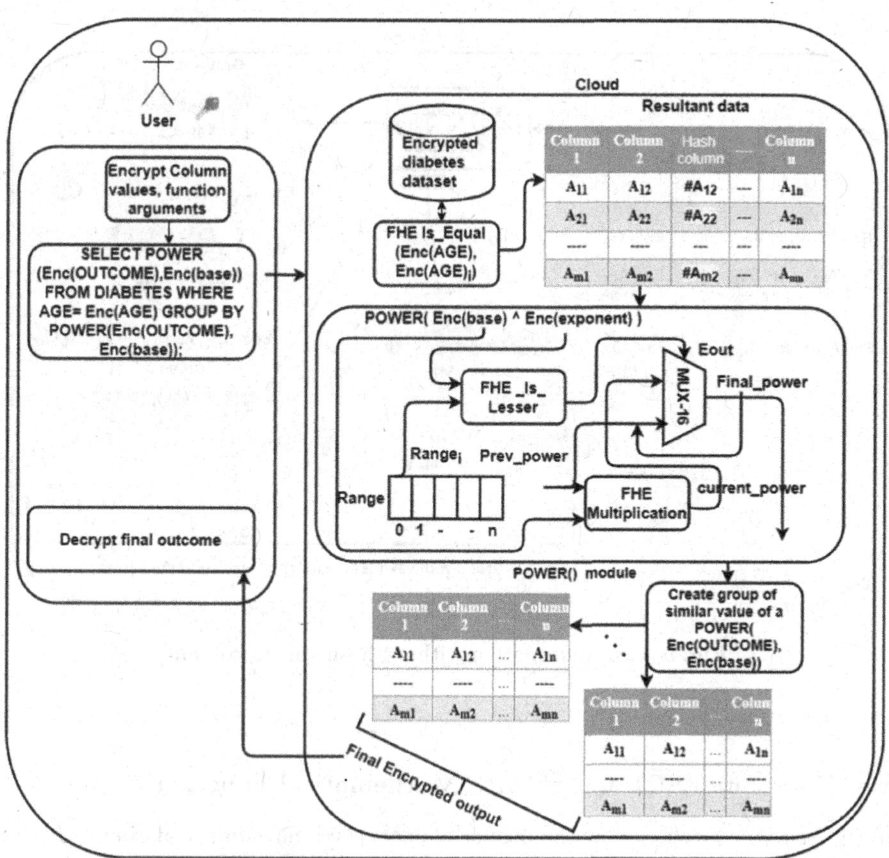

Fig. 8. Encrypted SQL with GROUP BY and POWER()

Initially, 'previous range offset' is set to $Enc(0)$. Next time, it will be updated by current range offset$_i$. Again, output of FHE_Is_Lesser module, $Eout1$ is taken as select input in MUX_2 and MUX_3 to find the last lower range perfect square value of $Enc(numeric\_expression)$ at which FHE_Is_Lesser condition is satisfied. Based on the output of this module, MUX_2 and MUX_3 generate nearest lower range perfect square value and its nearest square root value of given *numeric_expression*. Further, to calculate square root of a non-perfect square value, we find the difference between lower range value and *Enc*(*numeric_expression*) using FHE_Subtraction module [19]. The generated output of this module is used as an argument of ABS() (mentioned in Sect. 4.1) to find the absolute difference value. In the next step, ABS(difference) value is multiplied by range offset (output of MUX_1) using the multiplication module (shown in Fig. 4) to obtain *Multiplicative_result*. Finally, *SQRT_result* will be generated by performing FHE_Addition with *Multiplicative_result* and nearest square root value (output of MUX_3).

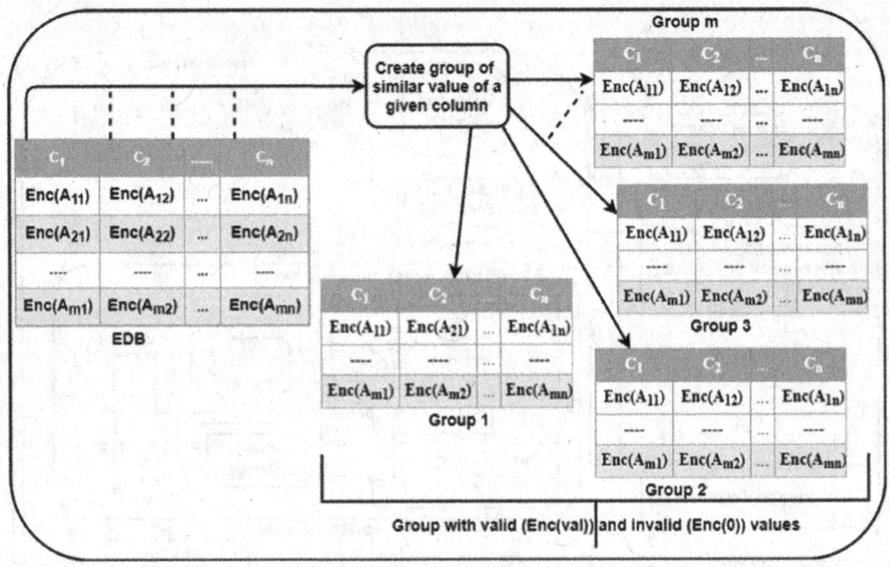

Fig. 9. Group formation without hash valued column

4.8 Encrypted SQL Query with Mathematical Function

In this section, we show how the proposed encrypted mathematical operators can be used with encrypted SQL query. For instance, we have tested our query execution on standard 'Pima-Indians-Diabetes-Database' [33] with encrypted column values. As an example, we consider the following SQL query with POWER() function:

SELECT POWER(Enc(OUTCOME),Enc(exponent)) FROM DIABETES WHERE AGE=Enc(AGE) GROUP BY POWER(Enc(OUTCOME),Enc (exponent));

User transmits this query to the cloud with all the field values encrypted. Cloud will perform homomorphic equality check with the given encrypted age value (Enc(AGE)) and stored AGE column values within encrypted database using FHE *Is_Equal* module [19]. Further, the cloud processing unit computes encrypted power() over generated resultant data, taking input the encrypted 'OUTCOME' and *Enc*(*exponent*) from this query. After that, GROUP BY operation is applied on the outputs of power() function to create groups of similar values (shown in Fig. 8). Final encrypted output is transmitted to the user. User decrypts this output and uses that result to specific applications.

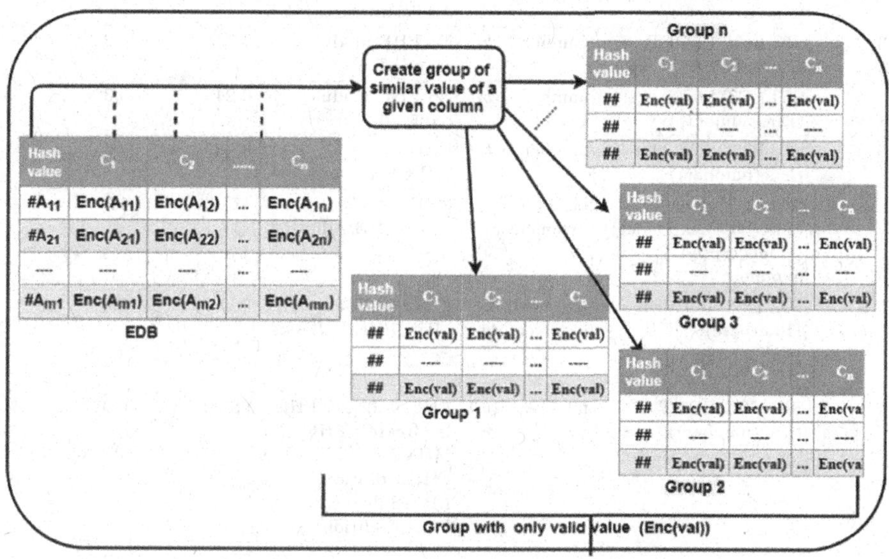

Fig. 10. Group formation with hash valued column

In general, the execution-time of GROUP BY operation grows rapidly in the homomorphic domain. To explain the reason, let us consider the GROUP BY operation is being done based on the values of a column C $(C(i))$. In this case, for all rows with $C(j) = C(i)$, $\forall j \neq i$, some valid rows will be produced with encrypted non-zero values and these rows are the valid members of the group. Otherwise, $\forall C(j) \neq C(i)$ cases, invalid rows (with all encrypted zeroes) will be generated. Thus, for each $C(i)$ based comparison, number of total rows (including valid and invalid rows) are always equal to m, where $m = total$ number of rows in actual database (shown in Fig. 9). Thus, GROUP BY operation over a particular column value generates m^2 rows in total as a resultant. That makes next-level processing infeasible. To alleviate this issue, GROUP BY operation is proposed in this work with the support of hash value comparison. Here, we append an extra hash column (for the columns whose values can be the key of GROUP BY operation) in the original database. Group formations are done by performing a hash equality check instead of homomorphic comparison (as shown in Fig. 10). Figure 10 also shows that hash equality check reduces the group size generating only valid row values for which the GROUP BY condition is getting satisfied.

Table 1. CPU and GPU based processing time of various functions including POWER() with 6 a) Unencrypted exponent and 6 b) Encrypted exponent.

Serial no.	SQL queries with mathematical functions	Input Details	Required FHE modules	CPU based execution time (sec)	GPU based execution time (sec)
1	SELECT ABS (Enc(number))	number:16 *bit*	FHE_Addition,FHE NOT,FHE MUX	0.97	0.09
2	SELECT CEILING (Enc(number))	number:16 *bit*	FHE_Is_Equal,FHE_Addition, FHE MUX	8.97	0.9
3	SELECT FLOOR (Enc(number))	number:16 *bit*	No FHE module required	0.13	0.2
4	SELECT SIGN (Enc(number))	number:16 *bit*	No FHE module required	0.24	0.3
5	SELECT SQUARE (Enc(number))	number:16 *bit*	FHE MUX,FHE_Addition	35.27	3.6
6 a)	SELECT POWER (Enc(base),exponent)) (Unenctypted exponent)	base:(16 *bit*), exponent:5	FHE MUX,FHE_Addition	177.30	17.8
6 b)	SELECT POWER (Enc(base), Enc(exponent)) (Encrypted exponent)	base:(16 *bit*), exponent:4 *bit*	FHE_Addition, FHE MUX,FHE_Is_Lesser	360.71	36.1
7	SELECT SQRT (Enc(number))	number:16 *bit*	FHE_Is_Lesser,FHE_Is_Greater, FHE MUX, FHE_Addition, FHE_Subtraction, FHE_Addition	63.92	6.39

However, non-deterministic homomorphic encrypted ciphertexts may not generate equal hash values. Hence, the main limitation of this proposed scheme is that GROUP BY operation only can be performed based on few selected columns for which hash values are already stored beforehand.

Similarly, cloud can evaluate encrypted ORDER BY with costly base and exponent encrypted POWER() function, which takes 115.83 min to execute 100 data rows with 9-columns, each of the column values having 8 bits of data. However, row-based parallelization can be easily incorporated in our implementation framework, since FHE operations in each rows are independent to each other and that can reduce the performance overhead further.

Table 2. Bit-wise performance of encrypted SQRT(), ABS(), SQUARE(), CEILING(), POWER() functions

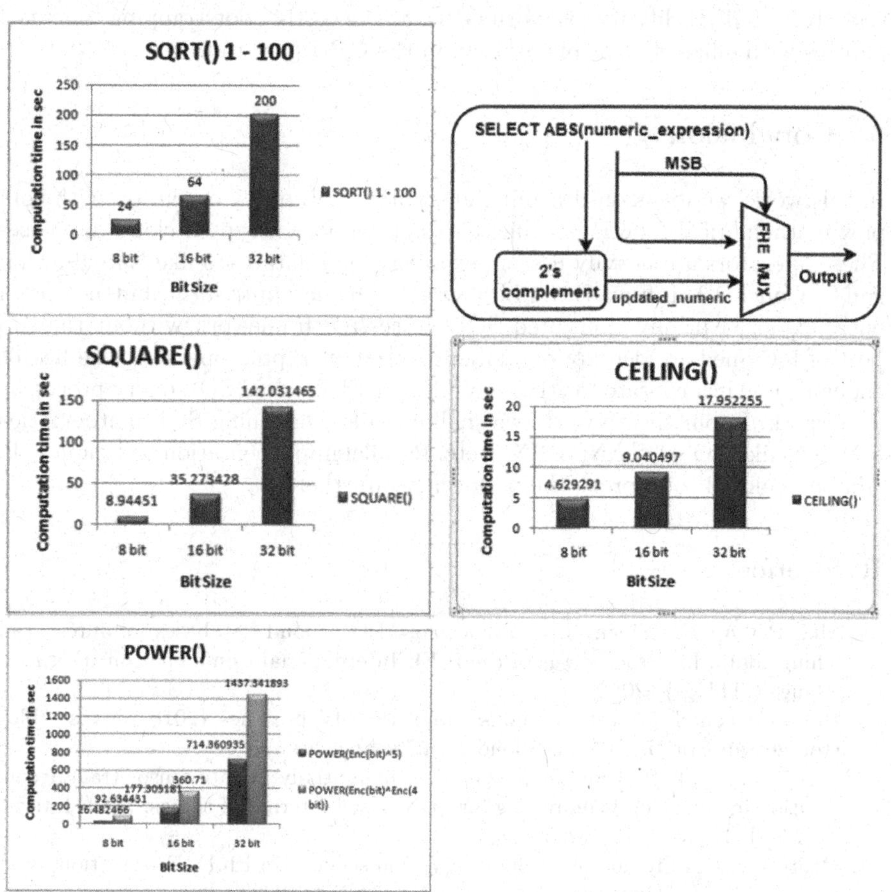

5 Performance Analysis

Table 1 shows the timing requirements for encrypted mathematical functions with TFHE [29] on 64 bit Intel(R) Xeon(R) E-2104G CPU clock speed 3.20 GHz, 64 GiB system memory with Ubuntu 16.04.3 platform and possible speed up with GPU based nuFHE library [34] in google colab platform. We have summarized a list of required FHE modules to implement several functions in that table. We also observe variations of processing time of these functions with respect to varying bit-lengths over 8-bits, 16-bits, and 32-bits encrypted numeric values as shown in Table 2.

This observation shows effective improvement in encrypted processing if input data of the application can be encoded with smaller bit-length. In case of POWER() implementation, we further observe the variation of timing with respect to bit-length of exponents (shown in Table 2). However, with suitable GPU support, same designs can exhibit improved timing requirements with underlying nuFHE library [34] with GPU, as the costly bootstrapping time itself reduces with efficient multiplier design in the GPU platform.

6 Conclusion

In this work, we focus on designing encrypted SQL query execution with complex mathematical functions, which are suitable for encrypted cloud databases. These operators are heavily used in existing cloud databases like NoSQL, MongoDB, CouchDB, InfluxDB, SQLite, etc., in unencrypted form, but not previously explored in any encrypted SQL processing framework without the support of intermediate decryption. The proposed encrypted operators are flexible enough to be incorporated within any LHE or FHE-based SQL query processing framework. In our future work, we shall consider remaining SQL mathematical functions like COS(), TAN(), SIN(), etc. Parallel implementation techniques also will be explored to improve the performance further.

References

1. Mai, P.T.A., Nurminen, J.K., Francesco, M.D.: Cloud databases for Internet-of-Things data. In: Proceedings of the IEEE International Conference on Internet of Things (iThings) (2014)
2. Bradford contel 7 most infamous cloud security breaches (2018). https://blog.storagecraft.com/7-infamous-cloud-security-breaches/
3. Nie, X., Yang, L.T., Feng, J., Zhang, S.: Differentially private tensor train decomposition in edge-cloud computing for SDN-based internet of things. IEEE Internet Things J. **7**, 5695–5705 (2020)
4. Gentry, C.: A fully homomorphic encryption scheme, in Ph.D. Dissertation, Stanford, CA, USA. Advisor(s) Boneh, D.: AAI3382729 (2009)
5. Acar, A., Aksu, H., Uluagac, A.S., Conti, M.: A Surveyon homomorphic encryption schemes: theory and implementation. arXiv:1704.03578v2 [cs.CR] (2017)
6. Vinayagamurthy, D., Gribov, A., Gorbunov, S.: StealthDB: a scalable encrypted database with full SQL query support. arXiv:1711.02279v2, [cs.CR] (2019)
7. Egorov, M., Wilkison, M.: Zerodb white paper. CoRR absarXiv : 1602.07168
8. Popa, R.A., Redfield, C.M.S., Zeldovich, N., Balakrishnan, H.: CryptDB: protecting confidentiality with encrypted query processing. In: Proceedings of the 23rd ACM Symposium on Operating System Principles, pp. 85–100 (2011)
9. Kumarage, H., Khalil, I., Alabdulatif, A., Tari, Z., Yi, X.: Secure data analytics for cloud-integrated Internet of Things applications. IEEE Cloud Comput. **3**(2), 46–56 (2016)
10. Always encrypted. https://www.cs.purdue.edu/homes/csjgwang/cloudb/EncrptedSQLSIGMOD20.pdf
11. Rivest, R.L., Shamir, A., Adleman, L.: A method for obtaining digital signatures and public-key cryptosystem. In: Proceedings of the Communication. ACM, pp. 120–126 (1978)

12. Gamal, T.: A public key cryptosystem and a signature scheme based on discrete logarithms. Inf. IEEE Trans. **31**(4), 469–472 (1985)
13. Paillier, P.: Public-key cryptosystems based on composite degree residuosity classes. In: Stern, J. (ed.) EUROCRYPT 1999. LNCS, vol. 1592, pp. 223–238. Springer, Heidelberg (1999). https://doi.org/10.1007/3-540-48910-X_16
14. Boneh, D., Goh, E.-J., Nissim, K.: Evaluating 2-DNF formulas on ciphertexts. In: Kilian, J. (ed.) TCC 2005. LNCS, vol. 3378, pp. 325–341. Springer, Heidelberg (2005). https://doi.org/10.1007/978-3-540-30576-7_18
15. Brakerski, Z., Gentry, C., Vaikuntanathan, V.: (Leveled) fully homo-morphic encryption without bootstrapping. In: Proceedings of the 3rd Innovations in Theoretical Computer Science Conference (ITCS 2012), pp. 309–325. ACM, NewYork (2012)
16. Grubbs, P., Ristenpart, T., Shmatikov, V.: Why your encrypted database is not secure. HotOS **2017**, 162–168 (2017)
17. Mathematical functions(transact-sql). https://docs.microsoft.com/en-us/sql/t-sql/functions/mathematical-functions-transact-sql?view=sql-server-ver15
18. Gentry, C.: Computing arbitrary functions of encrypted data. Commun. ACM **53**(3), 97–105 (2010)
19. Chatterjee, A., Aung, K.M.M.: Fully homomorphic encryption in real world application (2019)
20. Rass, S., Slamanig, D.: Cryptography for Security and Privacy in Cloud Computing. Artech House Inc., Norwood (2013)
21. Chatterjee, A., Sengupta, I.: Translating algorithms to handle fully homomorphic encrypted data on the cloud. IEEE Trans. Cloud Comput. **6**(1), 287–300 (2018)
22. Ghulam, A.: Top 5 databases to store data of IoT applications (2021). https://iot4beginners.com/top-5-databases-to-store-iot-data/
23. Influxdb design insights and tradeoffs. https://docs.influxdata.com/influxdb/v1.8/concepts/insights_tradeoffs/
24. Compare cratedb. https://crate.io/cratedb-comparison/cratedb-vs-mongodb/
25. RethinkDB: Rethinkdb https://rethinkdb.com/faq/
26. Xue, K., Li, S., Hong, J., Xue, Y., Yu, P., Hong, N.: Two-cloud secure database for numeric-related SQL range queries with privacy preserving. IEEE Trans. Inf. Forensics Secur. **12**(7), 1596–1608 (2017)
27. Xu, C., Chen, J., Wu, W., Feng, Y.: Homomorphically encrypted arithmetic operations over the integer ring, pp. 167–181 (2016)
28. Built-in mathematical SQL functions. https://www.sqlite.org/langmathfunc.html
29. Chillotti, I., Gama, N., Georgieva, M., Izabachne, M.: Faster fully homomorphic encryption : bootstrapping [1] in less than 0.1 seconds. Cryptology ePrint Archive Report 2016/870 (2016). https://eprint.iacr.org/2016/870
30. Shift-and-add multiplication. https://users.utcluj.ro/baruch/book_ssce/SSCE-Shift-Mult.pdf
31. Gosh, A., Chatterjee, A.: Practical performance improvement of domain aware encrypted computing. In: Proceedings of the ICMC (2021). Accepted
32. Jena, A., Panda, S.K.: Revision of various square-root algorithms for efficient VLSI signal processing applications. Proc. MCSP **2016**, 38–41 (2016)
33. Pima indians diabetes database. https://www.kaggle.com/uciml/pima-indians-diabetes-database
34. NuFHE. A GPU implementation of fully homomorphic encryption on torus. https://github.com/nucypher/nufhe

Robustness Against Adversarial Attacks Using Dimensionality

Nandish Chattopadhyay[1(✉)], Subhrojyoti Chatterjee[2], and Anupam Chattopadhyay[1]

[1] Nanyang Technological University, Jurong West, Singapore
nandish001@e.ntu.edu.sg

[2] Indian Institute of Technology, Kanpur, Kanpur, India

Abstract. Adversarial attacks have been a major deterrent towards the adoption of machine learning models reliably in many safety-critical applications. Structured perturbations introduced to test samples can fool high performing trained neural networks and force errors. We note that one of the key causes that facilitate adversarial attacks, is the curse of dimensionality or the behaviour of the high dimensional spaces. In this paper, we propose a machine learning infrastructure that is robust against adversarial attacks. The proposed pipeline uses a parallel pathway to carry out the primary machine learning task as well as identify adversarial samples. We use dimension reduction techniques to project adversarial samples into lower dimensions, thus eliminating adversarial perturbations. The end-to-end system has been tested to provide robustness, through different choices of neural architectures (VGG-19 [1], Inception ResNet v2 [2]), modes of adversarial attacks (FGSM [3] and PGD [4]) and multiple datasets (MNIST [5], CIFAR-10 and CIFAR-100 [6]). The overall accuracy of the end-to-end system was consistently found to be within a range of 1–2% (2%–4% in worst case scenarios) of what the accuracy would have been without the presence of any adversarial examples. We also show that this robustness is delivered without much compromise in time consumed for inference per sample.

Keywords: Adversarial attacks · Robustness · Adversarial defence · Dimensionality reduction · Neural networks

1 Introduction

Over the years, research in machine learning has seen improvements by leaps and bounces, particularly with the advancements in high performance neural networks, and the overall realm of deep learning. Some applications of neural architectures have reached and surpassed human accuracies, giving it a fresh start [7]. A variety of science and technology applications have adopted the data driven paradigm, both in academia and the industry. Historically, most statistical learning techniques consisted of significant data pre-processing requirements [8].

L. Batina et al. (Eds.): SPACE 2021, LNCS 13162, pp. 226–241, 2022.
https://doi.org/10.1007/978-3-030-95085-9_12

The accuracies of these models saturated over time and they typically lacked generalisation.

The much required breakthrough was provided by the emergence of deep learning models. Although the perceptron algorithm [9] was initially proposed long back, the idea did not receive much attention due to the lack of computing hardware, that was needed to sustain its operations. This problem was solved by the advent of high performing computational systems with multiple GPU cores. They could take advantage of the linear operations within neural architectures, and make multiple computations in parallel. Thus, enormous neural networks emerged into the scenes with tremendous learning capacities to solve problems which were not possible to have been addressed earlier.

1.1 Motivation

With the growth of machine learning applications, researchers found a new problem that proves to be a deterrent to reliable use of ML models. Adversarial attacks were first observed as an intriguing property [10] of neural networks, and over the years, many attack modes have been developed. Designing defence mechanisms against adversarial attacks has been a challenge for researchers as novel attacks emerge. Most mechanisms are quite ad-hoc in nature, and are successful against specific targets. The way this field of research has progressed is much like other domains in security, with every counter-measure proposed, a new attack is developed. We set out to take a step back from this loop, and understand one of the primary reasons behind the existence of such adversarial vulnerabilities, and use the learning to design the defence. We study the geometry of landscape in higher dimensions in which the neural network optimises, and note that its properties contribute to adversarial vulnerability. Dimension reduction therefore addresses this fundamental problem, and we observe that at lower dimensions, the attacks become significantly difficult. However, generic dimension reduction techniques are not able to specifically distinguish between adversarial noise and features of the clean sample. So, for a sample that doesn't have any adversarial perturbation, dimension reduction can potentially reduce its likelihood of correct classification. So the goal of this paper is to design a method that intelligently selects adversarial samples and subjects them to noise reduction through dimension reduction. Achieving that is important for a robust system that is able to correctly carry out the machine learning task, despite the presence of adversarial examples.

1.2 Contribution

In this paper, we propose a robust mechanism for fulfilling machine learning objectives by carrying out classification tasks and eliminating errors arising from adversarial attacks. Specifically, the end-to-end infrastructure that we have designed is able to accomplish the reliable functionality by leveraging the following:

- A parallel pathway of simultaneously carrying out the classification task and detection of adversarial perturbations in the samples to increase efficiency
- Using dimensionality reduction to eliminate adversarial perturbation from only those samples that are detected to be adversarial examples.

The proposed framework has been tested to generate satisfactory results, for multiple choices of neural architectures (VGG-19 [1], Inception ResNet v2 [2]), modes of adversarial attacks (FGSM [3] and PGD [4]) and multiple datasets (MNIST [5], CIFAR-10 and CIFAR-100 [6]). The overall accuracy of the end-to-end system was consistently found to be within a range of 1–2% of what the accuracy would have been without the presence of any adversarial examples.

1.3 Organization

In Sect. 2, we define adversarial attacks, and how the behaviour of high dimensions of the optimizing landscape of the neural networks impact them. We also provide the literature review on adversarial attacks and defences. In Sect. 3, we introduce our proposed adversarial defence mechanism using parallel pathways and dimensionality reduction. In Sect. 4, we describe the pipeline and the corresponding models and techniques used for the implementation. Then, the experimental results and findings are presented in Sect. 5. Finally, we conclude with some remarks on future scope and implications.

2 Adversarial Attacks

Adversarial attacks were first observed as anomalies in image classification systems [11]. For a specific classifier model trained on a particular dataset, and a particular correctly classified sample, the corresponding adversarial sample that can be generated using an adversarial attack, would be a sample with structured adversarial perturbation that would be invisible to the human vision, but picked up by the machine learning model, therefore creating a discrepancy at the inference decision.

There are some essential components of a machine learning system. Considering an image processing task, there are four aspects to look at. Firstly, the model of choice, which could be a neural network of some other parameterised model [12]. Next, a training dataset is necessary and for most tasks which are supervised, the dataset should also be annotated with labels. Then, there has to be a test dataset for inference. And in the end of the training process, we obtain a trained model, which is essentially the trained manifolds separated by the classifier [13].

To understand the process of the creation of adversarial examples, we explain the idea using the example of a simple binary image classification problem. First, is the notion of the dataset, for the task, which is a 2D approximation of some instances of what's observable in the real world, typically referred to as the population. We can not have the exhaustive set of the population at our disposal, and therefore have to work with the samples. There exists a true classifier, within the population, that correctly classifies all samples. However, that classifier is unknown, and therefore we have to use an approximation of it, using a machine learning model. A manifestation of the true classifier could be thought of as that of human vision annotator, while the ML model could be a neural network.

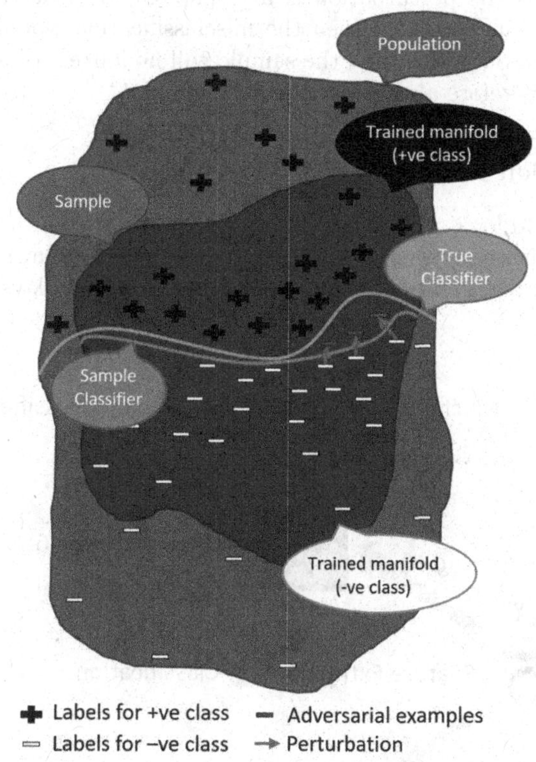

Fig. 1. Adversarial examples in context of a classifier.

Since we are trying to approximate the true classifier, we train the machine learning model to create the sample classifier, that is able to split the sample space into trained manifolds of the associated class labels. The sample space, in this case, is the labelled dataset of image samples derived from the population. One may assume that the true classifier within the population extends indistinguishably to the true classifier within the sample for simplicity. The sample classifier is an approximation of it for the dataset. As expected, this approximation can only be accurate up to a certain extent, and that might result is a notional 'gap' between the true classifier and the sample classifier trained on a definitely non-exhaustive dataset. In theory, this gap is responsible for creating an adversarial space, as any data point lying in that region would be associated with differing class labels with respect to the true and sample classifiers. And thus, the adversarial example is generated.

It is important to take note of the fact that if the data points are situated close to the boundaries of the individual trained manifolds, then the addition of a little adversarial perturbation facilitates the transfer of some of the samples to across the sample classifier, but not enough to cross the true classifier, as shown in Fig. 1. If the perturbation is high enough to make the sample cross over the true classifier as well, then the misclassification would hold good for the human annotator as well, and the sample will no longer be adversarial. This perturbation is therefore always bounded.

2.1 Formulation

Having had a good look at why the adversarial samples exist, it is important to formally define these adversarial examples, so that we can have a better understanding of how they are created and why dimensionality plays and important role (Fig. 2).

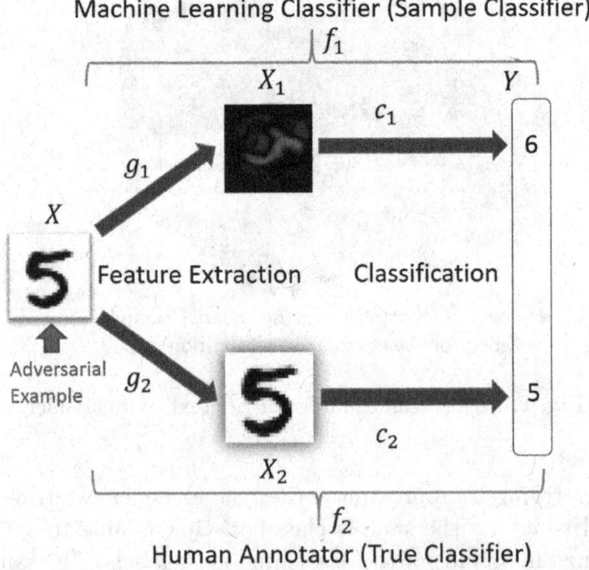

Fig. 2. Generation of adversarial examples.

We may consider X to be the space of input samples. When the system takes images as inputs, X may be thought of as the vector space of dimensions equal to the size of the image, that is pixels. The two classifiers being looked into are f_1 (sample classifier) and f_2 (human annotator). The classifiers have two components each, feature extraction and classification. We therefore have

X_1 to be the space of features for the sample classifier and X_2 to be the space of features for the human annotator, where d_1 and d_2 are norms defined in the spaces X_1 and X_2 respectively. As shown, $f_1 = c_1 \circ g_1$ and $f_2 = c_2 \circ g_2$.

We look at $x \in X$, to be a training sample. Given x, its corresponding adversarial example x^*, for a norm d_2 defined on the space X_2, and a predefined threshold $\delta > 0$, must satisfy:

$$\begin{aligned} f_1(x) \neq f_1(x^*) \quad &\text{and} \quad f_2(x) = f_2(x^*) \\ \text{such that} \quad &d_2(g_2(x), g_2(x^*)) < \delta \end{aligned}$$

2.2 Curse of Dimensionality

Our goal is to explain the creation of adversarial examples by understanding the geometry of the high dimensional spaces of the trained manifolds of the classed where they exist. We therefore pay particular attention to the behaviour of data points in such high dimensional settings, and look at their distribution within the manifolds. We take note of certain properties of objects in the high dimensional setting, like the fact that the majority of their volume lies near the surface. This is important is providing a theoretical explanation into why little structured perturbations are able to create adversarial samples [14] by pushing them across the sample classifier, as discussed earlier.

We look at an object A in a d-dimensional space, that is R^d. If we force to reduce it a little, that is bring down A by a small amount ϵ to create another object $(1-\epsilon)A = \{(1-\epsilon)x \mid x \in A\}$, Then we can note the following:

$$\text{volume}((1-\epsilon)A) = (1-\epsilon)^d \ \text{volume}(A)$$

In order to see if this holds or not, we begin by partitioning A into infinitesimal *cubes*. Then, we have $(1-\epsilon)A$ as the union of a set of cubes, which we have created by the shrinkage of the cubes in A by a factor of $(1-\epsilon)$. Upon the shrinkage of the $2d$ sides of a d-dimensional cube by a factor of $(1-\epsilon)$, it follows that the corresponding volume has a shrinkage by a factor of $(1-\epsilon)^d$. Therefore, considering any object A in R^d, we may note:

$$\frac{\text{volume}((1-\epsilon)A)}{\text{volume}(A)} = (1-\epsilon)^d \le e^{-\epsilon d}$$

Upon fixing the ϵ and letting $d \to \infty$, we see that the right hand side of the inequality in the equation rapidly approaches zero. The key takeaway from this is that almost all of the volume of A has to be present in that part of A which can not belong to the region $(1-\epsilon)A$. Therefore, in the high dimensional setting, almost all of the volume of A is present near its surface.

This property of the high-dimensional space is counter-intuitive, but it is one that tremendously facilitates the creation and existence of adversarial examples [15].

2.3 Attack and Defences Review

The research in this domain has led to competitive works in attacks and defences which have both improved over time. The first adversarial attack was studied as an interesting property of neural networks [10], but over time, different attack mechanisms have been developed like the Fast Gradient Sign method [3], the Momentum Iterative version of it [16], the Carlini Wagner attack [17] and the Projected Gradient Descent attack [4]. Similarly, multiple defence techniques have been proposed over time, to mitigate such attacks. Some prominent ones include the defensive distillation technique [18] and other filtering mechanisms [19]. Needless to say, as the attacks got stronger, it was imperative to come up with stronger defences and that serves as one of the primary motivations of this work, presented in this paper.

3 Defence Design

As discussed in the earlier sections, higher dimensionality facilitates adversarial example generation, and it is natural to try reducing dimensionality of the test samples as a defence. This may be effective in reducing, and in some cases eliminating adversarial perturbations. There is a sound theoretical explanation for the empirical results seen in experimental results of using techniques of reducing dimensionality as an adversarial defence. However, there are some issues which prevent it from being applied universally as a filter to deter adversarial attacks. They are as follows.

- Dimensionality reduction is not targeted, and therefore may reduce useful information from the samples along with adversarial noise. While being useful to eliminate adversarial noise, this process may at times make the original machine learning task (classification for example) difficult for a trained model. How much variability to preserve in the samples is therefore a critical design decision.
- It is also an unnecessary overhead for samples which are clean, and may slow down a system where there are many samples to deal with.

We seek to address this, by intelligently selecting which samples to expose to dimensionality reduction and which to remain as is, before sending them as inputs to the machine learning model. In particular, we adopt a design of parallel pathways, to simultaneously carry out the inference task and identify potential adversarial samples and apply dimensionality reduction to only those which have been picked up to contain adversarial noise. Our only assumption for choosing the parallel setup, as opposed to a serial setup is that most samples are clean, with some being adversarial.

3.1 Parallel Pathways

We consider a particular machine learning task as the primary objective, like classification. This is a trained neural network that is vulnerable to adversarial attacks. We design another classifier, that is specifically trained to identify samples that contain adversarial noise. The overall system is so designed that the input samples are fed to the two networks, in parallel. One network carries out the actual task (classification for instance) and we call that the Main Model. The other network determines whether the sample is clean or adversarial, and we call it the Adversarial Detector. If the sample is found to be clean, the output of the Main model is mapped to the output of the system. If the sample is found to be adversarial (that is it contains adversarial noise as identified by the Adversarial Detector), then the Dimensionality Reduction loop is activated. The sample is then fed to the Dimensionality Reducer and its result is further sent to the Main Model for carrying out the task (classification) again.

This design choice has been made keeping the following in mind:

- Adversarial samples, crafted by adversaries are fewer in number than naturally occurring clean samples. The system is likely to encounter many more clean samples and therefore not require dimensionality reduction.
- Since the dimensionality reduction loop will be activated for fewer adversarial samples, for most clean samples the throughput of the system will be comparable to what it would have been, without any defence mechanisms.
- By checking for the presence of adversarial perturbations and only then reducing dimension, we are ensuring that the model performance for clean samples is not hampered.

3.2 Detecting Adversarial Samples

Adversarial examples contain structured noise inserted as perturbation by attackers to fool the trained neural networks. This perturbations are bounded, because they are by design, imperceptible to human vision. The misclassification or simply mistake in the machine learning task by the model as opposed to correct classification by the human annotator leads to the discrepancy in class labels that generate adversarial attacks. In this work, we re-use the neural architecture that falls prey to adversarial attacks, by training it to differentiate between clean samples and adversarial samples. The intuition is that the model that picks up the adversarial noise to lead to an error, will also be able to detect that same noise, if it is trained to do so. We have generated pairs of adversarial samples for corresponding clean samples, and trained the network as a binary classifier. The sensitivity of the main model towards the attack is used in this classifier to identify adversarial samples. The experimental results later on vindicate the proposition.

3.3 Dimensionality

As a manifestation of the theoretical setup mentioned in the earlier section, high dimensionality of the optimizing landscape of the neural network classifier makes it vulnerable to adversarial attacks. It has been shown that the sensitivity of the model to adversarial perturbation grows with higher dimensions. As a natural extension of that idea, we propose to use dimension reduction to defend against such attacks. Essentially, we select the samples that have been detected to contain adversarial perturbation and then project them onto a lower dimension, eliminating a certain amount of information (measured through variability) to convert them into clean samples. The intuition is that such samples, with cropped information, will be classified to the correct classes when subjected to the Main Model. We have tested this idea through a series of thorough experiments.

4 Implementation

The adversarial defence mechanism has been implemented as an end-to-end system, that takes in samples, both clean and adversarial ones alike, and outputs the correct probability distribution over the classes with high accuracy. Internally, it is able to detect adversarial samples using a separate adversarial detector, and thereby activates a dimension reduction loop to eliminate noise that pertains to the attack. The implementation of the framework is shown in Fig. 3.

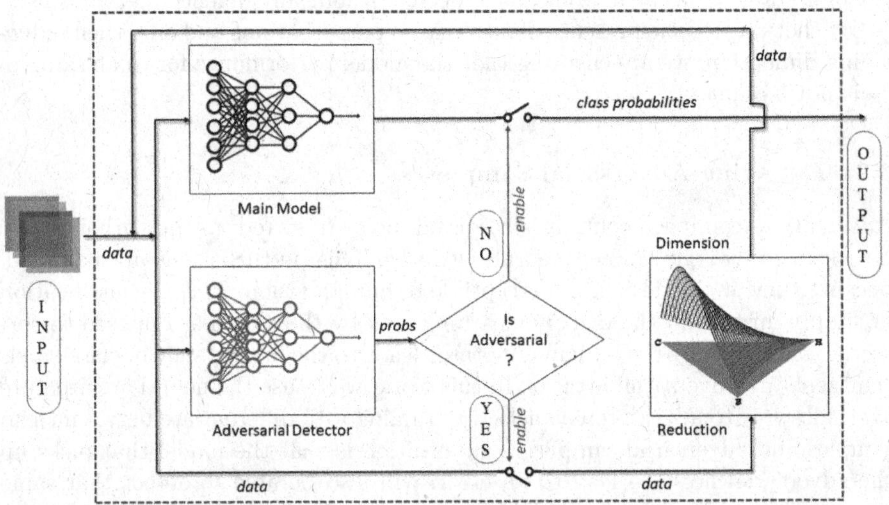

Fig. 3. Implementation of the framework pipeline. The flow of data samples is shown in black channels, the flow of output class probabilities is shown in blue channels and the flow of enable control is shown in red. (Color figure online)

4.1 Pipeline

The pipeline is setup using parallel pathways for the primary machine learning task of classification and the additional task of detecting adversarial samples. This is in accordance with the notion described in Sect. 3.1. The input samples are sent in parallel to both the networks, the Main Model and the Adversarial Detector. The have tested two different neural architectures for both these tasks. The Main Model generates the probability distribution over the classes and the Adversarial Detector labels the samples as clean or adversarial. If the sample is found to be clean, then the corresponding channel is enabled so as to map the output of the Main Model to the final output of the system. If the sample is found to be adversarial, then the other channel is enabled, which feeds the input sample to the Dimension Reduction block. This is where the sample is projected onto a lower dimension based on a tuning parameter, and then its output is again fed to the input of the overall system. This process ensures that the Main Model's predicted class probabilities are mapped to the final output only if the sample is deemed to be a clean one. The entire flow of data and control is shown in the diagram.

4.2 Models

In order to check if the proposed infrastructure's robustness against adversarial attacks is agnostic to any specific neural architecture or adversarial attack, we used multiple combinations of them and checked for performance. In particular, we used two state-of-the-art neural architectures (VGG-19 [1], Inception ResNet v2 [2]), two most widely used and effective modes of adversarial attacks (FGSM [3] and PGD [4]) and some benchmarking datasets (MNIST [5], CIFAR-10 and CIFAR-100 [6]) for making the results to comparable to the available literature.

4.3 Dimension Reduction

The process of transformation of data from a high dimensional space to a low dimensional space is carried out using dimensionality reduction algorithms. They ensure that the representation so created in the low dimensional setting, is able to retain as much meaningful properties as possible, of the data in the original high dimensional setting. This is particularly necessary for a variety of reasons, like avoiding the issues that arise due to the curse of dimensionality and other unfavourable behaviours of the high dimensional space. Reducing the dimension makes computation and analysis easier.

There are different ways of carrying out dimension reduction. Typically, techniques like principal components analysis or singular value decomposition [20] are used to reduce dimensions in a linear fashion, that is the new components so created are linear combinations of the original. There are some useful non-linear dimensionality reduction techniques as well, like the t-distributed stochastic neighbor embedding [21].

5 Experiments

In this section we discuss the experimental setup and corresponding results in details. The overall aim of the experiments is to study whether the proposed system is able to match the accuracies of the model when there are no adversarial examples, even when adversarial samples are introduced via attacks. The entire infrastructure has been built in TensorFlow [22] and the experiments were run on Google Colab with a NVIDIA Tesla K80 GPU. The attacks were taken from Google's Cleverhans [23] repository.

5.1 Design

We study each component of the infrastructure separately first, and then we look into the performance of the overall framework under specific circumstances. We note the accuracy of the Main Model when exposed to clean samples as the baseline (first row of the Tables 1, 2, 3, 4). This is the highest possible performance that we may have, given the neural architecture and a specific dataset. The rest of the accuracies will be compared to this benchmark.

Next, we look at the drop in performance of the Main Model when exposed to adversarial examples (second row of the Tables 1, 2, 3, 4). Then, we turn our attention to the Adversarial Detector. It is important to note that high accuracies of this component is extremely critical to the overall performance of the infrastructure. The error in Adversarial Detection, will be propagated to the overall output error of the system, as we apply the adversarial perturbation reduction loop to only those samples that are identified to be adversarial by this detector. Intuitively, a neural architecture that is vulnerable to picking up adversarial noise and thereby misclassifying, will also be sensitive to that exact same noise when trained as an Adversarial Detector rather than a regular classifier. We take a note of it in the third row of the Tables 1, 2, 3, 4.

In the next part of the experimental setup, we study the impact of using dimensionality reduction techniques and use two different techniques for the same. Note that only adversarial samples, detected by the Adversarial detector, are exposed to the dimensionality reduction. We report the corresponding performance of the Main Model when exposed to the projections of those samples on lower dimensions. We use two different techniques for doing the same, as shown in the fourth and fifth rows of the Tables 1, 2, 3, 4.

Finally, we check the performance of the overall framework. This is where we run the entire pipeline shown in Fig. 3. We use different scenarios here. One, where the test samples are 80% clean samples and 20% adversarial, this being a more likely situation from a practical perspective (results shown in the sixth row of the Tables 1, 2, 3, 4). And secondly, we consider a set of test samples which are 50% clean samples and 50% adversarial (results shown in the last row of the Tables 1, 2, 3, 4). We compare these accuracies to the baseline accuracy. Additionally, we also study how much time is consumed in the inference process for the aforementioned setups in Table 5. This gives us a good understanding of the efficiency of the infrastructure.

5.2 Results

The experimental results are presented in a tabulated form here. Each table is associated with a particular combination of neural architecture and adversarial attack pair. The performances of different settings are noted, for all three datasets (MNIST [5], CIFAR-10 and CIFAR-100 [6]). The bounds on adversarial perturbation, is set like this: $\epsilon = 1.0$ for MNIST and $\epsilon = 0.1$ for CIFAR -10 and CIFAR-100.

Considering a VGG-19 [1] neural architecture and the mode of adversarial attack being the FGSM [3] attack, the step by step results are shown in Table 1 and Fig. 4. We observe the drop in performance of the Main Model upon the introduction of the adversarial examples, while the Detector is able to correctly identify adversarial samples effectively. We also note that dimension reduction works well on adversarial samples to be correctly classified thereafter. In the end, the framework is able to perform almost as well (within a 1%–2% range) as the Main Model without the existence of any adversarial samples, thus fulfilling our objective.

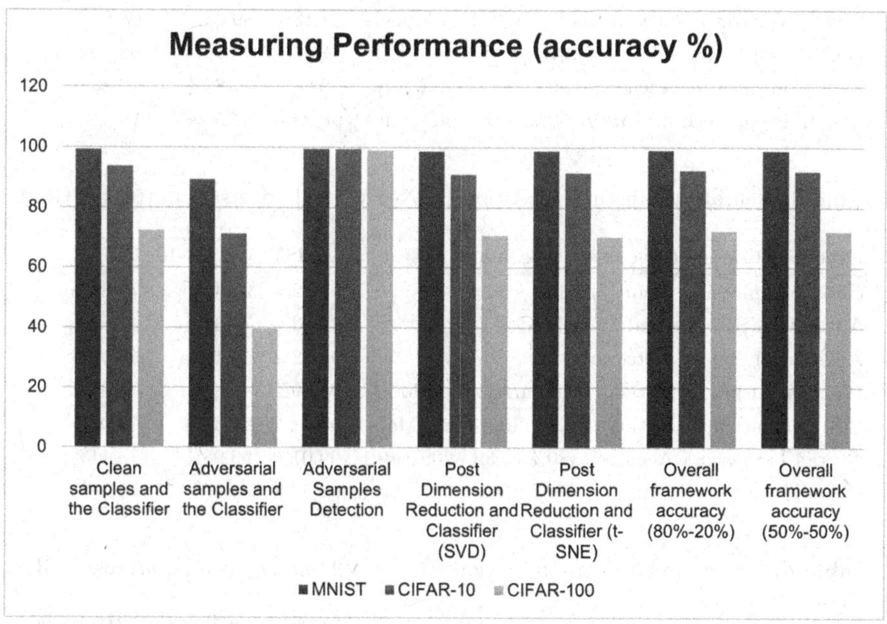

Fig. 4. Performances using a VGG-19 [1] neural architecture and the mode of adversarial attack is the FGSM [3] attack.

The exact same analysis is repeated for some different choices of neural architectures and adversarial attacks. Table 2 uses a VGG-19 [1] neural architecture and the mode of adversarial attack is the PGD [4] attack. Table 3 uses a Inception ResNet V2 [2] neural architecture and the mode of adversarial attack is the FGSM [3] attack. Table 4 uses a Inception ResNet V2 [2] neural architecture and the mode of adversarial attack is the PGD [4] attack.

Table 1. Neural architecture: VGG-19 and adversarial attack: FGSM

Experiment design (type of samples and model)	MNIST	CIFAR-10	CIFAR-100
Clean Samples and Main Model	99.12%	93.58%	72.14%
Adversarial Samples and Main Model	89.11%	71.04%	39.61%
Adversarial Sample Detector	99.24%	99.24%	98.89%
Post Dimension Reduction (SVD) and Main Model	98.51%	90.87%	70.66%
Post Dimension Reduction (t-SNE) and Main Model	98.66%	91.52%	70.04%
Overall Framework Accuracy (80% clean –20% adv)	98.79%	92.16%	72.05%
Overall Framework Accuracy (50% clean –50% adv)	98.66%	91.89%	71.95%

Table 2. Neural architecture: VGG-19 and adversarial attack: PGD

Experiment design (type of samples and model)	MNIST	CIFAR-10	CIFAR-100
Clean Samples and Main Model	99.12%	93.58%	72.14%
Adversarial Samples and Main Model	87.81%	70.01%	37.89%
Adversarial Sample Detector	99.27%	99.05%	98.11%
Post Dimension Reduction (SVD) and Main Model	97.18%	89.93%	68.91%
Post Dimension Reduction (t-SNE) and Main Model	97.84%	90.17%	68.76%
Overall Framework Accuracy (80% clean –20% adv)	98.88%	91.84%	70.88%
Overall Framework Accuracy (50% clean –50% adv)	98.22%	91.56%	70.41%

Table 3. Neural architecture: inception ResNet V2 and adversarial attack: FGSM

Experiment design (type of samples and model)	MNIST	CIFAR-10	CIFAR-100
Clean Samples and Main Model	99.32%	95.42%	79.89%
Adversarial Samples and Main Model	87.43%	72.36%	41.89%
Adversarial Sample Detector	99.28%	99.18%	99.02%
Post Dimension Reduction (SVD) and Main Model	98.49%	91.80%	72.86%
Post Dimension Reduction (t-SNE) and Main Model	98.23%	92.30%	74.01%
Overall Framework Accuracy (80% clean –20% adv)	99.01%	93.98%	78.11%
Overall Framework Accuracy (50% clean –50% adv)	98.77%	93.15%	75.18%

Table 4. Neural architecture: inception ResNet V2 and adversarial attack: PGD

Experiment design (type of samples and model)	MNIST	CIFAR-10	CIFAR-100
Clean Samples and Main Model	99.32%	95.42%	79.89%
Adversarial Samples and Main Model	86.15%	69.78%	38.45%
Adversarial Sample Detector	98.19%	98.16%	97.65%
Post Dimension Reduction (SVD) and Main Model	98.11%	90.41%	71.87%
Post Dimension Reduction (t-SNE) and Main Model	98.07%	90.59%	71.55%
Overall Framework Accuracy (80% clean –20% adv)	98.54%	93.66%	74.09%
Overall Framework Accuracy (50% clean –50% adv)	98.37%	92.89%	73.88%

Table 5 reports the amount of time taken for:

- just the Main Model to process the samples when they are in the proportion of 80% clean samples and 20% adversarial samples, as opposed to when they are equally likely to be clean or adversarial.
- the overall framework, that is the proposed pipeline, to process the samples when they are in the proportion of 80% clean samples and 20% adversarial samples, as opposed to when they are equally likely to be clean or adversarial.

Table 5. Inference time per sample (in ms)

Dataset composition	Model	MNIST	CIFAR-10	CIFAR-100
80% clean samples, 20% adversarial samples	Main Model	3.29	3.26	3.26
	Overall Pipeline	3.91	4.05	4.09
50% clean samples, 50% adversarial samples	Main Model	3.29	3.26	3.26
	Overall Pipeline	4.71	4.82	4.91

5.3 Key Findings

As evident form the data presented above, we have some important takeaways from the extensive set of experiments that we carried out. They are noted here.

- While the introduction of adversarial samples is able to bring down the accuracy of the Main Model (the image classifier) significantly (ranging from 15%–50% decline in performance), the use of dimensionality reduction successfully prevents it.
- Dimension Reduction works very well for reducing/eliminating adversarial perturbations and proves to be a good technique for correctly classifying adversarial samples (its performance being within 2%–5% within the range of accuracy of the classifier without any adversarial samples).
- The adversarial Detector, a model specifically trained to detect adversarial samples, is extremely efficient in doing so (accurate in excess of 98% for all combinations of models, attacks and datasets) and this is crucial for the successful working of the parallel nature of the pipeline (results shown in the third row of the Tables 1, 2, 3, 4).
- Since dimensionality reduction sometimes eliminates important information from clean samples, the parallel pipeline is necessary to increase overall accuracy of the framework when the input samples are a mix of clean and adversarial samples. There seems to be not much difference in using either of the techniques for dimension reduction though, both SVD and t-SNE generate similar performances (results shown in the fourth and fifth row of the Tables 1, 2, 3, 4).

- The overall framework is robust against adversarial attacks, whilst being functionality preserving for clean samples. For a practical scenario of an input set of samples consisting of some adversarial examples within clean samples (in a 80% clean and 20% adversarial split), the framework consistently generates good performance of accuracies within the range of 1%–2% of baseline (results shown in the sixth row of the Tables 1, 2, 3, 4).
- Even for an extreme scenario of a 50%–50% split in clean and adversarial samples (this is unlikely because adversarial samples are not naturally occurring), the framework is able to generate accuracies within a 2%–4% of baseline (results shown in the last row of the Tables 1, 2, 3, 4).
- The inference time per sample is comparable for the Main Model and the overall pipeline. This indicates that the framework is able to deliver robustness without much compromise on overheads (results shown in Table 5).

6 Concluding Remarks

Since adversarial attacks are capable of introducing structured perturbations into clean samples that are imperceptible to the human vision, they can easily be used to fool high performance trained neural networks. This is a major concern for adopting neural networks in critical operations. We address this problem by developing a frame work that delivers robustness against such attacks. We ensure that the framework is functionality preserving, that is it works as expected for clean samples and also is able to correctly classify adversarial samples, therefore preventing such attacks from disrupting the machine learning task. We approach the solution by first understanding one key property of neural networks, that is their vulnerability to attacks due to the high dimensional nature of the optimisation landscape. We use dimensionality reduction to tackle this problem, and aim to reduce/eliminate adversarial noise. However, we do not disturb the clean samples and therefore use a parallel pathway to detect adversarial samples and expose only those to the defence mechanism. The framework has been heavily tested with multiple neural architectures, datasets, dimensionality reduction techniques and adversarial attacks. Going ahead, we are looking to extend this idea to video streams instead of images and study the real-time applicability of the framework in greater detail, so as to find many more practical use-cases for it to be deployed in public.

Acknowledgement. This research is supported by the National Research Foundation (NRF, Prime Minister's Office, Singapore) as part of the "SoCure" project.

References

1. Simonyan, K., Zisserman, A.: Very deep convolutional networks for large-scale image recognition. arXiv preprint arXiv:1409.1556 (2014)
2. Szegedy, C., Ioffe, S., Vanhoucke, V., Alemi, A.A.: Inception-v4, inception-resnet and the impact of residual connections on learning. In: Thirty-First AAAI Conference on Artificial Intelligence (2017)

3. Kurakin, A., Goodfellow, I., Bengio, S.: Adversarial machine learning at scale. arXiv preprint arXiv:1611.01236 (2016)
4. Madry, A., Makelov, A., Schmidt, L., Tsipras, D., Vladu, A.: Towards deep learning models resistant to adversarial attacks. arXiv preprint arXiv:1706.06083 (2017)
5. LeCun, Y., Cortes, C., Burges, C.J.: MNIST handwritten digit database. AT&T Labs, p. 2 (2010). http://yann.lecun.com/exdb/mnist
6. Krizhevsky, A., Nair, V., Hinton, G.: The CIFAR-10 dataset (2014). http://www.cs.toronto.edu/kriz/cifar.html
7. Krizhevsky, A., Sutskever, I., Hinton, G.E.: Imagenet classification with deep convolutional neural networks. Adv. Neural Inf. Process. Syst. 1097–1105 (2012)
8. Friedman, J., Hastie, T., Tibshirani, R.: The Elements of Statistical Learning, vol. 1. Springer series in statistics, New York, NY, USA (2001)
9. Rosenblatt, F.: The perceptron: a probabilistic model for information storage and organization in the brain. Psychol. Rev. **65**(6), 386 (1958)
10. Szegedy, C., et al.: Intriguing properties of neural networks. arXiv preprint arXiv:1312.6199 (2013)
11. Goodfellow, I., Bengio, Y., Courville, A., Bengio, Y.: Deep Learning, vol. 1. MIT press, Cambridge (2016)
12. Cortes, C., Vapnik, V.: Support-vector networks. Mach. Learn. **20**(3), 273–297 (1995)
13. Bishop, C.M., et al.: Neural Networks for Pattern Recognition. Oxford University Press, Oxford (1995)
14. Dube, S.: High dimensional spaces, deep learning and adversarial examples. arXiv preprint arXiv:1801.00634 (2018)
15. Chattopadhyay, N., Chattopadhyay, A., Gupta, S.S., Kasper, M.: Curse of dimensionality in adversarial examples. In: 2019 International Joint Conference on Neural Networks (IJCNN), pp. 1–8. IEEE (2019)
16. Dong, Y., et al.: Boosting adversarial attacks with momentum. arXiv preprint arXiv:1710.06081 (2017)
17. Carlini, N., Wagner, D.: Towards evaluating the robustness of neural networks. In: 2017 IEEE Symposium on Security and Privacy (SP), pp. 39–57. IEEE (2017)
18. Papernot, N., McDaniel, P.: On the effectiveness of defensive distillation. arXiv preprint arXiv:1607.05113 (2016)
19. Chakraborty, A., Alam, M., Dey, V., Chattopadhyay, A., Mukhopadhyay, D.: Adversarial attacks and defences: a survey. CoRR, abs/1810.00069 (2018)
20. Golub, G.H., Reinsch, C.: Singular value decomposition and least squares solutions. In: Bauer, F.L. (eds.) Linear Algebra. Handbook for Automatic Computation, vol. 2, pp. 134–151. Springer, Berlin, Heidelberg (1971). https://doi.org/10.1007/978-3-662-39778-7_10
21. Van der Maaten, L., Hinton, G.: Visualizing data using t-SNE. J. Mach. Learn. Res. **9**(11) (2008)
22. Paszke, A., et al.: Pytorch: an imperative style, high-performance deep learning library. Adv. Neural Inf. Process. Syst. 8026–8037 (2019)
23. Papernot, N., et al.: cleverhans v2. 0.0: an adversarial machine learning library. arXiv preprint arXiv:1610.00768 (2016)

SoK - Network Intrusion Detection on FPGA

Laurens Le Jeune[1,2], Arish Sateesan[1], Md Masoom Rabbani[1], Toon Goedemé[2], Jo Vliegen[1], and Nele Mentens[1,3](✉)

[1] ES&S - imec-COSIC, ESAT, KU Leuven, Leuven, Belgium
{laurensle.jeune,arish.sateesan,mdmasoom.rabbani,jo.vliegen, nele.mentens}@kuleuven.be

[2] EAVISE - PSI, ESAT, KU Leuven, Leuven, Belgium
toon.goedem@kuleuven.be

[3] LIACS, Leiden University, Leiden, The Netherlands

Abstract. The amount of Internet traffic is ever increasing. With a well maintained network infrastructure, people find their way to Internet forums, video streaming services, social media and webshops on a day-to-day basis. With the growth of the online world, criminal activities have also spread out to the Internet. Security researchers and system administrators develop and maintain infrastructures to control these possible threats. This work focuses on one aspect of network security: intrusion detection. An Intrusion Detection System (IDS) is only one of the many components in the security engineer's toolbox. An IDS is a passive component that tries to detect malicious activities. With the increase of Internet traffic and bandwidth, the detection speed of IDSs needs to be improved accordingly. This work focuses on how Field-programmable Gate Arrays (FPGA) are used as hardware accelerators to assist the IDS in keeping up with high network speed. We give an overview of three approaches: Intrusion detection based on machine learning, pattern matching, and large flow detection. This work is concluded with a comparison between the three approaches on the most relevant metrics.

Keywords: Network intrusion detection · Deep learning · FPGA

1 Introduction

Stating that the amount of Internet traffic is increasing, is like kicking at an open door. The global COVID-19 pandemic contributed in raising the total amount of network traffic to unprecedented volumes. This was mainly due to the lock downs that were installed in various parts of the world, boosting video conferencing and on-line shopping. It should not come as a surprise that malicious individuals or groupings saw this as a lucrative evolution. Even without this evolution, network security is becoming increasingly important.

The simplest way to describe the Internet is calling it a network of networks. Figure 1 helps with introducing a number of concepts or components that are

L. Batina et al. (Eds.): SPACE 2021, LNCS 13162, pp. 242–261, 2022.
https://doi.org/10.1007/978-3-030-95085-9_13

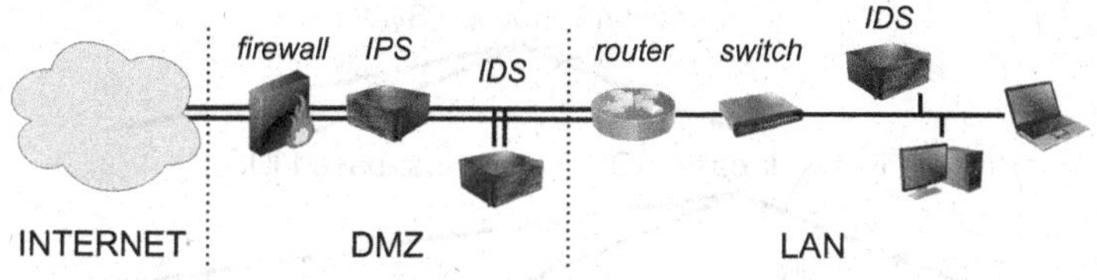

Fig. 1. General network setup

typically used in organising network security. The local network (e.g. the office network or a home network) is referred to as the Local Area Network (LAN). All the devices in the network can communicate with each other. When the LAN is hooked up to the Internet, a number of components are added in between. Generally these devices reside in a so-called demilitarised zone (DMZ).

The device, in the DMZ, that is positioned the closest to the Internet is the traditional firewall. This firewall uses a set of rules which it traverses sequentially. Depending on matches or mismatches to certain rules, incoming (or outgoing) traffic is allowed through or is denied passage. The firewall typically operates standalone and provides a first layer of network protection in an active way and focuses primarily in a single direction: from the Internet to the LAN. The actions taken by a firewall are typically also logged on the system.

An Intrusion Detection System (IDS) has a more passive role. Network traffic that is allowed by the firewall is examined by the IDS, as shown in Fig. 1. The IDS searches for signatures of network attacks. When such symptoms are detected, the system administrators can be notified. The logs of the passive IDS can be used to strengthen the active firewall. By using an IDS, additional defenses can be set up against threats like access of unauthorised clients or servers, Trojan horses, viruses, policy violations, SQL injections or Distributed Denial of Service (DDoS) attacks [35]. An IDS could also be placed in the local network to detect potential malicious activities from within the private network. In this work, we concentrate on network-based intrusion detection systems (NIDSs), which monitor the traffic in the network, as opposed to host-based intrusion detection systems (HIDSs) that monitor a specific host. In fact, the IDS in Fig. 1 is an NIDS. Figure 2 introduces this classification.

A challenge that comes with the design of an NIDS is that it should detect potential attacks as fast as possible in order to reduce the window of opportunity for an attack to be exploited. Therefore, this work focuses on NIDSs that are supported by dedicated hardware accelerators implemented on a Field-Programmable Gate Array (FPGA). Although with each new FPGA generation, larger designs can be supported, it is not always trivial to fit an NIDS in the configurable resources of one FPGA. When the FPGA needs additional external components, this has a detrimental effect on the processing speed. Moreover, the larger the utilized configurable resources, the longer it takes to run the toolchain for each new design. When frequent updates of the NIDS are needed, the redesign and reconfiguration delay plays an important role.

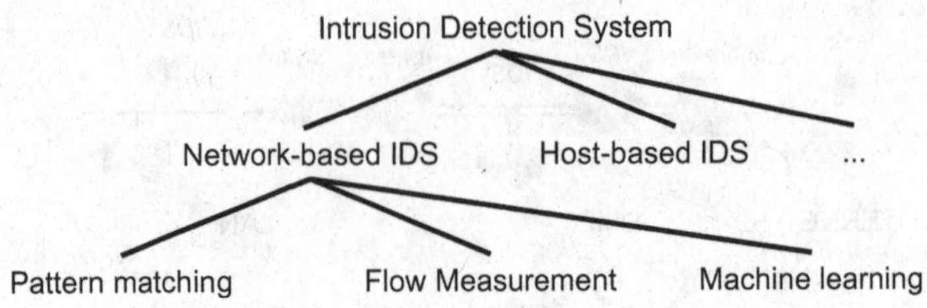

Fig. 2. IDS classification

Although many methods can be used, this work approaches the IDS from three different angles based on the technique that is used to make a decision: pattern matching, large flow detection, and machine learning (see Fig. 2). While related work typically concentrates on only one technique, the contribution of this paper is that it makes a qualitative comparison between the three approaches. This allows practitioners to make a decision on which method to use based on the specific application scenario. The three different approaches are discussed in Sect. 2, Sect. 3, and Sect. 4. Subsequently, a number of relevant properties are compared in Sect. 5 and the work is concluded in Sect. 6.

2 Pattern Matching-Based Network Intrusion Detection

When a network frame has been captured and has passed the firewall, it is inspected by the NIDS. An NIDS that follows the pattern matching approach then searches for signatures in the frame that belong to known network attacks in an extensive database. This database is generated (and maintained) by security engineers and contains a long list of *rules*. The number of rules can be as high as hundreds of thousands [54]. An example of a rule could be, for example, that an alarm should be triggered if network frames arrive, destined for port number 80 (which is the default port for an HTTP server). This rule could have been added because the policy states that only HTTPS traffic is allowed (which uses port 443).

Because of the large amount of rules that need to be verified, it becomes infeasible to linearly go over all of them. The main software suite that serves IDS or IDPS is Snort[1]. Other available systems include Zeek[2] (formerly known as Bro) and Suricata[3]. In Snort, the comparison with the active rule-set is done through string matching and/or regular expression (RegEx) string matching. Wang et al. published Hyperscan [70] which is a software-library to facilitate both. FPGA architectures for pattern matching-based NIDS are based on three different approaches: deterministic solutions, non-deterministic finite automata, and probabilistic architectures.

1 https://www.snort.org/.
2 https://zeek.org/.
3 https://suricata.io/.

Deterministic Solutions for Pattern Matching: Zhao et al. present the IDS/IPS Pigasus in [78]. They devise Pigasus as an FPGA-first implementation where the FPGA is not a co-processor to assist the main processor (which is doing the heavy lifting), but where the FPGA executes the majority of the processing. Pigasus can support a 100 Gbps network speed and consumes 38× less power than a CPU-first implementation. In their work, the authors present an FPGA implementation on an Intel FPGA.

Kang et al. presented in 2019 an FPGA-based implementation of a rule-based IDS [29]. This work is based on a 'whitelist' that can hold up to 256 entries. The ruleset can be updated through an on-chip processor. The latency is 0.032 µs which is mentioned to allow detection even before the complete packet has arrived.

Non-deterministic Finite Automata for Pattern Matching: Software IDSs heavily lean on the power of RegExs to provide flexible and high-performance searches. Unfortunately, checking RegExs on FPGAs is not straightforward. Luinaud et al. overcome the implementation challenge by using the reconfigurable nature of FPGAs [42]. This is achieved by using Non-deterministic Finite Automata (NFA), which is an approach to implement Finite State Machines (FSMs). In contrast with DFA (Deterministic Finite Automata), NFA can result in a different output state for a given input state and a set of inputs. Luinaud et al. use an intermediate layer on top of the classical reconfigurable fabric. Through this they are able to implement NFAs.

In [14], Češka et al. implement resource-efficient RegEx matching by approximately reducing NFAs based on the probabilistic distance between an automaton and its reduced counterpart. They propose heuristics to approximate this reduction, using a probabilistic model of the network traffic. Using this approach allows for significantly reducing automata while limiting the resulting error. As a result, they are able to accelerate the detection of Snort rules for 100 Gbps. Moreover, in [15], the authors implement multiple stages of over-approximating NFAs to push the possible throughput even further. Consider the traffic profile of the local networking environment they once again reducing the NFAs to limit the impact on accuracy. With their resulting multistage hardware accelerators, they are able to process traffic of up to 400 Gbps for some Snort modules.

Probabilistic Architectures for Pattern Matching: The most commonly used architectures for implementing of pattern matching algorithms on hardware are Bloom filters [12], content addressable memories (CAM), and ternary content addressable memories (TCAM) [2]. Even though CAMs and TCAMs are mighty accurate, disadvantages such as high cost per bit, storage inefficiency, limited scalability to long input keys, and large memory overhead put CAMs and TCAMs on the back foot [2]. In bloom filters, the length of the string has no effect on the memory requirements and the query time is not affected by the number of strings in the database. These advantages give a significant boost to bloom filters when it comes to hardware. These properties hold the same for other probabilistic lookup architectures such as Cuckoo filters [23] too.

Numerous hardware-focused researches on the implementation of signature-based IDS using deep packet inspection (DPI) and prefix matching schemes employ bloom filters as the main component. Dharmapurikar et al. [19] proposed a DPI system using parallel bloom filters, which employs a set of parallel bloom filters where each bloom filter contains predefined signature of a particular length. Considering the fact that there could be false positives, an analyzer based on a deterministic string matching algorithm, followed by the set of bloom filters ensures that false positives are eliminated. However, these analyzer units are slow and would affect the throughput when the false positive rates are high. Artan and Chao [9] proposed a chain heuristic method to reduce the false positive rate of Prefix bloom filters (PBF) without additional memory requirements, hence reducing the operation of the analyzer. Prefix bloom filters is the term given to the bloom filters stored with signatures and it used the same set of parallel bloom filters as in [19]. Additionally, this method also helps to detect signatures distributed over multiple packets, which [19] could not detect. A similar architecture using counting bloom filters as a system on chip (SoC) implementation is performed by Harwayne-Gidansky [26]. In this SoC, the operation of the analyzer part is performed by the PowerPC softcore processor.

Work by Dharmapurikar [20] extend the functionality of [19] to longest prefix matching (LPM) by employing additional off-chip hash tables. Based on the match vector from prefix bloom filter outputs, hash table lookups are performed for matching prefixes. However, this method would result in reduced throughput because of the multiple off-chip memory accesses. A slight modification to longest prefix matching using parallel counting bloom filters is put forward by Li [36], which requires less memory but at the cost of reduced speed. Extended bloom filter (EBF) proposed by Song and Lockwood [62] is a modified version of bloom filter for string matching. Each bucket in the bloom filter consists of 3 fields, hit-bit, a counter, and a pointer. Hit-bit is the same as in bloom filters whereas counter field is used to accelerate the matching process and pointer points to the signature storage location in the off-chip memory. In order to limit the false positive rate, either the number of EBF buckets or number of hash functions must be increased, which increases the memory consumption. The pointer field is 11-bits, which also adds to the high memory consumption compared to standard bloom filters. The use of off-chip memory in EBF also decreases the throughput.

Most of the deep packet inspection/string matching approaches based on bloom filters are static and also many of the techniques do suffer from a low throughput. Kefu et al. [30] proposed a counting bloom filter based architecture with two pipeline stages, fast and slow, on FPGA. The fast pipeline stage consisting of parallel counting bloom filter engines which is very much similar to [19], and the slow pipeline consists of a dynamic pattern matching algorithm. The fast pipeline ensures fast dynamic query and a high throughput whereas the slow pipeline validates the suspicious matches from the fast pipeline and at the same time updates the rule sets dynamically at run-time. Dharmapurikar and Lockwood [21] proposed another approach to improve the throughput by minimising the off-chip memory usage. In this work, prefix bloom filters are implemented in on-chip memory and hash tables in off-chip memory. The hash table lookup is performed only when there is a match in the bloom filters. This drastically reduces the off-chip memory access time and hence the throughput is improved. Aggregated bloom filter (AGF) [10] is a completely different approach than the parallel bloom filters. In AGF, each query is serialized into a queue and multiple queries can be performed simultaneously by one bloom filter, unlike parallel bloom filters where it can perform only one query at a time. Al-Dalky et al. [3] employed the NetFPGA as a hardware line of defense to accelerate the Snort NIDS. A bloom filter is used for matching the Snort rules and the most frequently triggered rules are dynamically offloaded to the NetFPGA. The NetFPGA replaces the Ethernet card and for every new incoming packet, the packet is passed to the slow Snort IDS module only if no matches are found in the NetFPGA. This minimizes the processing burden on the Snort IDS and improves the processing rate.

Even though not entirely specific to intrusion detection, there are numerous works available presenting the improvements of bloom filters for pattern matching applications on FPGA. The work by Wada [69] presents an FPGA implementation using UltraRAMs and rolling hash functions, providing a significant boost in performance. A sublinear time string matching algorithm using bloom filters is presented by Lin et al. [37] which allows skipping characters which are not matching, and proposed a bad-block heuristic to handover verification job to a verification module. An approach to improve the throughput of bloom filters on hardware is presented by Sateesan et al. [56], which showcases a high-throughput implementation of bloom filter having a single memory access and eliminates the disadvantages of hashing for bloom filters. Other than bloom filters, a few researches are available based on cuckoo filters. Works by Hisnawi and Ahmadi [4] which implements deep packet inspection system on CPU using cuckoo filters by storing the rule signatures on the filter, and the work by Ho [27] which proposes a deep packet inspection system on graphics processing units employing a pattern matching scheme on cuckoo filters provides showcases improved performance.

3 Flow Measurement-Based Network Intrusion Detection

With the emergence of high-speed networks and devices, flow measurement has become an important research challenge than ever before [22]. Real-time monitoring and storage of enormous amount of data pose the need of huge amount of resources and memory, which makes the implementation practically impossible and even more difficult on hardware. There has been numerous approaches to alleviate the complexities in flow measurements. Sampling based approaches [16,60] were commonly employed in many of the networking systems, which helped in significantly reducing the memory consumption compared to exact measurement approaches. Even though sampling techniques do achieve memory reduction, it has become obsolete with high-speed networks, and recent studies have pointed out the remarkable reduction in accuracy and loss of information caused by high sampling [39]. The proposal of an approximate counting algorithm in 1978 by Robert Morris [43] give rise to an alternate counting technique in database and networking applications. Along with approximate counting, the introduction of probabilistic counting algorithms based on hash tables [24] helped in significantly reducing the counting overhead while allowing a small error in accuracy. Sketches [17,39,74] in general significantly reduced the memory overhead of measurement and flow record generation tasks. An in-depth study of the role of sketches for traffic measurement is presented by Zhou in [79].

Sketch algorithms [74] and works employing sketches [72] have shown already that sketch based traffic monitoring schemes can deliver high throughput on FPGA. Work by Wellem et al. [72] employed a sketch data structure to extract the traffic features and the sketch-based monitoring part is implemented on a multi-core CPU. The hashing, bloom-filter based lookup and flow tables are implemented on the FPGA. The system is able to process a packet in every clock cycle at 210 MHz and is able to deliver a throughput of 53 Gbps assuming a minimum packet size of 64 bytes on a Virtex-5 platform. Approximation approaches such as self adaptive (SA) counters [73] on sketches for per-flow measurement proved to be effective reducing the memory footprint, but SA counters seem to be too complex for hardware. A more hardware efficient method to replace exact counting with approximate counting is proposed by Sateesan et al. [57]. This work proposes approximate CM ((A-CM) sketch and showed that the memory overhead can be reduced to half for CM sketch implementation and a high throughput can be obtained even without pipelining. With pipelining, A-CM sketch of width $w = 2^{16}$ and depth $d = 4$ can process a packet in every clock cycle at 454 MHz to achieve a throuhput of 233 Gbps on a Xilinx ultrascale+ device. Schweller et al. [59] proposes a reversible sketch architecture for traffic monitoring and change detection. Sketches in general are not reversible, which means we cannot track down flows having a large change estimate. This paper by Schweller presents reversible sketches with reverse hashing algorithms that provide an efficient way to network traffic monitoring for change detection. The FPGA implementation is able to produce a throughput of 16 Gbps on a virtex 2000E FPGA.

An intrusion detection model on FPGA using sketch-based feature extraction modules (FEM) is proposed by Das et al. [18]. The FEM is associated with an anomaly detection mechanism using principal component analysis (PCA). FEM summerizes the network behaviour and the PCA helps for detecting outliers. The FPGA implementations are performed on a Virtex-II device. The FEM implementation shows a throughput of 23.82 Gbps at 216 MHz with an accuracy of 97.61% for a sketch width of 2048 and the number of hash functions $h = 4$. But with increasing depth, the throughput and frequency decreases. Feature extraction modules and traffic classifiers also play a vital role in the network intrusion detection systems. Sketches have been the most hardware-friendly architecture for in-line feature extraction and classification applications. Similar to the work by Das et al. [18], another high speed feature extraction module using feature sketches is presented by Pati et al. [52] and the implementation on virtex-II fpga was able to produce a maximum throughput of 3.32 Gbps. Tong and Prasanna [65] proposed a method for anomaly detection on sketches. A generic architecture to accelerate sketches is proposed in this work and the analysis is performed on Count-Min (CM) sketch and K-ary sketch. The main design goal of this work is to enhance the throughput by parallel and pipelined combinations of components. In online network anomaly detection, the CM sketch serves the purpose of online heavy hitter detection and K-ary sketch performs the online change detection. Keeping the width of the sketch $w = 2^{16}$ and depth $d = 5$, the implementation of the sketch acceleration on a virtex ultrascale xcvu440 platform leverages a throughput of 159 Gbps for K-ary sketch and 155 Gbps for CM sketch, which is lower only to the implementation in [57]. Lai et al. [33] propose a work on sketch-based DDoS detection on the NetFPGA SUME platform. In this work, the complex and time consuming shannon entropy computations are pre-computed and stored in lookup tables on the FPGA, which considerably reduce the latency and is able to achieve a throughput of 40 Gbps.

Detection of heavy-hitters is very much relevant for DDoS, anomaly and intrusion detection. Tong and Prasanna [64] proposed an algorithm for an online heavy-hitter detection using CM sketch. With pipelining and parallel computing engines to accelerate the sketch, this architecture was able to achieve a throughput of 118 Gbps on a virtex-7 platform. Heavy hitter detection on FPGA using a CM-CU sketch is proposed by Saavedra [55], where the advantage with CM-CU algorithm is that the memory requirement is small and only a 2-stage pipeline is required for the update operation. This is somewhat advantageous than [65] because the deep-pipeline requires complex hazard detection and data forwarding unit. When running at 400 MHz, the CM-CU architecture of width $w = 2^{14}$ and depth $d = 4$ can achieve throughput of 128 Gbps with no false positives on a Kintex-7 XC7K325T platform. Not many works on FPGA are targeted for Terabit Ethernet and Zazo et al. [76] presents a heavy hitter detection architecture on 100 GbE links on a single FPGA. The detection architecture is based on Count Sketch (CS) and this work take advantage of the available 100 G Ethernet subsystem on Xilinx Ultrascale devices. The main components in this design are the CS sketch and a priority queue (PQ), where the CS sketch populates the PQ and PQ keeps track of the most active flows. The memory requirement of the design is so low that both the CS sketch and PQ are able to fit in the on-chip BRAM. The implementation also achieves a frequency of 322 MHz at 100 Gbps line-rate. Most of the recent works like LOFT [58] for detecting overuse flows and Jaqen [40] for volumetric DDoS attack detection also underlines the capability of sketches on hardware to support processing at line-rate for Terabit Ethernet.

4 Machine Learning-Based Network Intrusion Detection

Instead of defining rules to detect intrusions, it is possible to use learning algorithms. Before considering FPGA implementations of such approaches in Sect. 4.2 through 4.4, we will first start by providing a brief introduction to machine learning for network intrusion detection in the next section.

4.1 Machine Learning for Network Intrusion Detection

In a machine learning-based network intrusion detection system, a machine learning algorithm is responsible for deciding what network traffic is malicious. Concretely, the system is able to use specific features as input for a specific algorithm that as a result differentiates between benign traffic and attacks. While not necessarily new, this intrusion detection method remains challenging and is subject to continuous research. Initially, the detection algorithms mainly comprised traditional approaches such as Support Vector Machines (SVM) [5,6,32], decision trees (DT) [53,77] or simple neural networks (ANN) [41,45]. With the advent of Deep Learning (DL), larger and complexer architectures such as Convolutional Neural Networks (CNN), Long Short-Term Memory (LSTM) or autoencoders (AE) have become applicable for network intrusion detection. Some recent examples include [31,38,71]. Those learning algorithms are trained on datasets, usually publicly available, that present extracted traffic traces and/or features alongside their corresponding labels. Some frequently used examples include KDD99 [1], NSL-KDD [63], UNSW-NB15 [44] and CICIDS2017 [61]. While some datasets are outdated or consist of simulated traffic, they at least provide a common ground for comparison. Besides using published datasets, authors sometimes opt to instead use a custom dataset by combining other datasets [75] or using a custom testbed [25]. As these datasets are usually not available to other users, they can complicate comparison between different approaches.

The vast majority of research into machine learning for network intrusion detection however is limited to the design of software algorithms for improved detection of attacks through optimal feature and algorithm selection: Feature extraction and selection techniques are explored to obtain the features that best allow for distinguishing between normal and malicious traffic, while different machine learning models are investigated to optimally use the resulting features for decision making. Although this focus on software improvement is evidently important, it lacks consideration for the eventual implementation down the line. The resulting systems are often very resource intensive and have no innate support for feature extraction from raw network traffic. A complete NIDS should be able to interface with traffic in a network whilst consuming reasonable resources and returning feedback at an adequate rate. This is increasingly challenging as network bandwidths are ever increasing. Therefore, we investigate FPGA implementations of machine learning-based network intrusion detection systems as well as their capabilities and resource requirements. Section 4.2 considers traditional machine learning algorithms, while Sect. 4.3 lists current Deep Learning (DL) implementations on FPGA. Finally, Table 1 provides an overview of all discussed architectures with various metrics for comparison, which we will also discuss in Sect. 4.4.

4.2 Traditional Machine Learning Algorithms on FPGA

When it comes to traditional machine learning algorithms, it is possible to differentiate between (shallow) neural network implementations and other implementations. While neural networks use calculations that are very similar to the calculations used in DL networks, other algorithms such as k-means clustering incorporate a different way to turn the provided input into a classification. Before moving on to neural networks, we will therefore first consider other approaches.

One of the earliest machine-learning based network intrusion detection systems on FPGA is provided by Das *et al.* [18] in 2008. They introduce a new feature extraction module (FEM) to summarize network behaviour, the output of which is fed to a *Principal Component Analysis* (PCA) to detect anomalies. The FEM first extracts relevant information from the traffic flom by updating *Feature Sketches* that track various properties. Retrieving values from those sketches produces the features than can be processed in the PCA. Anomalies are then finally detected by considering the deviation from the mean of the normal data set, taking into account both the most and the least significant principal components. The authors report a Detection Rate (also known as recall) of 99% with a False Alarm Rate of 1.95% on samples from the KDDCup1999 dataset. As they manage to combine this with a throughput of 23.76 Gbps and a latency of 0.5 µs, the resulting system is both accurate and fast.

Maciel *et al.* [8] use a modified version of the k-means clustering algorithm, namely k-modes, that can deal with categorical data of the NSL-KDD dataset. For comparison, they implemented integer and floating-point alternatives for k-means as well, running the three different versions on different features (counters, percentages or categorical features). All three approaches obtain significant improvements over their CPU counterparts, both in number of clock cycles uses as well as in energy consumption. Moreover, of the three approaches, the *k-modes* algorithm on categorical data clearly outperforms the integer and floating-point alternatives. The authors however do not report the actual learning performance in terms of accuracy, or any other alternative metric.

Rather than k-means, Gordon *et al.* [25] use the k-nearest neighbours algorithm (KNN) to classify samples of a custom dataset on an FPGA. They propose a new sorting algorithm K-Min Sort to use during classification, which reduces resource overhead when compared to alternatives such as *Bubblesort*. For a training set size of 50%, they obtain an accuracy of 95% and a latency of 3.913 ms while using a limited amount of hardware.

Although alternative learning methods such as k-means and KNN are used in some amount, the majority of learning architectures comprises neural networks: Structures consisting of a least one hidden layer with neurons to process input data. While software solutions more often use large, multi-layer neural networks, most neural networks for network intrusion detection on FPGA only consist of one hidden layer.

Murovič *et al.* set out to train and synthesize hardwired Binary Neural Networks (BNN) [46] for real-time and high-speed applications on FPGA. After training a 1-layer BNN of 100 neurons on UNSW-NB15 and obtaining an accuracy of 90.74%, they built a parallel Verilog implementation in hardware that has a latency of only 19.6 ns. In [47] they propose a method to more efficiently implement BNN architectures in hardware. They replace the XNOR-popcount operation of binarized neurons with popcount operations preceded by precalculated masking. As a result, they reduce the hardware requirements for BNN layer computations. They also inclde a tool to map software BNNs to hardware. When reaccelerating their previous 1-layer network using this novel approach, they report an improvement of 38.1% when compared to their previous results. While their latency has slightly increased, the power consumption is further reduced to 0.72 W. In [48] they once again propose improved hardware acceleration methods, and they now train models for both NSL-KDD and UNSW-NB15. For their hardware, they introduce a ripple architecture based on the difference between neighbouring neurons in a layer. Moreover, as the hamming distance travelled when passing through a layer is correlated to the total number of summed bits, the authors use a genetic algorithm to minimize this distance. Using this approach, they manage to once improve upon their previous work. While the accuracy on NSL-KDD is rather limited at 77.77%, the hardware outperforms other work such as [8,28]. They also achieve very high throughputs of 256 Gbps for UNSW-NB15 and 288 Gbps for CICIDS2017 when considering packets of 576 bytes, which proves their architecture is very suited for high-speed applications.

Iannou *et al.* [28] implement a reconfigurable neural network on FPGA, that allows for updating coefficients at runtime. After selecting 29 input features from NSL-KDD, one-hot encoding them as necessary, they devise a model with 110 inputs, 29 hidden neurons and 2 outputs. They implement the model on a Xilinx Zynq Z-7020 FPGA using High-Level Synthesis (HLS), utilizing the included ARM to control the accelerator. Once the model is trained to reach an accuracy of 80.52%, they report a latency of 9.02 ms for the implemented accelerator at a clock frequency of 76 MHz.

Ngo *et al.* [50] design a decision tree and a neural network architecture on FPGA to classify NSL-KDD samples. They extract six features from input packets, and feed these features to the specific classifiers. While the neural network is very limited in size, using 6 inputs, two layers of 2 neurons and an output layer, it also features hardware for updating the weights using backpropagation. As the classifiers use 32-bit floating point precision arithmetic, the resource consumption is considerable. For packets of at least 512 bytes, the system manages a throughput of about 9.5 Gbps, which quickly collapses as the packet size decreases in the case of the neural network. However, the decision tree retains a throughput of near line-speed even for 64-byte packets. In [49], the same authors propose network intrusion engines to secure Software Defined Networking forwarding devices, implementing a neural network in an FPGA after training it on a GPU. A controller presents 10 features to a neural network with 10 input units, one hidden layer with 4 neurons and an output layer to perform classification. The model reaches a throughput of 4.84Gbps with a recall of 99.01% on a custom dataset.

Somewhat different from the other research, Tran *et al.* [66] decide to split the machine learning challenge in two seperate parts: They implement a feature extraction solution on an FPGA, but use a Graphical Processing Unit (GPU) to then perform neural network-based anomaly detection. On the FPGA, a *packet decoder* provides headers to the FEM, from which 10 features are extracted and normalized. An intermediate CPU facilitaties the transfer of normalized data from FPGA to GPU. Although the utilized FPGA supports up to 10Gbps, the bandwidth is limited to 200 Mbps due to hashing collisions when storing statistical information in memory. The authors report 80.42% accuracy on a custom dataset.

4.3 Deep Learning on FPGA

Contrary to traditional learning methods and shallow neural networks, DL incorporates neural networks with various layers to perform more complex computations. While this increase in complexity has more potential with regards to classification performance, it comes paired with an increased cost to FPGA resources: Larger data structures and an increased number of computations will have to be dealt with to implement DL on FPGA.

Alrawashdeh *et al.* [7] accelerate the training and inference of a Deep Belief Network (DBN) on FPGA. Their design is not only able to detect intrusions in the NSL-KDD dataset, but also to (re)train the model while still online. The 3-layer DBN reuses the same hardware for each Restricted Boltzmann Machine (RBM) layer to limit hardware usage. Moreover, they use dynamic fixed-point arithmetic and limit the bit width of the second and third RBMs to 8 bits while maintaining 16 bits for the first layer. This results in a 30% resource usage improvement in hardware over using just 16-bit fixed point arithmetic. In addition, using an approximation function to replace the sigmoid activation function constitutes another optimization. They then evaluate, among others, on the NSL-KDD dataset, obtaining an accuracy of 94.66%, about 1.5% worse than the corresponding software implementation.

Umuroglu *et al.* [67] accelerate Deep Neural Networks (DNN) on an FPGA through their *LogicNets* methodology. This methodology is based on representing neurons in a DNN as truth tables on an FPGA, and allows for training the DNNs in PyTorch after which they can be translated to hardware. Among potential evaluation scenarios, they select network intrusion detection with the UNSW-NB15 dataset at very high bandwidths. They report an accuracy of 91.30% and a latency of 10.5 ns when accelerating a 5-layer DNN with 593×256×128×128 neurons.

Le Jeune *et al.* [34] use two frameworks to quantize a convolutional neural network (CNN) and translate it to HLS. After using quantization aware training in Brevitas [51] to quantize their model's weights and activations to 2 bits, FINN [13,68] provides all the required steps to turn the resulting software model to hardware. Training on the CICIDS2017 dataset, they obtained an accuracy of 99.41%, with their reported hardware implementation obtaining a throughput of 90Mbps. While their throughput is significantly smaller than that of related work, the corresponding model complexity and classification performance is considerably higher than that of any other related work.

4.4 Discussion

The overview in Table 1 shows that FPGA implementations of machine learning algorithms for network intrusion detection vary greatly. Some implementations

Table 1. Overview of different FPGA implementations of machine learning algorithms for network intrusion detection. The columns feature, from left to right, the reference, the year of publishing, the used algorithm, the used dataset, the achieved accuracy, the supported network bandwidth, the model latency, the number of Lookup Tables, the number of registers, the power and the clock frequency.

Ref	Year	Algo	Dataset	Acc(%)	BW	Latency	LUTs	FF	P(W)	F(MHz)
[18]	2008	PCA	KDD99		23.76 Gbps	0.5 µs				93
[66]	2017	ANN	Custom	80.42	200 Mbps		58561	71860		102
[7]	2017	DBN	NSL-KDD	94.3		8 µs	121127	169290		
[50]	2019	ANN	NSL-KDD	87.30	9.58 Gbps	12 ms	107036	117078		104
[50]	2019	DT	NSL-KDD	95.10	9.58 Gbps	4 ms	67552	74059		100
[46]	2019	ANN	UNSW-NB15	90.74		19.6 ns	51353	0	1.57	
[28]	2019	ANN	NSL-KDD	80.52		9.0 ms	26463	56478		76
[8]	2020	k-means	NSL-KDD			1.2 ms		31864	1.50	50
[49]	2020	ANN	Custom		4.84 Gbps		99890	122085	11.00	100
[47]	2020	ANN	UNSW-NB15	90.74		23.5 ns	26879	0	0.72	43
[67]	2020	DNN	UNSW-NB15	91.3		10.5 ns	15949	1274		471
[48]	2021	ANN	NSL-KDD	77.77	288 Gbps	16 ns	26879	0	0.57	
[48]	2021	ANN	UNSW-NB15	92.04	256 Gbps	19 ns	26879	0	0.62	
[25]	2021	KNN	Custom	95		3.9 ms	3663	3886		
[34]	2021	CNN	CICIDS2017	99.41	90 Mbps		26615	27450		100

reach bandwidths of over 250 Gbps, some occupy a limited area, and some retain a very high accuracy. In the ideal NIDS, all these factors should be present, but the current situation is that trade-offs have to be made: It is possible to reach blazing speeds using techniques such as those demonstrated by Murovič *et al.* [48] or in LogicNets [67], but this severely limits the computational size of the models, both in number of neurons and layers as well as in arithmetic. Binary neural networks are the pinnacle of such an approach. On the other hand, more expensive algorithms such as the DBN [7] or CNN [34] increase the accuracy, and therefore the reliability of the resulting NIDS. This is also essential, as inaccurate NIDSs will just flood a system administrator with false alarms or not detect actual attacks. Future machine learning-based NIDS implementations on FPGA will have to somehow compromise between these seemingly opposite goals of resource efficiency and accuracy.

5 Main Takeaways

In this section, we compare the properties of the techniques covered in this paper as well as the limitations and open challenges in the state of the art.

5.1 Properties of the Compared NIDS Approaches

We will now compare the capabilities of pattern matching, large flow detection and machine learning through four key properties: detection capabilities, expert knowledge, detection speed and hardware efficiency. To help practitioners, Table 2 summarizes these properties and their effect on the three discussed approaches.

Detection Capabilities. The detection capabilities of an NIDS comprise both the range of detectable attacks, as well as the detection accuracy for those attacks. For pattern matching-based detection this is quite clear: They detect all attacks that are effectively described in their ruleset. Traffic either violates a rule, or it does not. Attacks that however are not incorporated in the ruleset will not trigger any alarm and remain unnoticed. Flow measurement approaches are more dynamic than pattern matching techniques, but probabilistic measurement could cause false positives and this in fact would reduce the detection accuracy. Machine learning systems, in contrast, can potentially detect a wide range of attacks. Not only can they detect whatever is present in a training dataset, they also have the potential to detect attacks that are unknown if those attacks deviate from the trained model. The downside to machine learning is that the resulting systems often produce myriad errors, both in the form of unseen attacks as well as false alarms. Such false alarms can also be dangerous, as they might form a distraction for actual attacks.

Expert Knowledge. Different approaches to NIDS also result in different requirements of expert knowledge. Pattern matching-based approaches rely on rules, which have to be defined by experts. Without those rules, the system is useless. Moreover, whenever a new attack is discovered, a new rule must be made that effectively detects the attack. Machine learning on the other hand is based on a dataset, which the training algorithm uses to create its own rules internally. This removes the need for experts defining the precise characteristics of an attack. Updating a machine learning model can be done through updating its weights, for example by retraining. Flow measurement-based approaches fall somewhat in the middle, where the rules not necessarily have to be defined by the experts, but setting the parameters such as the threshold bandwidth, measurement period, and memory sizes would require high level of expertise.

Detection Speed. Attack detection does not only need to be accurate, it also needs to be fast. Fast detection not only facilitates swift response, it also helps in processing larger amounts of data. Generally, pattern-matching approaches can be very quick, with sub-microsecond latencies possible. However, the speed is tied to the size of the ruleset: As a system wants to check against more rules, it becomes harder to maintain speed. This also goes for the throughput, which can reach up to 400 Gbps for limited rulesets. However, in probabilistic architectures the size of the ruleset does not affect the detection speed. In machine learning, the speed is tied to the model size rather than the number of rules. As model types and sizes vary wildly, so does the detection speed, with measurements both in the millisecond and the nanosecond range (see Table 1). While extremely fast models are certainly possible, these are often very limited in size, bit-width and accuracy. The most accurate models are therefore usually significantly slower and only support a limited bandwidth. The speed of online flow measurement-based systems is largely dependant on the speed of the measurement unit. Keeping the measurement unit within the on-chip memory of the FPGA reduces the latency to a minimum. However, with larger measurement period and higher memory requirement, offloading the storage to external memory significantly reduces the detection speed and even causes the monitoring to be performed offline.

Hardware Efficiency. The trade-offs that present themselves while considering detection speed, are similarly present when regarding hardware resource consumption. For pattern matching-based approaches, an increase in ruleset size implies an increase in resource consumption. In machine learning, the resources used depend strongly on the model used, considering the model size and the computational complexity. Once again, more accurate models will usually require more resources. It is however also possible to design models that are both accurate and (relatively) cheap in resource usage, but that might result in an increased latency instead. Similarly, the resource/memory requirement for measurement-based approaches is dependant on parameters like measurement period, traffic-rate, and accuracy.

Table 2. Summary of the most important properties of all three approaches

	Pattern matching	Flow measurement	Machine learning
Detection capabilities			
• Coverage	++	+	+++
• Accuracy	+++	++	+
Expert knowledge			
• Ease of maintenance	+	++	+++
• Ease of design	+++	++	+
Detection speed	+++	++	+
Hardware efficiency	+++	++	+

5.2 Limitations and Challenges of State-of-the-Art NIDSs

Encrypted Traffic. In the previous sections, different approaches to implement (parts of) IDS on FPGAs are discussed. One important remark to make is that, regardless of the approach, it is assumed that all network data are available to the IDS in plaintext. When connections use cryptography to encrypt the payload of network frames, pattern matching of this payload is infeasible. Depending on what type of encryption is used (e.g. IPSec in transport or tunnel mode or the new HTTP/3 (with QUIC[4])) a number of protocol fields, or even entire protocols headers, are no longer available for inspection. With new secure Internet Architectures like SCION [11], the packet headers of the available metadata also differ from what security experts are used to.

External Components. Most of the approaches that are mentioned earlier require a substantial amount of resources, and mainly memory resources. Going off-chip to external memory would cost too much time to achieve the required response times. It is therefore important to stay within the resources of one FPGA.

Update Speed. As network intrusion detection implies updates and changes at a quick pace, changes to the FPGA implementations also need to be fast. One way of speeding up the update process is through improving the FPGA toolchain. Another way is to use hierarchical or partial FPGA design and configuration.

6 Conclusion

Network intrusion detection systems on FPGA deal with the growing need for real-time intrusion detection in high-bandwidth networks. This paper discusses three important approaches, namely pattern matching, flow measurement and machine learning. An overview of both the employed techniques and the FPGA architectures is given, and the different methods are compared in terms of detection capabilities, expert knowledge, detection speed and hardware resources. Besides describing the clear potential of the different approaches, this paper also discusses the shortcomings and open challenges that need to be solved in order to be ready for the next generation of intrusion detection systems in high-speed networks.

Acknowledgements. This work is supported by CORNET and funded by VLAIO under grant number HBC.2018.0491. This work is also supported by the ESCALATE project, funded by FWO and SNSF (G0E0719N), and by Cybersecurity Initiative Flanders (VR20192203).

References

1. KDD Cup 1999 Data (1999). http://kdd.ics.uci.edu/databases/kddcup99/kddcup99.html
2. AbuHmed, T., Mohaisen, A., Nyang, D.: A survey on deep packet inspection for intrusion detection systems. arXiv preprint arXiv:0803.0037 (2008)
3. Al-Dalky, R., Salah, K., Otrok, H., Al-Qutayri, M.: Accelerating snort NIDS using NetFPGA-based Bloom filter. In: 2014 International Wireless Communications and Mobile Computing Conference (IWCMC). IEEE (2014)

[4] https://datatracker.ietf.org/doc/html/rfc9000.

4. Al-Hisnawi, M., Ahmadi, M.: Deep packet inspection using cuckoo filter. In: 2017 NTICT. IEEE (2017)
5. Al-Qatf, M., Lasheng, Y., Al-Habib, M., Al-Sabahi, K.: Deep learning approach combining sparse autoencoder with SVM for network intrusion detection. IEEE Access **6**, 52843–52856 (2018)
6. Al-Yaseen, W.L., Othman, Z.A., Nazri, M.Z.A.: Multi-level hybrid support vector machine and extreme learning machine based on modified K-means for intrusion detection system. Expert Syst. Appl. **67**, 296–303 (2017)
7. Alrawashdeh, K., Purdy, C.: Reducing calculation requirements in FPGA implementation of deep learning algorithms for online anomaly intrusion detection. In: 2017 IEEE National Aerospace and Electronics Conference (NAECON) (2017)
8. Maciel, L.A., Souza, M.A., de Freitas, H.C.: Reconfigurable FPGA-based K-means/K-modes architecture for network intrusion detection. IEEE Trans. Circ. Syst. II: Express Briefs **67**(8), 459–1463 (2020)
9. Artan, N.S., Chao, H.J.: Multi-packet signature detection using prefix bloom filters. In: GLOBECOM 2005, vol. 3. IEEE (2005)
10. Artan, N.S., Sinkar, K., Patel, J., Chao, H.J.: Aggregated bloom filters for intrusion detection and prevention hardware. In: IEEE GLOBECOM 2007-IEEE Global Telecommunications Conference. IEEE (2007)
11. Barrera, D., Chuat, L., Perrig, A., Reischuk, R.M., Szalachowski, P.: The scion internet architecture. Commun. ACM **60**(6), 56–65 (2017)
12. Bloom, B.H.: Space/time trade-offs in hash coding with allowable errors. Commun. ACM **13**(7), 422–426 (1970)
13. Blott, M., et al.: FINN-R: an end-to-end deep-learning framework for fast exploration of quantized neural networks. ACM TRETS **11**(3), 1–23 (2018)
14. Češka, M., Havlena, V., Holík, L., Lengál, O., Vojnar, T.: Approximate reduction of finite automata for high-speed network intrusion detection. In: Beyer, Dirk, Huisman, Marieke (eds.) TACAS 2018. LNCS, vol. 10806, pp. 155–175. Springer, Cham (2018). https://doi.org/10.1007/978-3-319-89963-3_9
15. Ceška, M., et al.: Deep packet inspection in FPGAs via approximate nondeterministic automata. In: 2019 IEEE 27th Annual International Symposium on Field-Programmable Custom Computing Machines (FCCM) (2019)
16. CISCO: CISCO IOS NetFlow Version 9 (2015). http://www.cisco.com/c/en/us/products/ios-nx-os-software/netflow-version-9/index.html
17. Cormode, G., Muthukrishnan, S.: An improved data stream summary: the count-min sketch and its applications. J. Algorithms **55**(1), 58–75 (2005)
18. Das, A., Nguyen, D., Zambreno, J., Memik, G., Choudhary, A.: An FPGA-based network intrusion detection architecture. IEEE Trans. Inf. Forensics Secur. **3**(1), 118–132 (2008)
19. Dharmapurikar, S., Krishnamurthy, P., Sproull, T., Lockwood, J.: Deep packet inspection using parallel bloom filters. In: 11th Symposium on High Performance Interconnects, 2003. Proceedings. IEEE (2003)
20. Dharmapurikar, S., Krishnamurthy, P., Taylor, D.E.: Longest prefix matching using bloom filters. In: Proceedings of the 2003 Conference on Applications, Technologies, Architectures, and Protocols for Computer Communications (2003)
21. Dharmapurikar, S., Lockwood, J.W.: Fast and scalable pattern matching for network intrusion detection systems. IEEE J. Sel. Areas Commun. **24**(10), 1781–1792 (2006)
22. Dreger, H., Feldmann, A., Paxson, V., Sommer, R.: Operational experiences with high-volume network intrusion detection. In: ACM CCS (2004)

23. Fan, B., Andersen, D.G., Kaminsky, M., Mitzenmacher, M.D.: Cuckoo filter: practically better than bloom. In: Proceedings of the 10th ACM International on Conference on Emerging Networking Experiments and Technologies (2014)
24. Flajolet, P., Martin, G.N.: Probabilistic counting algorithms for data base applications. J. Comput. Syst. Sci. **31**(2), 182–209 (1985)
25. Gordon, H., Park, C., Tushir, B., Liu, Y., Dezfouli, B.: An efficient SDN architecture for smart home security accelerated by FPGA. In: 2021 IEEE International Symposium on Local and Metropolitan Area Networks (LANMAN) (2021)
26. Harwayne-Gidansky, J., Stefan, D., Dalal, I.: FPGA-based SoC for real-time network intrusion detection using counting Bloom filters. In: IEEE Southeastcon 2009. IEEE (2009)
27. Ho, T., Cho, S.J., Oh, S.R.: Parallel multiple pattern matching schemes based on cuckoo filter for deep packet inspection on graphics processing units. IET Inf. Secur. **12**(4), 381–388 (2018)
28. Ioannou, L., Fahmy, S.A.: Network intrusion detection using neural networks on FPGA SoCs. In: 2019 29th International Conference on Field Programmable Logic and Applications (FPL) (2019)
29. Kang, J., Kim, T., Park, J.: FPGA-based real-time abnormal packet detector for critical industrial network. In: 2019 IEEE Symposium on Computers and Communications (ISCC) (2019)
30. Kefu, X., Deyu, Q., Zhengping, Q., Weiping, Z.: Fast dynamic pattern matching for deep packet inspection. In: 2008 IEEE ICNSC. IEEE (2008)
31. Khan, M.A.: HCRNNIDS: hybrid convolutional recurrent neural network-based network intrusion detection system. Processes **9**(5), 834 (2021)
32. Kim, D.S., Park, J.S.: Network-based intrusion detection with support vector machines. In: Kahng, H.-K. (ed.) ICOIN 2003. LNCS, vol. 2662, pp. 747–756. Springer, Heidelberg (2003). https://doi.org/10.1007/978-3-540-45235-5_73
33. Lai, Y.K., et al.: Real-time DDoS attack detection using sketch-based entropy estimation on the NetFPGA SUME platform. In: 2020 Asia-Pacific Signal and Information Processing Association Annual Summit and Conference (APSIPA ASC). IEEE (2020)
34. Le Jeune, L., Goedemé, T., Mentens, N.: Towards real-time deep learning-based network intrusion detection on FPGA. In: ACNS Workshops (2021)
35. Li, C., Li, J., Yang, J., Lin, J.: A novel workload scheduling framework for intrusion detection system in NFV scenario. Comput. Secur. **106**, 102271 (2021)
36. Li, Y.Z.: Memory efficient parallel bloom filters for string matching. In: 2009 International Conference on Networks Security, Wireless Communications and Trusted Computing, vol. 1. IEEE (2009)
37. Lin, P.C., Lin, Y.D., Lai, Y.C., Zheng, Y.J., Lee, T.H.: Realizing a sub-linear time string-matching algorithm with a hardware accelerator using bloom filters. IEEE Trans. Very. Large. Scale. Integr. (VLSI) Syst. **17**(8), 1008–1020 (2009)
38. Liu, L., Wang, P., Lin, J., Liu, L.: Intrusion detection of imbalanced network traffic based on machine learning and deep learning. IEEE Access **9**, 7550–7563 (2021)
39. Liu, Z., Manousis, A., Vorsanger, G., Sekar, V., Braverman, V.: One sketch to rule them all: Rethinking network flow monitoring with UnivMon. In: Proceedings of the ACM Special Interest Group Data Communication (SIGCOMM) (2016)
40. Liu, Z., et al.: Jaqen: a high-performance switch-native approach for detecting and mitigating volumetric DDoS attacks with programmable switches. In: 30th (USENIX Security 21) (2021)

41. Lopez-Martin, M., Carro, B., Sanchez-Esguevillas, A., Lloret, J.: Shallow neural network with kernel approximation for prediction problems in highly demanding data networks. Expert Syst. Appl. **124**, 196–208 (2019)
42. Luinaud, T., Savaria, Y., Langlois, J.P.: An FPGA coarse grained intermediate fabric for regular expression search. In: GLSVLSI 2017. ACM (2017)
43. Morris, R.: Counting large numbers of events in small registers. ACM Commun. (1978)
44. Moustafa, N., Slay, J.: UNSW-NB15: a comprehensive data set for network intrusion detection systems (UNSW-NB15 network data set). In: 2015 Military Communications and Information Systems Conference (MilCIS) (2015)
45. Mukkamala, S., Janoski, G., Sung, A.: Intrusion detection using neural networks and support vector machines. In: Proceedings of the 2002 International Joint Conference on Neural Networks. IJCNN 2002 (Cat. No.02CH37290), vol. 2 (2002)
46. Murovič, T., Trost, A.: Massively parallel combinational binary neural networks for edge processing. Electrotechnical Rev. **86**, 47–53 (01 2019)
47. Murovič, T., Trost, A.: Resource-optimized combinational binary neural network circuits. Microelectron. J. **97**, 104724 (2020)
48. Murovič, T., Trost, A.: Genetically optimized massively parallel binary neural networks for intrusion detection systems. Comput. Commun. **179**, 1–10 (2021)
49. Ngo, D.-M., Pham-Quoc, C., Thinh, T.N.: Heterogeneous hardware-based network intrusion detection system with multiple approaches for SDN. Mob. Netw. Appl. **25**(3), 1178–1192 (2019). https://doi.org/10.1007/s11036-019-01437-x
50. Ngo, D.-M., Tran-Thanh, B., Dang, T., Tran, T., Thinh, T.N., Pham-Quoc, C.: High-throughput machine learning approaches for network attacks detection on FPGA. In: Vinh, P.C., Rakib, A. (eds.) ICCASA/ICTCC -2019. LNICST, vol. 298, pp. 47–60. Springer, Cham (2019). https://doi.org/10.1007/978-3-030-34365-1_5
51. Pappalardo, A.: Xilinx/brevitas. https://doi.org/10.5281/zenodo.3333552
52. Pati, S., Narayanan, R., Memik, G., Choudhary, A., Zambreno, J.: Design and implementation of an FPGA architecture for high-speed network feature extraction. In: ICFPT. IEEE (2007)
53. Pfahringer, B.: Winning the KDD99 classification cup: bagged boosting. SIGKDD Explor. Newsl. **1**(2), 65–66 (2000)
54. Roh, J.h., Lee, S.k., Son, C.W., Hwang, C., Kang, J., Park, J.: Cyber security system with FPGA-based network intrusion detector for nuclear power plant. In: IECON 2020 The 46th Annual Conference of the IEEE Industrial Electronics Society. IEEE (2020)
55. Saavedra, A., Hernández, C., Figueroa, M.: Heavy-hitter detection using a hardware sketch with the countmin-cu algorithm. In: 2018 21st Euromicro Conference on Digital System Design (DSD). IEEE (2018)
56. Sateesan, A., Vliegen, J., Daemen, J., Mentens, N.: Novel bloom filter algorithms and architectures for ultra-high-speed network security applications. In: 2020 23rd Euromicro Conference on Digital System Design (DSD). IEEE (2020)
57. Sateesan, A., Vliegen, J., Scherrer, S., Hsiao, H.C., Perrig, A., Mentens, N.: Speed records in network flow measurement on FPGA. In: Proceedings of the International Conference on Field-Programmable Logic (FPL) (2021)
58. Scherrer, S., et al.: Low-rate Overuse Flow tracer (LOFT): an efficient and scalable algorithm for detecting overuse flows. arXiv preprint arXiv:2102.01397 (2021)
59. Schweller, R., et al.: Reversible sketches: enabling monitoring and analysis over high-speed data streams. IEEE/ACM Trans. Netw. **15**(5), 1059–1072 (2007)

60. sFlow: Traffic Monitoring using sFlow (2003). http://www.sflow.org/sFlowOverview.pdf
61. Sharafaldin, I., Lashkari, A.H., Ghorbani, A.: (2018)
62. Song, H., Lockwood, J.W.: Multi-pattern signature matching for hardware network intrusion detection systems. In: GLOBECOM 2005, vol. 3. IEEE (2005)
63. Tavallaee, M., Bagheri, E., Lu, W., Ghorbani, A.A.: A detailed analysis of the KDD CUP 99 data set. In: 2009 IEEE Symposium on Computational Intelligence for Security and Defense Applications (2009)
64. Tong, D., Prasanna, V.: High throughput sketch based online heavy hitter detection on FPGA. ACM SIGARCH Comput. Architect. News **43**(4), 70–75 (2016)
65. Tong, D., Prasanna, V.K.: Sketch acceleration on FPGA and its applications in network anomaly detection. IEEE TPDS **29**(4), 929–942 (2017)
66. Tran, C., Vo, T.N., Thinh, T.N.: HA-IDS: A heterogeneous anomaly-based intrusion detection system. In: NAFOSTED NICS 2017 (2017)
67. Umuroglu, Y., Akhauri, Y., Fraser, N.J., Blott, M.: LogicNets: co-designed neural networks and circuits for extreme-throughput applications. In: FPL 2020 (2020)
68. Umuroglu, Y., et al.: FINN: a framework for fast, scalable binarized neural network inference. In: Proceedings of the 2017 ACM/SIGDA FPGA. ACM (2017)
69. Wada, T., Matsumura, N., Nakano, K., Ito, Y.: Efficient byte stream pattern test using bloom filter with rolling hash functions on the FPGA. In: 2018 Sixth CANDAR. IEEE (2018)
70. Wang, X., et al.: Hyperscan: a fast multi-pattern regex matcher for modern CPUs. In: USENIX NSDI (2019)
71. Wang, Z., Zeng, Y., Liu, Y., Li, D.: Deep belief network integrating improved kernel-based extreme learning machine for network intrusion detection. IEEE Access **9**, 16062–16091 (2021)
72. Wellem, T., Lai, Y.K., Huang, C.Y., Chung, W.Y.: A hardware-accelerated infrastructure for flexible sketch-based network traffic monitoring. In: IEEE 17th HPSR. IEEE (2016)
73. Yang, T., et al.: A generic technique for sketches to adapt to different counting ranges. In: IEEE INFOCOM (2019)
74. Yang, T., et al.: Elastic sketch: Adaptive and fast network-wide measurements. In: Proceedings of the ACM Special Interest Group Data Communication (SIGCOMM) (2018)
75. Yu, Y., Long, J., Cai, Z.: Session-based network intrusion detection using a deep learning architecture. In: Torra, V., Narukawa, Y., Honda, A., Inoue, S. (eds.) MDAI 2017. LNCS (LNAI), vol. 10571, pp. 144–155. Springer, Cham (2017). https://doi.org/10.1007/978-3-319-67422-3_13
76. Zazo, J.F., Lopez-Buedo, S., Ruiz, M., Sutter, G.: A single-FPGA architecture for detecting heavy hitters in 100 Gbit/s ethernet links. In: 2017 International Conference on ReConFigurable Computing and FPGAs (ReConFig). IEEE (2017)
77. Zhang, J., Zulkernine, M., Haque, A.: Random-forests-based network intrusion detection systems. IEEE Trans. Syst. Man Cybern. Part C (Appl. Rev.) **38**(5), 649–659 (2008)
78. Zhao, Z., Sadok, H., Atre, N., Hoe, J.C., Sekar, V., Sherry, J.: Achieving 100Gbps intrusion prevention on a single server. In: 14th USENIX OSDI20 (2020)
79. Zhou, Y., Zhang, Y., Ma, C., Chen, S., Odegbile, O.O.: Generalized sketch families for network traffic measurement. POMACS **3**(3), 1–34 (2019). Kindly provide year of the publication for the Ref. [51]

Author Index

Printed in the United States
by Baker & Taylor Publisher Services